T&T Clark Handbook of Christian Eschatology

T&T Clark Handbook of Christian Eschatology

By Markus Mühling

Translated by Jennifer Adams-Maßmann and David Andrew Gilland

Bloomsbury T&T Clark
An imprint of Bloomsbury Publishing Plc

BLOOMSBURY

LONDON · NEW DELHI · NEW YORK · SYDNEY

Bloomsbury T&T Clark
An imprint of Bloomsbury Publishing Plc

Imprint previously known as T&T Clark

50 Bedford Square
London
WC1B 3DP
UK

1385 Broadway
New York
NY 10018
USA

www.bloomsbury.com

First published 2015

Markus Mühling, Original title: *Grundinformation Eschatologie. Systematische Theologie aus der Perspektive der Hoffnung*, Göttingen, 2007

British Library Cataloguing-in-Publication Data
A catalogue record for this book is available from the British Library.

ISBN: HB: 978-0-567-02343-8
PB: 978-0-567-63282-1
ePDF: 978-0-567-65567-7
ePub: 978-0-567-65568-4

Library of Congress Cataloging-in-Publication Data
Mühling, Markus.
T&T Clark handbook of Christian eschatology / by Markus Mühling.
pages cm
Includes bibliographical references and index.
ISBN 978-0-567-02343-8 (hardback) – ISBN 978-0-567-63282-1 (pbk) –
ISBN 978-0-567-65567-7 (ePDF) – ISBN 978-0-567-65568-4 (ePub)
1. Eschatology–Textbooks. I. Title. II. Title: Handbook of Christian eschatology.
BT821.3M84 2015
236–dc23
2014038577

Typeset by Integra Software Services Pvt. Ltd.
Printed and bound in Great Britain

In memoriam:
Hans Mühling
born unto eternity on 24 July 2013

Contents

Preface xiii

1 Introduction 1

1.1 Historical background of the term 'eschatology' 1
1.1.1 Our questions about the future 1
1.1.2 The origins of the term 'eschatology' 3
1.1.2.1 The *eschata* 3
1.1.2.2 The *eschaton* 7
1.1.2.3 The *eschatos* 11
1.1.3 Eschatology in the twentieth century 14
1.1.3.1 Eschatologies 'from above' 14
1.1.3.2 Eschatologies 'from ahead' 17
1.1.4 Eschatology and modernity 22
1.2 Eschatology and the concept of action 25
1.2.1 Action 25
1.2.2 Systematic theology as the self-reflection of Christian practice 30
1.2.3 Eschatology as reflection on Christian life 31
1.3 The logic of hope 32
1.3.1 Expectations and surprises 32
1.3.2 Hopes and fears 35
1.3.3 Volitions 37
1.3.4 The future in everyday language 37
1.3.5 The eschatic and the eschatological 38
1.4 Eschatology in outline 38

2 The Trinitarian Basis of Eschatology: The Eschatoi 41

2.1 Eschatological epistemology 41
2.1.1 Dead ends 41
2.1.2 The *eschatos* as basis? 43

2.2. The constitution of faith and Christian practice 46
2.2.1 Constitution and content 46
2.2.2 Justification and *promissio* 48
2.2.3 Minimal criteria of God-talk 49
2.2.4 The self-identification of the eschatic basis 54
2.2.4.1 Jesus' proclamation of the kingdom of his Father 54
2.2.4.2 Jesus' resurrection and the experience of Easter 56
2.2.4.3 The resurrection of Christ and the action of the Holy Spirit 60
2.2.4.4 Salvation by loving surrender 61
2.2.4.5 The triune self-identification 63
2.3 The Eschatoi as the basis of Christian faith and hope 66
2.3.1 Economic and immanent Trinity 66
2.3.2 God's action in the world and God's storied being 67
2.3.3 God's being as Trinitarian love 69
2.3.4 God's being as ordered love 72
2.3.5 The attributes of God 74
2.3.6 From the *eschatoi* to the *eschatos* 75

3 The Eschaton 79
3.1 Time and eternity 80
3.1.1 Models of time and eternity 80
3.1.1.1 Eternity as timelessness 80
3.1.1.2 Eternity as partial or complete simultaneity 88
3.1.1.3 Eternity as the flow of time without beginning or end 97
3.1.2 The eschatical basis of time and eternity 103
3.1.2.1 Time 103
3.1.2.2 Eternity 105
3.1.2.3 The relationship between time and eternity 106
3.2 Space and infinity 107
3.2.1 Models of space and infinity 107
3.2.1.1 Absolute space as an infinite container 108
3.2.1.2 Space as a finite container 111
3.2.1.3 Space as order of reversible relations 122
3.2.2 Space and infinity revisited 131

3.3 The good, the true and the beautiful 133
3.3.1 Suffering and divine omnipotence 133
3.3.2 God's omnipotence as all-embracing activity 138
3.3.3 The good, the bad and the ethically neutral 140
3.3.4 Divine–creaturely cooperation 141
3.3.5 Transformations 144
3.3.6 The good, the true and the beautiful 145
3.3.7 Multiple forms of the eschatic reality 149

4 The Pre-eschata 151

4.1 Annihilation or transformation? 151
4.1.1 The transformation of the world (*renovatio*) 152
4.1.1.1 Transformation in the tradition 152
4.1.1.2 Transformation in the philosophy of nature 154
4.1.1.3 Renewal as new creation 157
4.1.2 The annihilation of the world (*annihilatio*) 158
4.1.2.1 Annihilation in the tradition 158
4.1.2.2 A modern version of annihilation 160
4.1.3 Evaluative criteria 162
4.1.4 Guidance from the theology of creation 164
4.1.4.1 Thetic structures of love 164
4.1.4.2 Incomplete rules 165
4.1.5 Guidance from fundamental eschatology 167
4.1.6 The consummation of the world in God 168
4.1.7 Ethical relevance 169
4.2 Human death 172
4.2.1 Biological death 173
4.2.1.1 What is biological death? 173
4.2.1.2 Near-death experiences 178
4.2.1.3 Why is there biological death and aging? 179
4.2.2 Death as division of the body and soul 181
4.2.3 Humanity and death in the biblical tradition 183
4.2.4 Humanity and death in the theological tradition 187
4.2.5 Problems in the contemporary theological understanding of death 190
4.2.5.1 The total-death theory 190
4.2.5.2 Death and finitude, sin and creatureliness 195
4.2.5.3 Excursus: Reincarnation and absorption 201

4.2.6 Human being as *imago dei* 204
4.2.6.1 Human being as person in relation 204
4.2.6.2 Human being as creaturely love 207
4.2.7 Sin and death 211
4.2.7.1 Sin as misplaced love 211
4.2.7.2 Chaotic suffering and the confirmation of justification 214
4.2.8 Ethical, pastoral and liturgical aspects 218
4.3 The apocalyptic revelation of the future of history 223
4.3.1 Pre-modern and modern millennialism 224
4.3.2 Postmillennialism 229
4.3.2.1 Secular postmillennialism 229
4.3.2.2 Christianized postmillennialism 233
4.3.3 Premillennialism 236
4.3.3.1 Secular premillennialism 236
4.3.3.2 Christianized premillennialism 240
4.3.4 Amillennialist Christianity and the ethical consequences 243
4.3.5 Excursus: Omens of the end 248

5 The Eschata 251

5.1 The Parousia of Christ 252
5.1.1 The problem of the Parousia 252
5.1.2 Biblical conceptions of the Parousia 255
5.1.3 Parousia in the tradition 258
5.1.3.1 Ahistorical versions of the Parousia 259
5.1.3.2 Trans-historical versions of the Parousia 262
5.1.3.3 Historical versions of the Parousia 264
5.1.4 The eschatical assembly with the Lord 270
5.1.5 Ethical implications 274
5.2 The resurrection of the living body 276
5.2.1 Bodily resurrection in the early Christian tradition 278
5.2.2 Bodily resurrection in the history of theology 283
AA 'timeless-dualistic' versions of the resurrection 284
AB 'timeless-monistic' versions of the resurrection 285
BA 'simultaneous-dualistic' versions of the resurrection 286

BB 'simultaneous-monistic' versions of the resurrection 287
CA 'infinite-dualistic' versions of the resurrection 287
CB 'infinite-monistic' versions of the resurrection 290
5.2.3 Excursus: Intermediary states? 293
5.2.4 The living body as the medium of communicative relationality 297
5.2.5 Ethical implications 301
5.3 The judgement 302
5.3.1 The judgement in history 303
5.3.1.1 The judgement in the Bible 303
5.3.1.2 The judgement in tradition 306
5.3.2 The outcome of the judgement 307
5.3.2.1 Dual outcome: Eternal life and annihilation 308
5.3.2.2 Dual outcome: Eternal life and eternal punishment 310
5.3.2.3 Universal salvation 315
5.3.2.4 Election and selective judgement 321
5.3.3 The judgement as a process 325
5.3.3.1 The judgement as transformation and constitution of personal identity 325
5.3.3.2 Objects and criteria of the judgement 326
5.3.3.3 The judge and the process of judgement 330
5.3.3.4 The timing of the judgement 333
5.3.4 Ethical implications 336
5.4 The consummation of the Kingdom of God as the eschatical reality 338
5.4.1 The Kingdom of God in Scripture and history 340
5.4.2 Consummation considered 'conceptually' 345
5.4.3 Images of consummation 354
5.4.3.1 The new or heavenly Jerusalem (Rev. 21.10–27) 356
5.4.3.2 The peace of the animals (Is. 11.6–9) 357
5.4.3.3 Paradise (Lk. 23.43; Rev. 2.7) 357
5.4.3.4 A new heaven and a new earth (Rev. 21.1) 358
5.4.3.5 The eschatical vineyard (Mi. 4.4; Zech. 3.10) 358
5.4.3.6 Assembly with the Lord (1. Thes. 4.17) 360

5.4.3.7 Theosis (Rom. 8.14; Acts 17.28f.; 2 Pet. 1.4) 360
5.4.3.8 Seeing God 'face to face' (1 Cor. 15.28) 361
5.4.3.9 God is 'all in all' (1 Cor. 15.28) 361
5.4.3.10 Eternal life (Matt. 25.46; Mk 10.30; John 3.16; Rom. 6.22) 362
5.4.3.11 Music 366
5.4.3.12 The content of a good book 366
5.4.4 Back to the present 367

Bibliography 369
Scripture Index 389
Author Index 394
Subject Index 400

Preface

Eschatology experienced a very diverse fate in the twentieth century. Whereas at the beginning of the century it was claimed that the eschatological office of theology had been completely abandoned, in the midst of the century the same office was said to be working overtime. At present, in the twenty-first century, both extremes and many other evaluations of the role of eschatology in Christian Systematic Theology exist side by side. Whereas the classical locus *de novissimis* at the end of a contemporary dogmatics might not be as extensive as in the past, eschatological themes are as vivid as ever – though not necessarily discussed in a single locus at the end of dogmatics. Questions about the ultimate and eternal, and questions about what is persistent in our lives, are as vivid in theological reflection as they are in everyday life in our postmodern pluralist societies.

This situation can be best pictured by saying that eschatology is not so much a single locus or theme among others, but rather a dimension of theology as such: In eschatology, the whole of theology is perceived from the perspective of hope, or more precisely, from the relationship between everyday expectations and ultimate hope. The task of this book is to introduce Christian systematic theology from this point of view and to help broaden the reader's theological abilities. The purpose of this is threefold:

(1) Despite the fact that knowledge is indeed a necessary condition for systematic thinking, systematic theology is more a kind of action, meaning the task of systematic theological study is not so much learning things about theology, but becoming a theologian, i.e. developing different capabilities, skills and attitudes in order to be able to ask systematic theological questions, to see different kinds of answers, to recognize the relational framework between the different questions and their answers, and of course to evaluate them critically and to take responsibility for making theological decisions. These different skills and capabilities are no end in themselves but are part of the service of the church, or, more specifically, they are part of making intellectual and practical witness for the proclamation of the gospel in a methodical manner. Therefore, it is one purpose of this book to provide some help for the reader's development of these skills and capabilities.

(2) Knowledge about different theological themes, as well as responses to problems and positions, be they biblical, traditional or contemporary, are nevertheless a necessary condition for developing these skills and capabilities. This book therefore presents knowledge about eschatological topics in a thematic way that is oriented towards analysing and evaluating specific problems, which are grouped together into various models for comparison.

(3) Since there is no 'view from nowhere' and since developing the skills and attitudes necessary for making progress in developing a theological identity presupposes being confronted with actual, specific theological positions, this book does not pretend to present the material in a quasi-objective way, but rather explicitly from the standpoint of a particular position: This is the position of a decidedly relational kind of theology that is at the same time bound to an underlying relational-narrative mode of perception. It is this feature that is slightly more pronounced in this English version than in the German original which served as its template.

The means chosen for this project are realized in a dialogical form: After posing eschatological problems, presenting different kinds of solutions from Scripture and tradition, analysing and evaluating them, suggestions for our own solutions are made and, in Chapters 4 and 5, are exemplarily related to practical situations, be they ethical or liturgical. Eschatology is only partly about the future, but as reflection on the dimension of present hope, eschatology is eminently practical: Different kinds of hope also shape our present practice and life.

The outline of this book is shaped by the fact that eschatology is a dimension of systematic theology and by the task of introducing or improving the exercise of systematic theological capabilities: Chapter 1 introduces the history of the discipline of eschatology, discusses different meanings and ways to identify the subject matter of eschatology, as well as analyses the language we use for hope in everyday life. Chapter 2 asks about the different possibilities of the basis for ultimate or eschatical claims about Christian hope. The subject matter of Chapter 3 is different structural questions that shape the material answers to be provided in the later chapters. Questions about the relationship between time and eternity, and space and infinity are dealt with, as well as questions about the goodness, truth and beauty are features of the ultimate. Chapter 4 deals with penultimate or pre-eschatical phenomena that are occasions for asking about ultimate hope: Leading are the natural question about the future of our natural world, the social question about the future of history and the personal question about the future of human beings (or better: human becomings) in the face of death. The last chapter, Chapter 5, is about what are together traditionally called the classical *eschata*: The Parousia of Christ, the resurrection of the dead, the last judgement as well as models and pictures of the eschatical reality and life itself.

Among the many people who contributed to the publication of this book I am especially indebted to John Webster, Donald Wood, Paul Jones, Thomas Kraft and Anna Turton. Special thanks goes to Jennifer Adams-Maßmann for the translation of the first half of the book and to David A. Gilland, who not only translated the second half, but reworked the language of the entire book and contributed many theological suggestions that led to an overall improvement of the material. Finally, thanks to Annika Brunckhorst for her extensive and excellent proofreading.

Lüneburg 19 May 2014 *Markus Mühling*

1

Introduction

Chapter Outline

Historical background of the term 'eschatology' 1
Eschatology and the concept of action 25
The logic of hope 32
Eschatology in outline 38

1.1 Historical background of the term 'eschatology'

1.1.1 Our questions about the future

Throughout our lives we are confronted with situations that cause us to ask questions about the future: 'What will happen tomorrow? What will life be like in a few years? How will I live? How will my children live?' – to name a few. Aside from personal questions about our futures, we may also wonder about the future of society and what will happen to the natural world. Of course, these questions do not deal solely with a purely this-worldly future. As our lives unfold, we discover there are fewer and fewer possible courses of action: while we remain open to following certain paths, other options are no longer available. Everyone is thus confronted with the exhaustibility of existence. Natural resources are finite. To give a rather superficial example, one must begin to exercise starting around age 25 simply to maintain muscle mass. Of course, there are also much more pressing examples, including crisis situations, such as our experiences of suffering, illness or death, whether our own or that of loved ones. In such situations, the search for the meaning of our lives thrusts itself upon us, as do fundamental questions about a future that transcends the finitude of the world as we know it: 'What will happen after my death? Is my existence and that of my fellow human beings heading towards a particular goal or are we running, literally, straight into a wall? Is the world moving deliberately towards a final goal or will it run out of steam first?' Such questions are an everyday matter for those active in pastoral settings, whether the minister engaged in pastoral care, the religious educator instructing a class or simply church members who make pastoral calls to other parishioners.

To some extent, these are really everyday questions and there are two rough possibilities for dealing with them. One approach is to assume we cannot say anything about any of this because no one actually knows the answer. The other possibility is to assume Christian faith does in fact have something to say. In the first case, there are not really any answers to the specific questions raised, so answering the questions is left up to each individual, as there is nothing we can contribute from a Christian or theological perspective. In the second case, however, the theologian – regardless of whether that person speaks as a pastor, teacher, etc. – serves as a conversation partner from whom a certain expertise is expected. This does not mean the theologian ought to answer these questions for the conversation partner in an authoritative manner, but rather that he or she is able to offer expert advice. The role of the theologian in this case can be understood if we compare it with that of a doctor: when we are sick, we naively expect from a doctor that she will simply make us healthy again. We may also expect that the doctor will make a diagnosis, name some possible therapeutic approaches and predict how the disease is likely to progress under certain conditions. The latter would certainly be a reasonable expectation of a doctor. What virtually no one would expect is that the doctor would simply leave us alone when we are sick, naming the illness but not saying or doing anything else to help us: no prognosis, no treatment options, nothing at all. We would consider such a doctor to be fully incompetent and would presume she had neglected her duty to educate herself properly about the disease. An analogous situation exists when a pastor or religion teacher cannot provide any kind of answer – or gives only a sweeping, vague answer – to questions about the future, particularly those questions about the future which transcend the world. Responding with, 'Well, there is really nothing anyone can say about that', constitutes a breach of duty.

There is only one way to avoid such a situation: we have to engage these questions, and theologians need to do so in a methodologically controlled way. This necessity arises not only from the universal human questions we have mentioned, but from the experience of lived Christian faith itself. The practice of petitionary prayer is oriented towards the future. The petition for the coming of God's kingdom, for example, is an inalienable component of the Lord's Prayer. In the Apostle's Creed, both the second and third articles refer to future events: the second article, which focuses on Christ, speaks about the return (Parousia) of Christ and his judgement. The third article, focused on the Spirit, speaks about resurrection and eternal life. So, given how Christian faith understands itself, we are required to engage with the questions raised so far. The theological subsection dedicated to addressing these questions is called eschatology. But what is eschatology exactly? To examine this question, we must first consider the historical development of the term.

Both general anthropological concerns and the practical experience of Christian faith necessitate that theology deal with eschatology.

1.1.2 The origins of the term 'eschatology'

1.1.2.1 The *eschata*

The term 'eschatology' comes from Protestant Orthodoxy, from Lutheran Orthodoxy in particular. Protestant Orthodoxy describes a theological strand in the late sixteenth to eighteenth centuries and is characterized by its thorough, comprehensive and scientific approach to theology. The academic language of the time was still Latin. Johann Gerhard (d. 1637), an important early Lutheran exponent of Protestant Orthodoxy, concludes his dogmatics with the locus 'De novissimis' ('Regarding the last things'), in which he references a biblical passage – or rather, an apocryphal or deuterocanonical passage – from Sirach 7:36 (40).[1] A student of Gerhard named Philipp Heinrich Friedlieb (d. 1663) was one of the first to make use of the newly coined word 'eschatology'.[2] The term eschatology finally became established

[1]Cf. Sigurd Hjelde, *Das Eschaton und die Eschata: Eine Studie über Sprachgebrauch und Sprachverwirrung in protestantischer Theologie von der Orthodoxie bis zur Gegenwart* (Munich: Kaiser, 1987), p. 39.
[2]Cf. Hjelde, *Eschaton und Eschata*, p. 37.

after the decline of Protestant Orthodoxy, once German had become the standard academic language for theology. This transition from Latin to German took place during the Enlightenment. An example of this transition can be found in the theology of K.G. Bretschneider (d. 1848) among others.[3] The new term eschatology was later adopted by other confessions.

The meaning of the term was already not very clear in that time. On the one hand, it designated any kind of belief about the future and the afterlife, even non-Christian ones. On the other hand, as with Gerhard's term *novissima*, it referred to the specifically Christian doctrine 'of the Last Things', the *eschata* (in the plural). Determining just what these 'last things' include is a matter of controversy among theologians and the results are inconsistent. Gerhard was referring to the medieval doctrine of the *quattuor novissima*, the last four things: death, judgement, hell and eternal life. He added the resurrection of the dead to the list, since the Last Judgement presupposes that the dead are able to participate as living beings, and Gerhard also included the doctrine of the annihilation of the world, the *consummatio mundi* as the cosmic counterpart to the individual death of each person.[4] We might ask ourselves in which sense these topics deal with the 'last things'. Gerhard himself understood the *novissima* in a temporal sense: what comes last, chronologically speaking.

This makes it clear that, ultimately, we are not dealing with a universal Christian doctrine about the future. For if we consider the future as a whole, then we would have to speak not just about the last things but about the next-to-last or penultimate things, events with which we could actually be familiar. This is also the case, at least in part, because death, for example, is a next-to-last or penultimate matter, not a final matter, as Bretschneider later remarked.[5] One could certainly understand the term *eschata*, the last things, in a different way, not temporally but as the doctrine of logically or ontologically 'ultimate' things. This understanding was also maintained at the time, though the meaning is even older, at least if we do not focus on the technical term, for the term *finis ultimus*, the final goal of the world, has been used in dogmatics far longer than the discourse about the *novissima* or the *eschata*. Various subtopics can certainly be addressed within the framework of discourse about our final goal.[6]

---

[3]Cf. Hjelde, *Eschaton und Eschata*, pp. 102–05.
[4]Cf. Hjelde, *Eschaton und Eschata*, pp. 41–47.
[5]Cf. Hjelde, *Eschaton und Eschata*, p. 104.
[6]For more on the outline of this doctrinal point in the Middle Ages, see Ludwig Ott, *Eschatologie in der Scholastik* (ed. Erich Naab; Freiburg: Herder, 1990).

It is important to note that there has been little consistency about which subtopics are included under the rubric of the eschata. This depends not only on whether one has a temporal or ontological understanding of the eschata but is also a function of manifold formal discussions about what constitutes dogmatics as well as specific theological points of view. In late Protestant Orthodoxy, for example, there was an attempt, in keeping with the demands of science as was commonly conceived at the time, to understand theology as a positive academic field of study based on a goal or specific function: each academic field of study had to indicate the object and purpose it was seeking to achieve and the means with which this could happen. Because the stated goal was the eternal beatitude of the person, this topic was no longer addressed in the doctrine about the last things but ended up at the beginning of systematic theology, in the prolegomena (introduction) or fundamental theology, whereas, paradoxically, this final goal of salvation or eternal life was no longer discussed at all in the doctrine of the last things. Instead, eschatology then included only the 'next-to-last' or penultimate things.[7]

We can see that, from the beginning, when the term 'eschatology' was used, it was not at all certain what the object of this doctrine was intended to be. Nevertheless, the individual subjects of the classical eschata, even when they are not yet named explicitly as such, are highly important. For while they generally no longer appear as a self-contained chapter at the end of the dogmatics, they certainly do appear in other important places in the course of the entire dogmatics, such as the doctrine of God, christology or soteriology. This is significant, because it suggests that not only the classical eschata appear to be indispensible for dogmatics as a whole, but other classical subjects within dogmatics also appear to be indispensible for the doctrine of these 'last things'. It is debatable, however, whether we are dealing with a self-contained doctrinal unit, what in Protestant theology would be called a 'locus' or in Catholic theology a 'tractate'.

The concept of eschatology changed in the nineteenth century so that the eschata, the last things, no longer took centre stage. Before we trace this development, however, it should be noted that the designation of eschatology we have identified here as the 'doctrine of the last things' did not disappear. It continued on, under changed circumstances, for example, in confessional-conservative Lutheranism. The latter designation is somewhat misleading in that it generally is not a matter of a simple theology

---

[7]Cf. Hjelde, *Eschaton und Eschata*, pp. 69–80.

of repristination, that is, a theology which anxiously seeks to hold on to or restore the old in its pristine condition. Instead, it indicates a theology which aims to connect experience, the classical confessions, Scripture and piety (*praxis pietatis*). The most notable recent example comes from the so-called early Erlangen School. One of the later theologies of the early Erlangen School by Franz Hermann Reinhold von Frank (d. 1894) not only insisted on discussing the eschata, but was even able to reintroduce a subject which the Reformation confessions had banned from discussion: Frank spoke of a historical, thousand-year kingdom before the final end of time.[8] Because of the need to ward off the 'Radical Reformers' (known as the *Schwärmer*, which can be roughly translated as the 'Enthusiasts'), the magisterial Reformers were not only sceptical about the possibility of positively appropriating this doctrinal point, but Philipp Melanchthon (d. 1560) virtually forbade it in the *Confessio Augustana*,[9] and as a result Protestant Orthodoxy did not adopt it. Also known as chiliasm, this doctrine survived in popular Protestant piety, however, so that it did not seem implausible for the Erlangen School to take up this doctrine in the nineteenth century, because they represented an approach to theology that was mindful of personal piety. In fact, because of historical circumstances in church history, the Erlangen theologians in the nineteenth century had to fight for the unity of the Bavarian church and were successfully able to prevent the exodus of the 'awakened' circles associated with Wilhelm Löhe (d. 1872) who would otherwise have joined the so-called free (non-established) churches.[10]

- Eschatology, first, describes the doctrine of all the possible conceptions of the future and the afterlife.
- Second, eschatology can denote the doctrine of the Last Things, the final events. These can be understood in either a *temporal* or an *ontic* sense.

---

[8]Cf. Hjelde, *Eschaton und Eschata*, p. 164.

[9]Cf. Philipp Melanchthon, 'The Augsburg Confession (1530)', in Robert Kolb and Timothy J. Wengert (eds), *The Book of Concord: The Confessions of the Evangelical Lutheran Church* (trans. Charles Arand et al.; Minneapolis: Fortress, 2000), pp. 50–51 (XVIII: Concerning the Return of Christ to Judgment).

[10]For more on the Erlangen Theology, see Karlmann Beyschlag, *Die Erlanger Theologie* (Erlangen: Martin-Luther-Verlag, 1993).

1.1.2.2 The *eschaton*

Although the term 'eschatology' was widely used in the nineteenth century, this does not mean that there was a particular upsurge of interest in the actual object of eschatology. Rather, at this point in time, a series of changes ensued which finally resulted in a new concept of eschatology in the twentieth century.

In this historical context, the first person we should name is Friedrich Daniel Ernst Schleiermacher (d. 1834). In the first edition of his book, *The Christian Faith*, he does not yet use the term, although he does in the second edition, albeit sparingly. More importantly than Schleiermacher's explicit use of the term, however, is the way he deals with the subject of eschatology itself. Because Schleiermacher sees only those statements that describe a specific Christian state of consciousness as the true object of dogmatics – so that his theology can be characterized as a theology of experience in a broader sense – and because the object of Christian hope in the future cannot be experienced, Schleiermacher transforms eschatology. He understandably rejects the expression 'Last Things', because, based on his approach to theology, it cannot be a matter of objects having material substance or of real events.[11]

For Schleiermacher, however, eschatology cannot simply be excluded from dogmatics. First, the traditional subjects of eschatology, the eschata, must be critically examined based on the consciousness of truth. Thus, Schleiermacher engages in a critical and historical consideration of the concept of eschatology.[12] Second, there are important theological aspects to consider: Schleiermacher is writing within a new paradigm, the paradigm of a 'theology of consciousness'. Because of this, those not quite as familiar with Schleiermacher's theology may find some aspects strange, so it may be appropriate to review a few points of his thought briefly at this juncture.[13] Schleiermacher teaches that in Christ the constant strength of the God-consciousness appeared, meaning that immediate consciousness of absolute dependence on God invariably dominates over the consciousness of sin mediated by the temporal self-consciousness. Through the common spirit of the church, the constant strength of the God-consciousness is propagated historically in society. This approach has at least two implications: Both

---

[11] Friedrich Schleiermacher, *The Christian Faith* (trans. H.R. Mackintosh and J.S. Stewart; Berkley: Apocryphile, 2001, 2nd edn), pp. 703–07 (§159).

[12] Cf. Schleiermacher, *The Christian Faith*, pp. 703–07 (§158).

[13] Cf. Schleiermacher, *The Christian Faith*, §§3–6, 15–19, 91–112, 115–25.

the individual and collective dimensions of consciousness are united in Christ; the individual consciousness, because the constant strength of the God-consciousness is realized in a particular person, and the collective, as the constant strength of the God-consciousness is oriented towards the community of the church from the outset and does not exist for itself. In terms of eschatology, this means that Schleiermacher accords one topic in particular more prominence than it received in the tradition, even making it into its own particular doctrine: the return of Christ.[14] Important characteristics of his eschatology include the doctrine of the continuity of the individual human person, as this concept is included 'as the belief in the immutability of the union of the Divine Essence with human nature in the Person of Christ',[15] as well as of the church in its consummated state.[16] Schleiermacher refers to this eschatological subject area as the 'prophetic doctrines',[17] meaning eschatology cannot be derived from the experience of consciousness, in contrast to actual dogmatic doctrines.

The first line of argument discussed so far – the historicization of the concept of eschatology – was picked up and continued in the 1830s when Karl-Ludwig Weizel introduced the term 'eschatology' into historical and exegetical scholarship.[18] Towards the end of the nineteenth century, this was widely adopted, and scholars such as Johannes Weiss (d. 1914) and Albert Schweitzer (d. 1965) and many others even emphasized the eschatological character of the New Testament, particularly in the teachings of Jesus.[19] For our purposes, suffice it to say for now that the exegetical use of the term was borrowed from dogmatics, which led to new content associated with the term: Weiss and Schweitzer identified the kingdom of God as a central topic in the proclamation and actions of Jesus. They claimed that the kingdom of God denotes a transcendent, otherworldly entity, which is breaking in at any moment and will bring to an end the hitherto existing world and history. Schweitzer characterized this as a 'consistent eschatology'.[20] At the same time, he makes it seem unjustifiable to refer to the kingdom of God as an ethical undertaking since the expectation of the Parousia (i.e. the expectation of Christ's return) is apparently symptomatic of an incorrect

---

[14]Cf. Schleiermacher, *The Christian Faith*, pp. 707–09 (§160).
[15]Schleiermacher, *The Christian Faith*, p. 698 (§158).
[16]Cf. Schleiermacher, *The Christian Faith*, pp. 696–98 (§157).
[17]Cf. Schleiermacher, *The Christian Faith*, p. 706 (§159).
[18]Cf. Hjelde, *Eschaton und Eschata*, pp. 123–26.
[19]Cf. Hjelde, *Eschaton und Eschata*, pp. 221–33, 279–98.
[20]Cf. Hjelde, *Eschaton und Eschata*, p. 282.

relationship to God because the Parousia has not taken place yet in the last 2,000 years. According to Schweitzer, Christianity cannot use eschatology as a guide but needs to find a rationale for its morality by following other paths. Thus, Schweitzer perfects the consistent historical or historicizing concept of eschatology.

Scholars also adopted and further developed another aspect of how Schleiermacher uses the term eschatology – that is, the reduction of this doctrinal point to one single subject area within dogmatics as well as his reservations about or rejection of the doctrine of the last things – or rather its transformation. We can see this especially towards the end of the century in the thought of Albrecht Ritschl (d. 1889). Ritschl used the term eschatology in particular when he was speaking primarily as a historian and exegete, in the first and second volumes of his major work, the 'Critical History of the Christian Doctrine of Justification and Reconciliation', yet not in the third volume of his dogmatics.[21] Presumably, this is because he was writing before the inflationary interest in eschatology found in exegetical scholarship for which his son-in-law Johannes Weiss was a major catalyst. In fact, the implications of this volume are indeed eschatological, although they are transformed in an almost ingenious way, as we will later see in detail. Here, it suffices to note that Ritschl also worked within a new paradigm, although a different one from Schleiermacher. He draws on the works of his Göttingen colleague in philosophy, Hermann Lotze (d. 1881), as well as Immanuel Kant (d. 1804) and makes the idea of purpose and personality the foundation of his thought: God is personality and therefore always relates to a particular purpose. This is love and the object of this love is the kingdom of God, a kingdom whose purpose has never *not* already been actualized, from God's perspective. Only for humans can the means and the ends be separated.[22] With this, Ritschl is able to place a truly genuine 'last thing' – the kingdom of God – at the centre of his thought, although his theology is often described as an ellipse with two focal points.[23] The traditional idea of resurrection and eternal life can also be integrated, even though the topic appears only rarely in his work: eternal life means living in accordance with morality, a true end in itself,

---

[21]Cf. Albrecht Ritschl, *The Christian Doctrine of Justification and Reconciliation: The Positive Development of the Doctrine* (trans. and ed. H.R. Mackintosh and A.B. Macaulay; Edinburgh: T&T Clark, 1902, 2nd edn). The first two volumes of the three were not translated into English.

[22]Cf. Markus Mühling, *Versöhnendes Handeln – Handeln in Versöhnung: Gottes Opfer an die Menschen* (Göttingen: Vandenhoeck & Ruprecht, 2005), pp. 49–54.

[23]Cf. Ritschl, *Christian Doctrine*, p. 9.

and not allowing oneself to be constrained by the predicament of evil.[24] Certainly, this interpretation of the kingdom of God may not correspond to the results of exegetical research, as became clear just a few years later. But, Ritschl's thought represented a step away from eschatology as the doctrine of the last things towards eschatology as the doctrine of the *eschaton*.

We could name a whole host of other theologians who paved the way for this development. This idea was then fully realized at the end of the 1920s in the work of Paul Tillich (d. 1965). Tillich deliberately introduced the use of the now-familiar term 'eschaton' to theology. According to Tillich, it does not make sense to talk about the end of history and a time 'after' the eschaton, as this would perpetuate categories related to the progression of time which have ostensibly been abolished by the event in question.[25] Rather, one must assume that everything that exists at any moment in time is related to the transcendent meaning of an 'event', which cannot simply be described in terms of beginnings, but in terms of a goal, which should not be understood in a temporal way. Thus, Tillich provided a programmatic definition:

> The term 'eschaton' has been deliberately used instead of 'eschata', meaning the Last Things, as it is commonly called in biblical and theological language. The change is supposed to indicate that the eschato-logia are not things (meaning 'events' in this case) that will happen one after another at the end of time, but the focus is actually the meaning of the event as such, in so far as it is approaching something. That towards which the event is approaching, however, 'the last thing', is not again an event, but rather the transcendent meaning of the event. This is the reason for the use of the word eschaton.[26]

This understanding of the object of eschatology as singular became customary after Tillich and was also retained by theologians like Wolfhart Pannenberg, who uses the concept of an end of history.

---

[24]Cf. Albrecht Ritschl, 'Instruction in the Christian Religion', in *Three Essays* (trans. Philip Hefner; Eugene: Wipf and Stock, 2005), p. 230 (§23).

[25]Cf. Paul Tillich, 'Eschatology and History', in *The Interpretation of History* (trans. N.A. Rasetzki and Elsa L. Talmey; New York: Scribner's, 1936), pp. 266–84, esp. 280. The ET unfortunately renders Tillich's 'eschaton' with 'ultimate'. For the original, cf. Paul Tillich, *Main Works/ Hauptwerke*, vol. 6: *Theologische Schriften/Theological Writings* (ed. Carl Heinz Ratschow, Berlin: De Gruyter, 1992), pp. 107–25.

[26]Paul Tillich, 'Eschatologie und Geschichte', in idem, *Religiöse Verwirklichung* (Berlin: Furche-Verlag, 1930) p. 291, n. 4. The footnotes do not appear in the ET.

- Eschatology, third, can be understood as the doctrine of that which is ultimate, the ultimate things. This may be understood in a *temporal* sense but is generally expressed in other categories such as the ontically transcendent meaning of an event, as in Tillich.
- Fourth, eschatology can also be seen as a historical term for the future-oriented or apocalyptic character of the teachings and life of Christ, whether this is understood in a historicizing way (Albert Schweitzer) or in a systematic and positive way.

1.1.2.3 The *eschatos*

Unfortunately, this does not end the linguistic confusion about what the actual object of eschatology should be and, by extension, what eschatology itself is. Eschatology cannot simply relate to a singular, neuter, ultimate thing but must be a personal matter of 'the last things' or 'ultimate things'. Schleiermacher suggests this line of thought himself since he identified the return of Christ as a separate, new and important element of his 'prophetic doctrines'.

We find this expressed even more clearly in the theology of Isaak August Dorner (d. 1884), who was more oriented towards the work of Georg Wilhelm Friedrich Hegel (d. 1831) than Schleiermacher, but who was ultimately a highly independent theologian not to be underestimated. So-called 'mediating theology' is commonly ascribed to him. This was a movement in the nineteenth century that sought to connect traditional, confessional concerns with various elements adopted from contemporary paradigms. Dorner ascertained that eschatology is always related to christology as the doctrine of the person of Christ. Yet, because all existence is oriented teleologically and is moving towards a final goal, in eschatology both urgent contemporary concerns and practical action coincide with the centre of Christianity. At the same time, in its historical development, Christianity represents the acme of a teleological or eschatological religion and therefore adequately grasps truth and history. Through the close relationship of eschatology and christology, Dorner was also able to focus on the return of Christ, the Parousia. But in this, eschatology is not defined only in a one-sided way by christology, but the relationship is mutual so that eschatology also shapes christology. This becomes clear as Dorner was the first to speak about the incarnation, the 'becoming flesh' of the eternal Logos in Jesus Christ as the first parousia (as does the Eastern Orthodox tradition), so that the first and second parousias are connected. With this connection established, eschatology is accorded a central place in Christian faith and can develop an extremely sharp critical power.[27]

The object of eschatology – the eschatos, Christ – was defined even more clearly and explicitly by Martin Kähler (d. 1912) at the end of the nineteenth century. Kähler engaged in a theology of history and saw the meaning of eschatology as unlocking the meaning of history.[28] It is likely no coincidence that this reminds us at first of the later remarks of his student Tillich. Yet, in the end, his approach reflects a rather different interpretation, because Kähler cannot speak of the eschaton as an object in the same way Tillich does. For while history may be related to that which transcends history, the historical and that which transcends history are only united in the real person of the Christ. Kähler, who claimed to develop a decidedly biblical theology, is probably one of the most radically christocentric theologians one can imagine. He transforms and centralizes virtually all theological *loci* in Christ, starting with their foundation in fundamental theology. In terms of fundamental theology, one can speak of Christ having a three-part form: the historical Christ, the Christ who transcends history and the real Christ, who unites both.[29] Kähler thus attempted to solve the problem of the so-called 'ugly broad ditch'[30] of history, that is, the question of how contingent historical truths can have a validity that transcends time. As the historical eschatology of Johannes Weiss and Albert Schweitzer showed, the goal of the historical Christ, however, was irrefutably his return and the future kingdom of God, so there can be no eschatology without christology. The doctrine of the person of Christ is so central for Kähler that he personalizes theological terminology to refer everything to Christ: e.g. the doctrine of reconciliation is no longer 'soteriology', meaning the doctrine of salvation, but rather '*soter*ology', the doctrine of the saviour. Eschatology also undergoes the same christological centralization: 'Eschatological soteriology will now have

[27]Cf. Hjelde, *Eschaton und Eschata*, pp. 193–201.

[28]Cf. Martin Kähler, *Dogmatische Zeitfragen* (Leipzig: Deichert, 1908), p. 497.

[29]Cf. Martin Kähler, *Die Wissenschaft der christlichen Lehre von dem evangelischen Grundartikel aus im Abrisse dargestellt* (Waltrop: Spenner, 1994, 3rd edn), pp. 92–93, 217–18, 222; Martin Kähler, *Zur Lehre von der Versöhnung* (Gütersloh: Bertelsmann, 1998, 2nd edn), pp. 43–51, 54, 58 and 62.

[30]Cf. Gotthold Ephraim Lessing, 'On the Proof of the Spirit and of the Power', in Henry Chadwick (ed.), *Lessing's Theological Writings* (Stanford: Stanford, 1956), p. 55.

to be soteriology…. From this principle it follows that every eschatological dogma must be directly or indirectly a statement about the historical, living Christ.'[31] Thus, eschatology becomes 'in essence christology, statements about the person and work of Christ',[32] and Kähler can prove this claim by referring to the classical 'last things'. For apart from the topic of death it can be said: 'What was otherwise enumerated above are all statements about the living Christ: he comes, he judges, he consummates the world, he is our life, just as his return brings our resurrection. So we are not aware of a number of last things, but only one "last" person, who can only be the last person because he is also the "first".'[33]

This approach to personalizing the object of eschatology to focus on the person of Christ continued in the twentieth century, in part in the works of Karl Barth (d. 1968) or Walter Kreck,[34] (d. 2002) but above all in England with John A.T. Robinson (d. 1983), who in the 1960s spoke emphatically about the *eschatos*: 'Loyalty to the Christocentric nature of all New Testament theology would require us to speak always of *ho eschatos* – not the last Thing, but the last Man.'[35]

- Eschatology, fifthly, can also be understood as a description of the doctrine of the ultimate person, Jesus Christ.

By considering the history of the term specifically through the nineteenth century, we have uncovered at least five different understandings of the object and meaning of eschatology: eschatology as the doctrine of all possible concepts of the future, eschatology as the doctrine of the last things, eschatology as a historical concept for Jesus' proclamation, eschatology as the doctrine of the 'ultimate', understood either as some ultimate *thing* or condition, or as the ultimate person. In the end, these differing definitions of the term, which were all then brought together in the twentieth century, already existed alongside each other before.

---

[31]Kähler, *Wissenschaft*, pp. 441–42.
[32]Kähler, *Dogmatische Zeitfragen*, p. 500.
[33]Kähler, *Dogmatische Zeitfragen*, pp. 490–91.
[34]Cf. Walter Kreck, *Die Zukunft des Gekommenen: Grundprobleme der Eschatologie* (Munich: Kaiser, 1961).
[35]John A. T. Robinson, *In the End, God…A Study of the Christian Doctrine of the Last Things* (London: Clarke, 1958), p. 56, n. 1.

If we had to choose between them, we might discover that each has its own *particula veri*. Or, would we have to find a completely different definition of the object and meaning of the term eschatology? Before we can answer this question, it makes sense to turn our attention first to one more historical observation: the history of the concept of eschatology within the framework of Christian doctrine. Indeed, we can assume that determining this meaning will prove useful for ascertaining the object of eschatology.

1.1.3 Eschatology in the twentieth century

1.1.3.1 Eschatologies 'from above'

The fact that the various understandings of the term eschatology were already taking shape in the nineteenth century could lead us to believe eschatology was highly esteemed in this period, but this is not the case. Rather, Ernst Troeltsch (d. 1923) at the beginning of the twentieth century stated that 'the eschatological office [is...] mostly closed these days'.[36] Troeltsch names a few reasons for this: the eschatological office 'is closed' because it deals with things not relevant for Christian faith at the time and which do not have a sure foundation, 'for the ideas which led to the establishment of the office' have 'lost their roots'.[37] But, this situation had already changed completely by the middle of the century. Referring to the Troeltsch quote, the renowned Roman Catholic theologian Hans Urs von Balthasar (d. 1988) clearly stated that the eschatological office had been open and working overtime since the turn of the twentieth century.[38]

With the changes that took place in the theological landscape after the First World War – in particular the emergence of Dialectical Theology from liberal theology – the significance of eschatology grew. The ethical optimism of the outgoing nineteenth and early twentieth century appeared to have been completely shattered in the First World War, and with it the ideas that the values of Christianity were identical to those of society and that the West was truly Christian. As a result, eschatology moved into the foreground again. Thus, Karl Barth could make the claim in the famous second edition

[36] Ernst Troeltsch, Marta Troeltsch and Gertrud von Le Fort, *Glaubenslehre: Nach Heidelberger Vorlesungen aus den Jahren 1911 und 1912* (Munich: Duncker und Humblot, 1925), p. 36.
[37] Troeltsch et al., *Glaubenslehre*, p. 36.
[38] Cf. Hans Urs von Balthasar, 'Eschatologie', in Johnannes Feiner et al. (eds), *Fragen der Theologie heute* (Einsiedeln: Benziger, 1957), p. 403.

of his commentary on the Epistle to the Romans in 1922 that '[i]f Christianity be not altogether thoroughgoing eschatology, there remains in it no relationship whatsoever with Christ.'[39] With this, eschatology was no longer seen as a special topic within dogmatics, but as its comprehensive criterion. For dialectical theology, the reason was that Christianity is concerned with the inbreaking of eternity as fully transcendent into time and history, which judges every historical situation by sublating time in every moment, thus limiting time. This understanding of eternity also appeared in the work of theologians who cannot directly be called proponents of dialectical theology, such as Paul Tillich, who introduced the notion of an eschaton to theology as a neuter and singular noun. We already saw that for Tillich this denotes a transcendent meaning of history. Eternity can break into time at any moment so that moments in time gain a particular, heightened quality. Such a moment, in which eternity breaks into time, is described by Tillich as *kairos* and is not interpreted in a christological way at first. Here eternity happens in time.[40]

In the existential theology of Rudolf Bultmann (d. 1976), who drew inspiration from Martin Heidegger (d. 1976), one finds similar ideas: normally, human history and existence are subject to the conditions of the past, so that humanity is trapped in the world and determined in a worldly sense. This can be seen as an explanation of humanity's sinfulness. Christ liberates from sin because he represents the end of history, thus liberating humanity from being determined by its past. This happens in proclamation, in the *kerygma*, which calls us to let our existence be determined in every situation completely by God and thus no longer by the entanglements of the world.[41] In the work of all three theologians, the eschatological content of the relationship is determinative in a comprehensive way, because time and eternity are related to one another in a dialectical manner.

The historical use of the term eschatology was taken up in the twentieth century and completely reassessed: Charles Harold Dodd (d. 1973) emerged in 1935 with the thesis, later widely adopted, that Jesus' proclamation could not be understood in the apocalyptic sense that Weiss and Schweitzer had established. Rather, Jesus' message of the kingdom of God according to Mk 10:15 and Mk 1:14 is that the kingdom of God has already broken in as a

---

[39]Karl Barth, *The Epistle to the Romans* (trans. Edwyn C. Hoskyns; London: Oxford, 1968), p. 314.
[40]Cf. Paul Tillich, *Systematic Theology III* (Chicago: University of Chicago, 1967), pp. 369–72.
[41]Cf. Rudolf Bultmann, 'The Eschatology of the Gospel of John', in Robert W. Funk (ed.), *Faith and Understanding I* (trans. Louise Pettibone Smith; London: SCM, 1969), pp. 165–83.

present reality. Thus, the kingdom of God is a concrete circumstance that can be experienced in reality in the proclamation and actions of Christ, although its complete, universal realization is still pending. Yet, even here the meaning of eschatology changes: while in Schweitzer's theology eschatology refers to Jesus' belief about future events that did not actually occur, in Dodd's theology eschatology refers to a new experienceable reality in relation to Jesus.[42]

Following on this, Oscar Cullmann (d. 1999) attempted to determine more precisely the relationship between the 'already' and the 'not yet' of the kingdom of God, based on an investigation of how history is understood in Lukan theology. He came to the conclusion that the time of Jesus was an eschatically interpreted 'centre of time', redefining time and history. It is not secular history that determines salvation history but salvation history that determines what time really is.[43]

Yet, all these positions we have just discussed led to new problems. On the one hand, eschatology seemed to be radically occupied with eternity, which can only exist in a critical relationship to time. On the other hand, it seemed to relate to something that can be experienced in time, whether that means eternity is breaking into history in some way or the entire course of history needs to be re-evaluated based on the middle point of salvation history in Jesus Christ.

Many of the positions on eschatology in the twentieth century could be seen as attempts to engage with this problem. The eschatology of Lutheran theologian Paul Althaus (d. 1966) is one of the first to engage these problems. His book *Die letzten Dinge: Entwurf einer christlichen Eschatologie* ('The Last Things: Outline of a Christian Eschatology'),[44] of which four editions were published, is probably the most important textbook on eschatology in the twentieth century, although each of the editions included significant changes. In the earlier editions, Althaus differentiated between an axiological and a teleological concept of eschatology. The axiological concept derives from the fact that in every philosophy and worldview one must discuss ultimate values.[45] With the term 'axiology', Althaus is

---

[42]Cf. C.H. Dodd, *The Parables of the Kingdom* (London: Nisbet & Co, 1948).

[43]Cf. Oscar Cullmann, *Christ and Time* (London: SCM, 1963, 3rd edn). On Tillich, Bultmann, Dodd and Cullmann cf. Christoph Schwöbel, 'Die letzten Dinge zuerst?', in *Gott in Beziehung* (Tübingen: Mohr Siebeck, 2002), pp. 443–50.

[44]Cf. Paul Althaus, *Die letzten Dinge: Entwurf einer christlichen Eschatologie* (Gütersloh: Bertelsman, 1924, 2nd edn).

[45]Cf. Althaus, *Die letzten Dinge*, pp. 16–22.

adopting a term used frequently by Wilhelm Windelband (d. 1915).[46] In contrast, the teleological sense relates to what is specifically Christian about the goal of history, which Althaus, however, did not want to interpret as a part of history.[47] Because Althaus was criticized that his double concept of eschatology described such highly divergent objects that they could not be reconciled – especially as the axiological concept of eschatology lacks any basis in the experience of Christian revelation – Althaus finally abandoned this distinction in the fourth edition of his book, without revoking its theological point, however.[48] Regardless of how useful we may consider Althaus's efforts to be in the end, we must acknowledge that it represents an attempt to reconcile two different concepts of eschatology – a universal anthropological one and a specifically Christian one – and addresses both by framing the question in the same way.

1.1.3.2 Eschatologies 'from ahead'

Since the 1960s, Wolfhart Pannenberg has devoted himself to examining the problem of the universal validity of human knowledge, on the one hand, and Christian revelation, on the other. In his work, we find the most sophisticated and ambitious attempt to show that eschatology is not only a central doctrinal element of Christian faith but also determines the entirety of theology. Humans can only know about God when God chooses to be revealed. Pannenberg adopts this view from the late Karl Barth, an idea with which Barth attempted to overcome the radical contrast between time and eternity, human and God. In keeping with the view of the *Religionsgeschichtliche Schule* in the exegetical disciplines, Pannenberg assumes that God reveals God's self as history: the entire course of history must be understood as God's revealing of God's self. This means that the revelation of God is not complete or comprehensible until the end of history.[49] This end of history, however, is anticipated in the resurrection of Christ, which the early Pannenberg understood as a historical event, so that Christians can know the end of history and God can be manifest.[50] Thus, the resurrection of Christ is the only event in history whatsoever which can

---

[46]Cf. Hjelde, *Eschaton und Eschata*, p. 387.
[47]Cf. Althaus, *Die letzten Dinge*, p. 22.
[48]For more on this discussion, see Hjelde, *Eschaton und Eschata*, pp. 406–29.
[49]Cf. Wolfhart Pannenberg, 'Dogmatische Thesen zur Lehre von der Offenbarung', in *Offenbarung als Geschichte* (Göttingen: Vandenhoeck & Ruprecht, 1961), pp. 91–114, 95–98.
[50]Cf. Pannenberg, 'Dogmatische Thesen', pp. 103–06.

be accorded a truly universal meaning. Certainly, this universal meaning cannot be understood by the study of history, since it only functions by way of analogies and comparisons. By definition, the resurrection of Christ cannot be compared with anything else and must remain without analogy, precisely because it is a prolepsis, the anticipation of the unique end of history.[51]

The results of this way of thinking affected the entire field of dogmatics including fundamental theology, so that, for example, creation happens primarily in the future and approaches us from the future. Through Christ, who is the eternal Logos as the generative principle of particularity, that which is truly new is continually being realized throughout creation and in the process of evolution.[52] Pannenberg is able to appropriate critically several ideas from the process philosophy of Alfred North Whitehead (d. 1947) and from Pierre Teilhard de Chardin (d. 1955), whose theology positively incorporated evolutionary theory. According to this concept of truth, all that is acknowledged as true is characterized by universal coherence in the unity of truth in the eschaton.[53] If God is the all-determining reality – a term which Pannenberg adopts from Bultmann – then the essence of God cannot be comprehended without God's reign. Although the Christian claim is that this reign has already dawned through Jesus Christ, given the current situation this remains controversial. Only in the future will God be proved to be God.[54] In short: for Pannenberg God is the power of the future. God is God's own future, because God has the future in and of God's own self and is thus truly free.

While Pannenberg focuses on the conceptual analysis and presentation of an eschatologically grounded theology in its entirety, in Jürgen Moltmann's work, we find a project which likewise emphasizes the character of eschatology as one of the fundamentals of theology, in which the problem of the future as the object of Christian theology is identified,[55] but whose specific contribution lies in drawing attention to the practical

---

[51]Cf. Wolfhart Pannenberg, *Wissenschaftstheorie und Theologie* (Frankfurt am Main: Suhrkamp, 1973), pp. 60–73; Wolfhart Pannenberg, 'Dogmatische Erwägungen zur Auferstehung Jesu', in *Grundfragen systematischer Theologie II* (Göttingen: Vandenhoeck & Ruprecht, 1980).

[52]Cf. Wolfhart Pannenberg, *Systematic Theology II* (trans. Geoffrey W. Bromiley; Grand Rapids: Eerdmans, 1994), pp. 61–76, 109–15.

[53]Cf. Wolfhart Pannenberg, 'Wahrheit, Gewißheit und Glaube', in *Grundfragen systematischer Theologie*, vol. 2 (Göttingen: Vandenhoeck & Ruprecht, 1980), pp. 226–64 and Wolfhart Pannenberg, *Systematic Theology I* (trans. Geoffrey W. Bromiley; Grand Rapids: Eerdmans, 1991), pp. 48–61.

[54]Cf. Pannenberg, *Systematic Theology I*, pp. 230–57.

[55]Cf. Jürgen Moltmann, *Theology of Hope* (trans. James W. Leitch; London: SCM, 1967), p. 16: 'There is ... only one real problem in Christian theology, which its own object forces upon it ... : the problem of the future.'

and ethical implications of Christian eschatology. Moltmann is able to appropriate structures from the neo-Marxist philosophy of Ernst Bloch without having to agree with its materialistic basis. Christian hope is based instead on Jesus Christ, who remains the crucified one even though he is also the resurrected one, so that Christian eschatology is always an *eschatologia crucis*. From this revelation, we can recognize that the history of God is moving towards the kingdom of God as its goal. The discrepancy between this hope for the return of Christ and the actual experience of life now serves to strengthen Christians in their critique of the *status quo*. As a result of this hope for the future, Christians are sent out into the world and society, and their motivation does not simply derive from expectations defined and delimited by existing social roles. The full realization of the kingdom of God, however, remains under an eschatological *proviso*, because it is subject to the future of Christ. That the ethical impetus and motivation for action comes from the eschatological character of Christianity is an idea which Moltmann's theology shares with various contextual liberation theologies. So, for example, in the Black Theology of James H. Cone, hope in the future kingdom of God is the motivation to continue the struggle for liberation from oppression even in places where it seems futile, at least based on a this-worldly and pragmatic rationale.[56] For Gustavo Gutierrez, a classic Latin American liberation theologian, eschatology is the key to Christian faith, which simultaneously offers access to history, politics and redemption, as well as preventing misunderstandings of these terms: when seen in an eschatological light, history is not made by oppressive powers, politics is not the privilege of powerful oppressors and redemption cannot be spiritualized to make it apolitical.[57]

The theologians just named make an ethical appeal which seeks to address the entirety of society. This can be seen as an attempt to interpret specific Christian revelatory traditions in a way accessible to all people, albeit on the level of common, societal action. Another aspect of the problem of reconciling particular Christian beliefs with general societal convictions becomes clear when we consider the natural world. In the modern era and especially since the nineteenth century, the natural world has been the object of scientific inquiry by many highly specialized branches of the natural sciences. Within the natural sciences – which claim universal

---

[56]Cf. James H. Cone, *A Black Theology of Liberation* (Philadelphia: J.P. Lippencott, 1970), p. 249.
[57]Cf. Gustavo Gutiérrez, *A Theology of Liberation: History, Politics and Salvation* (London: SCM, 2001), pp. 198–224, esp. pp. 216–17.

validity based on their own methodological approach – this raises questions from natural philosophy about the unity of nature and reality, irrespective of the specialized area of each scientific branch. Thus, it is that much more necessary for theology to engage in dialogue with the natural sciences and natural philosophy, unless we are willing to abandon the idea of the unity of all reality.

This aspect of the challenge of reconciling Christian content with claims to universality also made eschatology in the twentieth century highly important, as exemplified in the comprehensive cosmic eschatology of Jesuit theologian Pierre Teilhard de Chardin. Teilhard supposes that the entire world is involved in an evolutionary process consisting of various stages. The various divisions of reality include the uninhabited 'Cosmosphere', the inhabited 'Biosphere', the conscious 'Noosphere' and finally the 'Christosphere'. The entire genesis of the cosmos is moving deliberately towards the eschatic, evolutionary Christogenesis. At this Omega point, 'the presence of Christ, which has been silently accruing in things, will suddenly be revealed'.[58] The completion of the Christogenesis of the world is anticipated proleptically in the Eucharist understood in terms of the classic Tridentine doctrine of transubstantiation, which, through the transformation of the wine and bread into the blood and flesh of Christ, anticipates Christogenesis as a transformation of the universe in Christ.

Towards the end of the twentieth century, Teilhard, Pannenberg and others provided the impetus for eschatologies which were not explicitly Christian but were the product of natural philosophy. Along the same lines, we find the 'physics of resurrection' by physicist Frank J. Tipler, who assumes that the evolutionary human progeny will manage to override the stipulations of natural law governing the cosmos, so that at the end, in the blink of an eye, sufficient energy will be available to raise all persons from the dead as simulations and to inaugurate the beginning of the history of the cosmos.[59] But, in mentioning Tipler, we have already arrived at the non-theological eschatologies, which we will need to postpone discussing for the time being. Aside from eschatologies that specifically value discussions with non-religious spheres of knowledge, at the end of the twentieth century, there were also eschatologies that attempted to include the existence of other religions in their hope for the future, particularly

[58]Pierre Teilhard de Chardin, *The Divine Milieu* (New York: Harper & Row, 1965), p. 133.
[59]Cf. Frank J. Tipler, *The Physics of Immortality: Modern Cosmology, God and the Resurrection of the Dead* (New York: Doubleday, 1994), pp. 214–16.

hope for Christianity's close relative Judaism. This was the case in the works of Friedrich Wilhelm Marquardt (d. 2002) and recently Henning Theissen, for example.[60]

To summarize:

- With the end of the First World War, the ethical optimism that Christianity could be realized within history in society collapsed. In Dialectical Theology and related currents of thought, eschatology was appreciated anew, because time and eternity were conceived of as strictly separated from one another, although eternity judges time at every moment.
- With the reappraisal of Jesus' message about the kingdom of God as something ultimate which can be realized and experienced but which is not yet perfected, the historical concept of eschatology also underwent a reassessment, as it was now capable of being built upon in a systematic way.
- This raised the question of how current eschatic experience and future eschatic hope, axiological and teleological eschatology, are related to one another. Because this problem touches on the question of how the universal human quest for truth relates to the recognition of revelation, eschatology became one of the fundamentals of theology.
- The most ambitious attempt to find a positive solution to these questions can be found in Wolfhart Pannenberg's works, in which the future of God – who has no future apart from Godself – and its anticipation in Christ determine all of history and nature.
- In Moltmann's theology, Black theology and liberation theology, eschatology is fundamental for understanding Christianity and serves as the engine for its world-changing power.
- In various evolutionary eschatologies, as exemplified in Christianity through the works of Teilhard de Chardin, the natural world is incorporated into a comprehensive concept of the future and centred on Christ.

[60]Cf. Friedrich-Wilhelm Marquardt, *Was dürfen wir hoffen, wenn wir hoffen dürfen? Eine Eschatologie*, vol. 1 (Gütersloh: Kaiser Gütersloher Verlagshaus, 1993); Henning Theißen, *Die evangelische Eschatologie und das Judentum: Strukturprobleme der Konzeption seit Schleiermacher* (Göttingen: Vandenhoeck & Ruprecht, 2004).

In all the examples mentioned thus far in the history of the concept of eschatology in the twentieth century, the emphasis has been on the eschatic. This eschatic, ultimate reality is interpreted in various ways, however:

> The 'ultimate' is understood in Barth, Tillich, Bultmann and to a limited extent in Althaus as transcendent and equally close at every (temporal) moment, while in Pannenberg, Moltmann, liberation theology and in Teilhard it is seen as specifically temporal or in the future. The former group of interpretations could thus be classified as eschatologies 'from above', while the latter could be typified as eschatologies 'from ahead'.

With this conclusion, our investigation of the historical significance of eschatology has not yet achieved the desired result: while we can see that eschatology became more important and experienced a revival in all areas of theology in the twentieth century, this did not yield a more precise and detailed definition of eschatology, nor have we answered the question about the object of this doctrine. On the contrary, the rapid increase in discourse about eschatology and eschatological terms has broadened the concept even more and made it seem virtually impossible to determine its meaning.

So, it will be necessary to use other methods than a historical overview of the use of the word to determine what eschatology means and what the object of this doctrine is supposed to be. Before we turn to other methods, however, we must first locate the development of eschatology in theology within the even wider context of modern intellectual history.

1.1.4 Eschatology and modernity

If we consider modernity as a whole, it is not easy to provide one common intellectual moniker for this entire period. Nevertheless, I would like to suggest a succinct interpretative framework, in order to understand better the development of Christian eschatology described above. One essential idea of the Enlightenment can be described as the deep-seated rejection of the concept of original sin as well as the principle of the perfectibility of humankind, meaning our ability to bring ourselves and our society to perfection in the course of history,[61] a view which may be

[61]See section 4.3 below.

even more important than a new faith in reason. This change also altered the awareness of time and history. If we can say that people in the Middle Ages and the early modern era saw the future as something that came towards them, then people were now stepping into the future. If Protestant Orthodoxy could still adopt the medieval doctrine of *quattuor novissima* – that is, the notion that events are coming towards humanity out of the future – then we could say that people now experienced themselves as open to the future and were stepping forward into the future. If the future is open as a matter of principle, then it makes sense that, in order to shape this future and themselves, people will look for various laws that regulate history and the future.

In the case of Kant, this may simply be the transcendent postulate of the immortality of the soul, which is not future-oriented and safeguards morality. Other thinkers focused on developing explicit theories of history. In the nineteenth century, we should mention Hegel in particular, who saw the laws of history at work in a dialectical process that had come to an end in his society. The left and right wing Hegelians took this same basic idea and constructed their own interpretation of the future and history based on Hegel. While the right wing Hegelians tended to conceive of the end of this process as transcendent in principal, the left wing Hegelians saw it as located in the historical process itself, even if in the future. Marxism is a particularly good example of this.[62] Even various theories of evolution can be seen as answers to this dilemma, whether classical Darwinism or epistemological evolutionism, which assumes that truth is realized in discourse through the course of history – even if history is an imagined ideal (C.S. Peirce, d. 1914).[63] We might see as various attempts to address this problem Lotze's neo-Kantian teleological concept of purpose[64] or Friedrich Nietzsche's idea (d. 1900) that he had found the key to history in the concept of power[65] or the abandoning of direct laws in history in favour of exploring history using the principle of analogy in historicism.[66]

---

[62]Cf. Hans Schwarz, *Die christliche Hoffnung: Grundkurs Eschatologie* (Göttingen: Vandenhoeck & Ruprecht, 2002), pp. 136–39.

[63]Cf. Charles Sanders Peirce, *Collected Papers*, vol. 5 (Cambridge, MA: Harvard, 1960), p. 407.

[64]For a brief introduction to Lotze cf. Johannes Wilhelm Schmidt-Japing, *Lotzes Religionsphilosophie in ihrer Entwicklung* (Göttingen: Vandenhoeck & Ruprecht, 1925).

[65]Cf. Margot Fleischer, 'Friedrich Nietzsche. Dionysische Bejahung der Welt', in Margot Fleischer and Jochen Hennigfeld (eds), *Philosophen des 19. Jahrhunderts* (Darmstadt: Primus Verlag, 2004, 2nd edn), pp. 179–98.

[66]Cf. Gunter Scholtz, 'Historismus', in Joachim Ritter et al. (eds), *Historisches Wörterbuch der Philosophie*, vol. 3, 13 vols (Basel: Schwabe & Co, 1974), pp. 1141–47.

What is interesting is that this new search for laws governing the historical experience of time was apparently inevitable, as it emerges even in those situations where the perfectibility of humanity is rejected as a matter of principle, as in Oswald Spengler (d. 1936), who spoke about the decline of the West due to the inexorable power of fate.[67] In the end, we might say the twentieth century represents nothing more than multiple and multiplying attempts to address this issue, trying to interpret the phenomenal course of history by means of principles or laws: we find observations from natural philosophy which in one way or another deny the experience of the openness of the future and thus advocate for a deterministic picture of history, as well as the unbridled optimism about progress in the 1970s, the renewed neo-Hegelian talk of the end of history in the implementation of democratization at the end of the Cold War in Francis Fukuyama,[68] or the pessimistic, neo-Spenglerian adoption of the idea of the decline of history in the so-called clash of cultures.[69]

Aside from a few extremely deterministic examples, the basis for each of these attempts to find the principles governing history and the future – in this case, the fundamental openness and contingency of the future – is not repudiated but seen as a necessary condition for the possibility of the future. After the end of optimism about progress in the 1970s and the awareness of ecological crises in the 1980s, the postmodern situation at the end of the twentieth century and beginning of the twenty-first century seems to be no exception to this rule. It may even introduce new problems, radicalizing the challenge of human interpretations of history: it could be that something like the end of paradigms has set in, because now within one culture we find varying concepts of history competing with one another, just as individual people are exposed to a plurality of ways to interpret their life stories and thus to understand their own identities. What is interesting is that, unlike in the time of Protestant Orthodoxy, in which one historical conception of Christian hope existed in competition with other interpretative frameworks or was developed through interacting with these theories, the eschatological concept today is subject to an internal pluralism: there is no longer *the* Christian understanding of history, *the* Christian understanding of time, or *the* Christian understanding of the kingdom of God, as these understandings themselves seem to have been

[67]See Section 4.3 below.
[68]See Section 4.3 below.
[69]See Section 4.3 below.

pluralized. The result of this development cannot be that we forgo striving to understand these eschatic problems adequately. For so long as reality is temporal or historical, and humanity has to make decisions and take action, then we will have – somehow or other – a concept of the future and history, and this concept may reflect reality more or less accurately. To borrow the terminology of Peter L. Berger,[70] we are subject to the necessity of choice, and this pertains even to how we interpret our historical existence. It is precisely because *not* choosing is not a real course of action that the reality principle is upheld.

A drastic increase in diverse interpretations of eschatology in Christian theology has taken place at the same time as the history of thought has experienced an inflation and pluralization of intellectual interpretative frameworks to understand the phenomena of temporality and the historicity of human culture.

1.2 Eschatology and the concept of action

Our historical consideration of the concept of eschatology so far has revealed a myriad of applications of the term still in use today. A systematic definition of the object of eschatology will thus need to take these into account at least in so far as it reflects their concerns. Therefore, we need first to seek a broad concept of eschatology that arises from the phenomenology of human experience or, more precisely, from the concept of human action.

1.2.1 Action

The specific difference between a concrete action and an event in general lies in the fact that an action is intentional. For an action, any description of the event contains the notion of intention: 'A man is the agent of an act if

---

[70]Cf. Peter L. Berger, *The Heretical Imperative: Contemporary Possibilities of Religious Affirmation* (New York: Doubleday, 1979), pp. 1–31, esp. p. 28.

what he does can be described under an aspect that makes it intentional.'[71] Purposefulness is among the 'intentional' capabilities humans possess, meaning those abilities with which we relate to other things and people. We are directly aware of intentions, whereas by definition we cannot be immediately aware of something we have done unintentionally: when we have done something unintentionally, we first need to detect it. Intentions are not predictions, because predictions are only true when that which was forecasted has actually taken place, but someone can have an intention which is not realized. Furthermore, intentions are not wishes. First, we do not always intend things that we wish for, e.g. I wish I could be a bird but I do not intend to be one. Second, wishes – in contrast to intentions – allow for differing degrees of intensity. For example, I wish to cross the Atlantic either by plane or by ship, but I prefer to travel by plane. Intentions, however, are not a matter of preference: As long as I am not sure by which means I will cross the Atlantic, I do not actually intend to use any particular means. But, after making the decision to take a plane, I also intend to take a plane, whereas I never intended to use a ship. And third, unlike wishes, intentions are always related to the speaker as an active subject. It is only in the first person perspective that intentions can be assessed without any doubt. Intentions are not motives, as the latter can also reflect affective attitudes. An intention is not the conviction that one can bring an event about, since one can also intend an event while remaining rather pessimistic about whether it will take place.[72]

Although intentionality is the decisive criteria for action, controversy exists about the role intention plays in the ontological definition of actions. Does the language of 'intention' presume a dualistic ontology that differentiates between a causal and a personal world?[73] With this question in mind, we can find reductionistic solutions, which avoid talking about intentions at all.[74] Other approaches which are not reductionistic as a

---

[71]Donald Davidson, 'Agency', in *Essays on Actions and Events* (Oxford: Clarendon, 2002), p. 47.

[72]For more on this, see Edmund Runggaldier, *Was sind Handlungen? Eine philosophische Auseinandersetzung mit dem Naturalismus* (Stuttgart: Kohlhammer, 1996), pp. 93–97.

[73]Cf. Runggaldier, *Handlungen*, pp. 17–23.

[74]So, e.g., Willard Van Orman Quine, *Word and Object* (Cambridge: MIT, 2013), pp. 198–203; Donald Davidson, 'Mental Events', in *Essays on Actions and Events* (Oxford: Clarendon, 2002), pp. 207–27. Davidson himself clearly does not see the approach to the problem reductionistically, p. 214: 'Anomalous monism shows an ontological bias only in that it allows the possibility that not all events are mental, while insisting that all events are physical. Such a bland monism, unbuttressed by correlating laws or conceptual economies, does not seem to merit the term "reductionism".' Cf. also Runggaldier, *Handlungen*, pp. 122–43, on this discussion.

matter of principle attempt to see the agent of an action, including his or her capabilities for intentionality, as a 'cause' – although not in the strictly deductive nomological[75] sense – and so they speak about 'agent causality'.[76]

Agents and their intentions are indispensable for explaining actions. So, we can now attempt to define the concept of action, which will then be examined in detail step-by-step:

> To say 'someone acts' means: A person intends an event (A) given a particular affective state and factual knowledge (B) and certainties based on a particular worldview (C). The action follows certain rules and means (E) to bring about the intended goal (F) with a particular expectation (G), and this agent is a necessary condition for this event to occur within the larger, overall context of the event (H).

A: Although *persons* are conscious of their actions and intentions, certain affective conditions are always present, such as feelings of desire or aversion. These feelings may play a role as a motivation for an action, but they can often also be circumvented. If I wish to climb a mountain, then I have various feelings such as a love of adventure and the excitement caused by an elevated level of adrenaline and so on.

B: Action always presumes *factual knowledge*. This refers to all the knowledge around the world which I can theoretically gain by following an empirically verifiable path. If I wish to climb a mountain, for example, I have to know where it is located, approximately how high it is, what the paths are like and where they are. This knowledge can be verified empirically, e.g. I could test various mountain paths for their practicality. Usually, such empirically verifiable knowledge is also knowledge in relation to conditions that have not come to be through human action, that is, the impersonal reality of the world. If we characterize these as natural or cosmic actualities, then action always has a natural or cosmic dimension as well.

[75]Cf. e.g. Carl G. Hempel and Paul Oppenheim, 'Studies in the Logic of Explanation', *Philosophy of Science* 15.2 (April 1948), pp. 135–75; Earl R. MacCormac, *Metaphor and Myth in Science and Religion* (Durham: Duke, 1976), pp. 4–21.

[76]Cf. Anthony Kenny, *Action, Emotion and Will* (London: Routledge, 1963); Roderick M. Chisholm, 'Events without Times: An Essay on Ontology', *Nous* 24 (1990), pp. 413–28; Georg Henrik von Wright, *Erklären und Verstehen* (Frankfurt am Main: Athäneum Fischer, 1974), p. 82, discusses passive and active personal components in describing causal reactions in scientific experiments.

C: Action always presupposes *beliefs based on a particular worldview* which one could also call *faith*. This means nothing more than particular assumptions implied by our actions, which are no longer empirically verifiable in principle. We must rely on a lot of facts without being able to verify them and without even being aware of this: I am not going to check the crampons needed for mountain climbing before every step to see if they still hold, but theoretically I could. However, I am certain of this knowledge in the sense that I rely on the crampon's hold or else I would not be able to go one step further. There are also certainties which in principle are no longer subject to review: I am sure, for example, that it is wise to climb this mountain. This belief is controversial, while other certainties are less so, such as the idea that it is wise to learn and to read. We might provide arguments in favour of the beliefs of a particular worldview but it cannot be empirically tested.

D: Actions are *events*. They are distinct from material things in that they are not subject to temporal change. An event requires a certain period of time to elapse. Events also cannot move about in space, but, when seen as a whole, they always involve a particular location. If I wish to climb a mountain, I move both in time – the duration I need from early in the morning until noon, for example – and in space as I displace myself from one place to another – say, the distance from the bottom of the glen to the summit. The event as such does not change, however.

E: The intention to cause an event is structured according to specific *rules* and *means*: Means can be material things such as instruments necessary for the action or else appropriate partial actions. 'Rules' refer to a category of norms and values that, due to the beliefs based on a given worldview, permit the adoption of means that do not derive solely from attaining a specific goal. Thus, it could be a sensible and very expedient means if, to quench my thirst while mountain climbing, I simply stole the water bottle of one of my fellow climbers. However, I will not do this because of certain rules, so I would rather wait until another opportunity presents itself to satisfy my thirst.

F: An event is intended to attain a particular *purpose*. The purpose can also be called the goal of the intended event. Every circumstance we can imagine in the future can become a possible goal. The intending person selects a goal from among this group of circumstances, for which the intended event is a means to achieving that end. As this selection from (in part unconscious) knowledge is dependent on the nature of the world and the person's affective state of desire or aversion, the person does not possess absolute freedom in choosing the goal. When the purpose of an action itself is no longer a means to achieving a higher purpose, one refers to an action as an end in itself. This would probably be the case for climbing a mountain if I were doing this during my vacation, but not if I were a geologist seeking to reach the summit in order to take pertinent measurements.

G: Every action takes place within a *horizon of expectations*. The expectation may simply be that the goal will be successful, but this is not necessary. As achieving the goal does not depend on the agent alone, there is the possibility the event will not take place and the goal will not be successful or even completely fail, or that it is only partially successful, or that success is based on certain likelihoods I can only estimate roughly. Finally, given the contingency of the world, something so surprising may happen that the goal may need to be modified completely. The range of expectations inherent in every action is thus not identical to the goal, as it likewise consists of imaginable events, that is, as something we can imagine in the future. Furthermore, this range of inherent expectations is connected to a certain assessment: I can either be optimistic (hoping an event will take place) or pessimistic (fearing an event will take place). In both cases, I can still carry out the action, but that is not necessary. In the case of mountain climbing, I have to judge how the weather is developing. But, even if I am concerned there will be a storm in the evening, I can still retain the goal of climbing the mountain, with the hope that I will get back before the storm.

H: So, we have now attempted to describe an individual action. An individual action occurs only within a larger *context of action* and can be classified based on whether it constitutes (1) a *master act* or (2) *basic* or *partial acts*. This distinction is firstly a relative one: a master act can include various aspects of basic or partial acts, and in several respects a basic act can also consist of other partial acts. Master and basic actions can be distinguished[77] in various ways. What is important here is only that this context for action means every action also leads to further actions in the future. This is the case even if, while trying to climb a mountain, I die and cease to be an agent of action myself. For then, other mountain climbers will orient themselves based on my failure, my family will have to plan my funeral, and so on. When we talk about the context for action, this involves not only the integration of the action within the context of the individual actions of a subject, but also the interactive context in relation to other actors. In short: action is always interaction and has a social dimension.

---

[77]Cf., for example, the detailed pattern in Richard Swinburne, *The Christian God* (Oxford: Oxford, 1994), pp. 56–62.

Action is thus a basic principle for fundamental anthropology, constituting the starting point for our own reflections, although it is also based on numerous other assumptions. In the process, it appears that three necessary elements of the concept of action are oriented towards the future and allow for temporal-historical existence: the goals of action, the horizon of expectations for each action and the embeddedness of actions in a larger context including consequences resulting in other actions.

It seems advisable to relate the concept of eschatology to these elements. Before we do, however, we ought to say a word about the structure of systematic theology.

1.2.2 Systematic theology as the self-reflection of Christian practice

If we assume that systematic theology deals with methodologically controlled self-reflection on the Christian life,[78] then systematic theology is itself an action that finds its subject matter in all areas of action. As we have seen, the concept of action always involves certain assumptions and certainties based on a given worldview so that it is ultimately impossible to examine a subject or reflect on an action that is neutral, that is, not influenced by a particular worldview. Thus, systematic theology is a form of reflection on actions which is not only aware of its own perspectival nature, but always explicitly reflects on this as well. The diverse classical disciplines of systematic theology cannot be viewed as various fields of knowledge but as the examination of one subject – Christian practice – always from differing perspectives drawn from elements of the concept of action: dogmatics deals with Christian action from the perspective of beliefs based on a certain worldview; ethics addresses Christian action from the perspective of its rules, means and goals as well as the affective circumstances of agents; ecumenical theology and missional studies are concerned with Christian action from the perspective of its location in an interactive context, in so far as agents always act together with other agents who have other beliefs based on their worldview; and finally, a Christian approach to the philosophy of religion addresses Christian action from the perspective of factual knowledge. The branch of theology known as fundamental theology or prolegomena does

[78]Cf. Christoph Schwöbel, 'Doing Systematic Theology – Das Handwerk der Systematischen Theologie', in *Gott in Beziehung* (Tübingen: Mohr Siebeck, 1992), pp. 9–22.

not deal with Christian action from one of these perspectives derived from the concept of action, but it reflects on the relationship between individual theological disciplines and the elements of the concept of action.

> Reflection on human action is ultimately a form of human action itself, and given the premise that human action always reflects presumptions based on a particular worldview, reflection cannot be neutral in terms of its own worldview either.
>
> Systematic theology is methodologically controlled self-reflection on human action, which explicitly addresses its own worldview presuppositions.
>
> Systematic theology can be done in terms of the philosophy of religion, fundamental theology, dogmatics, ethics, ecumenical theology, mission and religious studies, or eschatology.

1.2.3 Eschatology as reflection on Christian life

One element of action, however, remains outside the parameters of reflection: the consideration of Christian practice based on the inherent expectations associated with an action. We can define this as the subject of eschatology. If this definition is plausible, then it has immediate consequences for the concept of eschatology: The concept of eschatology is not just a single chapter in dogmatics. When eschatology appears in the context of dogmatics, it functions just like all the other perspectives examining the notion of action so that every individual perspective is relevant to every other perspective. This means eschatology is also concerned with the entirety of Christian practice or Christian belief. Eschatology must therefore also address all other elements of dogmatics including the classical *loci*, but now with regard to its own view on the inherent expectations of Christian action. Eschatology thus encompasses a much broader field than has traditionally been assumed and practised. Within the confines of this textbook, we will also be unable to carry out this agenda fully, so we will have to come to a pragmatic compromise in which the traditional themes of eschatology come to the fore and the basic idea that eschatology attempts to portray the entirety of Christian belief will only be implemented to the extent necessary.

The subject of eschatology is the entirety of Christian practice from the perspective of the inherent expectations associated with action.

Drawing on 1 Cor. 13:13 one could also say: while dogmatics relates to faith, and ethics to love, eschatology relates to the hope inherent in Christian practice.

Defining the object of eschatology in this way has two advantages: first, it can take up the concern of those theologians who argue that Christianity as a whole is eschatology such as Barth, Pannenberg, Moltmann and others. But, unlike Pannenberg, for example, this eschatological view of Christianity is not exclusive so that no other descriptions are conceivable. Rather, it is also able to address the concern of theologians such as Schleiermacher who argued that eschatology does not belong to the same realm as dogmatics, if the latter deals with Christian practice from the perspective of faith. In contrast to Schleiermacher, however, the subject of eschatology is not removed from the context of experience but rather systematic theology as dogmatics addresses the experience of hope in light of faith.

1.3 The logic of hope

We can now turn to the question of how to approach the range of inherent expectations generated by human action. In this case, we can start with everyday speech, since it contains numerous expressions relating to the realm of the future such as 'expecting, hoping for, fearing/worrying about, being surprised, dreaming, imagining, being disappointed, something being unhoped-for' and many more. Among these, two related conceptual pairs are particularly important, because we use them in everyday speech following a very fixed pattern: 'expecting – being surprised' and 'hoping for – fearing'.

1.3.1 Expectations and surprises

The phrases 'to expect' and 'to be surprised' are expressions of a secondary order that relates to a primary sentence or proposition. We use expressions such as 'I expect that…' and in place of the ellipses we can insert a full sentence. Surprise works the same way: 'I am surprised that … ' Both pairs of terms are thus oriented towards implied expectations about the future in such a way that they do not relate directly to events but to one of our attitudes towards possible future events. This attitude is thus an intentional intellectual stance, which, in the case of this conceptual pair, reflects how our reason – which involves the ability to estimate the probability of future events – judges these events. These conceptual pairs can be paraphrased as follows:

(1) 'it is expected that …'
(2) 'it is not expected that …' means 'it would be surprising if …'

Likewise we can say that:

(3) 'it would not be surprising if …' means 'it is expected that …'

In addition, two further negations are possible:

(4) 'it is expected that X will not happen …' means 'it would *not* be surprising if X does *not* happen'
(5) 'it is *not* expected that X will *not* happen …' means 'it would be surprising if X does not happen'[79]

To provide a concrete example: if I am not expecting a visit today, then it is surprising if someone comes to visit. If I am not surprised about receiving a visit today, then I have expected it, etc.

What is important is that these expressions can be combined or iterated to achieve new meanings. For example, on my birthday I can 'expect to be surprised'. Furthermore, there is a completely different use of the phrase 'to be surprised', which is not at all prospective and cannot be rendered as 'it *would be* surprising if …' but can only be rendered retrospectively as:

(6) 'it *is* surprising that …' meaning 'it was unexpected that …'

In expressions (1) – (5), the element of surprise lies before me prospectively within a range of inherent expectations, while the retrospective use of the term means that my range of inherent expectations has actually been altered. Although, according to the normal logic of a statement, a sentence cannot be simultaneously true and untrue as it would then be contradictory, we can express the retrospective use of 'being

---

[79]Ep = 'it is expected that …'; SPp = 'it would be suprising that …': –Ep=SPp; –SPp = Ep; –E–p = SP–p; –SP–p = E–p.

surprised' – that which could not have been unexpected – precisely by way of such a (seeming) contradiction:

> (7) 'it *is* surprising that…', or rather 'it was *completely unexpected* that…' means 'it was not expected that… and it would not have been surprising if…'[80]

Correspondingly, we can define what we presume will happen thus:

> (8) 'it was presumed that…' means 'it was expected that and/or it would have been surprising if…'

This last kind of surprise – that which could not have been expected at all – plays an important role in eschatology since we are dealing with ultimate things, or what is transcendent with regard to individual phenomena within the world but does not transcend the world itself. While events which are expected or prospectively surprising can always be derived from our current experience of the world, this is apparently not the case for things that are surprising in retrospect or completely unexpected. So, it appears at first we have a problem. In this case, would we not have to say with Wittgenstein: 'Whereof one cannot speak, thereof one must be silent?'[81] But this is not true, because combining these expressions can very likely happen in such a way that one *expects* a retrospective surprise or the completely unexpected: 'I expect to be surprised and do not know how.' Ostensibly, when we recombine these expressions, there is a reason why one expects to be surprised that arises from the range of inherent expectations so far. For example, the reason may be my upcoming birthday. The reason can also be that, within limits, the event which in retrospect is surprising or completely unexpected is, in fact, when seen prospectively, *relatively* surprising or relatively unexpected, as when I expect to be surprised with a present, for example. In this case, the surprise is conceived in a prospective way with respect to some qualities of the event – that is, its character as a gift – but with respect to its concrete manifestation, it remains surprising in a retrospective sense.

Christian eschatology is concerned precisely with this expectation of something surprising both in a relative sense and in retrospect. Based on their experience of faith, Christians have reason to expect something surprising in retrospect, something completely unexpected or unthought-of.

---

[80]SRp = –Ep & –SPp.

[81]Ludwig Wittgenstein, *Tractatus Logico-Philosophicus* (trans. C.K. Ogden; New York: Cosimo, 2007), p. 108 (Statement 7).

But, we can assume that this fully unexpected event will become a relatively unexpected event based on the nature of our experience of faith, meaning that certain qualities of the event – which one expected based on one's experience of faith – can be determined very precisely, although other qualities remain completely unexpected. Yet, Christian literature also describes, in part, the eschatic surprise, the unexpected. Admittedly, these statements function less on a conceptual level than in the realm of images. Because various Christian theologies interpret the distinction between these two idioms (concepts versus images) differently, it leads to different eschatologies. So, an important task of eschatology thus consists in specifying the reason for Christian hope and asking to what extent this reason alters the everyday range of inherent expectations in such a way that the completely unexpected becomes the relatively unexpected.

The expression of what one can expect and what one can find surprising prospectively constitute our range of inherent expectations. This range of inherent expectations can also be expanded, meaning one expects the unexpected, by being surprised in retrospect.

In our everyday lives, such expectations of the unexpected are based on our experiences, which may allow the completely unexpected to become the relatively unexpected.

Eschatology is faced with the task of naming the experiential background that shapes Christian expectation and the possibility of perceiving a distinction between the completely unexpected (*adventus*) and the relatively unexpected (*futurum*).

1.3.2 Hopes and fears

While expectation and surprise represent intentional or intellectual attitudes, which reason adopts towards our range of implied expectations about the future, the conceptual pair 'hoping for' and 'being afraid of' portray intentional attitudes which our emotions reflect in response to our future range of implied expectations. The use of both of these terms in our daily language follows a rather rigid but different logic. Both terms are used in the following ways:

(1) 'We hope for X not to happen…' means 'we fear that X will happen…'
(2) 'We fear that X will not happen…' means 'we hope that X will happen…'

In fact, yet another connotation is associated with these expressions, because in the negative form (2) one does not simply express a positive hope but considers it to be less likely. The linguistic use of both these expressions can sometimes be a bit confusing, because not only the negation of the hoped-for circumstance but also the negation of hope are depicted as fear:

(3) 'I hope that X does not happen...' means 'I fear that X will happen...'

These various interchangeable possibilities for expressing hope and fear make it necessary in practice to pay close attention to the context in which both expressions are used.

While 'expecting' and 'fearing' are generally used prospectively, the expressions 'to be satisfied or contented with something' and 'disappointed with something' are retrospective phrases related to the human attitudes of the prospective hope or fear. These expressions thereby diagnose the extent to which that which was hoped for or feared before actually took place, and they express our affective attitude of desire or aversion towards the events themselves:

(4) 'it is disappointing that...' means 'it was hoped that X would happen but X did not take place'
(5) 'it is satisfying that...' means 'it was hoped that X would happen and X did take place'

The creation of further possible combinations is here left to the reader. What is important is that eschatology is not simply concerned with the range of implied expectations in regard to what is expected, surprising, assumed or unsuspected – that is, with attitudes based on the reasonable probability of future events – but deals with the affective, emotional attitudes of hope, fear, contentment or disappointment. Christian eschatology generally contains both types: that which is hoped for, as expressed in language about eternal life, as well that which is feared, as expressed in traditional discourse about 'judgement', for example.

People look to the future prospectively with hope or fear and retrospectively with contentment or disappointment.

Christian eschatology deals with the hopes and fears as well as the satisfaction and disappointments of the horizon of expectations we have about our world viewed in light of the ultimate hopes and fears we have on the basis of the Christian faith.

1.3.3 Volitions

That which is hoped for or feared often conforms to our wishes or the goals of our actions. Both of these do not need to be identical, since we use the expression 'wish' or 'want' in two different ways: first, 'wish' or 'want' can mean to desire 'from the heart' and thus indicate what I really wish or want affectively, but it can also be a 'secondary wish' which, according to Harry G. Frankfurt,[82] means that which I am only striving for or putting up with for the sake of a primary wish. An example: My primary wish is not truly to run through the rain, but I need to satisfy this secondary wish in order to be able to fulfil my primary wish of locating a comfortable restaurant. Christian eschatology is also engaged with these wishes of primary and secondary importance and the question of how these come to be or are motivated. Because these primary and secondary wishes have a substantial impact on us, it ought to be clear that eschatology thereby has an eminently practical and ethical significance.

Secondary wishes describe something which is sought as the goal of certain actions in order to achieve a wish of primary importance – what one wishes from the heart.

By concerning itself with such wishes of primary and secondary significance and their causes, eschatology is a practical and ethical field of academic study.

1.3.4 The future in everyday language

In the last three subsections about the structure of everyday phrases that deal with the range of expectations inherent in action, we have tacitly assumed that the range of expectations distinguishes past and present from the future on which these expectations are focused. Furthermore, this future does not describe factual and current circumstances, but rather possible circumstances. In everyday language, we tend to assume that the future is the realm of possibility. This involves the tacit assumption that the future, at least to a certain extent, is open and not strictly predetermined. Yet, even this *prima facie* assumption can and has been disputed on both

[82]Cf. Harry G. Frankfurt, 'The Freedom of Will and the Concept of a Person', *The Journal of Philosophy* 68.1 (1971), pp. 5–20.

philosophical and theological grounds. Both positions would have differing effects on the possibility of eschatological statements.

Thus it is valid to say:

> Eschatology must deal not only with the attitudes people adopt as their range of implied expectations materializes, but it must also consider the necessary understandings of time and eternity.

1.3.5 The eschatic and the eschatological

To conclude our linguistic examination, we need to define one more term, used increasingly in theology,[83] which does not derive from our everyday language but is stipulated as a working hypothesis:

> In so far as we are referring to a transcendent and eternal range of expectations based on Christian faith which transcends the range of expectations we have about our world as well as the circumstances contained within this range of expectations, then we are speaking about the 'eschatic'. When we speak about the eschatic as the object of academic discourse, then we use the term 'eschatological'.

Thus, the eschatological is related to the eschatic in the same way as meta-discourse relates to first-order discourse.

1.4 Eschatology in outline

Having examined the systematic derivation of the concept of eschatology from the notion of action as well as its specific expression in those everyday phrases used to relate linguistically to the presumed range of expectations implicit in the notion of action, it is now possible to arrange the various aspects in the history of eschatology and to develop an outline for the present book.

Speaking about the *eschata* as temporally final or ontologically ultimate things expresses the idea that human action always takes place within the

[83]Cf. Wilfried Härle, *Dogmatik* (Berlin: De Gruyter, 1995), p. 605.

range of expectations inherent in future events, including the idea that the transcendent 'unexpected' is also expected. We must differentiate those pre-eschatic things that relate to the range of implied expectations in so far as they relate to conjectured future events. But, this presumes that human action always involves presuppositions based on a given worldview of which the agent is certain and which makes ultimate claims. Experience of our spatial and temporal world is thus always taking place within the framework of our notion of eternity, that is, of what is ultimate. Thus, discourse about the *eschaton* is warranted. But, if we wish to speak about the *eschata*, the pre-*eschata* and the *eschaton*, then we must search for the basis for discourse about the *eschata*, the pre-*eschata* and the *eschaton*. From a Christian perspective, this basis cannot be ascertained if we omit the person and work of Jesus Christ. So, discourse about the *eschatos*, the ultimate person, is warranted. Analyzing the basis for Christian hope will reveal that we must speak not about the *eschatos* as the 'last' or final person, but the *eschatoi* as the 'last' persons.

With this we have now sketched out the further outline of the book:

We must first speak about the *eschatoi*, the Trinitarian persons including Christ as the *eschatos*, as constituting the reason for Christian hope (Chapter 2).

After that, we must ask which notion of the *eschaton* – that is, which idea of the ultimate or eternity – this notion entails (Chapter 3).

Finally, we must investigate the concrete pre-*eschata*, the penultimate things (Chapter 4), as well as consider the *eschata*, the final things (Chapter 5) as individual subjects for Christian hope.

Because the concept of eschatology was derived from the concept of action – although the concept of action always includes personal, social and cosmic (natural) aspects – we can make the claim that:

The individual pre-*eschata* and *eschata* are examined from a personal, social and cosmic perspective.

After the problem has been formulated in various ways, possible types of solutions from the history of theology will be presented and illustrated in order to make a case for how to solve the problem.

2

The Trinitarian Basis of Eschatology: The Eschatoi

Chapter Outline

Eschatological epistemology	41
The constitution of faith and Christian practice	46
The Eschatoi as the basis of Christian faith and hope	66

2.1 Eschatological epistemology

2.1.1 Dead ends

Our reflections on the concept of action showed that action always takes place within a given set of expectations (the 'horizon of expectations'). These expectations can be altered and expanded due to future events that are surprising in retrospective, so that even an event described as surprising in retrospective – because it was not at all within the horizon of expectations before the event took place – *can* now at least be expected and thus becomes only relatively surprising in retrospective: One expects that something will happen, and one may even be able to identify specific characteristics of that event, but it cannot otherwise be identified more specifically. This is particularly true when considering Christian action within a Christian horizon of expectations. In this case, we can consider how to distinguish between what is definite versus what is indefinite in terms of the relatively surprising, or to put it another way: What is the reason for Christian expectations and why do we make this distinction with respect to what is surprising? The following approaches, among others, are conceivable:

(1) We orient ourselves based on biblical statements about the future.
(2) We orient ourselves based on the proclamation of Jesus relating to the future.
(3) We orient ourselves based on tradition and the creeds or confessions.
(4) We orient ourselves based on the person of Jesus.
(5) We orient ourselves based on our own experience of faith.

The first approach – using the biblical statements for orientation – is not a viable option. For within the multifaceted linguistic world of the Old and New Testaments, the distinction is only made occasionally between what is definite or indefinite with respect to the relatively unexpected. Much more often we see linguistic forms that do not make this distinction such as the powerful, imagery-laden language of the book of Revelation. Furthermore, Scripture does not have *one* theology but reflects a plurality of theological approaches by its individual authors. For this reason, we run up against different justifications for eschatology, each of which yields different expectations. So, we end up back at the beginning.

Yet, even if these objections were not true, the direct derivation of eschatological statements from Scripture would not be workable because of other fundamental objections: Scripture is not the same as Christian life, but rather interaction with Scripture is a part of Christian practice. Scripture is also not the direct word of God but is only the word of God in a derivative sense, to the extent that it witnesses to Jesus Christ, who is himself the Word. Furthermore, the boundary between Scripture and tradition is fluid: certain processes of tradition have given the canon of Scripture its current form. This still does not lead us to the third approach, however, in which we are to embrace the entire tradition as the basis for eschatological statements. Such an approach also falls short, as tradition is nothing more than Christian life in its historical form through the ages. So, when we search for the reason that eschatological statements about Christian life are possible, then this reason cannot be identical with Christian life itself.

Scripture is the word of God in so far as it points to Jesus Christ. Should it not be possible then to find the basis for eschatological statements in the proclamation of Jesus, as in approach number two? This means eschatological statements would be justified based on research about the historical Jesus. The problem is that this method yields a wide and diverse spectrum of results. Must we try somehow to find a positive connection to Albert Schweitzer's 'consistent eschatology' after all? Or, should Dodd's 'realized eschatology' be our starting point?

Apart from the potentially divergent results of historical research, a whole row of fundamental difficulties may ensue. For one thing, historical research is occupied with statements or texts related to Christian life and thus presupposes Christian practice, so it also cannot be the rationale for eschatological statements. Aside from this objection, the problem is that to be the better 'eschatological' theologian requires being the better historian. Even if this were possible, it would still not be a basis for eschatology, because historical research has always presumed that the proclamation of the person of *Jesus* yields relevant results, not the proclamation of other persons. Historical research alone cannot come to the conclusion that relevant results are produced by texts witnessing to this person and not others.

Deriving the rationale for eschatology directly from the experience of faith – meaning what Christians experience in their everyday lives – also does not work. Although the Christian life indeed entails eschatic expressions in all their diversity, if we take one aspect from this life, such as the experience of faith, and make it the subject matter of eschatology, then we would be making eschatology itself its own justification. In this case, we would be caught up in a tautology, and eschatology would be nothing more than a collection of different concepts about the future to which different Christians ascribe.

> Neither Scripture alone, nor the proclamation of the historical Jesus alone, nor tradition alone, nor the content of the experience of faith alone can be the basis of eschatological statements.

2.1.2 The *eschatos* as basis?

As all these alternate sources for eschatological statements have come up short so far, we now consider the option of taking the person of Christ himself as the foundation for responsible eschatological statements. This is the path often chosen by theologians, beginning with Dorner and Kähler and continuing on through Robinson. Furthermore, this option would be more consonant with attempts to justify eschatological statements within the Bible itself, as in Paul, for example, who follows this path in 1 Cor. 15. It may thus be worthwhile to examine this method more carefully, as seen in the example of Kähler, who offers one of the more sophisticated approaches.

For Kähler, eschatology is based entirely on the person of Christ whom Kähler speaks about in a threefold manner. The starting point for all theology is the individual Christian, who has certainty through her experience of community with God. This certainty, however, is the outcome of justification, which in turn is the effect of the exalted Christ who is present to the believer[1] as the one who brings about human faith in a particular situation. This Christ is the 'suprahistorical' Christ.[2]

This experience of Christ in the life of the believer also ties back, however, to the historical Christ identifiable in Scripture or, more precisely, in the proclamation of the gospel. The gospel always relates to a particular historical event in the past, the Christ-event, meaning Christ's work of reconciliation in his life, death and resurrection.[3] This is the historical aspect of Christ.

The historical Christ and the suprahistorical Christ who is now present (*Christus praesens)* are identical, for both are the biblical or real Christ, the reconciler. This can be described as the 'real principle' (*Realprinzip*) of Protestantism. Dogmatics as an academic statement about Christian faith[4] thus finds its 'material principle' (*Materialprinzip*) in 'soter*o*logy', in the doctrine about the reconciler. This includes both aspects of the work of Christ (the historical aspect) and the appropriation of the work of Christ (soter*io*logy, the suprahistorical aspect) as well as the doctrine of the person of Christ, which is derived from soteriology. It is crucial that neither aspect – formal or material – is overemphasized.[5]

The advantage of Kähler's approach appears to be that, in the person of Christ, he can integrate the other approaches to justifying eschatological statements that were recognized to be deficient. He acknowledges the present experience of faith as the result of the person of Christ, either by accessing the person of Christ via Scripture alone or by describing the suprahistorical Christ as the history of a cohesive principle and thus

---

[1]Cf. Kähler, *Die Wissenschaft der christlichen Lehre*, pp. 92f., 188.
[2]Cf. Kähler, *Wissenschaft*, pp. 217f., 222.
[3]Cf. Kähler, *Zur Lehre von der Versöhnung*, pp. 46–51.
[4]Cf. Kähler, *Lehre von der Versöhnung*, p. 58.
[5]Cf. Kähler, *Lehre von der Versöhnung*, p. 62. Here, Kähler names Schleiermacher and Menken each as examples of the respectively opposite errors.

integrating tradition. Nevertheless, there are a number of objections to this approach: Is Christ really the subject here in every case? Is the subjective effect of justification not traditionally ascribed to the Spirit? Is Christ truly the sole subject in eschatology or should we not also employ traditional statements that instead identify the Spirit (cf. 1 Cor. 15.44) or the Father (cf. Jn 14.2) as the subject?

The strength of Kähler's approach consists in organically linking into one principle the historical Christ-event, the proclamation of this event in the history of Scripture and tradition, and the present experience of faith, yet without pitting these elements against one another. A further strength is that he ultimately uses the experience of faith as his starting point and not its *facticity* – for then we would again lapse into circular reasoning about Christian life and end up making the factual into the normative. Instead, he asks how this Christian practice comes to exist. Although to a certain extent Kähler's approach is somewhere between Schleiermacher and Barth, he can avoid one-sidedness, because he does not need to pit experience against revelation.

The weakness of his approach, however, lies in the fact that, within this organic connection between the Christ-event, Scripture, tradition and experience, he is only able to identify the subject holding these elements together in an arbitrary way, identifying them with Christ. So, the problem suddenly arises that the individual elements of his organic eschatology do not point to the person of Christ when highlighting this integrative subject. Kähler's attempt to justify eschatology can thus be understood as an example of a falsely understood orientation of all theology towards Christ, that is, as an example of Christomonism.

Having learned from Kähler's attempt to find a foundation for eschatological statements, we can make the following assertion:

Eschatological statements are based on the condition that makes Christian practice possible, meaning the condition of the possibility of Christian thought, faith, love and hope.

The basis for eschatology cannot be identified with Christ too hastily, for elements appear within Christian life whose subject cannot simply be equated with Christ.

Seeking the basis for eschatological statements means posing the question of the nature of Christian practice, that is, seeking to understand the nature of Christian faith, hope and love.

2.2. The constitution of faith and Christian practice

2.2.1 Constitution and content

In order to describe what constitutes Christian practice, we will have to proceed in such a way that it closely corresponds to the actual content of Christian faith and hope. Given the premises of our analysis of the concept of action, we can see that faith and hope are not independent from one another but rather are different, interdependent and constitutive elements of the concept of action. This enables us to recognize that the question about the nature of Christian practice arises from the question about the nature of Christian faith. To put it more simply: because hope flows from faith, determining how Christian faith comes into existence also answers questions about the rationale of eschatological statements.

The answer provided by the Reformation tradition was that faith is not only an experience, but comes into existence because of a specific experience. The theory represented here – about how faith comes into existence through experience – is drawn from the current discussion among scholars such as Eilert Herms, Christoph Schwöbel and others.[6] Faith is one consequence of God's self-disclosure (*Selbsterschließung*) within the communication of the community of believers, whereby the structure of experience is crucial.

The experience of how reality discloses itself in Christian faith can be characterized in two ways: first, there is the experience leading to the creation and formation of Christian faith, which can be described as the self-disclosure of the Christian God. Faith, if it is not to contradict its own content, cannot be explained adequately using psychological, sociological or neurobiological paradigms but must be understandable as the product of God's action. But this would then mean that one can expect God to be identifiable in the experience of faith.

Second, we must define the situation in which God reveals God's self as a communal situation. A necessary condition for a situation in which revelation might occur is that the gospel be communicated and heard. Faith

---

[6]Cf. Eilert Herms, 'Offenbarung', in *Offenbarung und Glaube* (Tübingen: Mohr Siebeck, 1992), pp. 168–220; Eilert Herms, 'Offenbarung und Erfahrung', in *Offenbarung und Glaube*, pp. 246–72; Eilert Herms, 'Offenbarung V', in Gehard Müller et al. (eds), *Theologische Realenzyklopädie* (*TRE*) vol. 25 (Berlin: De Gruyter, 1995), pp. 146–210; Christoph Schwöbel, 'Revelation and Experience', in *God: Action and Revelation* (Kampen: Kok, 1992), pp. 83–120.

certainly does not arise without human participation, for it is people who come to faith as they are told about faith: in religion courses, in sermons, through discussions about faith or biblical stories that come alive for children as they are routinely recounted by fathers and mothers at bedtime. All these ways by which faith contributes to the socialization process are brought together in the Reformation tradition under the umbrella term 'external word' (*verbum externum*).

What this term imparts and communicates can be described in short form as the 'Good News' or, in other words, the gospel. The gospel is the narrative of the life (proclamation) and fate of Jesus Christ. The authenticity of any form of communication along these lines can be checked against Scripture, at least in principle. This has an important implication: an event that leads to the creation and formation of faith in a person in the present should exhibit the same conditions that led to the formation of the gospel. If God is identifiable in the experience of faith, then God is also identifiable in the events leading to the formation of the gospel and about which Scripture provides information. So, if we wish to explain how faith comes into existence, then we must describe this in such a way that it does not contradict the content of faith. Because the content is the proclamation of the gospel – although the gospel is communicated with the help of the Scriptures as a criterion of its Christian authenticity – then we can say in derivative form: the conditions leading to faith must be the same as those leading to the gospel and to the existence of Scripture and tradition.

Of course, other theories of how faith comes into existence are possible, that is, they can be internally consistent. But any theory that does not pay attention to the correspondence between the events leading to faith's formation and the content of faith cannot be a theological theory *per se*, because it would no longer have to do with the self-reflection of Christian life. Because we have already seen that it is not possible to understand an action as neutral (that is, as not reflecting a particular worldview), we would inevitably be dealing with an external theory the truth of which an individual cannot judge.

> The dilemma of how faith comes into existence can only be solved in such a way that we assume a correspondence between the explanation of how faith is constituted and the content of faith, meaning the content of the gospel.

The coming-into-being of faith therefore must be understood as an action of God which includes the human action of communicating faith (*verbum externum*).

2.2.2 Justification and *promissio*

The self-disclosure of the origin of this experience of faith involves not only the disclosure of the origin itself, but also the one receiving this revelation comes to experience himself or herself in relation to the initiator of this revelation as well as in relation to other objective circumstances. The content of the believer's self-experience naturally depends concretely on his or her life situation. If what we said in the last section about how faith comes into existence is correct, then all experiences of Christian faith in terms of content should share a common trait: believers do not experience their faith as constituted by themselves or as an object implied in the external relations of which they are a part, but rather as a gift or present. Because faith is related to truth as a whole, believers understand their existence, as well as the existence of the world, as dependent on the initiator of the disclosure, i.e. God. This also means, however, that faith is never at the disposal of the one who believes. Whether I still believe tomorrow (i.e. in the future) and live as a Christian does not depend on me or the people with whom I live together, at least not exclusively.[7] I can only hope that in the future I will still be able to live based on faith. Thus, the experience of the coming-into-existence of faith contains not only the element that faith is not at human disposal (i.e. I cannot produce it in myself, meaning that the character of faith is a gift), but also the character of hope. This is expressed through the form of the gospel called *promissio*. With regard to content, stories of the past are recounted which are not only meaningful in the present, but in fact promise the future of salvation, thus already allowing the present to be grasped in light of this future: 'I will be with you' (Gen. 26.3; Exod. 3.12; Is. 43.2).

[7]On this, see Wilfried Härle, 'Der Glaube als Gottes- und/oder Menschenwerk in der Theologie Martin Luthers', in Wilfried Härle et al. (eds), *Marburger Jahrbuch Theologie IV* (Marburg: Elwert, 1992), pp. 37–77.

Based on the experience that faith comes into existence as an event of disclosure, we can infer as the content of every Christian experience of faith (conscious or unconscious) that:

(1) Faith is never at anyone's disposal and has the character of a gift.
(2) Faith is never at the disposal of the believer and has the character of a promise, which interprets the present in light of the future.

Both points can be reformulated as follows: the uniform foundational experience of Christian faith and life is the experience of justification alone based on trust in the promise (*promissio*).

2.2.3 Minimal criteria of God-talk

In the last section, the implicit reason given for Christian faith and thus Christian hope was 'God'. However, in terms of semantic definitions associated with 'God', we were dealing only with the origin of our experience of faith which was not-of-this-world, which is certainly saying very little – *too* little, in fact – because what and who we imagine this 'God' to be depends on what this experience of faith looks like and the kind of salvation for which faith hopes. We must here distinguish between the question of *what* God is and *who* God is: the question of what God is ultimately aims at the essence of God, meaning all of those attributes which must necessarily be mentioned when the discussion is supposed to be about God. In contrast, the question of who God is aims at the identity of God which is not determined by any particular attributes. In this case, the question is about what something is, independent of the question of its identity. Normally, with entities of this world, the identity can be established through references. For example, I can point to an object, meaning I position myself in time and space in relation to an object and then investigate what it is with which I am dealing. Such a spatio-temporal relationship does not have to be established through deictic action, that is, through pointing, since elementary identification takes place through spatio-temporal localization, according to analytical philosopher Peter F. Strawson[8] (d. 2006). But the

[8]Cf. Peter Strawson, *Individuals: An Essay in Descriptive Metaphysics* (London: Routledge, 1971), pp. 23–30.

means for elementary identification can involve both giving proper names to the object identified and describing its identity, that is, narrating the events in which the object to be identified is involved. Descriptions of the identity to which the proper names relate are fundamental.[9] In terms of the concept of God, we will be able to localize God in a spatio-temporal sense through narrative descriptions of identity or proper names, if God is supposed to be identifiable. Ultimately, we are assuming that this identification of God is a matter of God's own self-identification, which humans now simply follow, if we are not to contradict the prerequisite of passivity implied in how faith is constituted as well as the idea that faith is not at our disposal.

We can further elucidate the interrelation between the identification and the essence of God with an example: The meaning of a sentence like 'God brings about salvation' becomes comprehensible for the first time when we clarify the identity of that which the word 'God' is supposed to convey. If we replace the word with the name 'Baal', then salvation relates primarily to the fertility of the land and the reliability of the weather. If we substitute 'the free market' for 'God', then salvation consists in material profit.[10]

Although the identification question comes before the question about the essence or characteristics of an entity, it is not complete. In the act of identification, some minimal characteristics must be presupposed or even appear in the act of identification itself, because we must presume the existence of a *universe of discourse* from which we can pick out the object we are seeking to identify. This is particularly true when identifying God, because in that case we cannot simply point to something. *Minimal* conditions are necessary that indicate in a universal and rather abstract way what might be intended by the word 'God'. These conditions can be met with a preliminary concept of God arising from the general concept of faith or rather, the understanding of reality.

Let us now consider the following statements which, among others, appear to fulfil these criteria.

(A) God is that on which we set our hearts, from which we hope for all good, or rather, that which is our ultimate concern.[11]

---

[9]Cf. Robert W. Jenson, 'The Triune God', in Robert W. Jenson and Carl E. Braaten (eds), *Christian Dogmatics* (Philadelphia: Fortress, 1984), p. 88.

[10]Cf. Robert W. Jenson, *Systematic Theology I: The Triune God* (New York: Oxford, 1997), p. 51.

[11]Cf. Luther, 'The Large Catechism', *Book of Concord*, p. 386; line 3; Paul Tillich, *Systematic Theology I* (Chicago: University of Chicago, 1967), pp. 211–15.

The first minimal condition comes from Martin Luther's (d. 1546) *Large Catechism* and Luther defines this more precisely, to say that that upon which we set our heart is that from which we hope for all good. This expression is a bit inaccurate because it uses the active voice instead of the passive. The actual meaning is: 'God is that on which our hearts have been set.' The difference is that we as humans appear to be the subjects of action in the first English translation of the text above, whereas according to the original meaning we or our hearts remain the objects of the action understood as justification and God remains the subject of the activity of 'setting'. This minimum definition emanates directly from the event through which Christian faith is constituted as trust in the future-oriented promises of the gospel. With this minimum condition from Luther, God is already related to the horizon of expectations of human action, specifically in the sense that, within this horizon of expectations, we are always hoping for something positive. The second minimum definition of God – that God is our ultimate concern – derives from Paul Tillich and can be interpreted as a modern paraphrase of Luther's definition. However, this definition does have the drawback that it is significantly more abstract, as the relation to the horizon of expectation of human action is not directly inherent. In both cases, we can say: faith guides action in so far as the believer trusts. Only that which one can ultimately and unconditionally trust can be a god.

(B) God is that than which nothing greater can be conceived.[12]

This definition, by Anselm of Canterbury (d. 1109), became the basis for Anselm's own argument for the existence of God. For our purposes, this last point is not relevant, but the following argument is: In our description of how faith came into existence, we determined that faith is dependent on a condition that is 'not-of-this-world', that is, God. In order to understand what a 'not-of-this-world' condition would be, Anselm's definition is helpful because it allows us to differentiate between things that are of-this-world or not-of-this-world, between the finite and the infinite, between the non-ultimate and the ultimate, meaning the eschatic: if God can be thought of as finite to such an extent that something even greater can be conceived, then we are not thinking about God but the world. Only when we are thinking of God in such a way that we cannot conceive of anything greater, then we are speaking about God. Although this definition certainly presents a

---

[12]Cf. Anselm of Canterbury, 'Proslogion' (trans. M.J. Charlesworth) in Brian Davies and G.R. Evans (eds), *Anselm of Canterbury: The Major Works* (Oxford: Oxford, 1998), pp. 87–8.

series of difficulties, such as the question of whether the infinite can even be imagined, let us put these questions aside for now.

(C) God is the all-determining reality.[13]

This definition originally comes from Bultmann, who used it to reformulate the classical predicate of God's omnipotence. It was taken up by Pannenberg[14] and intensified: in so far as reality should always be understood as historical reality, then God as the all-determining reality must be the one who determines all history. Because history should be understood temporally, however, we arrive at a further possible definition.

(D) God is what brackets time.[15]

This definition from Robert Jenson makes allowances for the temporal nature of history, which ought to be thought of as determined by God. Because the past no longer exists and the future does not exist yet, history is in danger of falling apart into non-being, for temporality causes each event to be detached from the others and lost in the past. This minimal understanding of God presumes that a meaningful interrelationship of events is not construed only subjectively by individual people, but can be experienced objectively in faith, if only through reconstructions. So, whatever does not 'hold time together' cannot be God. This definition accommodates this aspect and ties in with the Hebrew text from Exodus 3.14: 'I will be who I will be.' If we understand this as a minimal definition of God, then we are bringing together two points: God remains indefinable as a minimal condition, because only in the future will it be proven what God will be. But that which will be proven in the future will be coherent and consistent with that which has happened and is happening in history now. In this respect, God – whatever God is – is trustworthy. Thus, this definition also can be seen as derived from the way faith is constituted that we have already described.

The minimal understandings of God named so far are not mutually exclusive but relate to various aspects of how Christian practice is

[13]Cf. Rudolf Bultmann, 'What Does it Mean to Speak of God?', in *Faith and Understanding*, pp. 53–65; Pannenberg, *Wissenschaftstheorie und Theologie*, p. 304.

[14]Cf. Pannenberg, *Wissenschaftstheorie und Theologie*, p. 304.

[15]Cf. Jenson, *Systematic Theology I*, p. 54: '*gods* are eternities of a certain sort.... Just so also our actions and with them our lives threaten to fall or be torn between past and future, to become fantastic or empty, unplotted sequences of occurrence that merely happen to befall certain otherwise constituted entities. Human life is possible only if past and future are bracketed by reality that reconciles them in present meaning.'

constituted. An essential attribute of all these definitions is that they are rules describing how to think about God. These rules of thought each exhibit the character of *necessary* conditions: whenever an understanding of God is found that corresponds to a rule, several rules or all rules, we may nevertheless be dealing with an understanding that does not correspond to the reality of God, however, so that the corresponding faith would therefore be superstition.[16]

The careful reader may have noticed that an important minimal definition may be missing in this list: God as being itself.[17] This definition in this form also comes from Tillich, who was thereby engaging with a wide scholastic and philosophical tradition. This minimal definition can also refer to a biblical text, namely the Greek version of Exod. 3.14 of the Septuagint: 'I am the one who is' or 'I am the one being.' But we will pass on this minimal definition here, because it is superfluous and capable of being misunderstood. If God is being itself, then God is the ground of all beings. Provided the 'being' is historical and real, then this definition of God as being itself is merely saying that God is the all-determining reality or that which holds time together. Thus, the concept is superfluous for our purposes. Of course, the concept can also be understood in another way. God as being itself could designate that which, in the course of changing events, is enduring and immutable, quasi an 'eternal present'. Such an understanding can be found, for example, in Parmenides[18] (fifth century BCE). If one were to understand God as being itself in this way, this would only be compatible with the minimal definitions so far if we define that which is changeable as that which is *not* being. But, since changeability is a characteristic of the historical sequence of events and because this historical sequence of events is a necessary precondition of our approach to the experience of how Christian practice comes into existence, then an understanding of God along the lines of Parmenides would mean, from the outset, that we could deduce absolutely nothing about God from our experience of faith. To avoid this misunderstanding, we will not adopt this definition of God here.

The list of these minimal definitions of God provides an instrument with which to decide how to proceed to answer the question of who God is, that is, of how God is identifiable. Whatever we encounter in our further attempts to identify God that does not fulfil these criteria cannot be God.

---

[16]Luther discusses this in relation to concept [A] in 'The Large Catechism', *Book of Concord*, p. 386ff.
[17]Cf. Tillich, *Systematic Theology I*, p. 235.
[18]Cf. Sextus Empiricus, *Adversus Mathematicos – Gegen die Wissenschaftler* (Würzburg: Königshausen & Neumann, 2001), p. 193 (IX).

In the experience of how Christian faith and hope is constituted, certain minimal provisions of the concept of God are implied as the eschatic basis for faith and hope. These are:

God as that on which we set our hearts, and from which we hope for all good;
God as that than which nothing greater can be conceived;
God as that reality which determines all historical reality completely;
God as what brackets time.

These minimal definitions of God serve as the criteria of a narrative identification of God, which will be a self-identification of God and answer the question of who God is.

The answer to the question of who God is determines the answer to the question of what God's essence or nature is.

2.2.4 The self-identification of the eschatic basis

The identification of God should take place in accord with the events that are constitutive for the creation of the gospel or of Scripture. This does not mean individual Scriptural texts can serve to identify God alone, however. It also does not mean we need to examine the conditions in which individual biblical texts originated. Rather, the focus is on those events that unleashed a Christian process involving tradition and communication, which is, in turn, a necessary precondition for the existence of Christian life today. This means that eschatology here is particularly dependent on the results of Old and New Testament research.

2.2.4.1 Jesus' proclamation of the kingdom of his Father

Because we are dealing with a theory of how Christian faith and hope come into existence, it is appropriate that we begin with our first correlated set of events: Jesus' proclamation. So, we will start with the proclamation of God's reign or the kingdom of God by Jesus as a fundamental event in his life. Although Jesus could be seen as within the tradition of judgement prophecy of John the Baptist, his proclamation also reflects other, original characteristics. One point of continuity to the John the Baptist tradition lies in the fact that Jesus' message of salvation no longer relied primarily on the tradition of election as its rationale. Instead, the basis of Jesus' understanding of the reign of God should more likely be sought in those traditions of early Judaism describing the God of Israel – eschatologized – as the creator and sustainer of the world.[19] Jesus' proclamation of God's reign thus has two constitutive aspects: one reflecting the future and the other the present. The future aspect consists in the final and perfect state of God's reign understood as a feast of communion, that is, as the communal enjoyment of creation's gifts in the future.[20] The present aspect consists in Jesus' claim that God's rule is breaking in and is present now in and through his proclamation itself. This claim is primarily expressed in Jesus' actions, meaning in his table fellowship, the parable stories and his miracles as central aspects of God's reign. These are intertwined with the final and perfect state of God's reign, which can be seen particularly in the singular meaning of the table fellowship,[21] which also corresponds to the assimilation of tradition as they 'represent the creative lifeworld'.[22] Jesus' proclamation of God's reign allows us to elicit the significance of Jesus himself for God's reign. If he understood his proclamation as a turning point in salvation, then it is this inbreaking reign of God, 'through which everything else – including the Torah ... derives its dimensions and interpretation'.[23] On the one hand, the inbreaking reign of God is thus inseparable from Jesus' action, so that Jesus' action expresses an implicit, unspoken but very clear claim about his own significance. This claim appears to be intensified further because for Jesus the future reign of God (cf. Mk 14.25) also 'cannot be imagined without him'.[24] Although we can only reconstruct with difficulty which individual events actually led to Jesus' death, it is nevertheless apparent that Jesus probably expected his own death as a result of his own actions and proclamation and may even have 'consciously' accepted it. For Jesus' implied personal claim – that in him the eschatic reality of the kingdom of God is breaking in – inevitably brings him into conflict with the ideas of those around him who share the

[19]E.g. Pss. 8, 23, 84 and 104; 1 Enoch. 84.2-4; Is. 24–27, 33; Mic. 4.1ff.; As. Mos. 10. Cf. Jürgen Becker, *Das Urchristentum als gegliederte Epoche* (Stuttgart: Katholisches Bibelwerk, 1993), p. 21.

[20]Matt. 8.11 par. Cf. Becker, *Urchristentum*, p. 20.

[21]Cf. Becker, *Urchristentum*, p. 22.

[22]Becker, *Urchristentum*, p. 23.

[23]Becker, *Urchristentum*, p. 27.

[24]Becker, *Urchristentum*, p. 27. We should mention here Jesus as a criterion for judgement, Lk. 12.8-9 par., and Jesus' expectation in the face of death that he would participate in the future meal, Mk 14.25 par.

opinion that the law is the final – that is, the eschatic – revelation of God, so that this conflict leads him to the cross: 'You are human and make yourself equal to God' (cf. Jn 5.18 as an interpretation). With the event of Jesus' death, it appears Jesus' proclamation of God's reign, as well as the implicit claim Jesus makes about himself, has been falsified, which is made clear in the fleeing of the disciples[25] among other things. If it had ended there, we would likely know nothing about the events described. But, then the disciples of Jesus unexpectedly and excitedly experienced Christophanies, or appearances of Jesus, in which they came to see the identity of his resurrection and exaltation,[26] such that Jesus was no longer dead but was indeed very much alive.

In Jesus's proclamation of the kingdom of God, Jesus references the inbreaking reign of the God of Israel active in his own ministry.

This claim of Jesus transcends the horizon of expectations of his own context, bringing him into conflict with those around him and thus leading to the cross.

2.2.4.2 Jesus' resurrection and the experience of Easter

We have now come to the point that the resurrection can be recognized as a constitutive moment in the search for the basis of Christian faith and hope. Its significance, which should not be underestimated, is presupposed in Scripture itself, as when Paul acknowledges in 1 Cor. 15.14, 19 that Christians are taking a major risk: 'And if Christ has not been raised, then our proclamation has been in vain and your faith has been in vain [...]. If for this life only we have hoped in Christ, we are of all people most to be pitied.'

So, how are we to understand the resurrection of Christ? We can distinguish between two opposing views, while recognizing that a broad spectrum of interpretations exists between these two extremes:

1. Jesus' resurrection did not take place.
2. Jesus' resurrection is a historical event.

---

[25]Cf. Becker, *Urchristentum*, p. 29, 72.
[26]Cf. Becker, *Urchristentum*, p. 31.

The thesis that Jesus' resurrection did not take place is not new. It can be traced to early Enlightenment theology and was adopted again at the end of the twentieth century by Lüdemann,[27] but its content is even older and goes back all the way to early Christian Gnosis, as seen with Basilides (second century BCE), who claimed Jesus switched places with Simon of Cyrene before the crucifixion. In the system of the Orphic Gnostics, it was the human Jesus who had died without being resurrected, while the spiritual Christ had already left his body.[28] Later Heinrich Paulus (d. 1851) argued Christ did not die on the cross at all but only appeared to be dead. Hermann Reimarus (d. 1768), on the other hand, did not deny Jesus' death on the cross but assumed Jesus' disciples stole the body in order to invent the resurrection. This would have been necessary so as not to admit defeat and thus lose face within their context, especially in front of their families. While Reimarus' thesis amounts to believing the disciples intentionally engaged in deception, David Friedrich Strauss (d. 1874) assumed that the resurrection appearances reported in the Scriptures should be interpreted as intra-psychic, unconscious processes. All these interpretations share a common methodological approach: they attempt to explain the resurrection reports in Scripture based on a horizon of expectation and interpretation that does not require any shift in terms of what kind of events one might anticipate or suspect based on the traditional academic study of history. From the outset, they denied the resurrection could be an actual event that would have been retrospectively and thus absolutely surprising, as well as leading to the constitution of a new horizon of expectations. Neither the resurrection nor the life or proclamation of Jesus could possess any kind of eschatic relevance in this case for, according to the usual methods of historical research, all these theses are vacuous as the texts do not support the idea the disciples engaged in deceit or were experiencing purely inner-psychic processes, nor that Jesus faked his death. Thus, these theses cannot be seen as dependent on an academic approach to history. They are only explanatory attempts within the framework of another (in this case non-Christian) horizon of expectations and another (non-Christian) understanding of reality.

Let us now consider the opposing thesis about the resurrection: that it is a historical event. This thesis is normally attributed to Wolfhart Pannenberg

[27]For more on the discussion related to Lüdemann's theses, see, for example, Hansjürgen Verweyen, *Osterglaube ohne Auferstehung* (Freiburg: Herder, 1995).
[28]Cf. Karlmann Beyschlag, *Grundriß der Dogmengeschichte I* (Darmstadt: Wissenschaftliche Buchgesellschaft, 1987), pp. 39, 141.

who argued the resurrection would have been visible to anyone with eyes.[29] Pannenberg presupposes there are no historical sources contesting the emptiness of the tomb. This interpretation actually forces people to choose between two alternatives: accepting the deception theory represented in several quite late polemical texts or accepting the historicity of the resurrection which is much better attested. The resurrection is thus being taken seriously as a historical thesis according to the methods associated with the academic study of history.[30] The evidence becomes even more convincing when we pay attention to the character of the study of history. If we engage in the academic study of history with a worldview of historicism, then history can only be drawn with analogies between events and thus *per definitionem* cannot comprehend what is truly singular. But, despite all the analogies between historical events, history is distinguished by a certain amount of singularity and newness, so that the purely historical study of history is deficient in relation to its object.[31] A study of history that is not deficient would also have to consider the concept of singularity, which can only be understood in conjunction with the truly universal. But, under historical conditions, universality can only express the entirety of history – which, in turn, can only be understood with the knowledge of its end. For this reason, an adequate study of history presupposes an anticipation of the totality of history. Given the conditions of history itself, such an anticipation can only appear historical and thus would have to be an event that cannot be understood by way of analogies, because there are no analogies to the end of history. If the resurrection is understood as an event without analogies, a singular event that anticipates the end of history, then we are no longer forced to examine the resurrection of Jesus using the methods of the conventional academic study of history. A study of history which is not deficient conversely presupposes the resurrection of Christ and God's activity.[32]

The question of whether the resurrection can be regarded as such an event is answered positively by Pannenberg when he points out that intertestamental apocalyptic texts describe the end of history with the idea of the universal resurrection of the dead. This approach, however, defines the resurrection of Christ as a proleptically anticipated eschatic event, or, to be more precise, as the anticipated end of history.

---

[29]See Pannenberg, 'Dogmatische Thesen zur Lehre von der Offenbarung', in *Offenbarung als Geschichte*, pp. 91–114 (98).

[30]See Pannenberg, 'Dogmatische Erwägungen zur Auferstehung Jesu', in *Grundfragen systematischer Theologie II*, pp. 160–73.

[31]Cf. Pannenberg, 'Dogmatische Erwägungen', p. 164.

[32]Cf. Wolfhart Pannenberg, 'Der Gott der Geschichte', in *Grundfragen systematischer Theologie II* (Göttingen: Vandenhoeck & Ruprecht, 1980), p. 117.

Given all this, we cannot determine *per definitionem* what the resurrection of Christ means semantically, because it can only be elucidated by way of analogies, which is not possible *per se*. Yet, in order not to remain silent about what has happened in this singular event, we must use the metaphor of arising from sleep.[33] Pannenberg's thesis is impressively thorough and self-contained, but it ultimately depends on whether we share his understanding of the study of history. Yet, even then problems remain. An absolutely trustworthy witness of a resurrection from the dead would not necessarily have the effect which Pannenberg presumes – the creation of a new comprehensive horizon of expectations. For if we knew that someone was truly resurrected, we would probably be less likely to revise our ideas based on our religious convictions or worldview than our factual knowledge about natural science. We would be more likely under such circumstances to change our relative, but not our absolute horizon of expectations.

Because both theses are polar opposites, we do not need to choose between them but can vote for a third option represented by Ingolf Ulrich Dalferth who characterized the resurrection of Christ as an eschatological or, rather, eschatic event.[34] If this is right, then the resurrection of Christ is an absolutely surprising event in comparison to all previous horizons of expectations and thus should be categorized as retrospectively surprising. As such, it cannot be derived from the previous horizon of expectations *per definitionem* and also cannot be proved based on this horizon of expectations. Instead, it actually shifts the horizon of expectations of human practice. Precisely for this reason, it cannot be experienced independently from the reconstitution of a person's eschatic horizon of expectations, and it cannot be experienced independently from human persons obtaining Christian hope, faith and action,[35] as can be shown paradigmatically with the Easter witness, Paul.

Thus, the resurrection of Jesus responds to two experiences of those who witness to it: 'Jesus is dead' and 'Jesus is alive'. The statement: 'The Lord is risen' is thus based on experience, although it is not at one's disposal. Therefore, we might ask ourselves why people accept the resurrection of Christ – even if this is not an object of human understanding and remains elusive – as an absolutely surprising or eschatic event.

---

[33]Cf. Pannenberg, 'Dogmatische Erwägungen', p. 168; Pannenberg, *Systematic Theology II*, p. 346.
[34]Cf. Ingolf U. Dalferth, *Der auferweckte Gekreuzigte: Zur Grammatik der Christologie* (Tübingen: Mohr Siebeck, 1994), p. 82.
[35]Cf. Dalferth, *Der gekreuzigte*, p. 69.

Both diametrically opposed theses – that the resurrection of Christ did not take place or that the resurrection of Christ is a historical event – can be abandoned in favour of the thesis that the resurrection of Christ is an eschatic event. This means the resurrection is an event that does not originate in the previous horizon of expectations and thus transforms the horizon of expectations for human action into a Christian horizon of expectations.

2.2.4.3 The resurrection of Christ and the action of the Holy Spirit

According to the New Testament witnesses, the raising of Jesus is not simply a matter of the continuation of one human life, but rather being raised and being exalted can be interpreted as differing descriptions of one circumstance.

This is not only suggested in the various traditions about Jesus' raising, indicating both that God awoke Jesus from the dead and that Jesus consequently leads a personal life as the exalted one,[36] but there is in fact a broadly attested set of circumstances unambiguously naming the Spirit as having brought about this conviction. As becomes apparent, the experience of the Spirit begins with the experience of the resurrection and then follows on in various ways into every early Christian experience of faith. Originally, in the tradition of the words and deeds of Jesus, we can find no reference to the Spirit; and where such a reference exceptionally appears, it is most properly a secondary, later clarification: 'Jesus did not ground his authority … by claiming to have received a gift of the Spirit.'[37] Most notably, however, there was no giving of the Spirit to Jesus' disciples prior to Easter, standing in conspicuous contrast to the inflation of statements about the Spirit after Easter.[38] One consequence of this experience of the Spirit was the occasioning of the development of implicit and explicit christologies, from the invocation, by means of the Aramaic *marana-tha* (1 Cor. 16.22), of the

---

[36]For example, through the participial resurrection formula, 'who raised Jesus from the dead' as predication of God in Rom. 1.3b–4, 4.24b, 8.11, 2 Cor. 4.14, Gal 1.1; explicit confessional formulas 1 Cor. 15.3b–4, 1 Thess. 4.14a, Rom. 4.25, 6.3f and 8f; prayers to the one who was raised 1. Cor. 16.22, Rev. 22.20; acclamations Rom. 10.9, I Cor. 8.4–6 and 13.3; the Christ hymn Phil 2.6–11, 1 Tim. 3.16; a 'sketch for a sermon' (Becker) 1 Thess. 1.9–10; and finally through narrative texts.
[37]Becker, *Urchristentum*, p. 30.
[38]Becker, *Urchristentum*, pp. 29–38.

crucified one who had been exalted and raised as the bearer of salvation through to expressions about Christ as the sovereign ruler of the end-times, as representative of humanity, as pre-existent mediator of creation and expressions about Jesus' equality with God[39] all the way to the initial appearance of Christian occasional writings (letters). If these are now combined with the expressions from Scripture that designate the action of the Spirit (e.g. Rom. 1.4) as the source of Christ's raising, then it is possible to justify the view that both the resurrection as an eschatic event and the assurance of the believer with regard to the resurrection have the same origin in the action of the Holy Spirit. As a consequence, the answer to the question of why Christians believe in the resurrection of Christ can be put briefly thus: 'Because God the Holy Spirit has confirmed it to them.' The conditions that make possible both the raising of Christ and the assurance creating activity of the Holy Spirit, also constituting the community of the church, are by no means purely eschatological, but also 'protological': Both, the raising of Jesus and the action that makes up faith, are to be understood as God's action, in so far as this action is not bound to any presuppositions deriving from the world, or only bound to presuppositions deriving from the world in so far as divine action itself allows them. Traditional dogmatics designates this by the concept of creation without any worldly presuppositions, or *creatio ex nihilo*. This characteristic trait of the entirety of God's action is also found in Paul, who parallels resurrection from the dead and the constitution of faith in Rom. 4.17 (in connection to 2 Macc. 7.14-28).

In the Scriptural witness, the same ground is given for both the raising of Christ and the believer's assurance about this raising, which is the action of God the Holy Spirit. This action has eschatical, ultimate character and is not bound to any worldly presupposition – with the exception of those presuppositions that it posits itself.

2.2.4.4 Salvation by loving surrender

Christ's life, cross and resurrection, however, are not only the ground of faith and have revelatory character, they are also the ground of reconciliation and have redemptive character. According to Martin Kähler, eschatology is always *soter*ology, the doctrine of the redeemer. We have already seen how

[39] Becker, *Urchristentum*, pp. 38–76.

Kähler applies a Christocentric reductionism materially unsuitable for its task in so far as the Father and the Spirit are undervalued in his thought; this, however, does not have to lead to a devaluation of Kähler's insight that eschatology must be based upon the centre of the Christian faith in the cross and resurrection together as an *event of salvation*. As a result, we will have to interrogate and compare various theories[40] of reconciliation if we are to dedicate ourselves to this line of questioning from the perspective of faith, i.e. according to the dogmatic meaning of the term. At this point, then, we will sketch out an introduction to the doctrine of reconciliation stipulated for this purpose from the perspective of hope, thus, from eschatology.[41]

As made clear by the cross and resurrection: Humans always live within provisional horizons of expectation, with their actions directed towards provisional hopes, expectations and purposes. These horizons of expectation determine the interactional activity of humans, in which their own identity claims come to expression. Cross and resurrection transcend all prior human horizons of expectation and constitute the horizon of expectation of Christian faith and hope as the eschatic, ultimate, horizon of expectation. As the ultimate horizon of expectation, the Christian horizon of expectations transcends all foregoing horizons of expectation and judges them: The foregoing horizons of expectation are now perceived as sinful and not in line with reality, as well as the identity claims that humans make for themselves and the identity expectations that humans apply towards each other. However, while the resurrection is a confirmation of Christ's claim about himself and Christ's horizon of expectations, if Christ's claim about himself is nothing other than universal love (Matt. 5. 45), then the cross and resurrection can be interpreted in the following way: Whereas Christ abides in love to all human persons, the sinful claims humans make about themselves repudiate this as false love, and Christ goes to the cross for the sake of the lack of love or false love of sin, i.e. it is an act of devotion to humanity by the person of Christ. Christ's resurrection through the Spirit and the constitution of faith and hope of the faithful that originates from the same source can now in any case be interpreted as devotion based in love: The Spirit gives himself over to the dead Christ, by raising him from

[40]For a brief overview over various types of the doctrine of reconciliation, cf. Markus Mühling, *A Theological Journey into Narnia: An analysis of the message beneath the text of the 'Lion, the Witch and the Wardrobe' by C.S. Lewis* (trans. Sarah Draper; Göttingen: Vandenhoeck & Ruprecht, 2006), pp. 106–15.

[41]The theory of atonement adduced here takes elements from various theologians such as Martin Luther, Thomas Erskine of Linlathen, Rudolf Bultmann, Wolfhart Pannenberg and Eberhard Jüngel.

the dead, and he gives himself over to humanity as sisters and brothers of Christ, by which he also acts in them. An action only upon the dead Christ but not upon humanity would be out of the question because in that case it would be precisely the self-definition of Christ by means of the claim to love that would be damaged. This resurrecting, Easter action of the Spirit on humanity now has a doubly eschatical character: a present-eschatical character and a promisive eschatical character. The present-eschatical character consists in the fact that the action of the Spirit creates the horizon of expectations of the Christian faith that is in line with reality and therefore frees Christians from their past-oriented, sinful horizon of expectations and the claims they make about themselves and frees them from them as such, that is to say it reveals them to be sinful. The promisive character, however, is included in this constitution of the Christian horizon of expectations as the ultimate horizon of expectations, in which humans know that what happened to Christ in the resurrection will also happen to them and to that of the world: Whatever cross and resurrection mean as eschatical events, this is also promised to us for the future; what happened to Christ in the resurrection will also happen to us.

In the cross and resurrection of Christ, the disorder sin is adjusted in that Christ and the Spirit surrender themselves to humanity, with the effect that all sinful and contradictory human horizons of expectation are relativized and judged by the constitution of the horizon of expectations which is Christian faith and hope.

It is in this manner that the sole horizon of expectations in line with reality, that is the Christian faith, arises, including within itself the *promissio* and accordingly the confidence that what happened to Christ in the resurrection will also happen to us.

2.2.4.5 The triune self-identification

The constitutive conditions that have been depicted fulfil all the presuppositions which have been named as necessary for establishing the identity of the eschatic ground of Christian faith and hope. At issue is a narrative structure, which has its concrete location in space and time with the person of Jesus Christ, with the result that the person Jesus is identifiable. Jesus' self-understanding is certainly not to be narrated without its relation to the kingdom of God, that is to say to the God of the Old Testament who Jesus called *Abba* ('father', in the sense of 'papa'). The identity description that is identifiable by spatio-temporal and localizable historical means, and with which the proper name of Jesus is linked, consequently points to the identity descriptions that in tradition of the Old Testament and of early Judaism are linked with Yahweh and which cannot be placed in a specific location in time and space using historical means. At the same time through the breaking in of the Kingdom of God in the action of Jesus and of the danger of foundering on the cross, this determination of the identity of the God of the Old Testament is bound constitutively to the determination of the identity of Jesus. The identification of Jesus is in this case only viable in the context of the identification of the God of Israel, and the identification of the God of Israel is only viable in the context of the identification of Jesus. The fact that it is not a case of mistaken identification from among the various possibilities of identifying the God called Abba by Jesus presupposes however an additional identity description that is linked to a proper name. This identity description consists in the fact that in the history of the church, the faithful experience the action of the one called the spirit in such a way that this identification supports the correlation of the first two identity descriptions named in the formation of assurance in the resurrection.

But, does it also come down to an issue of the conjunction of identity descriptions that could be valid as determinations of *God's* identity? In order to be able to make a judgement in this matter, we have named minimal determinations of the eschatical ground as criteria: The criterion according to which God is that on which one's heart is set and is everything one hopes for [A] is fulfilled, because the Kingdom of God that Jesus proclaims or the Christ, who the church proclaims, is proclaimed precisely as something which demands that those called to faith set their 'whole heart' on it. The criterion according to which God is designated the all-determining reality [C] is fulfilled, because the three identity descriptions are descriptions of something that explicitly claims to be the all-determining reality, in which an eschatical-ultimate horizon of expectations is constituted. One could show this in detail by the fact that the Kingdom of God proclaimed by Jesus includes a constitutive reference to creation or by the fact that the early church recognized this all-determining role of Christ in their proclamation of the cosmic Christ. The criterion that God is that which holds time together [D] is fulfilled, since on the one hand the descriptions of the identification of Jesus point towards the past, and on the other hand the identity descriptions of the Spirit have eschatological valence so that here God is actually 'described as that which holds time together', what e.g. the community's utterance of *marana-tha* through the Holy Spirit has in view. Even the criterion of God as 'that than which nothing greater can be conceived' is fulfilled, since by definition the ultimate eschatical horizon must be one that cannot be surpassed by other experiences. In this case, however, the originator identified in this way must be unsurpassable by others.

The existence of Christian faith and hope presupposes a relation of three identity descriptions consisting of the three meta-narratives of the history of God with Israel, the history of God in Jesus Christ and the history of God with the church, and which were later given the proper name 'Father, Son and Spirit'.[42] The conditions for the constitution accordingly yield a 'proto-Trinitarian depth structure', which also appears in individual texts.[43]

What is of particular interest is the interconnection of the identity descriptions elicited from the conditions of the constitution of Scripture with the conditions of the constitution of Christian hope and faith to all spatio-temporal locations. This would indicate that human communication of the gospel is a necessary condition for the constitution of faith, but that it could not be named as a sufficient condition for the appearance of the Christian faith. The sufficient condition, however, can now itself be given in the identity descriptions implied by the gospel: It is the unmanipulable action of the Holy Spirit, the sufficient condition of the emergence of Christian hope and faith as the 'Easter experience'. The identity descriptions of this *identifying* Trinity thereby allow the disclosure experiences of Christian hope and faith as a whole to be attested as the *experienced* Trinity.

---

[42]The name for God as Father is therefore not an expression for the direct self-assertion of God as it is frequently criticized by feminist theology. For an understanding of the significance of the doctrine of the Trinity for the conversation with feminist theology with especial consideration of Christian thinking on love, cf. Christine Axt-Piscalar, 'Trinitarische Entzauberung des patriarchalen Vatergottes', *Zeitschrift für Theologie und Kirche* 91 (1994), pp. 476–86.

[43]Cf. the study in Christoph Schwöbel, 'Trinitätslehre als Rahmentheorie des christlichen Glaubens', in Wilfried Härle et al. (eds), *Marburger Jahrbuch Theologie* X (Marburg: Elwert, 1998), pp. 129–54, esp. 138–9, 141–2; Christoph Schwöbel, 'Christology and Trinitarian Thought', in Christoph Schwöbel (ed.), *Trinitarian Theology Today* (Edinburgh: T&T Clark, 1995), pp. 113–46, 127.

2.3 The Eschatoi as the basis of Christian faith and hope

2.3.1 Economic and immanent Trinity

If the preceding description of the nature of hope and faith is correct, then this description contains within itself not only a self-identification of God, but also permits the joining together of expressions about God's action and God's being, i.e. what must be said about God necessarily, beyond this self-identification of God. The condition of the possibility for this is the following: If this disclosure event is to pertain to an understanding of God as that than which nothing greater can be conceived, i.e. to the eschatical, then God's reality must correspond to God's revelation. One could also say: based on the faithfulness and truthfulness of God, God's identification in the constitution of faith is God's *self*-revelation.[44]

Karl Rahner (d. 1970) expressed this connection between the action of God in the world and the being of God in his much noted, discussed, modified, but altogether positively received thesis on the identity of the immanent and economic Trinity. The thesis runs as follows: 'The "economic" Trinity is the "immanent" Trinity' and vice-versa.[45] What does this mean? The immanent Trinity is God's being in and for itself; the economic Trinity is the totality of God's action in and with the world. The thesis therefore implies that God's action in the world is indicative of God's being. This is the reason why it is no wonder that theologians like Jürgen Moltmann, Wolfhart Pannenberg or Eberhard Jüngel, who speak of God's revelation as history, in the future, or of God's being in becoming, must take on this thesis more or less positively.[46] One certainly cannot simply adopt this thesis in this way as a thesis of *identity*. As such, it would not only convey that God's being is knowable from God's action, but that God's action *is* God's being. In this case, however, the objects of God's action, the world, would necessarily belong to

[44]The fact that revelation is invariably a matter of self-revelation is an insight that has gained wide acceptance, especially since Hegel and Barth. On the significance of the concept of revelation, cf. Herms, 'Offenbarung V'.

[45]Karl Rahner, *The Trinity* (trans. Joseph Donceel; ed. Catherine Mowry LaCugna; New York: Crossroad, 2010), esp. pp. 21–4.

[46]Cf. Eberhard Jüngel, 'The Relationship between "Economic" and "Immanent" Trinity', in *Theology Digest* 24 (1976), pp. 179–84; Pannenberg, *Systematic Theology I*, pp. 327–8; Jürgen Moltmann, *The Trinity and the Kingdom* (trans. Margaret Kohl; Minneapolis: Fortress, 1993).

God's own self. Yet, even more, this would also mean that what happens in the world – including all provisional horizons of expectation of humans and their sin – would necessarily and constitutively belong to the eschatical, not to the provisional. This, however, is obviously a contradiction, since in this case the eschatic would not be the eschatic. God would then be merged into the world and not only be in a relationship with it. Further, it belongs to the condition of the possibility of relationality that something must also remain undisclosed between those who are in relationship; otherwise the relation would become identity. In the eschatical horizon of expectations of Christian faith and hope, this is clear: On the one hand, it is eschatic and unsurpassable, having a solid grounding in the Trinitarian action of God, on the other hand, however, as a horizon of *expectations* it is nonetheless also *per definitionem* undisclosed and inaccessible. Revelation does not mean the reduction of alterity.

However, this contradiction can easily be avoided with the following thesis:

> The economic Trinity, God's action in the world, is *epistemic.* This means the economic Trinity is the condition of the possibility for human knowledge of the immanent Trinity, and conversely, God's immanent Trinity, God's being, is the ontic condition of the possibility of human knowledge of the economic Trinity, God's action in the world.

The question is now in which way this principle is to be applied, i.e. how God's action in the world and how God in God's own essence are to be described.

2.3.2 God's action in the world and God's storied being

It goes without saying that God's action in the world, i.e. the economic Trinity, can be described in a variety of ways. For our eschatological perspective, it is sufficient to provide a description of divine action that pays especial attention to the temporality and historicity of the world. Such a description will also render more alternatives than could be discussed from the dogmatic point of view. However, one example from the eschatological perspective is sufficient: the reconstruction of the American Lutheran Robert W. Jenson. Jenson describes God's action in such a way that the Father is always the origin of every divine action, the Son is always the present and the Holy Spirit is always the future. In this way, the Father is the source who has no source, sending the action of the Son and the Spirit out from himself. Conversely, the Spirit is the absolute future, who cannot be surpassed, and who frees the action of Father and Son out from falling into the past. This example can suffice for now.

God's action on and in the world takes place as action on and in a historical and temporal world. Consequently, it is expected that God's being is to be thought of in such a way that it is what affords this possibility.

The tradition of post-liberal, narrative theology in its different branches among different denominational forms[47] has insisted that God's very being has to be described as a storied being: If God is disclosed in a historical and temporal world, that can only be described by narratives, being a narrative cannot be foreign to the being of God. The branch of the Roman Catholic tradition relying on Hans Urs von Balthasar has argued[48] that there are two kinds of narratives: epics, where the outcome and the plot of the story is already set from the beginning, and dramatic narratives that provide space for openness, interaction and – as I would like to suggest – contingency[49] in God. This kind of narrative theology often appears to be opposed to what are more properly conceptual approaches. The question therefore arises whether this impression of opposition is a necessary or an accidental one. It is most likely that the latter is the case. This would mean that proper conceptual work and an approach through dramatic narratives are not contradictory. Furthermore, it gives contemporary theology a decisive

[47]Cf. e.g. Robert W. Jenson, *Systematic Theology I & II* (New York: Oxford, 1997 & 1999); Stanley Hauerwas, *A Community of Character* (Notre Dame: Notre Dame, 1981); Hans Frei, *Theology and Narrative* (New York: Oxford, 1993); George A. Lindbeck, *The Nature of Doctrine* (Philadelphia: Westminster, 1984); Hans Urs von Balthasar, *Theo-Drama I–V* (San Francisco: Ignatius, 1988–1998);Celia Deane-Drummond, *Christ and Evolution* (Minneapolis: Fortress, 2009).
[48]Cf. Deane-Drummond, *Christ and Evolution*, pp. 48–53.
[49]Cf. Markus Mühling, *Liebesgeschichte Gott* (Göttingen: Vandenhoeck & Ruprecht, 2013), pp. 135–59.

research task: to work on developing a narrative ontology that can help us avoid unnecessary antagonism. I have elsewhere tried to propose guidelines for such an ontology, culminating in the claim that not only God's action towards and in the world, but also God's very being and becoming in itself has to be understood as a love-story or as an adventure of love.[50] The term adventure signifies storied being including a process and an outcome that is partly open but also partly subject to directedness. Specifying the respects in which openness and directedness are applicable is one of the pre-eminent tasks for contemporary research on the doctrine of God. Such research cannot only be built on the innovations of the past few decades, but has also to consider the insights of the broader tradition. It is not possible to draw out the main features of such an ontology at this point. But, in so far as the broader tradition is concerned, the following sections present decisive cornerstones.

> It belongs to the condition of the possibility of God's revelation in a historical and temporal world that both the being and becoming of the world and the being and becoming of God can be described in dramatic-narrative ways. In so far as God is concerned, God's essence can be understood as storied, as a love-story or as an adventure of love. This kind of narrative theology is not opposed to conceptual theology, but it is in need of further research in the fields of narrative ontology.

2.3.3 God's being as Trinitarian love

Church tradition was already aware of the issues addressed by Rahner long before the twentieth century and had clarified responses to them in the traditional Eastern and Western doctrinal formulations on the Trinity. Since God's action in the world is a unified occurrence of love, but Father, Son and Spirit are all identifiable[51] in God's action as three centres of action,

[50]Cf. Markus Mühling, *Resonances: Neurobiology, Evolution and Theology: Evolutionary Niche Construction, the Ecological Brain and Relational-Narrative Theology* (Göttingen: Vandenhoeck & Ruprecht, 2014).

[51]The discussion of the Trinitarian persons as centres was profiled in particular by Pannenberg, *Systematic Theology I*, p. 319.

God must be thought of in one respect as three and in another respect as one. And this is precisely what the tradition did, though in two different types.

The Eastern type[52] assumes that God in God's self can be described by means of the relations of birth or begetting on the one hand and proceeding on the other. God acts not only on the world, but God's action is constitutive for God's own being even in itself, in which the Father bears or begets the Son and causes the Spirit to proceed. This action is thought to be constitutive for both the Son and the Spirit, as well as for the Father, so that both the being of the divine persons and the essence of God as community depend on this action. Now, what is important is that begetting and proceeding are distinguished from each other, i.e. as two different kinds of action, since otherwise the Son and Spirit would not be distinguishable. There is a difficulty, however: How is one to conceptualize a distinction between begetting and proceeding and everything that these terms imply about God, without also necessarily having to consider the existence of the world?

The Western model can virtually be read as an answer to the foregoing question: Here one speaks of *processiones* in both cases. The Spirit proceeds from the Father as well as from the Son. Now, in order to distinguish between the two processions, the so-called *filioque*[53] was introduced into the Nicene Creed at the time of Charlemagne: The Spirit proceeds from the Father *and the Son* (in Latin, *filioque*). What does this achieve? It is now the case that the Father proceeds from *no one*, the Son proceeds from *one* other and the Spirit proceeds from *two* others. As a result, Father, Son and Spirit remain distinguishable – even if in very abstract ways – though also without any necessary associations with the world.[54]

The controversies over which model is more commensurable to the being of God ultimately led to the separation of the Eastern and Western churches. For our purposes, however, a decision as to which model is most appropriate is completely irrelevant: In both cases, what is retained is the fact that even in a purely Trinitarian fashion the divine persons

---

[52]Cf. John Zizioulas, 'The Doctrine of the Holy Trinity: The Significance of the Cappadocian Contribution', in Christoph Schwöbel (ed.), *Trinitarian Theology Today* (Edinburgh: T&T Clark, 1995), pp. 44–60.

[53]On the problem of the *filioque*, see Bernd Oberdorfer, *Filioque: Geschichte und Theologie eines ökumenischen Problems* (Göttingen: Vandenhoeck & Ruprecht, 2001).

[54]Cf. e.g. Richard of St. Victor, *On the Trinity* (trans. and ed. Ruben Angelici; Eugene: Cascade, 2011), pp. 182–8 (5,IX–XIII).

are distinguishable and related constitutively to one another. Accordingly, the unity of God is something that happens, an event; one could even say: God's being is always action and interaction, and this is the case even if one does not also consider the existence of the world. Thus, this event, 'God', is actually much more suited to being designated by the terms 'community' or 'love' than by 'begetting' or 'proceeding'. This is because if the character of the action of God in the world is that of love, then one must also refer to God's essence as an event which is love. But, further, this love also does not blur the distinction between Father, Son and Spirit. God actually is like what God shows God's self to be, because love requires differentiation and otherness, not reducing down to what is undifferentiated, abstract unity. This event or this interaction, however, remains to be specified. What is meant then is an interaction in which a lover is related through a co-lover[55] to a loved one as a common *project*[56] in faithfulness, veracity and trust in a way such that the lover wants to realize the real good for the beloved one. As a result, the roles of the lover, the loved and the co-loved are not simply allocated to Father, Son and Spirit, but they are rather individually always lover, co-loved and beloved.[57] In defining love in part as the desire to see the realization of the good of the other, Eberhard Jüngel has best characterized this particular relation as that of surrender.[58] We can define surrender specifically as love from the perspective of the lover expressing a disposition opposite of that of Kant's

---

[55]Richard of St. Victor, *On the Trinity*, pp. 125–6 (3,XI).

[56]The concept of a common project has precisely the advantage that it can involve a third personal relatum but does not have to, so that the triadic basic structure of Trinitarian love also comprehensively applies to the creaturely sphere.

[57]Cf. Markus Mühling, *Gott ist Liebe: Studien zum Verständnis der Liebe als Modell trinitarischen Redens von Gott* (Marburg: Elwert, 2005, 2nd edn), pp. 271–326.

[58]Cf. Eberhard Jüngel, *God as the Mystery of the World: On the Foundation of the Theology of the Crucified One in the Dispute between Theism and Atheism* (Grand Rapids: Eerdmans, 1983), p. 319: 'What is then of great significance ontologically and theologically is that the fact that the loving I wants to have the beloved Thou and only then wants to have itself transforms the structure of having. For the beloved Thou is desired by the loving I only as one to whom it may *surrender* itself. Love is mutual surrender, and the desire of love is the most extreme enemy of violent assault. The exchange of mutual surrender means then, with regard to the element of having in love, that the loving I wants to have itself only in the form of being had by someone else.' Cf. Jüngel, *God as the Mystery of the World*, p. 321: 'In surrender, I don't promise myself anything; rather, I promise myself nothing at all because I do not want to have anything from anyone, not even myself; I don't even want to have and to hold myself. Rather, I want to be had. Self-possession, self-having, is replaced by being possessed. But the same is true of the beloved I. Thus the structure of having is changed as the active side of being had . . . . In the event of loving surrender, then, a radical self-distancing takes place *in favour* of a new nearness to oneself – a nearness, to be sure, in which the beloved Thou is closer to me than I am to myself.'

famous second formulation[59] of the categorical imperative: Now one's disposition is directed towards providing one's own self or something that is at one's disposal to be a means for the end of the beloved. To be sure: It is only possible to provide something to someone else that is at one's own disposal. And since no created person 'owns' their personhood but is dependent on the triune God, this disposition towards surrender is strictly speaking only possible for Father, Son and Holy Spirit.

God's essence is love, in which the highest unity and the highest differentiation are bound together.

2.3.4 God's being as ordered love

The condition of the possibility for what is this highest differentiation in highest unity can even be clarified by means of a mathematical 'trick'. This consists in the fact that one can describe the relations in the eternity of God as mathematical 'ordered relations'. While this procedure certainly has the apparent disadvantage of sounding extremely abstract, in actuality this disadvantage can also be an advantage. Since we have no experience of the eschatical reality except in the mode of hope, we cannot actually imagine its shape. But since the eschatical reality is disclosed in the life, death and resurrection of Christ – who is himself the eschatical reality in person – it must be possible to conceive of some of its decisive features. What is interesting about this procedure is the fact that based on revelation, one can *think* something about God that one cannot actually *imagine* on one's own. Thus, this introduces the possibility that one can think about more than what one can independently imagine. How does this procedure look now?

All descriptions of the immanent Trinity, as they are want to appear in detail, presuppose that the relations between the Trinitarian persons are 'ordered relations'. An ordered relation is a relation that is *asymmetric* and

[59]Cf. Immanuel Kant, *Groundwork of The metaphysics of morals*, in *Practical Philosophy* (trans. and ed. Mary J. Gregor; Cambridge: Cambridge, 1996), p. 80: 'So act that you use humanity, whether in your own person or in the person of any other, always at the same time as an end, never merely as a means.'

irreflexive, as well as *transitive*. This is best explained with the help of an example. An ordered relation is generated for example by the alphanumeric sorting of a lexicon or dictionary, which one can well describe by the phrase 'comes after'. It is asymmetric because 'motorboat' always comes before 'motorcycle' and never the reverse. It is also irreflexive because 'motorboat' never comes after 'motorboat'. It is also transitive because if 'motorboat' comes after 'motor', and 'motorcycle' comes after 'motorboat', then 'motorcycle' also comes after 'motor'. What does this example have to do with God? Well, nothing, except for the fact that the Trinitarian relations as relations must also possess these properties, allowing for the possibility of making an ordered distinction in God. We cannot specify a particular semantic content as in the case of 'comes after', apart perhaps from suggesting that this ordering in God can be nothing other than one of love, assuming that Christian faith and hope is really constituted by disclosure experiences. Traditionally speaking, both the Eastern and Western models possess these logical properties in that they speak of 'processions' in God. The error, however, arises in the fact that the words 'procession' or 'beget' are filled with a semantic content in such a way that in what this actually consists remains unspecified.

The essence of God is ordered love in the sense of the characteristics of an asymmetric, irreflexive, transitive relation.

This analysis works as such, but we still have to see that it is also decisive for an entire range of eschatological issues.

However, by means of these excurses from dogmatics, we have now answered the question of what can ultimately be the only ground of Christian hope, allowing us to sum up the results with the following:

It is not simply that Christ is the person of the *eschatos*, but it is rather the persons of the Father, of the Son and of the Holy Spirit, in their differentiation and community of love, that are themselves the *eschatoi*: That than which nothing with greater ultimacy can be said.

2.3.5 The attributes of God

Here, the term 'attributes' should be understood as referring to attributes of the essence of God, that is, attributes which *cannot not* apply to God. At issue then are attributes that arise resulting from God's essence as a set of specifically arranged interactions, namely, from God's being as love. For the most part, these attributes have already been named: perfect commitment, perfect faithfulness and trustworthiness, as well as perfect truthfulness. From the concept of perfect love further arises God's freedom, which, however, is not the freedom of a *potentia absoluta*. The concept of *potentia absoluta* stems from the voluntarism of late scholasticism and denotes the idea of God's completely unconstrained omnipotence. If the concept of the God's freedom or omnipotence is applied to doing what is logically impossible, then it is a self-contradictory and, accordingly, a meaningless concept. If it refers only to the ability to do what is logically possible but stands in contradiction to God's essence as love, then we are dealing with a notion that is abstract and in any case to be rejected accordingly. It is certainly not the case that God could not do this, but rather the case that God does not do this, indeed, could not do this, without also contradicting God's own self. From the character of love as ordered love arises the attribute of reliability, which is traditionally rendered with the concept of God's righteousness. From the concept of love as interaction arises further the concept of God's power, which is to be understood as the divine person's capacity for action. From this capacity for action arise further the attributes of intentionality and of the self-consciousness of the Trinitarian persons.

More interesting than the question of what attributes are to be ascribed to God is the question of which attributes are not to be attributed to God, or at least not in the sense of the essential attributes as we are using the term here. At this point, it is worth decisively adopting the insight of Gottfried Thomasius[60] (d. 1875), that the classical attributes of omnipotence, omniscience and omnipresence are not attributes of the essence of God because they instead refer to God's relation to the world; but, since the world as creation does not belong to God's essence, God is therefore to be thought of *etsi mundus non daretur* (as if the world did not exist). If this insight is correct, then omnipotence, omniscience and omnipresence are not instances of essential attributes, which it would be impossible *not*

[60]Cf. Gottfried Thomasius, *Christi Person und Werk: Darstellung der evangelisch-lutherischen Dogmatik vom Mittelpunkt der Christologie aus*, vol. 1 (Erlangen: Bläsing, 1856, 2nd edn), pp. 47–54.

to ascribe to God. As a consequence, these attributes are also not to be discussed within the scope of the doctrine of God, but within the scope of the discussion of God's relation to the world.

> The attributes of God as of the eschatical ground arise out of the perfect love, which is God, as devotion, faithfulness, trust, truthfulness, freedom, justice, reliability, power, ability, intentionality and consciousness. Omnipotence, omniscience and omnipresence are not attributes of the *essence* of God. These can only be understood as attributes of God's relationship to the world.

2.3.6 From the *eschatoi* to the *eschatos*

Having begun with the emergence of the Christian practice of proclamation and what happened to Jesus in the resurrection, we then worked our way towards the self-identification of the Triune God. Now looking in the other direction, we have to ask what this self-identification means for our understanding of the person of Christ. Classically speaking, it is this question that is the object of christology, i.e. the question asking who Christ is. This presupposes that Christ is the eternal Logos, the second person of the Trinity. And yet, as Christ is also human, the question arises as to whether these two affirmations can be reconciled with one another and what possible solutions lie before us.

There are roughly two types to be distinguished here. One type is of a christology of separation (*Trennungschristologie*), represented by the Antiochene school of theology in the early church, most theologians of the Middle Ages, e.g. Anselm of Canterbury (d. 1109), and the Reformed side of the Reformation. This type holds to an understanding of the concepts of 'divinity' and 'humanity' antecedent to, i.e. *before*, the fixing of the knowledge of the person of Christ. Thus, these concepts are virtually extrapolated from the worldly provisional horizons of expectation and frameworks of interpretation. As a result, this can be called a christology of separation, because divinity and humanity are construed as mutually exclusive on principle, with the danger consisting in a loss of the unity of the person of Christ in favour of the full integrity of the natures of Christ.

The other type, represented by parts of the Alexandrian school of the early church, the new Chalcedonian theology of the second council of

Constantinople (553) and the Lutheran tradition, assumes that the meaning of the concepts of divinity and humanity only first become apparent in the one person of Christ. These concepts will only be intelligible within the eschatical horizon of expectations, which materializes through the constitution of faith and hope. This can be called a christology of unity (*Einigungschristologie*), because it presupposes that the unity of the person of Christ is antecedent and that the discussion of the two natures is properly reached by way of extension from this foundational maxim.

The way in which we have described the occurrence of faith through the self-identification of the Triune God leads us into alignment with the latter of the two foregoing models: Christ is primarily the eternal Logos, the second person of the Trinity. In the incarnation, he takes on a human nature, that is, he changes the structure of his relations with respect to creation: whereas before the incarnation, the Logos, like the Father and the Spirit, stood only as a whole in relation to creation, with the incarnation he enters into the structure of creaturely relations himself.[61] This does not constitute a relinquishment of divinity, thus no *kenosis* (emptying), and apart from that is unproblematic because the attributes such as omnipotence, omniscience etc., which induce the conflict between human and divine attributes, have not in any case proven to be attributes pertaining to God's essence itself. Thus, as already delineated by Ernst Wilhelm Sartorius (d. 1859), the incarnation makes for nothing other than a change in perspective:

> The eye that comprehends heaven and earth with the beams of its view does not relinquish its sight when it betakes to the dark or closes the eyelid, but rather only relinquishes its co-dominant efficacy; thus the Son of God on earth lowers his all-encompassing gaze and betakes to human darkness and opens his eyes therein as a human being who is the gradually rising light of the world of humanity, until that point in which he is permitted to shine at the right of the Father in full majesty.[62]

It is at this point that the Logos no longer stands in relation to all created entities as if to a class as a whole, but rather the Logos stands in relation to creation by entering into the human structure of relations including into what are the relational particularities of a concrete spatio-temporal

---

[61]Cf. Christoph Schwöbel, *Gott in Beziehung: Studien zur Dogmatik* (Tübingen: Mohr Siebeck, 2002), p. 289.

[62]Ernst Wilhelm Sartorius, *Die Lehre von der Heiligen Liebe oder Grundzüge der evangelisch-kirchlichen Moraltheologie* (Stuttgart: Liesching, 1861, 2nd edn), pp. 126–7.

place. Vital to grasp is that the incarnation is irreversible on the basis of the faithfulness of God: from now on, humanity belongs constitutively to the identity of God the Son.

The second divine person of the Trinity, the eternal Logos, is not only related to the other two divine persons, but, also like them, to the world as a whole. In the incarnation, he assumes humanity, that is, he enters into the system of the world's relations, into the concrete spatio-temporal location of Palestine in the first century. As an action of God, this assumption of a human 'nature' is not reversible.

3
The Eschaton

Chapter Outline

Time and eternity 80
Space and infinity 107
The good, the true and the beautiful 133

Having occupied ourselves with the basis for eschatological statements about the Trinitarian God – the *eschatoi* – and identified the foundational event of all eschatological statements in the work of reconciliation of this Trinitarian God in Jesus Christ, we can now turn our attention to the 'eschaton', that is, to the ultimate reality presupposed in Christian faith, hope and action. By this, we mean concepts which may not affect our images of hope directly, yet shape how these images of hope might appear: What are time and space and what is their relationship to the ultimate, if this appears as eternity and endlessness? What is truth in this world and what is its relationship to the ultimate, if this is defined as truth? And what is the relationship of this truth to other definitions of the ultimate, expressed for example in discourse about the three classical transcendentals: goodness, truth and beauty? What conceptual models should we use to reconstruct our understanding of reality? All these questions touch on the relationship of God to the world from one principal point of view without actually addressing the horizon of expectations of Christian practice itself. Instead, certain preconditions and criteria are established here for how the horizon of expectations of Christian practice can be described in a responsible way.

With the first three sets of problems, we are asking questions which, within the framework of dogmatic reflection, often deal with one part of the doctrine of God's characteristics: the first question frames the question in terms of God's providence, the second in terms of God's omnipresence, and the third in terms of God's omnipotence. These do not appear as characteristics of God's essence but as particular modalities of God's action in the world.

This chapter, whose focus is on the conditions necessary for us to be able to talk about relationship to God, or the conditions for a relationship between ultimate and non-ultimate things, functions in part as a bridge and has been intentionally placed between the chapter on the *eschatoi*, as the basis of Christian hope, and the chapter on the pre-*eschata* and *eschata*, as the content of Christian hope. This arrangement allows the meaning of the term *eschaton* to be rendered more precisely, but also in distinction from the standard unspecific terminology of the Judgement Day or the perfected world, which will become central themes later in our treatment of the *eschata*.

3.1 Time and eternity

3.1.1 Models of time and eternity

By considering the works of Augustine (d. 430), Boethius (d. 524) and Richard Swinburne, we can identify three (or four) models that describe the relationship between time and eternity: (1) eternity as timelessness, (2) eternity as either complete or partial simultaneity and (3) eternity as an unending progression of time. The corresponding notions were chosen because they can be used effectively to depict the basic problems related to each understanding of time and eternity. Within the individual types, it is still necessary to name their derivatives, that is, those concepts connected to each type. Finally, after connecting the description of each problem to the definition of the ground of eschatological statements, one must consider a solution to the problems identified.

3.1.1.1 Eternity as timelessness

The textual basis for the following understanding of time is drawn from Augustine's depiction in the famous 11th book of his *Confessions*. This is not the only way Augustine understands time, so the choice of text has already determined the typecast being made here.

After ascribing eternity to God in the form of a prayer,[1] Augustine begins his meditation on Genesis 1.1 in which he explicates what we typically call *creatio ex nihilo* (creation without worldly preconditions) (XI,1,1–XI,9,11). In XI,10,12, Augustine then introduces the subject of time asking: 'Lo, are they not clinging too much to the past, those who say to us: "What was God doing before He made heaven and earth?"'[2] Although Augustine does not want simply to respond in a lapidary way with the oft-used joke which he quotes ('He was getting hell ready for people who inquisitively peer into deep matters'[3]), he finds this inadmissible given the strictly incomparable nature of time and eternity and asks: 'Who shall see … that it cannot be compared; and that a long time cannot become long, but out of many motions passing by, which cannot be prolonged altogether; but that in the Eternal nothing passeth, but the whole is present (*totum praesens*); whereas no time is all at once present (*nullum tempus totum praesens*)?'[4] This quote is illustrative because we see how, before Augustine has even asked what time is, he has already made the move from describing time and eternity as not comparable to viewing them as mutually exclusive: The *totum praesens* of eternity is not the present of all time as a whole. This is expressly out of the question.

With this, Augustine has already managed to assign time to the side of creaturely existence, which owes its existence to God's activity in creation, although he has certainly not shown yet why that is possible. Augustine now attempts to show this in the following Book (XI) by means of the question: 'What is time?'[5] Augustine even insists: 'I desire to know the force and nature of time.'[6] This indirect question specifies the topic of Augustine's investigation. It is also an ontological question. It is not a question drawn from natural philosophy, so in this respect, it cannot be compared to Aristotle's treatment of time in the fourth chapter of his 'Physics'. It is also

---

[1]Cf. Augustine, *The Confessions* (trans. Maria Boulding; ed. John E. Rotelle; New York: New City Press, 2012, 2nd edn), p. 284 (XI,1,1): 'Eternity belongs to you, O Lord.'

[2]Augustine, *Confessions*, p. 293 (XI,10,12): 'People who ask us, "What was God doing before he made heaven and earth?" are obviously full of their stale old nature.'

[3]Augustine, *Confessions*, p. 294 (XI,12,14).

[4]Augustine, *Confessions*, p. 293 (XI,11,13): 'Who is to … find it incomparable, and come to see that a long time is not long except in virtue of a great number of passing moments which cannot all run their course at once? They would see that in eternity nothing, passes, for the whole is present, whereas time cannot be present all at once.'

[5]Augustine, *Confessions*, p. 295 (XI,14,17).

[6]Augustine, *Confessions*, p. 303 (XI,23,30): 'I want to know the essence and nature of time.'

not, as we will see, a psychologizing interpretation of an inner time as opposed to an external time, nor is it about making time dependent on the subject the way transcendental philosophy does and as modern interpreters often want to assume. Rather, in *Confessions* Book XI, we see an ontological theory of what time really is. It is about time's 'reality status', that is, what kind of reality can be ascribed to time. For Augustine, it is clear time exists. He is attempting to examine various diverse ways of understanding time as real and transforms these various possibilities into *aporiae*.

Augustine's remarks are only comprehensible in the context of his explanation of substance, essence and accident from *De Trinitate* Books V–VII. In this work, Augustine alludes to *Isagoge* (*The Introduction*) by Porphyry (d. 301) with whom he was likely familiar in the translation by Marius Victorinus (d. 363) and whose explanations he adopts and then completely reconfigures. What is most obvious at first is the concept of accident as he defines it: an accident is what is changeable.[7] This is striking because Augustine adopts only one of three definitions from Porphyry.[8] The result is significant for how he conceives of substance and essence. Substance is defined in contrast to accidents: substance in the broadest sense is what is not an accident. But, there are two more possibilities: (1) substance can be that to which accident is necessarily attributed[9] or (2) that which is not an accident and that to which accident cannot be attributed by any means, although Augustine considers the term 'essence' more appropriate.[10]

With this in mind, let us now turn back to *Confessions* Book XI and to the question of what time is, or rather the kind of 'reality status' time should be accorded. In section 14,17, Augustine first ascertains that the future is not yet and the past is no more. But, since the present seems to be merely a constantly moving threshold between past and future, the present also does not exist. This argument already appears in Aristotle's writing, although he did not consider it worth discussing; the Skeptics, on the other hand, considered it particularly important for time's irreality. Augustine argues against this idea

---

[7]Cf. Augustine, *The Trinity* (trans. Edmund Hill; ed. John E. Rotelle; New York: New City Press, 2002), p. 191 (V,1,5). The ET unfortunately uses 'modification' in lieu of the more appropriate philosophical term 'accident'. Cf. Augustine, *De Trinitate* I–XII (ed. W.J. Mountain; *Corpus Christianorum Series Latina*, vol. 50 [*CChr.SL* 50]; Turnhout: Brepols, 1968), p. 209 (V,IV.[IV 5],1f.).

[8]Porphyry, 'The Introduction', in *The Organon, or Logical Treatises of Aristotle* (trans. and ed. Octavius Freire Owen; London: Bell, 1902), pp. 623–24: 1. 'Accident is that which is present and absent', 2. 'Accident is that which may be present and not present to the same thing', 3. 'Accident is that which is neither genus, nor difference, nor species, nor property, yet is always inherent in a subject.'

[9]Augustine, *Trinity*, p. 227 (VII,3,10). *CChr.SL* 50, p. 260 (VII,V.,1–9).

[10]Augustine, *Trinity*, pp. 227–8 (VII,3,10). *CChr.SL* 50, p. 260 (VII,V.,10–26).

altogether because he is convinced of the existence of time which he derives from its measurability.[11] What is achieved thus far? Augustine shows with this argument that time is not substance, yet is nevertheless real.

In section 23,29 Augustine then ascertains that time also cannot be the sum of all movements of all bodies, not only heavenly bodies: 'I was once told by a certain learned man that the movements of the sun, moon and stars themselves constitute time. I did not agree with him. Why, in that case, should not the movements of all corporeal things constitute time?'[12] This argument becomes moot when Augustine determines that movement always takes place in time. Incidentally, he is not positioning himself with this argument against Aristotle, who did not identify time with its movement but with its measurement.[13] This is a crucial difference. Augustine can use time in the sense of the extent of movement in a positive way, although this consideration, which originates in physics, does not provide a positive answer to the ontological question but a negative one: time is not only *not* a substance, but is also not a characteristic of substances with bodies.

In the end, Augustine arrives at a solution through a process of elimination: time is *distentio animi*, an extension of created souls, which, in the strong sense, only exists in the present as it is evident to us. There is therefore no past, present and future, but the present of things past as memories (*praesens de praeteritis* as *memoria*), the present of present things as attention or sight (*praesens de praesentibus* as *contuitus*) and the present of future things as expectation (*praesens de futuris* as *exspectatio*).[14] Time therefore has its reality in the soul, and, as Augustine says, nowhere else.[15] If we read this conclusion against the background of what is explained about substance and accident in *De Trinitate*, we can then say: time is real in so far as it is a characteristic – as an accident – of a created, bodiless substance, of the created soul, or concretely a *distentio animi*.

If we spring over Augustine's remarks about the measurability of time and jump to the end of Book XI, Augustine returns to his initial question and concludes that the question of what God was doing before creation is futile,

---

[11]Cf. Augustine, *Confessions*, p. 296 (XI,15,18).

[12]Augustine, *Confessions*, p. 302 (XI,23,29).

[13]Cf. Kurt Flasch, *Was ist Zeit? Augustinus von Hippo Das XI. Book der Confessiones: Historisch-philosophische Studie: Text – Übersetzung – Kommentar* (Frankfurt am Main: Klostermann, 1993), pp. 117–24.

[14]Cf. Augustine, *Confessions*, p. 300 (XI,20,26).

[15]Augustine, *Confessions*, p. 300 (XI,20,26).

because in eternity there is no extension, no *distentio*.[16] With this, Augustine returns to the strict opposition between time and eternity established at the outset, but not without pointing out that the soul also has a hope for eternity, which is to be freed from this *distentio*.[17]

> We can extract from Book XI of Augustine's *Confessions* a definition of the relationship between time and eternity, according to which time is merely a trait of the created world and is real only in the extension of the present which is experienced by the created soul. As an accidental characteristic, the soul primarily knows only the present, but in three forms: as the present of the past (in memory), as the present of the present (in perception) and as the present of the future (in expectation). Eternity is primarily timelessness, in radical antithesis to time.

What hope can created souls have for eternity? The soul's hope for eternity consists only in being freed from this extension of time (from *distentio* to *intentio*). What this kind of participation in eternity might look like cannot be imagined.[18]

> Because time is accorded to the fallen soul in the same way that accidents are understood to be attributed to substances – meaning time does not belong to the soul necessarily – the soul's hope for eternity consists in being freed from time.

To what extent is this 'purified' Augustinian understanding of time and eternity a prototype for other understandings of eternity? It is a type or example of all those understandings of eternity which describe eternity

---

[16]Augustine, *Confessions*, p. 310 (XI,30,40): 'The word never has no meaning where time does not exist'.

[17]See Augustine, *Confessions*, p. 310 (XI,29,39). Here, the ET renders *distensio* with 'distraction' and 'dispersion.'

[18]In contrast to other neo-Platonic sources, however, there is an unresolved problem in *Confessions* XI: An important element is missing between the atemporal One and time, what in neo-Platonic terminology would be defined as the eternal life of the *nous* as an intermediary stage between the One and the temporal world. Cf. Werner Beierwaltes, 'Einleitung', in Plotin, *Über Ewigkeit und Zeit (Enneade III, 7)* (trans. and ed. Werner Beierwaltes; Frankfurt am Main: Klostermann, 1995, 4th edn), pp. 43–9.

primarily as timelessness. The advantage of talking about types or models is that it enables us to perceive similar structures without our having to engage in questionable retrojections. We can include both Christian and pre-Christian thinkers within this framework:

The understanding of eternity as an 'eternal now' (*nunc stans*) already surfaces in the pre-Socratic thought of Parmenides.[19] Since the Middle Ages, the understanding of eternity as timelessness has frequently appeared in mystical strands of theology. In this context, Meister Eckhardt (d. 1328) and Heinrich Seuse (d. 1366) could be considered paradigmatic.[20] If we take a look at modernity, then diverse thinkers such as Immanuel Kant and Schleiermacher would fall in this category, and we can also find this understanding in English Romanticism, in the works of Samuel Taylor Coleridge (d. 1834),[21] for example.

Kant understands time and space to be forms of intuition, which are present in the knowing subject *a priori* (before any experience),[22] because even if we tried to think away all objects of appearance and experience, time would still remain as a constant. But time is not itself a *concept of understanding*, since it would then be formed by abstraction and generalization. Therefore, time is antecedent, existing as a form of perception. Kant thus falls within the Augustinian paradigm in so far as time is made dependent on the knowing subject. But, in contrast to Augustine, time as a form of intuition could not be an accidental attribute of fallen souls, since a subject conceived as being timeless does not make sense for him.

For Schleiermacher, God as absolute causality is also the timeless origin of time, so that in his conception a different aspect of the Augustinian model receives emphasis than in Kant: it is not so much about the experience of time as it is the understanding of eternity as timelessness. Another interesting parallel could be identified in the way Schleiermacher understands redemption as consisting in the constant strength of the

---

[19]Cf. G.E.L. Owen, 'Plato and Parmenides on the Timeless Present', *The Monist* 50 (1966), pp. 317–40.

[20]Cf. Heinrich Seuse, *Das Buch der Wahrheit: Mittelhochdt.-dt.= Daz buechli der warheit* (eds Loris Sturlese and Rüdiger Blumrich; Hamburg: Meiner, 1993); Alois Haas, 'Meister Eckharts Auffassungen von der Zeit', in Evangelische Studiengemeinschaft (ed.), *Naturphilosophische Studien* Heidelberg: Forschungsstätte d. Evang. Studiengemeinschaft, 1982), pp. 27–62.

[21]Cf. Georges Poulet, 'Timelessness and Romanticism', *Journal of the History of Ideas* 15.1 (1954), pp. 3–22.

[22]Cf. Immanuel Kant, 'The End of all Things', in *Religion and Rational Theology* (trans. and ed. Allen W. Wood and George di Giovanni; Cambridge: Cambridge, 1996), pp. 221–31; Immanuel Kant, *Critique of Pure Reason* (trans. and ed. Paul Guyer and Allen W. Wood; Cambridge: Cambridge, 1998), pp. 162–7.

God-consciousness, which dominates over the timely consciousness.[23] The sense consciousness is always understood temporally and, to the extent that it affects the sense consciousness in the back and forth between its various temporal conflicts, this is a mark of its sinfulness. Whereas Schleiermacher certainly does not view redemption as liberation from the temporal sensory self-consciousness – Augustine hopes for the liberation of souls from the experience of time – he sees it rather in terms of the dominance of the consciousness of God over sensory, temporal self-consciousness. Both Augustine's and Schleiermacher's concepts are comparable, however, in that time constitutes an essential factor of the fallen world and thus of sin, and not just creation.

Augustine's model is not indebted to an understanding of time or eternity based on a theory of subjectivity. This is suggested in the contemporary situation by theologian Eberhard Wölfel, who incorporates the theory of relativity into his theory of time and eternity. Although we are unable to examine this more closely at this point, it should be pointed out here that in the theory of relativity space and time are no longer forms of perception as in Kant or objectively existing facts of the external world as in Newton. Rather, they are empirically accessible phenomena which are themselves dependent on other things. In our case, this factor is chiefly the speed of light as the constant, to which the phenomenon of time dilatation (the extension of time) is related: seen objectively, time passes more slowly as speed increases until you reach the speed of light, at which point it is no longer possible to speak of the passage of time in an objective sense. Eberhard Wölfel takes this as an inducement to ask – standing in the mystical tradition – whether light (or the speed of light) is not a clear image of God's eternity.[24]

> In various ways, we can see Parmenidian models of eternity, assorted mystical models of eternity, Kant's understanding of time and Schleiermacher's understanding of eternity as variations on the Augustinian model.

---

[23]Cf. Schleiermacher, *The Christian Faith*, pp. 203–6 (§52).

[24]Cf. Eberhard Wölfel, 'Endet die Zeit? Bemerkungen zum Zeitproblem im Aspekt naturwissenschaftlicher Erschließung', in Konrad Stock (ed.), *Zeit und Schöpfung* (Gütersloh: Gütersloher Verlagshaus, 1997), pp. 11–40.

Let us return to our original Augustinian model and consider the consequences of this understanding of eternity. For one, an important advantage is that the Christian understanding of creation, in which the eternal God is not reliant on worldly things in the act of creation (*creatio ex nihilo*), is very clearly expressed: time as an attribute of creation is part of being created. Time and eternity are categorically distinct. This argument has the further advantage of making the claim that eternity is not dependent on time. Nevertheless, it is not positively conceptualized as being based solely on itself, as Karl Barth had demanded,[25] but always remains in relationship to time, namely as its negation.

What are the drawbacks of such an understanding? First, there can be no positive relationship of a timeless and inalterable God to the temporal world. In fact, a suffering or compassionate God is hardly conceivable. Even an action by God is not conceivable in the strictest sense, because action presupposes at the very least alterity and change. Compared to the eternity of God, the temporal world is a starkly deficient mode of being. The religious practice of prayer can then hardly be understood as real – ironically, we might add, for Augustine continually avails himself of prayer in *Confessions* XI. Furthermore, the biblical evidence also comes up rather short: Augustine hardly quotes Scripture in *Confessions* XI aside from the 'in the beginning' of Genesis 1.1. All in all we can say that Augustine's concept of eternity can hardly secure the relevance of temporal events for eternity, which we diagnosed in relation to the spatio-temporal self-identification of the Triune God as being the eschatic ground for Christian hope.

We can identify one advantage of the Augustinian model as preservation of the categorical difference between God and the world, creator and creation.

Disadvantages of the model include that it is not possible to conceive of an action of God in eternity, time has no positive meaning for eternity and neither alterity (differentness) nor novelty (newness) are conceivable in eternity.

---

[25]Cf. Karl Barth, *Church Dogmatics II/1: The Doctrine of God, Part 1* (trans. T.H.L. Parker et al.; eds G.W. Bromiley and T.F. Torrance; London: T&T Clark, 2004), p. 611.

3.1.1.2 Eternity as partial or complete simultaneity

The second type of understanding of eternity to address is complete simultaneity which can be found, for example, in Book V of *The Consolation of Philosophy* by Boethius (d. 524). Boethius' definition of eternity is given in the context of answering the question of whether both human freedom and divine providence can be posited without contradiction. We will begin with Boethius' definition and then draw on some of his arguments.

First, the Boethian definition: 'Eternity, then, is the whole simultaneous and perfect possession of boundless life.'[26] This definition very strongly calls to mind the definition of Plotinus (d. ca. 270), the founder of neo-Platonism: eternity is 'a Life changelessly motionless and ever holding the Universal content in actual presence; not this now and now that other, but always all; not existing now in one mode and now in another, but a consummation without part or interval'.[27] There can be no denying that Boethius is a late neo-Platonist. One decisive difference becomes apparent when we compare Boethius and Plotinus, however: when Plotinus interprets the concept of eternity as the life of the Spirit (*nous*) which develops from the One through self-reflection, he does not make reference to time at all. Time emerges only in a third step as the life of the soul as the image of eternity.[28] In contrast, Boethius relates his definition to the temporal world directly: eternity as the possession of infinite life 'becomes clearer by comparison with temporal things'.[29] This comparison does not turn out to be a mutually exclusive relationship between eternity and time as in Augustine, nor is it a correspondence between archetype and ectype or image as in Plato, but rather the simultaneity of all temporal events:

> Whatever therefore comprehends and possesses at once the whole fullness of boundless life, and is such that neither is anything future lacking from it, nor has anything past flowed away, that is rightly held to be eternal, and that must necessarily both always be present to itself, possessing itself in the present, and hold as present the infinity of moving time.[30]

---

[26]Boethius, *The Theological Tractates and The Consolation of Philosophy* (trans. S.J. Tester; Loeb Classic Library; Cambridge: Harvard, 1973), p. 423 (V,6).
[27]Plotinus, *The Enneads* (trans. Stephen MacKenna; London: Penguin, 1991), pp. 216 (Ennead III,7: Time and Eternity, Chap. 3).
[28]Cf. Beierwaltes, *Ewigkeit und Zeit*, pp. 62–74.
[29]Boethius, *Consolation*, p. 423 (V,6).
[30]Boethius, *Consolation*, pp. 423–5 (V,6).

Unlike Augustine, Boethius does not immediately relate the idea of *creatio ex nihilo* to time, for a beginning of time would not disrupt his argument. What is decisive is this: in contrast to Augustine, eternity is immediately accorded a very positive relationship to time, an even stronger relationship than the correspondence between archetype and image in Plato. The reason Boethius argues for such a strong relationship between time and eternity lies in the context of his explication of the problem of providence. Boethius identifies a very clear challenge: if God foresees (*praevidere*) everything in a quasi-primordial (original) way, there can be no absolute retention of human freedom.[31] The idea that God's foresight could involve foreknowing human decisions is expressly rejected. This would not change the fact that all that follows would still happen by necessity. Boethius seems to believe he has solved this problem in a new way, for he says that the matter has not been adequately explored so far;[32] he is now trying to illuminate this problem anew. His solution essentially consists in saying that one cannot speak of looking forward (*praevidere*), but only looking forth (*pro-vidence*), a concept wrapped up in Boethius' definition of eternity. While all temporal events happen by necessity if we adhere to the idea of 'looking forward', if we accept the idea of looking forth or *providence* instead, it now becomes possible to say that some events happen by necessity while others occur only by *relative* necessity.

Boethius illustrates this eternal providence with an analogy: the relationship of time and eternity can be compared to an observer who sees the sun rising and a person walking at the same time. While the rising of the sun can be attributed to an intrinsic necessity, only a hypothetical necessity can be imputed to the walker: If [A] the observer truly perceives a walker, then a person is truly going [B] for a walk. B is not intrinsically necessary but only in so far as A is true. In this way[33] then, God in eternity would see the past, present and especially the future together simultaneously – these are divergent for humans – without meaning that all temporal events happen by necessity:

> In the same way, if providence sees anything as present, that must necessarily be, even if it possesses no necessity of its nature. But God beholds those future events which happen because of freedom of the will, as present; they therefore, related to the divine perception, become necessary through the

[31]Cf. Boethius, *Consolation*, p. 395 (V,3).
[32]Cf. Boethius, *Consolation*, p. 405 (V,4).
[33]Cf. Boethius, *Consolation*, p. 429 (V,6).

> condition of the divine knowledge, but considered in themselves do not lose the absolute freedom of their nature.[34]

For this analogy to work, it requires yet another epistemological premise: the possession of knowledge or perception is hierarchized in such a way that the highest natural power of understanding includes the lower, but the lower never rises to the higher. Humans only possess *ratio*, but God possesses *intelligentia*.[35] This true intelligence can know everything that *ratio* does, but not the other way around. The Boethian explanation of eternity or 'looking forth' (providence) as distinguished from 'looking forward' takes place in *ratio*, however, and is thus inadequate. Taken literally, according to the Boethian explication of eternity, the relative and absolute necessity of events one sees would thus ultimately collapse back into pure necessity. The distinction can only be sustained with the caveat that it does not happen by way of human reason but by way of the much more capable divine intelligence. This means, however, that Boethius ultimately refuses to give a solution to the problem: the freedom and necessity of all times can exist together in the simultaneity of eternity, but we do not know why. We can say, however, why we do *not* know it: we are not God. The Boethian understanding of eternity can thus rightly be considered unsatisfactory.

Interestingly, in the history of the philosophy of religion in the twentieth century, the Boethian understanding of the relationship between time and eternity is described using an image which is hinted at but not explicitly provided in Boethius' own work. Apparently, various scholars quoting this story are actually referencing each other without checking into the original. Since this twentieth-century explanation is easily understandable, however, it is helpful to mention here. It states that the flow of time is like a group of walkers in a mountain glen. Just as they cannot see beyond the next curve in the trail in front of them, temporal humanity does not know the future, and just as one can no longer look back behind the last curve, the past is also forgotten in memory. God's eternity, on the other hand, is similar to an observer on the highest mountain peak who always has all of time in front of him at the same time.[36] Or to give a somewhat more modern example,

---

[34]Boethius, *Consolation*, p. 431 (V,6).

[35]Cf. Boethius, *Consolation*, p. 417 (V,5).

[36]This attribution of the story of the mountain peak to Boethius can be found explicitly for example in the work of Vincent Brümmer, *What are we doing when we pray? On prayer and the nature of faith* (Burlington: Ashgate, 2008), p. 46. In Boethius we find only the suggestion of the idea in the following statement in *Consolation*, p. (V,6): 'It is called … providence (*providentia*), because set far from the lowest of things it looks forward on all things as though from the highest peak of the world'.

we could think of a roll of film. A temporal perspective is like playing the film in its chronological sequence, while the eternity of God would be like having all of the images from the film laid out and looking at all of them at the same time.

We can therefore say:

> According to the Boethian model, time and eternity are related to each other in such a way that the temporal sequence in eternity is simultaneous, but in their ordered succession they are all but translated from temporal into spatial dimensions.

Boethius' model can be found in diverse forms throughout the course of intellectual history. Thomas of Aquinas, who was the model for a broad tradition that developed in the Middle Ages,[37] expressly aligned himself with Boethius' convictions.[38] An extremely interesting variation can be found towards the end of the nineteenth century in the works of Albrecht Ritschl.[39] Ritschl thinks in terms of Herrmann Lotze's system in which the concept of purpose plays a decisive role. God and humanity are defined based on their purpose. The purpose of God is the kingdom of God, which is also humanity's purpose. In God's eternity, this purpose is always realized, so there is no difference between purpose and goal. From the human perspective, purpose and goal are different from one another, however, because human purposes are inhibited by other contradictory goals and purposes. Ritschl characterizes these inhibitions of personal purposes as 'evils'. The temporal experience of humanity is the result of purpose and goal now being different from one another. Ritschl's concept resembles the Boethian model in so far as Ritschl also relates eternity to the entirety of time. His epistemological starting point is different, however. While Boethius takes the experience of time as his starting point and then derives eternity from time, Ritschl takes as his starting point the realization of purpose and makes inferences about time as the differentiation of purpose and goal.

---

[37]This is expressed particularly clearly with the term '*sempiternitas*'; Cf. Helmut Echternach, 'Ewigkeit', in *Historisches Wörterbuch der Philosophie*, vol. 2 (Joachim Ritter et al.; 13 vols; Basel: Schwabe & Co., 1972), p. 842.

[38]Cf. Thomas Aquinas, *Summa Theologica*, vol. 1 (trans. Fathers of the English Dominican Province; 5 vols; Notre Dame: Ave Maria, 1981), pp. 40–1 (1a, Q.10, Art.1).

[39]Cf. Albrecht Ritschl, *The Christian Doctrine of Creation and Redemption*, pp. 305–6, 513.

Variations on this model can be found as well in the modern relativistic notion of time which ought to be mentioned here briefly. The phenomenon of time dilation (the *distentio* of time), which has emerged with the special theory of relativity mentioned earlier, means that an absolutely valid time for all places in the world is no longer an option. If the flow of time is dependent on the speed of the observer, then it is certainly conceivable that there could be two observers moving at different speeds, observer A and observer B, in which observer A sees observer B as simultaneous, and vice versa. It is possible, however, that A observes a further event C which is simultaneous for him, although it lies in the past or future for B.[40] This possibility led Hermann Minkowski (d. 1909) to understand time as a further, quasi-spatial dimension. Yet, in the writings of Minkowski, Albert Einstein (d. 1955) and many other natural scientists interested in natural philosophy, this four dimensional space-time is ultimately interpreted in terms of the Boethian model, in which the future is already determined, so one is forced to accept a deterministic world.[41]

The Cambridge idealist philosopher John M.E. McTaggart (d. 1925) also thought along these lines. He made the important observation that we must speak of time in two different ways: on the one hand, we use terms such as 'is present', 'is past' or 'is future'. These are related temporally to the present of the speaker, so that each person's experience of the present is granted a distinct position. McTaggart names this the 'A-series'. On the other hand, we use terms such as 'before' and 'after', which simply identify a chronological sequence of events, for example, when we say that the Second World War took place *before* the second Iraq war, but *after* the second Peloponnesian war. McTaggart calls this the 'B-series'. Such statements do not provide clues as to the current 'present' of the speaker, because this linguistic measure of time is independent of any characterization of the present. If McTaggart were to stop there, his analysis would show simply that he is a good observer of reality and his approach could certainly be very helpful for understanding time. But, instead, he goes on to claim that this B-series is adequate for comprehending the phenomenon of time,

[40]Cf. Cornelius W. Rietdijk, 'A Rigorous Proof of Determinism Derived from the Special Theory of Relativity', *Philosophy of Science* 33 (1966), pp. 341–4.

[41]Cf. Hermann Minkowski, 'Raum und Zeit', in Hendrik A. Lorentz, Albert Einstein and Hermann Minkowski (eds), *Das Relativitätsprinzip: Eine Sammlung von Abhandlungen* (Darmstadt: Wissenschaftliche Buchgesellschaft, 1958, 6th edn), pp. 54–66; Hermann Weyl, *Was ist Materie?* (Berlin: Julius Springer, 1924), p. 87; Rietdijk, 'A Rigorous Proof of Determinism'; Cornelius W. Rietdijk, 'Special Relativity and Determinism', *Philosophy of Science* 43 (1976), pp. 598–609.

while the A-series is expendable. Thus, he ultimately reconstructs the Boethian understanding of time in his own way. For if we do not need to speak of a present characterized in a specific way, then all events in the future, past and present are ultimately the same; furthermore, discourse about present, future and past presupposes the existence of the A series, which was declared expendable.[42]

Variations on the model of eternity as complete simultaneity include diverse medieval understandings such as that of Aquinas, in addition to Albrecht Ritschl in the nineteenth century, various natural philosophical interpretations of relativistic understandings of time and McTaggart's philosophy of time.

If we put aside some of the particularities of McTaggart's philosophical interpretation, his view of the linguistic perception of time using the distinction between the 'A-series' (past, present and future) and 'B-series' (before-after) is helpful.

Let us return to our original model and consider first the advantages of this understanding of time: in comparison to the model of eternity as timelessness, this model has the benefit that supporting documents may be more easily found, for example in early Jewish tradition, such as the apocalyptic seer in heaven who not only sees what lies in the future but also into the past (1 Enoch 33.6). In contrast to our very first model, this one relates much more strongly to the temporal world, because we find a positive meaning for what happens in time for eternity. At the same time, it preserves the categorical difference between time and eternity. Furthermore, the eternal God can now be understood as acting in time as well.

This last point also turns us to the model's disadvantages. While God acts, this ultimately only happens once, so God's activity can be understood solely as the establishment of the world, which creates all the time of the world including all its events all at once. Nothing can happen in the future which is not already real for the eternal God. This limits the freedom of God to a one-time action. Additionally, unless we follow Boethius' distinction between *ratio* and *intelligentia*, this translates into determinism for the temporal world. Therefore, God's freedom to act and human freedom are ultimately both lost with this model.

---

[42]Cf. John M.E. McTaggart, 'The Unreality of Time', *Mind* 17 (1908), pp. 456–73.

Furthermore, the problem of the origin of evil must either remain an open question or must be traced back to the one-time action of God. In particularly simplistic forms of this model, the problem may also arise that this evil is 'eternalized', although this does not generally happen: we already saw with Ritschl that evil is understood as the inhibition of purpose and thus can constitute time. Yet, it is excluded from the concept of eternity from the outset. Of course, in other models as well, the eternalization of evil is not a necessary consequence if we make use of the concept of a final judgement. The Final Judgement could be understood in such a way that, in addition to the protological action of God establishing the entire world, there would be a second, eschatic action of God. This would be comparable to the work of a film director who takes a finished movie and then edits out selected scenes. However, this hypothetical first and second action does not alter the fact that there is still only one single action of God. Hence, from the perspective of eternity, when we observe the passage of time, we would have to say that some sequences simply do not exist, although they do exist from another temporal perspective, namely evil. If more happens in time than in eternity, however, can such an understanding of eternity still be considered eschatic?

Some advantages of this model are that the categorical distinction between God and the world is maintained, alterity is possible even in eternity and time has a positive meaning for eternity.

Disadvantages of this model are its fundamental determinism (precluding contingency), the problematic understanding of what can ultimately only be a single divine action as well as the exclusion of novelty (newness) from eternity.

Given the disadvantages just mentioned, this model has been modified in various ways. The modified version can be called eternity as *partial* simultaneity. Vincent Brümmer[43] and Richard Swinburne[44] levelled criticism against the model of complete simultaneity arguing that its mistake lies in a spatialization of time, in a reduction of quasi-spatial relations – particularly when one thinks of the image of the observer looking over a glen from the highest mountain peak. Although it upholds the distinction between

[43]Cf. Brümmer, *What Are We Doing When We Pray?*, pp. 46–55.
[44]Cf. Swinburne, *The Christian God*, pp. 138–9.

before and after from 'the B-series' of time in eternity, this does not work for characterizing the respective present of each observer at the same time. If one wishes to maintain both, then the Boethian model can be applied only to the past and present but not the future: although God in God's eternity as simultaneity necessarily sees all that has happened as simultaneous, in simultaneity God sees the future only as possibility.[45]

We can use another image to grasp this, comparing this modified Boethian model to an observer who accompanies the walkers in the glen. On the one hand, he can see all the walkers behind him at the same time, because he is flying along with a paraglider and thus views them from a higher perspective. At the same time, he can see the way ahead in the glen and even has an overview of all the diverging paths ahead, but he cannot see which path the group will take. We could also describe this modified Boethian model as follows: a view of eternity in accordance with McTaggart's B-series of events would supplement the indexical A-series, and eternity would be assigned its own perspective.

These modifications are found for the first time in the work of John Duns Scotus (d. 1308).[46] This understanding of eternity as partial simultaneity is further reflected in a broad theological and extra-theological tradition. We find elements cropping up in various theories in the twentieth century including in Paul Tillich,[47] in process philosophy,[48] in the work of philosophical theologian Vincent Brümmer[49] or in the philosopher of religion Peter T. Geach, who drew inspiration from Wittgenstein.[50]

In the model of eternity as partial simultaneity, the divine eternity accompanies the respective present of each time, in which the past and present of eternity are simultaneously existent, while the future of the respective present is only available as a multiplicity of possibilities.

---

[45]Cf. Brümmer, *What Are We Doing When We Pray?*, pp. 46–55.

[46]Cf. Calvin Normore, Norman Kretzmann, Anthony Kenny and Jan Pinborg (eds), *The Cambridge History of Later Medieval Philosophy* (Cambridge: Cambridge, 1982), p. 367.

[47]Cf. Tillich, *Systematic Theology III*, pp. 419–23.

[48]Cf. Michael Welker, *Universalität Gottes und Relativität der Welt* (Neukirchen–Vluyn: Neukirchener Verlag, 1988, 2nd edn), pp. 109–37.

[49]Cf. Brümmer, *What Are We Doing When We Pray?*, pp. 46–55.

[50]Cf. Peter T. Geach, *Providence and Evil* (Cambridge: Cambridge, 1977), pp. 57–8.

Since the twentieth century, the model derived from Duns Scotus has been widely adopted as seen in Tillich, process-philosophy and theology as well as in the works of Vincent Brümmer and Peter Geach.

With this seemingly minor modification to the model of absolute simultaneity, it is possible to abandon a deterministic worldview so an eternal God and humankind are both able to act. True contingency is possible. Prayer between temporal humans and an eternal God can now be understood as real communication.

But, besides these advantages, this concept also has some disadvantages, for the distinction between eternity and temporality has now clearly been minimized. Furthermore, this image does not enable us to posit any kind of true innovation above and beyond events in the temporal world. A philosophical difficulty lies in the fact that the insights of the theory of relativity – according to which there can no longer be any distinct absolute frame of reference and thus no unified present – must be reconciled with the idea of God accompanying humanity through time. This certainly may be possible, but only at the cost of certain frames of reference within the world having to coincide with this divine perspective. We might think, for example, of the frame of reference of the earth which could be justified christologically through the incarnation but also appears in specifically non-religious natural philosophical interpretations[51] and is based on a Big Bang theory of the beginning of the world, which cannot be reconstructed.

Advantages of the model of eternity as partial simultaneity include that it makes it possible to speak of true contingency in the world and it rejects a deterministic universe, it makes alterity (differentness) between time and eternity possible, results in a positive meaning of time for eternity and makes it possible to conceive of God acting in the world.

[51]Cf. the description of a relativistic logic based on one's standpoint Thomas Müller, 'Arthur Priors Zeitlogik' (Unpublished doctoral dissertation, Freiburg, 2001), pp. 195–6.

The disadvantages are that eternity still precludes novelty (newness); furthermore, the categorical distinction between God and world is in danger of being blurred. This model has additional conceptual problems in integrating the understanding of time drawn from the special theory of relativity.

If we search for humanity's hope for eternity given the conditions of these models of eternity (as either absolute or partial simultaneity), this may be found in the idea that human experiences in time are eternalized, so to speak. To borrow the terminology of the process philosophy of Whitehead, it is preserved in the consequent nature of God; nothing is lost in God's memory or it will be, according to Tillich, essentialized.[52] Within these conceptions of the eternalization of the temporal, there is still room for the idea of judgement: not everything from temporal eternity will be preserved, but only that which is coherent. The eternalization of the temporal is thus simultaneously a process of purification. This type of hope for eternity does not offer humanity the hope for something truly new and qualitatively different. Eternity does not add anything new to temporality; it only takes something away from it. So, it remains questionable whether this type of eternity can really be described as eternal life that retains the full valency of time.

3.1.1.3 Eternity as the flow of time without beginning or end

Boethius mentions a further understanding of eternity, which he curtly dismisses: the seemingly naive understanding of eternity as an endless flow of time.[53] This understanding of eternity should also be considered with due diligence. Rather than taking a classical author, however, we will turn to the example of contemporary Oxford philosopher of religion Richard Swinburne, who has presented one of the most philosophically sophisticated designs of this type. Swinburne laid out his ideas in two works: in *Space and*

---

[52]Cf. Tillich, *Systematic Theology III*, pp. 419–23 and Alfred North Whitehead, *Process and Reality: An Essay in Cosmology* (eds David Ray Griffin and Donald W. Sherburne; New York: Macmillan, 1978), pp. 342–51.

[53]Cf. Boethius, *Consolation*, p. 425 (V,6).

Time (1968) and *The Christian God* (1994). We will first consider Swinburne's understanding of time, in order to then discuss his concept of eternity.

Swinburne begins his discussion with the four principles of the essence of time. The first principle is that events occur over periods of time, never at particular instants in time, as these only have the character of boundary points: 'Everything that happens, every event that is – including the mere existence of a substance with its properties – happens over a period of time and never at an instant of time.'[54] One consequence of this principle is that moments are seen as merely boundary points between periods and that any time period can be divided up into an infinite number of time periods.

The second principle distinguishes topology from a metric of time: 'Topology is concerned with the ordering of events, metric with the size of interval between them.'[55] Topology is concerned with the pure sequence of real or possible events and is independent of the laws of nature. Metric relates to the measurable length of time periods and is based on laws of nature. While metric presupposes topology, topology does not presuppose metric: 'While time has a topology, independently of whether there are laws of nature, it has a metric only if there are laws of nature.'[56] Metric presupposes the existence of natural or artificial clocks, while topology does not. Without metric, the various periods cannot be distinguished with respect to their length; the concept of the measurability of time is then meaningless. One consequence of this principle is that the metric of time can have a beginning and an end, while a typology cannot: if there were an initial boundary point at which substances would appear, then it would simultaneously be the end of a metric-less period before: 'So if there were no God and the universe had a beginning, then before then there would be no substances and hence no laws of nature; and then although one could talk of the time before there was a universe … one could not distinguish any one such period from another.'[57] As a result, Swinburne relates the Augustinian view of the creatureliness of time to the metric, not to topology.

The third principle is concerned with a causal reduction of time: the future is that which can be causally affected, while the past is that which has been causally affected: 'A period of time is future if it is logically possible that an agent now can causally affect what happens then; and a period of time is past if it is logically possible that an agent acting then could have

---

[54]Swinburne, *The Christian God*, p. 72.
[55]Swinburne, *The Christian God*, p. 75.
[56]Swinburne, *The Christian God*, p. 75.
[57]Swinburne, *The Christian God*, p. 79.

causally affected what happens now.'[58] One consequence of both this and the first principle is that there is only past and future. An Augustinian present is not conceivable. The distinction between the remembrance of what is past and perception of what is present is not of a categorical, but of a contingent and biological nature. Both involve an awareness of what is past: perception is related to what is past, which is inevitably and constantly connected causally and surfaces in consciousness. Memory, however, is related to what is past which is not consciously before us all the time but appears in consciousness only erratically. This consciousness remembers the sequence of events in a fragmentary way. For personal individuals with non-human brain structures, according to Swinburne, the distinction between perception and memory may not hold:

> Both memory and perception must be of things past .... Those experiences of a kind which arise by an immediate causal chain from an event ... experiences unavoidable if our organs are operative and we direct them aright, we call perceptions. Memories, by contrast, are not constantly before us; they come to us erratically .... These differences between perceptions and memories in humans clearly have their source in the different brain structures which mediate our experience of the world. Individuals of a very different kind from ourselves might not have a similar twofold scheme of awareness of the past.[59]

Another consequence of the causal reduction is that the progression of time is irreversible. A third consequence is the exclusion of the possibility that the existence of parallel timelines could be a meaningful concept.

Finally, the fourth principle is concerned with the indexicality of time, according to which the distinction between earlier and later is dependent on the observer. Swinburne adopts McTaggart's differentiation between an A-series of events and a B-series of events: as mentioned already, the B-series deals only with the ordering of events, independent of the indexical standpoint of the observer, while the A-series factors in the order of earlier-later relative to the observer indexically.[60]

Let us now turn to Swinburne's concept of eternity. Swinburne distinguishes between two possible ways of understanding eternity: first, the naive understanding of eternity as an unending flow of time, expressed explicitly or implicitly in the New Testament as well as until the third-century

[58]Swinburne, *The Christian God*, p. 81.
[59]Swinburne, *The Christian God*, p. 90.
[60]Cf. John M.E. McTaggart, *The Nature of Existence*, vol. 2 (Cambridge: Cambridge, 1927), Chap. 33.

CE, and second, the concept of eternity as timelessness that has existed since neo-Platonic times and is also predominant within Christianity. We should note that under this heading, he includes both the Augustinian and Boethian types but focuses primarily on the Boethian. The shift from a biblical to an Augustian–Boethian type can be explained based on the apparent deficiencies of the first concept that God had subordinated God's self to the transience of time and become time's prisoner: 'It seems to imply that time stands outside God, who is caught in its stream. The cosmic clock ticks inexorably away, and God can do nothing about it.... Let us call the view of God's relation to time stated in the last paragraph, the view of "God as time's prisoner".'[61]

Swinburne continues by attempting to show that the Boethian type is incoherent: If the entire course of temporal events is present in God's present, this can either mean that God's present is here for a moment or a period. The first option is precluded by the first principle of time, according to which moments solely have a boundary point character: 'The most natural reading of the tradition seems to me to read "moment" as "instant", and in that case, the doctrine is in conflict with the first principle. A state of affairs must last for a period of time; it cannot occur at an instant!'[62] If God's eternal present could be interpreted as a period, this would have to be identical with the entire progression of time. If God is supposed to act in a causal way, however, this would mean a *backward causality*, which Swinburne already considers logically incoherent, or a simultaneous causation or it would be the essentially meaningless possibility of a parallel timeline which would not be related to ours at all. For this reason, however, Swinburne considers the Boethian type to have been disproven.

So, the only remaining option is to return to the model of eternity as an infinite progression of time and show that this does not necessarily mean God is time's prisoner. Swinburne achieves this through the distinction between the metric and topology of time. The topology of time is God's eternity. It is thus pointless to speak of periods of varying lengths: 'There would be no difference between a divine act of self-awareness which lasted a millisecond and one which lasted a million years.'[63] But, it may be that before there was a universe of created substances and laws of nature – and thus a metric of time – there could have been a topology related to ordered mental events within God without a cosmic clock ceaselessly ticking away to which God would

[61]Swinburne, *The Christian God*, p. 138.
[62]Swinburne, *The Christian God*, p. 139.
[63]Swinburne, *The Christian God*, p. 140.

be subordinated: 'There would be no cosmic clock ticking away – for there would be no laws of nature.'[64] Furthermore, in contrast to us, there is no difference for God between perception and memory, so God is conscious of all 'past events' in the same way. The future, however, 'remains under God's total control; he need not make free creatures – in which case nothing will surprise him.'[65] But, if God has decided to create the laws of nature and thus to create a world which includes a metric of time, this does not mean time is ontically superior to God, since God has made a choice based on free will to subject God's self to time. For God's past, the same consciousness without the distinction between perception and memory would be valid, while for God's future, we can say the possibility absolutely exists for the future to hold surprises. Yet, God is not therefore the prisoner of time: 'The unwelcome features of time – the increase of events that cannot be changed, the cosmic clock ticking away as they happen, the possibility of surprise in the future – may indeed invade God's time; but they come by invitation, not by force – and they continue for such periods of time as God chooses that they shall.'[66]

Let us put aside for now the question of whether Swinburne's view really contradicts the Boethian type as clearly as he assumes, or whether the lack of a distinction between memory and perception does not actually affirm a concern of the Boethian understanding of time after all. Given Swinburne's idea that God has a time before and after the metric of time, so there is the possibility of continued novelty and surprise, we can say that Swinburne's view is probably an example of an understanding of time as an infinite progression.

Swinburne distinguishes between a topology, the ordering of earlier and later which is identical to McTaggart's B-series, and a metric of time, which is concerned with the length of periods. While topology is God's eternity and does not presuppose the existence of a world, metric presupposes the world as creation. Past and present are equally present to God, because for us they differ logically only as two varying forms of perception of the past. God remains the Lord of time, and, yet, since the creation of the world, the future remains open for God also, because God desires this state of affairs.

[64]Swinburne, *The Christian God*, p. 142.
[65]Swinburne, *The Christian God*, p. 142.
[66]Swinburne, *The Christian God*, p. 143.

A broad tradition has adopted this understanding of time. In the twentieth century, for example, we find it in the works of New Testament scholar Oscar Cullmann,[67] who considers it to be the most adequate biblical understanding of time, in the works of the philosopher of religion Nelson Pike[68] and in modified form in the physicalist and reductionistic understanding of reality expressed by physicist Frank F. Tipler.[69]

While the understanding of eternity as an infinite flow of time is widely attested in the Bible, it is mostly rejected by the theological and philosophical tradition and is only rarely advanced.

The advantages of this understanding of time and eternity are obvious: God and the world can be conceived of as being both active and passive. Novelty is possible again and again. Even Christian practices such as prayer are now conceivable as being real communication.

The disadvantages are also equally obvious: the categorical distinction between time and eternity can be largely thought to have disappeared; instead, the temporal world is now an aspect of the eternity of God. Although God does not merge completely with the temporal world – because God existed infinitely before and after the world – God does not transcend the world within time.

The advantages of this understanding of eternity as an unending flow of time can be identified as contingency through the rejection of determinism, a positive meaning of time for eternity as well as alterity and novelty for time and eternity.

The disadvantage is that the categorical distinction between time and eternity seems to be lost.

So, what does humanity's hope for eternity look like with this model? It could involve the infinite continuation of what we experience and do here, but with a new quality. Yet, even then the relevance of temporal events cannot

[67]Cf. Oscar Cullmann, *Christus und die Zeit* (Zurich: Evangelischer Verlag, 1963, 3rd edn), p. 69.
[68]Cf. Nelson Pike, *God and Timelessness* (London: Routledge, 1970), pp. 121–9.
[69]Cf. Tipler, *The Physics of Immortality*, pp. 128–38. The modification in Tipler is that he presumes a universe with an objective finiteness as a condition for a subjective infiniteness of life.

be fully preserved, because, were we to consider the eternal life of human individuals, these events would also sink into the past unless human life was transformed.

3.1.2 The eschatical basis of time and eternity

The question now arises of whether is it possible to conceive of eternity in a way that can secure the ontic relevance of temporal events? In all three forgoing cases, conceptions of eternity are derived from experience of the temporal world. But, theologically, this constitutes a problem. If the human being is temporal and not eternal, can there then actually be a circumstance in which he or she can grasp eternity? This circumstance does exist, but only when eternity discloses itself to humanity. A necessary condition of a suitable concept of eternity from the perspective of Christian faith therefore presupposes the revelation of eternity in time.

A brief reflection on time is nonetheless necessary in order to be able to identify which aspects of revelation are relevant for the relationship between time and eternity. This presupposes not only involving philosophical considerations of time, but should also be in resonance with features of contemporary understandings of time as treated in natural philosophy, in order to relate these to the self-disclosure of God. Subsequently, it would also have to be possible to propose a few conditions for an understanding of eternity in relation to time.

3.1.2.1 Time

Proceeding from the modern conception of time in relativity theory, one can ascertain that time itself does not constitute a constant, as in classical mechanics, but is rather dependent upon what has become the new constant, the speed of light.[70] The extension of time[71] resulting from this might unsettle us, but the consequences are not as significant as one might think. As a result, something like absolute simultaneity is no longer conceivable, but the sequence of time, before and after, McTaggart's B-series, is preserved.

---

[70]Cf. Wölfel, 'Endet die Zeit?', in *Zeit und Schöpfung*, pp. 22–30.
[71]Cf. Wölfel, 'Endet die Zeit?', in *Zeit und Schöpfung*, pp. 25–16.

Now, if we add quantum theory to this, a further unsettling occurs, because the possibility of a discontinuous 'dropleting' of time appears, since it is meaningless to speak of periods shorter than Planck time (10^{-43} seconds). Time now appears to be constructed atomistically.[72] It appears only *prima facie* conceivable that any period of time can be split into ever-smaller periods of time. If all the factors are taken into consideration and quantum theory is held to conform to reality, then time also appears to be atomistic. The philosophical interpretations are remarkable, because for this reason and with the help of other aspects of quantum theory, it can be shown that time and space cannot actually be the frameworks of individuation encompassing all things, or what actually makes individual objects individual things. This does mean that time indeed makes it possible for us to *identify* things with the help of our consciousness, including the narrative self-identification of God, but that not only God, but objects in the world as well cannot actually be *individuated* by time itself. We can certainly only identify what is also individuated, but the actual individuation of objects in the world surpasses what we are able to identify in the world. As God's economic Trinity cannot be identical with the immanent Trinity, but rather only constitutes its epistemic presupposition, then the identification of objects in the world is also not identical with their individuation, but only with their epistemic presupposition.

Now adding thermodynamics to this, time appears to be irreversible, so that it is possible to refer to differences between past, present and future. McTaggart's reduction of time to the B-series does not therefore appear to be appropriate. Thus, our intuitive experience of time can be confirmed in a manner suitable to that of the natural sciences. This has certainly not yet answered the Augustinian question about what time actually is – that is, the question of the essence of time. But this is not strictly necessary. Whatever time may actually be, we now know a few of its characteristics and we can also specify its capacities and function: time makes it possible for us to identify distinct events and objects. It affords the perception of differentiation and relatedness between different entities, actually making alterity possible. This is not, however, couched in the essence of time, but rather in its character as a logical ordered relation, i.e. as a relationship that is asymmetric, irreflexive and transitive. By way of reminder: 2004 comes after 2003, not the reverse. Time is therefore asymmetric. 2004 never comes after 2004. Time is therefore irreflexive. If 2005 comes after 2004 and 2004 comes after 2003,

[72]Cf. Volker Weidemann, 'Das inflationäre Universum', in Helmut A. Müller (ed.), *Naturwissenschaft und Glaube* (Bern: Scherz, 1988), pp. 346–65.

then 2005 also comes after 2003. This means time is transitive. Although we have not discovered the essence of time in these formulations, we can establish an important postulate for any potential concept of eternity: If there is a concept of eternity that can be set into a meaningful relationship to the temporal world, eternity will have to correspond to this logical character of the ordered relation in the case that eternity is not to mean the negation of created time and the creatures living within it.

Considerations of time in natural philosophy do not manifest its actual essence, but rather its logical character as an ordered relation (in the B-series) as well as a few additional features, from which the irreversibility of time with the possibility of an open future, as it is linguistically conceived in the A-series, is of especial significance.

3.1.2.2 Eternity

With this we are at the second question of the self-disclosure of God, which we have already pursued in the context of the question of the basis for eschatological hope. At that point, we determined that God in and for Godself – God's immanent or individuated Trinity – likewise possesses the character of an ordered relation, making alterity in God possible. Similarly to the analysis of time, we can also not indicate with reference to God in what this ordered relation between the Trinitarian persons consists, with the exception of the fact that it must be a matter of love. Martin Luther described this communication as an inner-Trinitarian conversation. 'As the Father is Speaker from eternity, and just as the Son is spoken from eternity, so the Holy Spirit is the Listener from eternity.'[73] That this Trinitarian communication itself is an ordered relation means for the eternity of God, that:

The eternity of God is God's being itself and therefore the Trinitarian communicative relational structure itself.

[73]Martin Luther, 'Sermons on the Gospel of St. John Chapters 14–16', in Jaroslav Pelikan and Daniel E. Poellot, (eds) *Luther's Works*, vol. 24 (St Louis: Concordia, 1961), p. 365. This Lutheran conception of the Trinity as communication plays a decisive role for the understanding of God proposed by Christoph Schwöbel, *Gott im Gespräch* (Tübingen: Mohr Siebeck 2011), pp. 451–78.

3.1.2.3 The relationship between time and eternity

The following then applies to the relationship between eternity to time: As God brings forth a free creation, he brings about a creation that corresponds to his eternity, which finds its own character as an asymmetrical, irreflexive and transitive relation, among others things, in the temporality of the world, whatever the 'essence' of time might also be. However, it is therefore also possible for the eternity of God to stand in a positive relation to this creation and yet remain categorically distinct from it. The eternal God can lovingly be company to the world, without otherwise infringing upon its independence and alterity. This involves the world possessing an irreversible progression of time, in which the Triune God knows the past and present as to their facticity, but the future as a qualified range of possibilities that God can steer with more strength and precision than can creatures within time. This affords both the freedom of the eternal God and the freedom of persons and the contingency of events in the temporal world: both God and his personal creation can actually be thought of as acting, and, as a result, a personal relationship between God and the personal creation is possible. In short, the relation of eternity and time corresponds to the relationship between the immanent and economic Trinity: The immanent Trinity is the ontic condition of the possibility for the economic Trinity; the economic Trinity is the epistemically sufficient condition of the possibility for the immanent Trinity. As God in eternity stands positively in connection with time, one problem with the relativistic understanding of time does however remain: It is no longer the case that all frames of reference appear to be of equal value; the divine perspective has ostensibly bound itself to one framework in particular, and not just to any frame of reference, but rather, through the incarnation of the Word, to that of the cross and the manger.

What does this understanding of eternity now mean for our hopes about eternity? It means that our eschatic eternal hope consists in the fact that through the action of God we are to be relocated from the ordered relation of the temporal world into the inner-Trinitarian relational events, not by necessity, but rather by grace. This means we participate eschatically in the eternal inner-Trinitarian conversation. In this case, our alterity is preserved because we do not turn into Father, Son or Spirit. Furthermore, our identity, which we live out in our history in the temporal world, is preserved: it is actually we ourselves and no one else who will lead our eschatic eternal life. The possibility of genuine newness is also given: the eschatical inner-Trinitarian life is not confined to a recapitulation of the temporal world. And, the notion of judgement is made possible: not everything we are in this temporal world must be eternalized.

In this understanding of eternity, in which the connection of eternity and time occurs through the interconnection of two sets of ordered relations, the ontic relevance of temporal events can accordingly be secured. Indeed, what is more, we can even describe how the eschatic eternity is experienced in the world of temporal events: If, as Luther says, God's eternity consists in God's inner-Trinitarian communication, then we could not actually be able to experience eternity under the conditions of time through meditation or ecstatic experiences, which attempt to block out the human experience of time, but rather in what is altogether the everyday communication of the gospel occurring in and to our earthen vessels. Or, to use Luther's words: 'Where and with whomever God speaks, whether in anger or in grace, that person is surely immortal.'[74]

> Both eternity and time have the same logical structure as asymmetric, irreflexive and transitive ordered relations and are thereby compatible. The difference consists in the fact that eternity must be understood as the ontic condition of the possibility of time.

3.2 Space and infinity

3.2.1 Models of space and infinity

Just as time and eternity can be seen in relationship to one another, a reflection on space and infinity is indispensable for eschatology, because beings that hope and believe such as humans are always corporeal beings, who occupy a certain amount of space and move within a specific space. One might expect that the problem of space could be addressed in a similar way to time. The history of theology and philosophy shows us, however,

[74]Martin Luther, 'Lectures on Genesis: Chapters 26–30', in Jaroslav Pelikan and Walter A. Hansen (eds), *Luther's Works*, vol. 5 (St Louis: Concordia, 1968), p. 76.

that this is only true within certain limits. While it is possible to take the distinctions made about the time-eternity relationship and make analogous claims with reference to space, the theological discussion goes beyond this, however, in so far as the problem of space plays a much stronger role in the doctrine of sacraments than is the case with the problem of time and eternity.

If we consider the history of philosophy, there appear to be two fundamental options for talking about space. Interestingly, these two options have been understood as being mutually exclusive instead of complimentary. One is the container model and the other is the relational model.

The container model of space presumes that space is the universal stage on which – or in which – at least the natural events of the world are playing out. In this model it makes perfect sense to assume that there is something like empty space. This model of space can also be understood in such a way that space is considered to be either infinite on the one hand, or finite and limited on the other. The understanding of God and infinity varies depending on which model of space is predominant.

3.2.1.1 Absolute space as an infinite container

This model of space is ancient and can already be found, for example, in the pre-Socratic thinkers, such as the atomists Democritus (d. 371 BCE) and Leucippus (d. 5 BCE), who considered empty space to be the background of a material made up of atomic particles, and principally as infinite space.[75] To borrow an image from the mathematician Bernhard Riemann (d. 1866): space is understood here as a 'tenement building', though perhaps an infinite one, which the entities of the world inhabit.[76] This space is nothingness, which is thus to be accorded existence in the same way as the material world. According to this model, space is homogeneous and isotropic, that is, without a centre, without a border and without distinct directions. In this way, space is a continuum, meaning a specific section of space can be divided infinitely in any order. This space is interpreted by the atomists as created and eternal. Space is ultimately a condition of the possibility of speaking about objects and their movements. Although this concept traces back to

---

[75]Cf. Hermann Diels, *Die Fragmente der Vorsokratiker*, vol. 2 (Hamburg: Rowohlt, 1964), pp. 75, 168.
[76]Cf. Bernhard Riemann, 'Über die Hypothesen, welche der Geometrie zugrunde liegen', in Richard Dedekind and Heinrich Weber (eds), *Gesammelte mathematische Werke, wissenschaftlicher Nachlass und Nachträge* (Berlin: Springer, 1990), p. 318.

the atomists and appears to have *prima facie* plausibility, it was surprisingly lost on antiquity and the Middle Ages.[77]

First of all, it is not connected to the mathematical notion of three-dimensional structures in Euclid which could not yet be labelled 'Euclidean space' and in this respect does not have natural philosophical or ontic valence.[78] The complete integration of Euclidean geometry into the understanding of space as an infinite container was carried out by Isaac Newton (d. 1727), who distinguished absolute space from metric space. Infinite space has the characteristics already mentioned, while metric space is concerned with measurements and is dependent on various scales or coordinate systems which are imposed on absolute space. The introduction of absolute infinite space as a container through Newton turned out to be pragmatic but remained controversial and was always understood as an ontological conjecture, since this absolute space could not be empirically proven. After a long process of development[79] in which he attempted to reconcile Newton's absolute space with various divergent understandings of space, Immanuel Kant (d. 1804) eventually subscribed to the Newtonian understanding but conceived of its reality differently: while Newton presumed the ontological existence of absolute space, for Kant it is an *a priori* form of perception like time. Infinite, three-dimensional space no longer belongs to the realm of empirical reality but rather arises from the subject's cognitive faculty[80] as a condition of possibility antecedent to every experience. For our purposes, as we examine different models of space, it is ultimately beside the point whether three-dimensional space is real or not.

The fascinating question now is how and whether we can mediate a concept of the infinity of God with this notion of space. For this notion of space with its concept of infinity already has clear divine or rather eschatic characteristics: it establishes the universal horizon of expectations in which all that happens and can happen takes place, and this horizon of expectations is no longer movable *per se*, nor can it be surpassed by another horizon of expectations. An understanding of the infinity of God can thus be developed with two possible types which respond to this understanding of space: identification or strict negation.

---

[77]Cf. Dirk Evers, *Raum – Materie – Zeit: Schöpfungstheologie im Dialog mit naturwissenschaftlicher Kosmologie* (Tübingen: Mohr Siebeck, 2000), p. 15.
[78]Cf. Evers, *Raum – Materie – Zeit*, p. 19.
[79]Cf. Elisabeth Jooss, *Raum: Eine theologische Interpretation* (Gütersloh: Gütersloher Verlagshaus, 2005), pp. 29–42.
[80]Cf. Jooss, *Raum*, p. 36.

The way to the identification of God with space can be found in Newton with the incorporation of the ideas of Henry More (d. 1687), although we should add that Newton did not fully identify space with God but designated space as the sensorium of God, as God's organ of perception.[81] Ultimately, it was Baruch de Spinoza (d. 1677) who followed the idea of identification to its logical conclusion and who saw the entire world as the one ultimate, eschatic reality (*deus sive natura*), in which the divine aspect is substance and the changeable phenomena in the world are considered to be accidents as they are attributes of this substance.[82] This approach towards identification is thus pantheistic and has seldom been adopted by the Christian tradition, in addition to the fact that biblical exegesis does not strongly support it. Nevertheless, Samuel Clarke tried to reconcile this Newtonian notion of infinity with biblical faith: 'For "in him we live and move and have our being"; as even some of your own poets have said, "For we too are his offspring"' (Acts 17:28).[83]

The other option is strict negation, in which one denies that religion and faith can be related in this way to the concept of space in natural philosophy. This presupposes an approach with a subjectivisitic starting point. This approach is probably employed most consistently in the late Schleiermacher. By defining God as nothing other than the source of the consciousness of absolute dependence that constitutes the subject, Christian statements about concepts of space within the doctrine of creation are ultimately reduced to reflecting the finitude of the human subject necessarily established by the concept of absolute dependence. As Ulrich Barth has consistently argued, religious notions of such matters related to creation theology thus become reflections on finitude, making it possible for religion to eschew any explanation of the world and thereby to be freed for its own essence. As a result, conflict between natural philosophy and theology is ruled out.[84]

How should we evaluate this model of space and the associated notion of infinity? It must be said that both attempts to conceive of the infinite

---

[81]Cf. Isaac Newton, 'Optics', in *Opera quae exstant omnia*, vol. 4 (London: 1782), p. 238.

[82]Cf. Baruch de Spinoza, 'Ethics', in *The Essential Spinoza: Ethics and Related Writings* (trans. Samuel Shirley; ed. Michael L. Morgan; Indianapolis: Hackett, 2006), p. 8: '*God, or substance consisting of infinite attributes, each of which expresses eternal and infinite essence, necessarily exists*'.

[83]Cf. Samuel Clarke and Gottfried Wilhelm Leibniz, *Der Briefwechsel mit G.W. Leibniz von 1715/1716 = A collection of papers which passed between the late learned Mr. Leibniz and Dr. Clarke in the years 1715/1716 relating to the principles of natural philosophy and religion* (ed. Ed Dellian; Hamburg: Meiner, 1990), p. 154.

[84]Cf. Ulrich Barth, 'Abschied von der Kosmologie – Befreiung der Religion zu sich selbst', in Wilhelm Gräb (ed.), *Urknall oder Schöpfung? Zum Dialog von Naturwissenschaft und Theologie* (Gütersloh: Kaiser, 1995), pp. 14–42.

God based on the idea of space as an infinite container are, despite their dichotomy, rigorous and coherent and thus impressive. While the negation type can fully preserve the categorical difference between God and the world, this is no longer the case with the identification type. True alterity cannot be conceived in either type, ultimately due to the notion of space being assumed. The identification type does not allow God to act, or if God does act those actions can only be God's actions towards God's self, and furthermore, creatures are ultimately also incapable of action. So, we can say this view tends towards a mechanistic view of the world. The negation type cannot directly conceive of an *action* (*Handeln*) of God, implying agency, but only an *influence* (*Wirken*), or to be more precise, the one absolute causality which cannot be comprehended by natural sciences or natural philosophy.[85] The major problems with this model are found in its underlying notion of space as infinite container – a metaphysical not an empirical notion – although this can also be called into question by empirical facts, as we shall see.

> Space can be understood as a three-dimensional, infinite and empty container. For Isaac Newton, this absolute space exists in reality, while in Kant, space is only a form of the intuition of our cognitive faculties. In this model, the infinity of God can be seen as either identifying or negating: in the first case, space must be identified with God or parts of God (*God's sensorium*), implying pantheistic tendencies. In the second case, the infinity of God cannot be related in any way to space and therefore also not to nature.

3.2.1.2 Space as a finite container

The second model can be understood in a sense as a modification of the first model, but, as we shall see, it is really a blend of the first and third models. In the second model, space is still interpreted in terms of a container, though it is no longer infinite and limitless, but finite. This

---

[85]For more on the question of whether the concept of action constitutively presupposes spatial categories, see the discussion between Reiner Preul, 'Problemskizze zur Rede vom Handeln Gottes', in Wilfried Härle and Reiner Preul (eds), *Marburger Jahrbuch Theologie I: Handeln Gottes* (Marburg: Elwert, 1987), pp. 3–11, who responds affirmatively and Christoph Schwöbel, 'Die Rede vom Handeln Gottes im christlichen Glauben', in Preul, *Marburger Jahrbuch Theologie I*, pp. 56–81, who responds negatively.

understanding of time is thus a modification of the first model and represents a transition to the third model, as we will see towards the end of this section. With respect to the intellectual history of this model, it is striking to note that this was not only the leading model in Greek antiquity, but also the predominant model in the Hebrew tradition.

In Greek tradition, it traces all the way back to Parmenides (fifth century BCE), who thought of space as a sphere.[86] It eventually became prevalent through the influence of the Aristotelian view of the world, although the understanding of space itself in Aristotle (d. 322 BCE) does not belong to this second model but rather corresponds to the third type we will discuss later. Which elements of the Aristotelian view of the world lead to modification? Fundamental for Aristotle is the distinction between movement and the 'Unmoved Mover'. This is reflected in Aristotle's notion of space to the extent that he does not presume the equality of all directions in the atomistic understanding of space but uses the distinctions (over, under, etc.) to specify directions. These, in turn, make it possible for bodies to take up the appropriate space and to be in a particular location.[87] In the final analysis, this leads to the Aristotelian view of the world, which in the time after Christ became the basis for the more strongly empirically oriented Ptolemaic view of the world: the earth is found at the centre, surrounded by various spheres out of which the lunar sphere is accorded special importance as the sphere closest to the earth. On the one hand, the gap between moon and earth, in contrast to the trans-lunar spheres, is not entirely inaccessible for humanity. At the same time, it exerts a force that can influence human life in a particular way. In the popular piety of antiquity in particular, this space is seen as populated partly by personal beings (like the classical gods, for example) who can be seen in a positive and negative light and who can exercise this influence. Traces of this belief are found in Rom. 8.38 as well as the Christ-hymn in Colossians 1.16. The planetary spheres follow after the lunar sphere, and the outermost sphere is the fixed star sphere, followed by the empyreal heaven. This entire world structure is seen as moving, kept in motion by an unmoved mover transcending the spherical structure. The extent to which the unmoved mover residing outside of the spherical structure – identified with God in the Middle Ages by Thomas Aquinas – should be understood as spatial (or personal at all) was a major point of

[86]Cf. Diels, *Die Fragmente der Vorsokratiker*, p. 238.
[87]Cf. Evers, *Raum – Materie – Zeit*, p. 17.

controversy. In principal, however, a series of thinkers understood the outer sphere as the limit of space.[88]

This concept of space reveals, as mentioned already, astonishing parallels to the Hebrew concept of space – although the Near Eastern view of the world presupposed in the Priestly account of creation is different in that a *rakia* ('dome', cf. Gen. 1.6) appears to protect the earth, understood as a disk, from the waters of chaos above and below.[89] Apart from this view, however, we can say that the typical Hebrew concept of space corresponds to the same type as the Greek one. While the Hebrew version does not have any abstract concept for space, it does make use of various expressions such as 'heaven and earth' in which space is conceived of as finite and is described in its entirety. This designation is more than just a merism, a type of synecdoche in which parts of a thing stand for the whole. In fact, various texts suggest the earth denotes the space available to humanity, while heaven designates the space which remains inaccessible to creation. Thus, heaven (or 'the heavens' as the plural in the Greek translation in particular seems to suggest) appears capable of gradations and reflects various levels of inaccessibility. Heaven is also seen as finite. God as infinity surpasses even heaven, as already mentioned, even if God also fills it. In part, heaven can be interpreted as the blue, royal robe of God.[90]

Given the similarity between the concepts of space named already, in the Middle Ages both concepts could easily be connected to one another. Thomas Aquinas (d. 1274) identifies, for example, three uses of the word 'heaven' which should be strictly distinguished based on semantic criteria: the word can designate the sublunary sphere of the sky, the outer space between planetary spheres and the final sphere, or it can be used in a metaphorical way to designate the triune God, although the latter use no longer relies on a view of the world as comprising different levels.[91] One can see that his model of space as a finite container must be understood as independent of one's view of the world. This is confirmed with the Copernican Revolution, which certainly did not introduce a different

---

[88]Cf. Wolfgang Breidert, 'Raum II', in Joachim Ritter et al. (eds), *Historisches Wörterbuch der Philosophie*, vol. 8, 13 vols (Basel: Schwabe & Co, 1992), pp. 82–8.

[89]Cf. Odil Hannes Steck, *Der Schöpfungsbericht der Priesterschrift* (Göttingen: Vandenhoeck & Ruprecht, 1981, 2nd edn), pp. 76–83.

[90]For more on heaven in the Old Testament, see Rüdiger Bartelmus, 'Himmel', in G.J. Botterweck, H.-J. Fabry and H. Ringgren (eds), *Theologisches Wörterbuch zum Alten Testament*, 10 vols (Stuttgart: Kohlhammer, 1995), pp. 204–39.

[91]Cf. Evers, *Raum – Materie – Zeit*, p. 119.

notion of space. Although the sun was now at the centre, Kepler (d. 1630) still thought of the fixed star sphere as the outer edge of space.[92]

In fact, the model of space as a container is even defensible within the parameters of modern relativistic cosmology. This happens only rarely but is not impossible, and it is even possible to conceive of the finitude of space at the same time. For in the wake of Riemann, who created a non-Euclidean, curved geometry, it is possible to distinguish between finitude and limitedness and to understand space as finite but unlimited. At first, this distinction may strike us as strange, but we can not only conceive of it and calculate it, but also even imaging it concretely.[93]

First, however, we have to ask how it is possible to conceptualize infinity under the conditions of space as a limited container. The problem is initially a conceptual one: Is it even possible to imagine a finite space without always having to imagine an additional space beyond it? We saw how, according to Kant, three-dimensional infinite space is a form of perception. If Kant is right, then a finite space could at best be conceivable but not actually depicted. This problem was frequently debated in medieval scholasticism using the following intellectual exercise: if one were to sit at the most outer sphere of the physical world, would it be possible to stretch out one's hand?[94] Framing the problem this way resulted in diverse answers, including one which, in principle, overcame the concept of space as a container. But we will get to that one later. For now, let it suffice to say that infinity should be strictly understood within the premises of this model. A threefold approach makes this possible: through identification, through negation similar to the first model and through the postulation of infinity as limited by finite space.

The identification model of infinity within the framework of the model of space as limited container seems to be fairly rare. A prominent example, however, would be Johannes Kepler who adopted a spherical model of the Trinity from Nicholas of Cusa (d. 1464) unrelated to real space. In this model, the centre point of the world is the sun, which is to be identified with the Father, the outer fixed sphere of the stars with the Son and the gap

---

[92]Cf. Jürgen Hübner, *Die Theologie Johannes Keplers zwischen Orthodoxie und Naturwissenschaft* (Tübingen: Mohr Siebeck, 1975), p. 186.

[93]Cf. Riemann, 'Über die Hypothesen, welche der Geometrie zugrunde liegen', p. 316. This concept can be illustrated with the concept of the Mobius strip, which has an infinite surface because it is unidirectional if limited. This can easily be demonstrated by taking a strip of paper, twisting it along its axis 180 degrees, gluing it together and then cutting it through its axis.

[94]Cf. Johannes Buridanus, *Kommentar zur Aristotelischen Physik* (Paris: 1509), IV.10.

between both with the Holy Spirit.[95] Such a model would be pantheistic, like the identification model of the unlimited container. In contrast to the latter, however, it begs the question of whether we are actually thinking about infinity at all, since this model has to view anything 'beyond' this limited space as being meaningless. But if Kant is right, we are then forced to always imagine a 'beyond' for any assumed limit.

The second possible response is that of negation: God could be conceived as being beyond space in principle, so that the category of space cannot be applied to the infinity of God at all. In this case, one would have to assume that infinity is not a spatial category. This does not present any difficulties since infinity can be understood as a second-order logical predicate: To speak of infinity in and of itself is meaningless in principle, because infinity must always be related to a first-order predicate: one ought to be able to specify *what* is infinite. This does not have to be space; other things might be possible: wisdom, goodness, power, etc. We learned about some representatives of this position already when discussing the first model of space. Ulrich Barth made the claim that this model allows one to be neutral in terms of a view of the world. This is confirmed here as notions of space are undoubtedly one aspect of a view of the world. The appearance of this model within the context of two different models of space sufficiently proves neutrality. Admittedly, the negation model within the framework of the model of space as limited container – in contrast to its use within the framework of the first, infinite model of space – does not lead to the question of the relationship of space to the infinity of space but in fact avoids it altogether.

A much more promising option appears to be postulating an infinity which is limited by finite space. This concept can be easily conceived and depicted in fact if you imagine an infinite line of numbers from minus to plus with the interval -1 to $+1$. The interval -1 to $+1$ symbolizes the finite as it is clearly limited. Both limited but infinite intervals -1 to $-\infty$ and $+1$ to $+\infty$ are now limited by the finite interval but would be just as infinite themselves and equally comprehensive as the infinite interval $-\infty$ to $+\infty$. A variation on this understanding of infinity, which we could call relatively limited infinity, looks like this: it encompasses both the infinite and limited space as well as that which transcends it. In fact, both these concepts of God as the infinite limited by finitude appear often in

[95]Cf. Johannes Kepler, *Mysterium Cosmographicum* (Munich: Beck, 1938), p. 23 as well as Hübner, *Theologie Keplers*, p. 168 and Evers, *Raum – Materie – Zeit*, p. 126.

various guises in Christian tradition. This was already suggested through the examination of the Old Testament (Hebrew Bible), in which that part of creation named heaven includes God but cannot contain God. Augustine also appears to have this view,[96] which was also prominent in the Middle Ages. Additionally, it is affirmed in the Reformed and Tridentine understandings of Holy Communion and even acquired a quite practical and visible value.

To illustrate this, we need to go back further to examine the understanding of Holy Communion in Huldrych Zwingli (d. 1531) and John Calvin (d. 1564), the Council of Trent and finally also in the Eastern Church in terms of their significance for the understanding of infinity.

Furthermore, space can be conceived of as a finite, empty container. Infinity can then be viewed in terms of identification or negation. It is also possible to imagine infinity as limited by finite space, whether that means infinity is that which transcends space or infinity encompasses space.

3.2.1.2.1 The Lord's Supper and finitude – Zwingli

As is well known, Zwingli views the 'Lord's Supper' as a celebration of remembrance for Christ's one-time sacrifice on the cross:

> This memorial is a thanksgiving and a rejoicing before Almighty God for the benefit which He has manifested to us through His Son; and whoever appears at this feast, meal or thanksgiving bears witness that he belongs to those who believe that they are redeemed by the death and blood of our Lord Jesus Christ.[97]

But, as a 'memorial' or 'remembrance' (*Wiedergedächtnis*), it does not have the character of a means of salvation that can mediate salvation. This is expressly rejected, in fact:

> I believe, indeed I know, that all the sacraments are so far from conferring grace that they do not even convey or dispense it.... For as grace comes

[96]Cf. Augustine, *Confessions*, p. 163 (VII,5,7).

[97]Huldrych Zwingli, 'Action or Use of the Lord's Supper, Easter 1525', in Bard Thompson (ed.), *Liturgies of the Western Church* (Philadelphia: Fortress, 1980), p. 150.

> from or is given by the Divine Spirit . . . so this gift pertains to the Spirit alone. Moreover, a channel or vehicle is not necessary to the Spirit.[98]

Correspondingly, a real presence of the person of Christ in communion is also rejected: 'The body of Christ in essence and really, i.e., the natural body itself, is neither present in the supper or masticated with our mouth and teeth.'[99]

This does not mean, however, that it has nothing to do with the presence of Christ. For, according to Zwingli, Christ's presence is in the contemplation of faith: 'I believe that in the holy Eucharist, i.e., the supper of thanksgiving, the true body of Christ is present by the contemplation of faith.'[100] Furthermore, we should keep in mind that a Reformed christological idea that corresponds to the so-called Antiochene type, along with the majority of medieval Christian tradition, distinguishes strictly between the divine and human natures. The characteristics of God and humanity are to be kept separate. Because humans are not omnipresent but God is, the divine nature of Christ can be present in communion, because it is present anyway in accordance with the model of relatively limited infinity. This is not the case for human nature and thus not for the person of Christ.

3.2.1.2.2 The Lord's Supper and finitude – Calvin

Calvin's position differs from Zwingli's in terms of the significance of communion. The integrity of both Christ's natures is also important to Calvin, even more than the unity of his person. And because Christ's human nature must now be fixed to one location, he can say:

> For as we do not doubt that Christ's body is limited by the general characteristics common to all human bodies, and is contained in heaven (where it was once for all received) until Christ return in judgment, so we deem it utterly unlawful to drawn it back under these corruptible elements or to imagine it to be present elsewhere[101]

---

[98]Huldrych Zwingli, 'An Account of the Faith (*Fidei Ratio*, 1530)', in *The Latin Works and Correspondence of Huldreich Zwingli*, vol. 2 (trans. S.M. Macauley; Philadelphia: Heidelberg Press, 1922), pp. 46.

[99]Zwingli, 'An Account of the Faith', in *The Latin Works and Correspondence of Huldreich Zwingli*, p. 49.

[100]Zwingli, 'An Account of the Faith', in *The Latin Works and Correspondence of Huldreich Zwingli*, p. 49.

[101]John Calvin, *Institutes of the Christian Religion*, vol. 2 (trans. Ford Lewis Battles; ed. John T. McNeill; Louisville: Westminster, 1960), p. 1373 (IV,XVII,12).

Heaven is imagined here as the location in space where Christ is residing, at the right hand of the Father.[102] Nevertheless, the Lord's Supper is not a mere meal of remembrance, but in communion one might say:

> Even though it is unbelievable that Christ's flesh, separated from us by such a great distance, penetrates to us, so that it becomes our food, let us remember how far the secret power of the Holy Spirit towers above all our senses ... the Spirit truly unites things separated by space.[103]

Communion in visible signs thus corresponds to the invisible spiritual event in which our spirits through the Holy Spirit are led in communion to Christ who 'lifts us up to himself'.[104] Christ has two natures: divine and human. Communion has two natures: visible and invisible. Human beings have two natures: body and soul. And, so that we not only come into contact with the divine nature of Christ in communion but also the human, the Holy Spirit brings our souls together with the whole Christ in heaven. The Holy Spirit allows our spirit to 'ride the elevator' in a manner of speaking. 'Our souls are fed by the flesh and blood of Christ in the same way that bread and wine keep and sustain physical life.'[105]

3.2.1.2.3 Infinity and finitude – the Tridentine and Orthodox understanding

According to the Roman Catholic notion, all of Christ is indeed present in communion including both his natures: divine and human. Thus, the canons and degrees of the Council of Trent state that:

> To begin with, the holy council teaches and openly and straightforwardly professes that in the Blessed Sacrament of the Holy Eucharist, after the consecration of the bread and wine, our Lord Jesus Christ, true God and man, is truly, really, and substantially contained under the appearances of those perceptible realities [can. 1].[106]

This can be more precisely illustrated with the well-known doctrine of transubstantiation, which became dogma in the Fourth Lateran Council and was reaffirmed at the Council of Trent:

---

[102] Cf. Calvin, *Institutes*, vol. 2, pp. 1380–1 (IV,XVII,18).
[103] Calvin, *Institutes*, vol. 2, p. 1370 (IV,XVII,10).
[104] Calvin, *Institutes*, vol. 2, p. 1379 (IV,XVII,16).
[105] Calvin, *Institutes*, vol. 2, p. 1370 (IV,XVII,10).
[106] Heinrich Denzinger, *Compendium of Creeds, Definitions and Declarations on Matters of Faith and Morals* (ed. Peter Hünermann et al.; San Francisco: Ignatius Press, 2012), pp. 392–3 (1636).

> By the consecration of the bread and wine, there takes place a change of the whole substance of bread into the substance of the body of Christ our Lord and of the whole substance of wine into the substance of his blood. This change the holy Catholic Church has fittingly and properly named transubstantiation [can. 2].[107]

Substance is that which accounts for the essence of a thing, in contrast to the accidents, meaning those things which are not constitutive of the essence. This means that after the consecration in communion, only Christ is present: the flesh and blood of Christ are present, but wine and bread no longer are. The fact that the 'chewing coefficient', taste and appearance of bread and wine all remain after consecration is purely accidental and inessential.

Let us now turn to the Orthodox notion: while the Orthodox Church has always had reservations about the doctrine of transubstantiation and would prefer to dispense with a philosophical-ontological *explanation* of the transformation, but not the *transformation* or *metabole* itself. According to John of Damascus (d. 749), bread and wine are 'the body and blood of God', in that 'they are … supernaturally changed … by the invocation and coming down of the Holy Ghost'.[108]

We can summarize as follows:

> According to the Council of Trent and the theologian John of Damascus, the divine and human nature of Christ – flesh and blood – are present in communion, but no longer the bread and wine.

Let us now draw the explicit connection of these statements of the various doctrines of communions to the concept of infinity:

> In the Reformed notions of both Zwingli and Calvin, the whole Christ is not present in communion within the limits of bread and wine, for Christ has both a divine nature, which is present everywhere according to the model of a relatively limited infinity, and a human nature, which

---

[107]Denzinger, *Compendium of Creeds*, p. 395 (1642).
[108]John of Damascus, 'The Orthodox Faith', in *Writings: The Fount of Knowledge: The Philosophical Chapters, On Heresies and On the Orthodox Faith* (trans. Frederic H. Chase; The Fathers of the Church, vol. 37; Washington D.C.: Catholic University, 1958), p. 358 (IV,13(86)).

is believed to be present at a particular place in heaven understood as a location in space. This also makes it clear why infinity that can incorporate the finite must still be described as relatively limited by the finite. This is because it cannot lead to such a unity of the person of Christ that the infinite can be completely present in its infinity in the finite.

Similar statements can be made to summarize the Roman Catholic and Orthodox understandings: although all of Christ is present in communion, bread and wine are no longer there, but only appear that way. While infinity comes to us in communion, it only works if the finite is omitted so that where bread and wine used to be there is now no longer bread and wine; when, aside from the human nature of Christ, nothing created is still there. This leads to a punctiform presence of finite and infinite. This model of a punctiform connection can also be found in Jewish Kabbalah: in this case, we might turn to the doctrine of *Tzimtzum*, which initially meant that the infinite God could contract in order to be present entirely at the one location of the Temple.[109]

In the Tridentine understanding of communion, the Orthodox understanding of communion and the original *Tzimtzum* teaching in Jewish Kabbalah, the relative infinity limited by the finite is capable of becoming a punctiform presence in the finite to the exclusion of the finite.

The concept of *Tzimtzum* is also interesting in so far as it can be understood the other way around as in the Jewish version of Isaac Luria (d. 1572): the infinite does not contract to one point, but on the contrary, it pulls back into its infinity in such a way that it creates a void of infinity and thus limits itself. This void, however, is nothing other than the finite space provided for God's creation.[110] Among Christian theologians, Jürgen Moltmann has most extensively and positively incorporated the idea of the self-limitation of the infinite into his theology.[111]

---

[109]Cf. Evers, *Raum – Materie – Zeit*, p. 146.
[110]Cf. Evers, *Raum – Materie – Zeit*, p. 146.
[111]Cf. for example Jürgen Moltmann, *The Trinity and the Kingdom*, pp. 109–10.

As a variation of the *Tzimtzum* teaching, the self-contraction of the infinite can also be understood in such a way that the finite space of creation is formed within the infinite.

In fact, if one wishes to conceive of space and God together in this model, one will be able to understand the limitation of the infinite (even if only relatively) through the finite only as a self-limitation and vouchsafing of the void, if one wishes to hold onto the concept of God as the all-determining reality. This self-limitation does not have to be understood within the model of spatiality. We have already seen, in fact, that finite and infinite can be understood as second-order characteristics, which always relate to another characteristic. This does not necessarily have to be understood as spatiality, however. In this sense, Eberhard Jüngel also agreed with the self-limitation model as an instrument for maintaining God's sovereignty.[112]

With the introduction of the figure of thought of the self-limitation of God, we have neither solved the problems with the understandings of space as finite container nor those defining its relationship to the infinite. On the contrary, these problems now culminate in a multiplicity of aspects: even as that which is only relatively limited by finite space, infinity is still construed in opposition to finite space. This leads to further problems.

If the problem of the negative concept of infinity consists in saying that the infinite cannot show itself in the finite or rather cannot be placed in any kind of positive relationship to it – which is presumed, however, in the self-identification of the *eschatoi* and especially the adoption of a human nature through the Son as eternal Logos – then God is being understood from the outset as spatial in the sense of container-like. Due to the idea of self-limitation, this does not lead to pantheism, but to *panentheism*: real space can only be understood as a finite container, because it is a subspace of the entire space which is God or the infinite. In this sense, such a concept of space proves to be a variation on the idea of space as an infinite container and thus as a variation on the pantheistic understanding of infinity.

In both biblical tradition and in the debate in the Middle Ages about the problem of space, approaches emerge which led to a completely different

[112]Cf. Eberhard Jüngel, 'Gottes ursprüngliches Anfangen als schöpferische Selbstbegrenzung', in *Wertlose Wahrheit: Zur Identität und Relevanz des christlichen Glaubens* (Munich: Kaiser, 1990), pp. 151–62.

notion of space: space as the essence of simultaneous relations. Let us now turn to examine this notion.

3.2.1.3 Space as order of reversible relations

A third model of space does not start with the idea of space as a container but sees space as the very essence of all simultaneous relations between entities. In this model, space is no longer the condition of the possibility of objects, states of affairs and processes in the world, but rather states of affairs in the world, meaning the worldly elements of relationships and their relationships themselves are conversely the condition of possibility of space itself. This notion of space was most likely the one for which Aristotle himself argued.[113] With respect to the Bible, we find approaches to a relational understanding of space, or to be more precise, such modes of speaking about spatial concepts which can only be explained with the help of the model of space as the essence of relations. The most prominent examples are the pericopes about the baptism of Jesus, in which heaven is described as standing open and the divine and earthly worlds are solely connected through the person of Jesus as depicted concretely with the figure of the dove (Mk 1.9–11 and synoptic parallels). The Middle Ages finally came closer to a solution in answering the question of whether one could stretch out one's hand past the last sphere of the finite world structure by saying that this would be possible, but not because there is more space behind the world structure, as this would compromise the finitude of space, but that by stretching out one's hand space would be extended around it.[114] The most prominent concept of space as the essence of relations was advanced by Gottfried Wilhelm Leibniz (d. 1716) against Newton. In his correspondence with Samuel Clarke, Leibniz wrote that 'space denotes, in terms of possibility, an order to things which exist at the same time, considered as existing together'.[115] This relational understanding of space can also be harmonized with the relativistic notion of space and is generally accepted by its supporters although the relativistic notion of space does not inevitably presume the relational notion of space. In order to understand this, we must first describe more clearly the modern relativistic notion of space in terms of its history.

---

[113]Cf. Evers, *Raum – Materie – Zeit*, pp. 17–19.
[114]Cf. Buridanus, *Aristotelische Physik*, IV,10.
[115]Clarke and Leibniz, *Briefwechsel*, p. 72.

Newton's understanding of absolute space as infinite container had the disadvantage that it was not empirically verifiable and was mathematically limited to three-dimensional Euclidean space. Carl Friedrich Gauss (d. 1855), however, already suspected that real space did not conform to Euclidean geometry, but his efforts failed due to the precision of measurements available to him at the time which were needed for empirical verification. Bernhard Riemann (d. 1866) finally provided the necessary mathematical theory by extending Gauss' notion of curved spaces to n-dimensional multiplicities, that is, he expanded it for theoretical spaces with any number of dimensions. Albert Einstein (d. 1955) combined the instruments thus created with the idea of Ernst Mach (d. 1916), that there are only relative movements so that the Newtonian space therefore must be rejected in favour of the special and later general theory of relativity which is empirically well verified.[116] General relativity implies that both time and space are dependent on acceleration and gravitation. Just as there is time dilation (*distention*), there is also a longitudinal contraction. This understanding at first appears better able to be explained with the relational notion of space but also introduces a problem: because time is also no longer a constant, space can also no longer be considered the essence of all those relations which are *simultaneous* as it is in Leibniz, because the concept of absolute simultaneity no longer appears to make sense. This difficulty can be resolved, however, with Minkowski's model of space-time, which he simply labels 'world', in which space and time are connected to space-time and can no longer be considered separately from one another.[117] If we understand this relativistic model of space-time in terms of the model of the relational understanding of space, then time certainly does not inevitably become a further dimension of space. Instead, while spatial relations now also have the character of asymmetry, irreflexivity and transitivity like temporal relations – which we can easily see already if we consider the colloquial use of expressions like 'before' and 'above' – space lacks the attribute of irreversibility: A body can be moved from location A to location B and can be moved back to A, while a body that has progressed from time t to time t+1 cannot go back to time t. According to natural philosophy, the definition of space in the relational model that makes the most sense would be that space is the essence of those relations between objects, which have the irreflexive, asymmetrical and transitive character of an ordered relation but are also reversible.

[116]Cf. Evers, *Raum – Materie – Zeit*, pp. 42–63.
[117]Cf. Minkowski, 'Raum und Zeit', in *Das Relativitätsprinzip*.

Space can be understood as the essence of those relations between bodily entities which not only form an ordered relation but are also reversible.

So, considering the model of space as the essence of reversible relations, what notions of infinity are now possible? For one, the solution of negation is available to us: God or infinity can be defined as that which is not space itself, that is, as that which is not structured relationally and ultimately is not capable of being in relation. This way of thinking certainly cannot be carried out consistently, because at least one relational statement is necessary, namely, that 'infinity' understood in this way is at least related to space as the 'condition of its possibility'. This understanding was explicitly advocated by Karl Heim (d. 1958).[118] However, we can also see at this point the limitations of the attempt to think of infinity in terms of negation: for if we take a radical enough approach, then we must deny that the infinite has any relation at all to the world as a network of relationships. This means it is no longer meaningful to say, as some have, that religion can be freed for its true purpose once spatial views of the world have been eliminated: for now, the infinite would simply hold no meaning for either the world or for human subjectivity. The other option is exemplified by Karl Heim, who remains in the mode of negation but reintroduced relational and thus spatial figures of thought.

It therefore seems more reasonable to think of the infinite itself as a network of relationships, which is capable of establishing relationships with the world's network of relationships and is able to do this in such a way that it is not thereby limited by this finite network of relationships. This option is already imagined and expressed biblically in terms of the intersection of heaven and earth, as found in the pericopes containing Jesus' baptism (Mk 1.9–11 and Synoptic parallels). Luther's doctrines of Holy Communion and Christ's ascension in particular laid out this interpretation by adopting and expanding medieval definitions. Its abstract content was taken up again and reconfigured in the nineteenth century by Georg Wilhelm Friedrich Hegel (d. 1831).

---

[118]Cf. Karl Heim, *Die Wandlung im naturwissenschaftlichen Weltbild: Die modern Naturwissenschaft vor der Gottesfrage* (Hamburg: Furche, 1954), pp. 110–1.

3.2.1.3.1 The Eucharist and infinity – Luther

According to Luther, the hypostatic union in Christ is the essential point, while for Calvin the integrity of both natures was central. Christ is one person. If he has two natures, this means the characteristics of both natures must be attributable to both natures alike (*communicatio idiomatum*). This means the whole Christ must be present in communion, both his divine and human natures. Thus far, we could say Luther's views seem to coincide with the Roman Catholic and Orthodox traditions. But – this is where it gets interesting – Christ is present in, with and 'under' the bread and wine, as we see in the Lutheran confessional writings and statements of faith.[119] In communion, bread and wine are present as well as the body and blood of Christ. Let us listen to Luther himself discussing the words of institution at communion and addressing two complementary mistakes: the belief that either the body of Christ alone is present or that bread and wine alone are present:

> It is undeniably true that two diverse substances cannot be one substance. For example, an ass cannot be an ox . . . . Now when we approach the Supper with this conception, reason takes offence, for here it discovers that in these words, 'This is my body', two distinct substances, bread and body, are spoken of as one object or substance. It shakes its head and exclaims, 'Oh, it is quite impossible that bread should be body! If it is bread, it is bread; if it is body, it is body – take your choice'. In this case the sophists have retained the body and let the bread go, saying that the bread disappears and sheds its substance when the words of institution are spoken, and the word 'this' indicates not the bread but the body of Christ, since the text says, 'This is my body'. Wycliff, on the other contrary, opposes this and retains the bread, rejecting the body, and says the word 'this' indicates the bread and not the body.[120]

These complementary mistakes derive from a linguistic misunderstanding:

> Logic rightly teaches that bread and body . . . God and man are divers beings. But it should first seek the aid of grammar, which lays down a rule of expression applicable to all languages: when two divers beings become

[119]Luther himself speaks in the 'Larger Catechism' (*Book of Concord*, p. 463; lines 8–9) about 'in' and 'under', and the 'Formula of Concord' explicitly uses 'in', 'with' and 'under' (*The Book of Concord*, p. 599; §38).

[120]Martin Luther, 'Confession Concerning Christ's Supper, 1528', in *Luther's Works*, vol. 37: *Word and Sacrament III* (trans. and ed. Robert Fischer; Philadelphia: Fortress, 1961), p. 295 ('The Law of Identical Predication').

> one being, grammar embraces these two beings in a single expression, and as it views the union of the two beings, it refers to the two in one term…. This mode of speaking about diverse beings as one the grammarians call synechdoche…. For instance, if I point to or hand over a bag or purse and say, 'This is a hundred gulden', both the gesture and the word 'this' refer to the purse. But since the purse and the money in some degree constitute one object, one lump, my words apply at the same time to the money…. Now a subtle Wycliffe or a sophist may laugh and say, 'You show me a purse, saying, 'This is a hundred gulden'; but how can a purse be a hundred gulden?'…At such a remark even the children would laugh as they do at a fool or jester… [for] here we have to do with two substances which have become one substance… the purse here is no longer mere leather or a mere purse but a money purse, leather containing money.[121]

Luther draws parallels between this problem and the Christological problem: if we point to the human person of Christ and say, 'this man is God's Son', then we must also speak of two natures or classes which were inseparably connected in the former unity of the person.[122] In communion, something similar happens in a sacramental unity between the body of Christ and the elements:

> As they become one, they are called and designated one object…and by virtue of the sacramental unity it is correct to say, 'This is my body', designating the bread with 'this'. For now it is no longer ordinary bread in the oven but 'flesh-bread' or 'body-bread', i.e. a bread which has become one sacramental substance, one with the body of Christ.[123]

Luther's position is thus sufficiently clear. It is obvious this is connected to extensive revisions with respect to how we understand God and the world. But, for our descriptive purposes, it suffices to say for now: In the Eucharist, the whole Christ, undivided, is present at the same time with the bread and wine.

It is possible for Luther to think this way because he is familiar with the scholastic tradition of three concepts of possible presence, of which we must reject the first two: presence that is defined as *circumscriptive (Lat.)* or *localiter* means the presence of a body in space according to its extension. Presence understood as *definitive* means the presence of space-less objects, such as a specific idea at one location. Both types of presence

[121] Luther, 'Confession Concerning Christ's Supper', in *Luther's Works*, pp. 301–2.
[122] Cf. Luther, 'Confession Concerning Christ's Supper', in *Luther's Works*, p. 297.
[123] Luther, 'Confession Concerning Christ's Supper', in *Luther's Works*, p. 303.

obviously cannot help us explain the dilemma of the presence of Christ in communion. Luther is also aware of a third possibility, however: presence which is defined as *repletive* means something is completely present in all places, yet cannot be contained by any one place. This is what Luther applies to God and hence to the one Christ including his divinity and humanity.[124] Apparently, this repletive presence, unless it ends in an antinomy, should not be understood with a container model of space, only with relational models of space. And, in fact, in his understanding of heaven, Luther also is critical of the idea of heaven as a location in space.

In the tradition of Luther, the whole Christ is completely present in both his divinity and his humanity in Holy Communion in, with and under the bread and wine.

3.2.1.3.2 The ascension of Christ, space and infinity

While thinkers in the early church primarily associated the Christ's ascension with the *sessio ad dextram*, Jesus Christ sitting at the right hand of the Father, in order to express Christ's equality in essence with God the Father, for the Middle Ages the ascension was interpreted predominantly within the framework of a Ptolemaic view of the world. Heaven was the outermost sphere of the world structure from which God was equidistant to all locations on earth. Thomas Aquinas understood heaven as a place beyond the creaturely realms of body and mind to which the human nature of Christ ascended by changing location, whereas Christ's divine nature could not be localized.[125] Such concepts were only overcome sporadically, as in Albert the Great (d. 1280), who did not understand heaven as a place but as the Trinity itself.[126] This concept can also be found in Thomas Aquinas but was not applied fruitfully to the concept of the ascension of Christ.

For the Reformers, ascension was closely associated with diverse Christological concepts, as expressed in the conflicts over communion. We already saw that Calvin ultimately understood ascension in the medieval

---

[124] Luther, 'Confession Concerning Christ's Supper', in *Luther's Works*, pp. 216–18.

[125] Cf. Aquinas, *Summa Theologica*, vol. IV, p. 2321–6 (IIIa, Q. 57).

[126] Cf. Albertus Magnus, 'De ressurectione', in Bernhard Geyer (ed.), *Opera Omnia*, vol. 26 (Münster: Aschendorff, 1958), pp. 286–7 (tr.2 q.9 a.3).

tradition as Christ's vanishing into heaven understood as another location in space.[127] This Reformed concept entails some difficulties in maintaining the personhood of Christ since his divine and human 'natures' are separated from one another. Luther, along with Swabian Reformer Johannes Brenz (d. 1570) and large parts of Lutheran Orthodoxy, emphasized instead the personhood of Jesus Christ in such a way that the entire person including his human 'nature' participates in the divine omnipresence.[128] A spatial concept of heaven thus became impossible. Ascension, including *sessio ad dextram*, was interpreted in such a way that the right hand of the Father was not a place but God's power, which 'at one and same the time can be nowhere and yet must be everywhere'.[129] With the ascension, Christ is internal and external to all creatures.[130] Ascension is therefore a means by which Christ comes closer to us instead of moving further away. This concept, later dubbed 'ubiquity', made it possible to argue for the Christ's real presence in communion. While the Reformed concept of ascension came into conflict with the new Copernican worldview and with the development of modern natural science, the Lutheran notion was compatible with the new view of the world, although it was not developed further at the time.

Starting with the Enlightenment and running through Friedrich Schleiermacher (d. 1834) and Rudolf Bultmann (d. 1976),[131] the doctrine of the ascension was sidelined as a mythological assertion and was ultimately discarded. A countermovement began, however, with the neo-Lutheranism of the nineteenth century and continued in numerous theological movements in the twentieth century, in which the idea of ascension was positively adopted once again. In Karl Barth (d. 1968), the ascension is the 'terminating point' of the history of revelation.[132] In Paul Tillich (d. 1965),

---

[127]Cf. Calvin, *Institutes*, vol. 2, pp. 1372–3 (IV,XVII,12) and pp. 1393–4 (IV,XVII,26).

[128]Cf. Johannes Brenz, 'De personali unione duarum naturam in Christo', in Theodor Mahlmann (ed.), *Die christologischen Schriften, Teil 1* (Tübingen: Mohr Siebeck, 1981).

[129]Martin Luther, 'That These Words of Christ, "This Is My Body," etc., Still Stand Firm Against the Fanatics, 1527', in *Word and Sacrament III*, vol. 37: *Word and Sacrament III* (trans. and ed. Robert Fischer; Philadelphia: Fortress, 1961), p. 57.

[130]Cf. Markus Mühling, 'Ascension of Christ IV: History of Dogma and Dogmatics: Protestantism', in Hans Dieter Betz et al. (ed.), *Religion Past and Present (RPP)*, vol. 1, 14 vols (Leiden: Brill, 2006–2013).

[131]Cf. Schleiermacher, *The Christian Faith*, pp. 417–24 (§99) and Rudolf Bultmann, 'New Testament and Mythology', in *New Testament and Mythology and Other Basic Writings* (Minneapolis: Fortress, 1990), pp. 1–44.

[132]Cf. Barth, *Church Dogmatics IV/2*, p. 153.

it is the 'participation of the New Being in divine creativity',[133] and in Michael Welker, we see the incorporation of biblical insights and the partial incorporation of ideas from process philosophy so that the ascension is the presence of Christ in a part of creation which remains spatially and temporally indeterminate and inaccessible for us.[134]

Yet, none of these attempts have truly caught up to Luther's approach, as they either continue to think in terms of the model of space as container or seek to do without any spatial concepts at all. A spatial interpretation, however, is crucial, because space is an important aspect of life. With the relational model of space, spatial distance between two locations is an important instrument for expressing personal transcendence. It is the very first condition making personality possible, for in personal transcendence various persons are separate from one another and thus able to relate to one another, making them open to mutual communication. Following a similar train of thought to that used in determining the relationship between time and eternity, we can now assume it is not space itself making this possible but its underlying logical characteristic as a ordered relation. We have already seen that the Triune God is in essence also such an ordered relation. We also saw that the incarnation can be understood as an intersection of both networks of relationships of God and the world from the world's perspective. Conversely, ascension means the intersection of God's and humanity's networks of relationships under God's conditions: the eternal Logos in the incarnation participates in the concrete spatio-temporal perspective of Palestine, while the humanity of Christ participates through the ascension in the divine perspective, that is, the relation of God to the spatial world as a whole.

'Heaven', to be precise, means God's reciprocal but asymmetrical possibility of relationship to creation and individual creatures in all locations. Ascension then means that this possibility for relationship is mediated in the person of Jesus Christ, who is the only one of the Trinitarian persons to have become human. It is because Christ is in heaven that he is close to us.

---

[133]Cf. Tillich, *Systematic Theology II*, p. 162.
[134]Cf. Welker, *Universaler Gott, Relative Welt*, pp. 224–8.

3.2.1.3.3 Hegel on space and infinity

We have not yet resolved the problem of how the finite and infinite intersect. Under the relational model of space, the infinite is to be thought of as present in the finite, that it can be present *as a whole* in the finite, without being limited by the finite. In the container model of space, this concept would be simply incoherent.

With help from the historical doctrine *finitum capax infiniti* (the finite is capable of the infinite), we can emphatically state that the Lutheran view is that the infinite, meaning God, is capable of appearing in the finite. This applies to the person of the eternal divine Logos, who is able to appear in Christ's human nature, and this also applies for the understanding of communion and ascension in the Lutheran tradition. Luther even expresses this in his Christmas hymn 'From Heaven Above to Earth I come' in verses 9–11:

> Ah, Lord, who hast created all, How hast thou made thee weak and small, To lie upon the coarse dry grass, The food of humble ox and ass.
>
> Were earth a thousand times as fair, Beset with gold and jewels rare, It yet were far too poor to be, A narrow cradle, Lord, for Thee.
>
> Thy silk and velvet are coarse hay, Thy swaddling bands the mean array, With which even thou, a King so great, Art clad as with a robe of state.[135]

If we consider models of space that do not depict space as a container, the presumed basic principle – that the infinite can appear completely within the finite yet without being limited by it – is at least understandable, although we may not be able to picture it to ourselves. Thinkers have traditionally employed this logic of the infinite by borrowing from Hegel's distinction between true infinity and bad infinity.[136] The bad infinite is the infinite I am able to independently imagine *and* conceive, but cannot appear in the finite. But this means that it actually is limited – by the finite in fact! Yet, true infinity can only be understood in such a way that it is not limited by the finite and in so far as it is capable of completely entering the finite and still comprising the antithesis between finite and infinite.

---

[135]From the 1855 translation of 'Vom Himmel hoch da komm ich her' by Catherine Winkworth.

[136]Cf. Georg Wilhelm Friedrich Hegel, 'Wissenschaft der Logik I/1: Die Objektive Logic: Erstes Buch: Die Lehre vom Sein (1832)', in Walter Jaeschke and Friedrich Hogemann (eds), *Gesammelte Werke*, vol. 21 (Hamburg: Felix Meiner, 1984), pp. 124–37; see also Wolfhart Pannenberg, 'Unendlichkeit', in Joachim Ritter et al. (eds), *Historisches Wörterbuch der Philosophie*, vol. 11, 13 vols (Basel: Schwabe & Co, 2001), pp. 140–5.

This is the point of the Lutheran notion of the person of Christ and the Lutheran understanding of communion.

> According to Hegel, bad infinity is still limited because it is constructed as an antithesis to the finite. Only the infinite that can exist completely in the finite is no longer limited by the finite and thus the true infinity.

3.2.2 Space and infinity revisited

Since the twentieth century, various concepts of God's infinity as a structured network of relationships related in diverse ways to the world's spatial network of relationships have appeared repeatedly in theology. Listing them all in detail is beyond the scope of our project here, but we should mention at least two more recent conceptions by Dirk Evers and Luco van den Brom. Both describe God as a Trinitarian network of relationships that is structurally related to the world's relational structure.

Evers, in particular, points out how this relationship between the two structural arrangements of God and the world cannot be understood on its own with the model of space, but rather temporality is always implied within its eschatic dimension, without the danger of spatial infinity turning into temporality.[137]

Van den Brom emphasizes the importance of thinking about the concept of worldly space only as a concept derived from the Trinitarian network of relationships in a metaphorical way. He delineates a relational understanding of God's omnipresence[138] in which he provides an account of both the Trinitarian relationships and worldly network of relationships and the relationship between the two by talking about three or four kinds of spaces: primary space is God in God's Trinity, secondary space is created space, and tertiary space is the activity of the Holy Spirit as the connection between the primary and secondary spaces. By designating tertiary space as an attribute of the Holy Spirit's activity, Luco van den Brom is able to show that the relationship between God's infinity and the finitude of the

---

[137]Cf. Evers, *Raum - Materie - Zeit*, pp. 152–60.

[138]Cf. Luco Johan van den Brom, *Divine Presence in the World: A Critical Analysis of the Notion of Divine Omnipresence* (Kampen: Kok, 1993).

world is not simply a relation which is static or constitutive. Rather, with the image of tertiary space, he is able to integrate two aspects: the reign of God which is beginning and the reign of God which is consummated eschatically:

> Through the power of the Holy Spirit a new space is created within the secondary, created, intermediary space for the believers, made up of a community of persons, that is, the people of Israel or the church as a special communicative space *in via* .... Here the Holy Spirit raises the hope of the eschatological or ultimate space of the final, irrevocable unification with the primary space of God, that is, 'heaven' as a reciprocal communicative community between God and a recreated humanity. Thus, the intermediary space in God which makes personality possible will not disappear ... but will rather be constituted anew through the infinite dimension of this eternal communication.[139]

What is not entirely clear is whether van den Brom is designating the space of the present activity of the Spirit and eschatic space as one or two kinds of space, although this is immaterial for our purposes at this point at least.

For now, let us go along with Evers' and van den Brom's models while noting that this solution of the space-infinity problem corresponds to the solution proposed to the time-eternity problem. Because the revelation-event of the eschatic ground happens through self-identification, we can add a few specifications to our model:

> The network of relationships which is God should be understood as multiple asymmetric, irreflexive and transitive relations between the Father, Son and Holy Spirit. It is identical with eternity and infinity or, rather, with divine time and divine space. As such a network of relationships, God is the condition of possibility for worldly space-time: manifold, equally asymmetrical, irreflexive and transitive relations, in which the three dimensions of space known to us are reversible while the sole dimension of time we know is irreversible. Due to these structural possibilities, we can conceive of both God's companionship in relation to God's creatures in time and God's presence in the world. These make novelty and alterity possible.

[139]Luco Johan van den Brom, 'Space I. Philosophy of Religion; Space II. Dogmatics', in Hans Dieter Betz et al. ed. *Religion Past and Present*, vol. 12, 14 vols (Leiden: Brill, 2006–2013), pp. 179–80.

3.3 The good, the true and the beautiful

Having considered the question of the relationship of time and space to eternity and infinity, we now turn to the search for what is good, true, and beautiful. All these aspects are important for different reasons, above all because of an important theological question. When we identified the basis of eschatic hope, we did not reference the persons of the *eschatoi*, as they are in their eternity in and of themselves, but we presupposed the triune action of God in creation, redemption and consummation. But, if the relation between God and the world cannot be defined solely in terms of the creation of the world but also its redemption and consummation, then we can postulate that there is a contradiction in sin, evil and that which is unconsummated or imperfect. These are the 'negative' presuppositions, so to speak, of every eschatology. 'Negative' is being used in an epistemological, not an ethical sense. But, if there were nothing bad or evil or the world were perfect, then eschatology could deal with the *eschaton* and the *eschatoi*, but not with the *eschata*, because there would be nothing to hope for: the world as it is would already be the eschatic reality. An imperfect world in which there is evil raises the question of where this evil comes from and how God relates to it. This question (*unde malum*) is related but not identical to the theodicy problem, which does not seek to address the origins of evil but, given its existence, seeks to acquit God. Therefore, the question of the origins of evil should not determine our primary approach to our topic. However, before we formulate the question more precisely, we should briefly mention what the theodicy problem is generally perceived to be.

3.3.1 Suffering and divine omnipotence

Named the 'theodicy problem' by G.W. Leibniz[140] (d. 1716), this is a philosophical problem which will be treated here only selectively with regard to different strategies for its resolution. These in fact lead to solutions that are satisfactory in a purely formal sense. To be able to comprehend this,

[140]Cf. Gottfried Wilhelm Leibniz, *Theodicy: Essays on the Goodness of God, the Freedom of Man, and the Origin of Evil* (trans. E.M. Huggard; La Salle: Open Court, 1985).

we must first understand how the problem has come to be. It arises from the combination of (at the very least) the following sentences:

A. There is suffering (evil) in the world.
B. God is good.
C. God is omnipotent (and omniscient).
D. God exists.

It is easy to see that statements A–C appear contradictory, which is the source of the problem. If we did not agree with even one of the statements or were able to negate any one of them, then the problem would thereby be resolved. The history of attempts to solve this problem can thus be categorized according to the way in which various statements are negated.

(A) One can deny that there is bad or evil in the world, or one can downplay its existence. If one can argue that suffering attests to a higher, positive purpose, then the problem is resolved and there is no contradiction between statements B–C. We can assign to this category all those approaches that presuppose evil ultimately does not have any existence of its own and is simply a lack of goodness (*privatio boni*). This approach can be found principally in the neo-Platonic tradition, as well as in Augustine (d. 430). In the debate about universals, neo-Platonism argued in a realist way that the good, the true and the beautiful are identical with being. Hence, evil is ultimately a lack of being to which one cannot ascribe any reality of its own.[141] One could also place Leibniz in this category as he attempted to show why the various types of evil are meaningful and thus the world as it is now actually represents the best of all possible worlds.[142]

(B) If we can deny the goodness of God, there is no longer any problem because then God's essence would not exclude evil. This does not mean that one has to teach a monism of evil; it would suffice to accept that God is partially good and partially evil or that there are two equally powerful principles which are opposed to one another, and which only make up the all-determining reality when taken together. Apart from numerous films in popular culture, this notion found its classical expression in Zoroastrianism, in which a good god (Ahura Mazda) and an evil god are pitted against one

[141]For more on the history of *privatio boni* thought, see Friedrich Hermanni, *Das Böse und die Theodizee: Eine philosophisch-theologische Grundlegung* (Gütersloh: Gütersloher Verlagshaus, 2002).
[142]Cf. Leibniz, 'Theodicy', p. 228, 249.

another.[143] In Christianity, this thesis has almost always been rejected. We find dualistic elements only in Manicheism, a mixed religion that was popular in parts of the early church at times. Polemics against certain heretical movements in the Middle Ages also included accusations of dualism.[144] It is also possible to conceive of Luther's discussion of the hidden God so that it no longer relates to the hiddenness of the revealing God in which everything that is yet to be discovered about God eschatically would be coherent with this revelation, but instead in such a way that the hidden God is the God active in death and life and is all in all, who stands in contrast to the revealed God as a God who affirms life. So in this case, it might be possible to find dualistic solutions to the problem of theodicy within Christianity after all,[145] as in the works of Werner Elert (d. 1954).

(C) One might also solve the problem by denying the omnipotence of God. This approach has been particularly popular more recently and can be found, for example, in process philosophy, which traces back to Alfred North Whitehead (d. 1947) and in process theology which has been influenced by process philosophy[146] and in popular form in Hans Jonas (d. 1993).[147] In process thought, God is assumed to have a double nature: a 'primordial nature' and a 'consequent nature'. Primordial nature is nothing other than pure, apersonal causality, which sets in motion the processes of the course of the world. This consists of '*actual entities*' both passively connected to each other and able to enjoy one another, on the one hand, and actively influencing one another, on the other. Events which take place do not get lost in the course of time but are preserved in the *consequent nature* of God. The originally empty causality of God is expanded through the world, so that God gains personality yet without merging with the world.[148] According to Charles Hartshorne (d. 2000), in neoclassical theism, God is still perfect, although God is capable of growth. God can be surpassed, yet God can be surpassed only by later stages of God's own *consequent nature*.[149] Structural similarities can be identified in the work of Hans Jonas, who, as a Jew, has to

[143]For more on Zoroastrianism, see Michael Stausberg, *Zarathustra und seine Religion* (Munich: C.H. Beck, 2005).

[144]Cf. Johannes van Oort, 'Manichaeism', in Hans Dieter Betz et al. (eds), *Religion Past and Present*, vol. 8, 14 vols (Leiden: Brill, 2006–2013), pp. 25–30.

[145]Cf. Volkmann, *Der Zorn Gottes*.

[146]Cf. David Ray Griffin, *God, Power and Evil: A Process Theodicy* (Philadelphia: Westminster, 1976).

[147]Cf. Hans Jonas, 'The Concept of God after Auschwitz: A Jewish Voice', *The Journal of Religion* 67.1 (Jan. 1987), pp. 1–13.

[148]For more on Whitehead's thought, see Welker, *Universaler Gott, Relative Welt*.

[149]Cf. Hubertus Gezinus Hubbeling, *Einführung in die Religionsphilosophie* (Göttingen: Vandenhoeck & Ruprecht, 1981), p. 180.

deal with much more substantial difficulties with respect to theodicy. For if Yahweh is the all-determining historical reality and has chosen this Israel as God's people, then the Holocaust cannot simply be the sole responsibility of the German people, but God must also be responsible in some way, for God chose God's own people and is the Lord of history. Election and annihilation are apparently not mutually exclusive. Jonas attempts to resolve the theodicy problem – in a more literary than formal way – by narrating a new creation myth in which he suggests that, by creating the world, God completely divested God's self of omnipotence (and ultimately also of personality) which can only be regained through the course of the world with its events and developments, as described in process thought.

In Christianity, there have also been several approaches along these lines in which thinkers have presupposed that God suffers with humanity when God divests God's self in the cross and in Christ. This concept, which has always been especially widespread in Lutheranism, was not developed as a solution to the theodicy problem *per se* but was interpreted in this respect in the twentieth century by Jürgen Moltmann, among others. Of course, it cannot remain there with the sheer empathy of a God who has divested God's self of all omnipotence, for empathic suffering does not overcome suffering.[150]

(D) One could also reject the existence of God altogether. This option is nothing special within the history of modernity, so it is not necessary here to list examples. Furthermore, this solution is still problematic because in effect it simply entails a shifting of the problem. Odo Marquard has pointed out that with the death of God, the problem has been shifted, so that humanity is to be held solely responsible – at least for moral evil – and now stands in front of the judgement seat itself. Thus, modern people feel the perpetual compulsion to justify themselves for everything and are accountable with regards to evil. The only way to prevent this is to avoid any contact or confrontation.[151]

Thus, the majority of solutions dealing with the theodicy problem can be classified according to this typology. Yet, we have not offered a Christian solution in the true sense so far. Above all, a Christian solution must insist that the theodicy problem reflects just one aspect of a more comprehensive set of problems. The theodicy problem is not identical with the question '*unde malum?*' and is not identical with the search for a possible meaning

---

[150]Cf. Dorothee Sölle, 'Gott und das Leiden', in Michael Welker (ed.), *Diskussion über Jürgen Moltmanns Buch 'Der gekreuzigte Gott'* (Munich: Kaiser, 1979), pp. 114–17.

[151]Cf. Odo Marquard, 'Rechtfertigung: Bemerkungen zum Interesse der Philosophie an der Theologie', *Gießener Universitätsblätter* 13.1 (1980), pp. 78–87.

of suffering and a possible overcoming of suffering. Every attempt to solve the problem within Christian theology will have to factor in these aspects, especially the last one. Martin Luther offers a few insights in his famous doctrine of lights at the end of *De servo arbitrio*. Absolutely no solution can be found in the light of reason. In the light of grace – that is, God's self-disclosure in the cross and resurrection – one can find some personal comfort for one's self at least, because one can be sure of being saved, no matter whatever happens. The problem that some will be rejected by God can be solved according to Luther in the *lumen gloriae*, in the eschatic light of perfection, because one will then recognize that rejection means the highest form of grace even for the rejected. With this, Luther attempts to resolve this set of problems with an eschatic approach by postulating that human reason will be able to comprehend coherence once it has been eschatically restored.[152] We can merely point out that in creation, redemption and consummation, God's action aims to overcome suffering, and thus every Christian attempt to solve the theodicy problem must always take place within an eschatological perspective, so it cannot be subsumed within the types listed so far to address the otherwise abstract theodicy problem. As a defence against the potential accusation that this only represents an empty promise about the future, we can remain steadfast: while this may in fact be the case, it does make it possible to act differently in the here-and-now. We certainly do not always have to act with resignation in the face of suffering and there is also the possibility of accusing God (Job), which is generally taken to be a sign of faith as *fiducia*, since the speech-act of accusation only makes sense if one also holds the accused to be responsible for that which they are accused.

The theodicy problem results from the incompatibility of simultaneously asserting four of the following claims: (1) God is. (2) God is good. (3) God is all-powerful. (4) There is evil. The theodicy problem can easily be resolved by negating any of the four statements. The various solutions throughout the history of philosophy can be subdivided into types depending on the kind of negation. When it is claimed that the theodicy problem cannot be resolved, what is usually meant is not the philosophical problem of theodicy, but the existential experience of suffering.

---

[152]Cf. Martin Luther, *On the Bondage of the Will*, in *Luther and Erasmus: Free Will and Salvation* (eds and trans. E. Gordon Rupp et al.; Philadelphia: Westminster, 1969), pp. 329–32.

Thus we can conclude our excursus into the theodicy problem and return to our more comprehensive, global question, which can be posed in various ways:

- Why did God create a world with the possibility (or even the necessity?) of a fall, a world with the possibility and reality of suffering, and not the perfect world right away or rather the eschatological reality?
- Why did God make us in order 'to redeem us and make us holy'[153]?
- If the triune God discloses God's own self in the cross and manger, if God discloses God's self under the appearance of the opposite of what one would expect as the divine (*sub contraria*) – which would mean that in the cross and resurrection evil is included at least as evil that has been overcome – then why does the resurrected eschatic Christ, who is the image of our eschatic hope, still bear the scars of crucifixion? Should it not be the crucified one alone – and not the resurrected one – who bears the wounds and scars?
- How should we understand discourse about the omnipotence of God?

By way of addressing these questions, we can narrow down the much broader question of what is ultimately good, true and beautiful in order to answer it. Nevertheless, this question still remains so broad that within the frame of this textbook, we must forgo an examination of the history of its meaning or various approaches to answering it. Instead, we will consider a solution that can tie in with the Reformation tradition.

3.3.2 God's omnipotence as all-embracing activity

According to Luther, 'creatures are only the hands, channels, and means through which God bestows all blessings'.[154] Consequently, God acts in all events and God's omnipotence as a description of God's action in the world is continually actualized and not a mere potentiality. Nevertheless, one can interpret Luther's position in different ways. One option is to understand omnipotence as meaning God's sole efficacy (*Alleinwirksamkeit*).[155] The

[153]Luther, 'The Large Catechism', in *Book of Concord*, p. 439; line 64.
[154]Luther, 'The Large Catechism', in *The Book of Concord*, p. 389; line 26.
[155]Cf. Paul Althaus, *Die Theologie Martin Luthers* (Gütersloh: Gütersloher Verlagshaus, 1984, 7th edn), pp. 101–7; Bernhard Lohse, *Martin Luther's Theology: Its Historical and Systematic Development* (trans. and ed. Roy A. Harrisville; Minneapolis: Fortress, 1999), p. 209.

other option is to speak of God's all-embracing activity (*Allwirksamkeit*) and forgo thinking of God alone as being the sole agent. Even in *De servo arbitrio* – the text in which Luther describes God's omnipotence in the most radical way – we find the idea of cooperation between divine and human action.[156] To choose between these two interpretations, we must first define them in more detail and identify wherein the true differences lie. Secondly, we must make a systematic, phenomenon-oriented decision, rather than an exegetical one derived from Luther or other traditions.

All-embracing activity means that God's actual action is a necessary condition of every actual event that happens in the world, including those actions of intentional creatures. By contrast, God's sole efficacy (*Alleinwirksamkeit*) means God's actual action is a necessary and sufficient condition for every actual event. Thus, it follows that God is the sole agent in everything, even if God can make use of other agents – including the intentions of personal creatures – as mere instruments. Another option would be to accept that there are yet other causes, including the intentions of personal creatures, but that God's intentions are most important. God's sole efficacy means that God is the agent behind everything that happens.[157]

One cannot go so far as to assume that Luther would describe the action of God in such a way that God should be held responsible for sin or that Luther would teach a double predestination. While some may welcome this for theological or religious reasons, it is logically incoherent.[158] In the argumentation that follows, we will see why we should choose the interpretation of God's omnipotence as all-embracing activity for both theological and logical reasons, while rejecting the notion of God's omnipotence as sole efficacy as contradictory and meaningless.

We will have to accept the necessity of introducing the idea of the elusiveness or hiddenness of God in some sense. If one wishes to speak of a God who is revealed and hidden at the same time, then we must reject the interpretation of omnipotence as sole efficacy. For if we were to presume sole efficacy, not only would certain particular events in the world be God's self-identification, but God would have to be revealed in all the events of the world. But, then, God and the world would in fact be conceived of

---

[156] Cf. Thomas Reinhuber, *Kämpfender Glaube: Studien zu Luthers Bekenntnis am Ende von de servo arbitrio* (Berlin: De Gruyter, 2000), p. 118.

[157] For a comprehensive explanation see Schwöbel, 'Revelation and Experience', in *God: Action and Revelation.*

[158] Cf. Althaus, *Die Theologie Martin Luthers*, pp. 106–7.

as identical in a pantheistic way, or the concept of revelation or the self-identification of God would become meaningless. For this reason, we can only speak of God as revealed, when we also speak of God as hidden.

> Luther speaks in various places of how God is all in all. This understanding of omnipotence can be understood in various ways: it can be understood to say that God acts in all the events of the world, in which case we would call this all-embracing activity (*Allwirksamkeit*). It can also be understood so that *only* God is acting – mediated or unmediated – in all the events of the world, which we might call *sole efficacy (Alleinwirksamkeit)*. Only the notion of God's all-embracing activity is coherent.

3.3.3 The good, the bad and the ethically neutral

Luther begins with the assumption that the goodness of human acts does not depend alone or primarily on the act itself, but on the person who is acting. In one sense, the goodness of an action does depend in part on the action itself: An act can only be designated as good if it is commanded by God, meaning, for example, those acts performed for the sake of one's neighbour. As a result, there must be acts that are ethically neutral because they are not bad but neither are they commanded by God. Nevertheless, they can become good acts if the person is a believer. Luther gives an example in *De servo arbitrio*:

> But if we are unwilling to let this term go altogether – though that would be the safest and most god-fearing thing to do – let us at least teach men to use it honestly, so that free choice is allowed to man only with respect to what is beneath him and not what it above him. That is to say, a man should know that with regard to his faculties and possessions he has the right to use, to do, or to leave undone, according to his free choice, though even this is controlled by the free choice of God alone, who acts in whatever way he pleases.[159]

Therefore, Luther distinguishes between the good, evil and those human actions that are probably neutral. For there are matters in which humans

[159]Luther, *On the Bondage of the Will*, p. 143.

can exercise free will, namely in those situations where humans ultimately cannot cause damage, matters which are not relevant to salvation. This set of human actions is just one subset of all worldly events. If, according to this, there are not only good and evil events but also ethically neutral events with respect to human action, then as a result there are not only good and evil events but also neutral ones throughout the world. We will see that the existence of this category of the 'ethically neutral' is a decisive condition for the concept of beauty and thus for aesthetics in general. If we connect this insight with the meaning of the omnipotence of God as all-embracing activity from the last section, then clearly God's action towards the world is a necessary condition for good, bad and indifferent events, although God is not the responsible agent for every single event. Even if we can determine whether particular actions are really good, bad or neutral, we still cannot identify God as the agent responsible for particular actions, whether they are good, bad or ethically neutral.

There are two options for understanding the ethically neutral: absolute neutrality and relative neutrality. Absolute neutrality means an event is neither good nor bad. Relative neutrality means an event may have ethical value as good or bad, but nevertheless be ethically neutral in relation to one or more other events so that none of the events is better than the others. The only thing being rejected is the idea that all events can be organized strictly in an ethical hierarchy based on some being 'better than' others. Different levels of goodness can entail multiple events that are all equally good. For our purposes, it suffices to use the concept of relative neutrality.

In the world, there are good, bad and indifferent events. This ethical indifference allows us to imagine that there is no absolute hierarchy of the goodness of events. Relative ethical neutrality means multiple different events can have the same goodness. The action of the triune God towards the world is necessary for all these events to take place.

3.3.4 Divine–creaturely cooperation

The concept of divine and creaturely action, as developed in the last two sections, presupposes a specific interpretation of God's eternity in relation to time. If God is to be understood as an agent in particular worldly events, then God's eternity should not be understood in terms of the Augustinian model of timelessness. We also cannot adopt the Boethian concept of eternity which presumes that all events in the world happen at the same time from the perspective of God's eternity, because within this understanding of eternity it is logically necessary to interpret all events in the world as one single action of God, including a single intention of God.

If we presume the understanding of eternity explicated above instead – in which God can be understood as an eternal event but which is logically structured as an ordered relation and which is the condition of possibility for the creaturely spatio-temporal structure – then we can imagine a corresponding action of God. God's eternity allows for the process of events in the world, precisely because God is a process of events in God's self, although one that differs from the world.

How can we understand this divine–creaturely cooperation? Peter T. Geach develops an interpretation by means of the well-known example of a chess game: God behaves like a chess grand master, while the creaturely players are beginners. The chess master does not know exactly what the beginner will do next, for a beginner is significantly more unpredictable for him than an advanced player would be. Nevertheless, the chess master knows he will win no matter what the beginner does.[160] While Geach's analogy of the chess game can be considered expedient, it has a major disadvantage: divine–creaturely cooperation is depicted as a battle.

To avoid this conflictual model of the relationship between God and humanity, one can easily adopt another image instead. The idea of genius or the importance of individuality did not exist yet in the Renaissance (it gained prominence in the nineteenth century). So, Renaissance painters such as Lucas Cranach, Albrecht Dürer and the great Italian masters often – but not always – designed the most important elements and themes of their paintings themselves. The details of the painting, however, as well as the actual execution of the painting were handed over to their assistants to complete. The finished painting could be understood as the product of the master, but also as a product of his assistants and ultimately also of contingent factors. Nevertheless, the master already knew before its completion that his work would be good in the end and the desired results would be achieved.

This image can be applied to the relationship between divine and human action: God chooses human actors and true contingency as co-operators in the knowledge that the entire process of the world will turn out nothing but good eschatologically.

---

[160]Cf. Geach, *Providence and Evil*, pp. 57–8.

To explain divine–creaturely cooperation, true contingency also has to be taken into account in addition to divine and human intentions, that is, events which are not completely predetermined, either through natural causes or intentional action. This understanding of true contingency can be seen as a necessary precondition for speaking about both human and divine freedom. Within an eschatological rather than a dogmatic framework, this cannot be fully developed, but we can offer a few considerations: dogmatic tradition presupposes that God created a world or at least humankind in God's image and likeness. If God is love, then it is plausible to assume God not only created the world out of love, but also determined it for love. This was traditionally expressed in the double commandments of love, which can be understood as a rule which is constitutive for the being[161] of the world and its creatures. Thus, love determines the being of the world. So that love can be love, it must include the possibility of contradiction, that is the freedom of creatures. The double commandment of love is a deontic rule, a rule that can be broken. Thus, love contains not only contingency, but also freedom in a double sense. This freedom includes spontaneity and affectivity as well as the freedom to choose in a specific sense, as we shall see. While this rule of love cannot be rescinded for personal creatures, it can be violated. If this rule of love could not be violated, it would not be love.

Now, we can seek the conditions that must be logically possible so that this violability of the rule of love and thus its deontic character can be given. We can connect the answer to this question with the answer to the question about the imperfection of cosmic regularities, that is, the natural world, by offering the following thesis: the imperfection of cosmic regularities is a necessary condition for the deontic character of the double commandment of creaturely love. This thesis cannot be completely proven, but its plausibility can be ascertained if we consider the following thought experiment: the natural regulating system contains contingency: suffering and death. For sentient creatures, contingency necessarily entails a distinction between desire and suffering. Just imagine a natural world in which there were no contingency, no suffering and no death. In such a world, could some creatures be understood as personal who could break the rule of love? The most likely answer seems to be no: with a natural set of rules in which there

[161]For more on the distinction between constitutive and regulative rules as well as the difference between deontic and adeontic rules, see Amedeo G. Conte, 'Konstitutive Regeln und Deontik', in Edgar Morscher and Rudolf Stranzinger (eds), *Ethik: Grundlagen, Probleme, Anwendungen* (Vienna: Hölder-Pichler-Tempsky, 1981), pp. 82–6.

is contingency and no suffering, creatures could not develop who would be unable to love. These creatures would be constitutively incorporated into a cosmic set of rules or a continuous regular flow of events, in which they would only experience good and in this way could not have any idea or concept of a negative choice. The concept of choice or freedom would therefore be an empty concept if not self-contradictory – as would the understanding of love.

In this way, we can show that the concept of true contingency is a part of the order of creation. This true contingency does not contradict God's actual all-embracing activity (*aktuale Allwirksamkeit*). For if God can choose to allow human intentions, then God can also allow undetermined actual events, that is, true contingency. Nevertheless, God's action towards the world remains a necessary condition for every individual event to become actual.

This conception of cooperation between divine, human and contingent factors implies that God can respond appropriately whatever creatures do or whatever happens due to true contingency so that the eschatic *telos* of all worldly events is guaranteed: it will correspond to God's intention that the eschatic reality is good and nothing but good.

3.3.5 Transformations

Christian hope must think of the consummation of the kingdom of God as a life without ethical differences, without the predicates of 'better' and 'worse'. One might ask then what contribution the world and its history will make towards shaping the consummated state of the kingdom of God. Such a contribution is only possible if we presume a final judgement. Traditionally, the assumption has been that that only the good will survive, while there will be no place for evil. This, in turn, can be understood in one of two ways: on the one hand, one can believe that only good persons can survive in the consummated state and that bad persons must undergo eternal suffering or be annihilated (see Chapter 5). On the other hand, this idea might also mean that only the good events enter into the eschatic life and contribute in some way to its eschatic life, while there is no (eschatic) place for bad events including bad human acts and their effects (see Chapter 5). The second option appears more appropriate than the first, given the precondition of the doctrine of justification and reconciliation on the cross which shows that God distinguishes between sin and sinner in such a way that God loves the sinner and hates the sin.

In the past few sections, we sketched out an understanding of God's action which makes it necessary to alter even this second interpretation of the final judgement. This is because we ascertained that there are not only good and evil events, but also neutral events and actions, at least some that are relatively ethically neutral in relation to one another. If it is right that good and neutral actions can contribute something to the eschatic reality, while bad actions and events must be rejected since what is really evil cannot be understood as good and vice versa, then it must be possible for the evil – and perhaps, but not necessarily, for the good – to be transformed into the relatively ethically neutral. If it were possible, this would have one advantage: without humans having to achieve something on their own and without the world being able to contribute something to its soteriological *telos* (i.e. that it will be good) so that it does not contradict the doctrine of justification by grace alone, we could say that the world and humanity could in fact contribute something to the eschatic *telos*, that is, in so far as this is ethically neutral.

All human actions, including their good and evil deeds, will become ethically indifferent with respect to the *eschaton*, without damaging their pre-eschatic ethical value.

3.3.6 The good, the true and the beautiful

In neo-Platonic metaphysics, as well as in German Romanticism, the good, the true and the beautiful coincide. In neo-Platonic metaphysics, this is possible because of the presupposition of a strong realism of universals: If we find good things in the world, and perceive good and true states of affairs in our experience of the world, then the true, the good and the beautiful must be a reality in our world. For in late antiquity, people thought in terms of the scheme of classification called the 'tree of Porphyry'.

This tree of Porphyry or the *arbor porphyriana* – named for the pagan neo-Platonic thinker Porphyry, who wrote an elementary textbook in late antiquity – is a classification scheme in which terms can be divided up into *genus* and *species*. Thus, 'humanity' can be understood as a *species* whose next higher *genus* would be 'living creature'. Humanity can be differentiated from other animals *species* by a specific difference (*differentia specifica*), such as 'gifted with reason'. This is how definitions are made up: a definition is formed by the proximate genus and the specific difference (*definitio fit per genus proximum et differentiam specificam*). If terms are defined, then they are always treated as *species in* which one can be categorized by indicating a next higher *genus* and a specific difference. What is important is that *genus* and *species* are relative terms. What is a *genus* at one level can be a *species* at another: the term 'living creature' can be understood as a *species* of the next higher *genus* (for example, 'material body'). Here we can also supply a *differentia specifica* such as 'animate'. In this way, we can organize all possible terms and the result is a pyramid of terms or rather, the other way around, a tree with branches. At the very bottom at the root of the tree (or at the acme of the pyramid) there is Being itself, and at the very top of the crown of the tree (or at the base of the pyramid), there would be individuals. Since there is no higher *genus* for being, and since individuals, unlike terms, cannot be defined through a specific difference, we can say: *esse non in genere* (being is not a *genus*) and *individuum est ineffabile* (the individual cannot be defined).[162]

In this case, the term realism applies when we ascribe reality to the actual universals themselves, while nominalism applies when such universals are not considered to be real in themselves, but only abstractions from individuals. In neo-Platonism, this pyramid of terms was understood in terms of the reality of universals as a pyramid of being, and in such a way that the closer a level is to Being itself – that is, the closer a level is to the top of the pyramid or the root of the tree – then the higher the ontological status ascribed to it.[163]

According to the classification system of *arbor porphyriana*, it is possible to ascend to the higher categories until we reach that which is really good, really true and really beautiful, because higher categories possess a higher degree of reality. In both neo-Platonist metaphysics and Christian neo-Platonism, existence and essence coincide with the divine One. Consequently, although we as people can describe the good, the true and the beautiful with various linguistic means, the terms of the good, the true and the beautiful must ultimately have the same extension: the One or God who is Being itself.

---

[162]Cf. Wilfried Härle, *Systematische Philosophie* (Munich: Kaiser, 1987, 2nd edn), pp. 76–8.

[163]For more on the problem of universals, see Wolfgang Stegmüller, *Das Universalienproblem einst und jetzt* (Darmstadt: Wissenschaftliche Buchgesellschaft, 1974, 3rd edn).

This approach is highly problematic for various reasons. The main reason is that this understanding depends on presumptions which are not necessarily Christian, such as the reality of universals. While this view is not necessarily un-Christian, if we accept it at this point, then we have made our understanding of God dependent on philosophical and external decisions at a central point. Let us attempt to solve this problem step-by-step.

First, in terms of the relationship of the true to the good: All events in the world can be understood as the outcome of divine–human cooperation, in such a way that divine action permits the actions of personal creatures and permitted effects of true contingency. This includes human understanding and human language as subsets of human action.

Traditionally, truth is the correspondence between language and reality.[164] This definition is problematic because it presupposes a relation of correspondence between two *relata*, which belong to different categories of entities: language and reality. But, entities belonging to differing categories of things are not comparable. One cannot speak in a meaningful way about a correspondence between apples and pears.

Alternative theories of reality such as Tarski's semantic theory of truth, theories of coherence or pragmatic theories of reality can be seen as answers to this specific problem of classical theory. The semantic theory of Tarski does not modify the description of the relation (correspondence). This remains a relation of correspondence. But, instead, what is changed are the two *relata*. Both relations belong to the same set, the category of speech: the sentence 'snow is white' is true precisely when 'snow is white' as formulated at another linguistic level.[165] Coherence theories likewise operate with one set of language-based *relata*, but without distinguishing between object language and meta-language. The result is that now the description of the relationship also has to be modified. It is no longer the relation of correspondence but of coherence, free from contradictions between statements.[166] While both semantic theories of truth and coherence theories modify the description of the reality-*relata* in such a way that one is speaking only of language, pragmatic theories claim we cannot avoid also talking about reality if we wish to speak about truth. So, pragmatic theories

[164]For a short overview about theories of truth, see Christoph Schwöbel, 'Wahrheit', in E. Fahlbusch (ed.), *Taschenlexikon Religion und Theologie*, vol. 5 (Göttingen: Vandenhoeck & Ruprecht, 1983, 4th edn), pp. 283–89.
[165]Cf. Lorenz Bruno Puntel, *Wahrheitstheorien in der neueren Philosophie. Eine kritisch-systematische Darstellung* (Darmstadt: Wissenschaftliche Buchgesellschaft, 1993, 3rd edn), pp. 41–69.
[166]Cf. Puntel, *Wahrheitstheorien*, pp. 172–204.

consider those linguistics concepts which are the most viable, which prove themselves to be the best in practical action.[167]

Within the framework of a Christian event-based ontology, which assumes cooperation between divine and human action, we can reformulate the classical correspondence theory of truth by avoiding its contradictions. Now, both *relata* – human speech and reality –belong to the same set of objects. Both are events which are speech-acts: reality belongs to the class of events known as divine speech-acts and language to the class of human speech-acts. With Colin E. Gunton (d. 2003) we can thus say: 'The world is a kind of object that can be interpreted with language. It is or has itself – metaphorically – a kind of language.'[168] There is thus, according to Jüngel, 'an interplay between humanity and world, in which humanity understands itself in a cosmomorphic way and the world anthropomorphically'.[169] Thus, both could stand in a relation similar to correspondence: in a relation of resonance. If we pay attention to categorical difference between human action and divine action, between *actio Dei* and *actio hominum*, we could define truth in the following way:

> Truth is the resonance of creaturely personal speech-acts with divine speech-acts and its event-like results.[170]

This definition of truth is conceptualized within the Christian internal perspective. This theory not only provides a definition of truth, but makes it possible to explain why the only operable proof of truth consists in pragmatic justification. Furthermore, this theory explains why pragmatic justification is only a necessary condition but cannot be a sufficient condition for truth: This theory provides an ontological description of various relations of resonance between various kinds of action and thus it is an ethical theory of truth. As such, it must always account for human action including human

---

[167]Cf. Puntel, *Wahrheitstheorien*, pp. 142–71.

[168]Colin E. Gunton, *The Actuality of Atonement: A Study of Metaphor, Rationality and the Christian Tradition* (Edinburgh: T&T Clark, 1988), p. 37.

[169]Eberhard Jüngel and Paul Ricoeur, 'Thesen zur theologischen Metaphorologie', in Jean-Pierre von Noppen (ed.), *Erinnern um Neues zu sagen* (Frankfurt am Main: Athenaeum, 1988), p. 63.

[170]A detailed resonance theory of truth with special reference to William James is provided in Markus Mühling, '"Voller Gnade und Wahrheit": Eine theologische Resonanztheorie der Wahrheit', in Ulrich Beuttler and Martin Rothgangel (eds), *Glaube und Denken, Jahrbuch der Karl Heim Gesellschaft*, vol. 27 (2014), pp. 81–102.

speech-acts and observe it in light of the fall of creation and reconciliation, that is, from the perspective of Law and Gospel. The human search for truth and its discovery in all areas of human knowledge and science does not depend solely on the creative action of God but also the reconciling and perfecting action of Father, Son and Holy Spirit. And, thus, the human search for truth is under an eschatological reserve. Notwithstanding, however, one consequence of this theory of truth is that truth now becomes a subject for ethics: our metaphors are true if they resonate with the divine action. And that could certainly mean diverse linguistic answers in the communication with God's speech-acts. If they do not fit, i.e. if they are dissonant with God's communicative action, then they are false. We must wait until we are face to face with the Father, Son and Holy Spirit to see to which actions this applies. Nevertheless, this theory has an important implication: now, the true becomes a subject of ethics and eschatology, for the true and the good ultimately coincide.

If we try to find similarities between the beautiful and the good (or the true), then we encounter difficulties that hinder such a correlation. In our everyday language, we follow a decisive rule, when it comes to aesthetics: *De gustibus non est disputandum* – there is no arguing about matters of taste. The beauty of things may vary, but we cannot decide which is more beautiful. But, if the transcendentals of the good, the true and the beautiful form a complete disjunction – so that there is nothing in the world which cannot be comprehended with the categories of the true, the good and the beautiful – then it is logically necessary that the realm of the beautiful is the realm of things which share the same ethical value, that is, the realm of that which is ethically neutral, at least in terms of relative neutrality. Thus, the existence of the ethically neutral is a necessary condition for the existence of beauty.

> The transcendentals of the good, the true and the beautiful do not have the same extension: the good and the true may coincide, but not the beautiful.

3.3.7 Multiple forms of the eschatic reality

If we were to summarize this chapter so far, we could say that the process of the world is determined through God's all-embracing activity and the permitted actions of God's creatures and their outcomes. It is important to maintain that creatures cannot contribute anything to the soteriological outcome of the world. It is foreseeable for God this outcome – the *eschaton* – will be good. But, because there are ethically neutral events, there are several conceivable ends of the world which are equally good. Furthermore, in the final judgement, the evil acts of humanity – and possibly even their good actions – will be judged, that is, they will be transformed into ethically neutral actions and their outcomes. Nevertheless, they can contribute something to the eschatic identity of both the individual personal creatures and the whole shape of the eschatic world, as the one realized outcome of those different – yet ethically equivalent – possibilities. These possibilities differ not in goodness or truth, but in beauty, and not in the sense that one possibility is more beautiful than others, but in the sense of *de gustibus non est disputandum*.

> Pre-eschatic, ethically relevant events will be transformed into events of aesthetic difference by the triune God as the eschatic ground. Humanity and contingency will be co-operators with respect to the aesthetic shape of the eschatic world, as with a work of art. This is the case because of the possibility that the world can have several conceivable goals, all of which have the same ethical value: in theory, then, there is more than one 'best' world. With respect to aesthetics, however, these multiple 'best' possibilities differ from one another. Which possibility will be realized is something not even God can foresee.

With this, we have answered our initial question and can present the following thesis:

> God created the pre-eschatic world (and did not create the eschatic reality immediately) with the goal of creating specific beauty in cooperation with God's creatures. The identity of the *eschaton* as the final shape of the kingdom of God is an effect of divine–human cooperation with respect to its beauty, but not with respect to its goodness. This can be seen in the resurrected eschatical Christ: the crucified Christ bears the wounds and scars caused by the sins of the world. The risen Christ bears these scars of suffering, which has been overcome, as signs of beauty.

4 The Pre-eschata

Chapter Outline

Annihilation or transformation? 151
Human death 172
The apocalyptic revelation of the future of history 223

4.1 Annihilation or transformation?

As mentioned previously, in what follows we will first attend to the *eschata*, which in the proper sense are not at all last things, but rather penultimate things since they only concern an end that is immanent to the state of the world, persons and society as they are at present. We will therefore begin with the cosmic aspect, the ultimate destiny of the world, which can be subdivided into two different types that then connect to a third: conceptions of the transformation or of the annihilation of the world. A third model only apparently arises in assuming that concepts like transformation or annihilation of the world do not have any religious or eschatological relevance. After reviewing these particular answers for the problem of the question of the ultimate destiny of the world, a reformulation of the problem and potential solutions will need to be sought out.

Before addressing the material problem, however, it is first necessary to look at the Biblical evidence, which does not by any means use unequivocal language on this matter.

To begin, we can cite passages that assume a transformation of the world. According to John 3.16–17, the reason for God's sending of the

Son into the world is God's love for the world and the goal is the world's salvation. In so far as the discussion in 1 Cor. 15 concerns the transformation of humanity, indicating that the corruptible will be clothed with the incorruptible, these formulations also appear to include the possibility of the transformation of the world as a whole. This can be confirmed through Rom. 8.19–23, where the discussion centres on the yearning for redemption of the whole creation, which is enslaved because of humanity. This appears to presuppose that there can be no eschatic fulfilment of redemption without the inclusion of the non-personal creation, therefore not a redemption from the world, but rather a redemption of the world.

On the other hand, there is also a series of passages that speak of a radical end of the world, in the sense that they ultimately have to be understood to entail the annihilation of the world (Ps. 102.25f., Is. 51.6, 1 Cor. 7.31, Heb. 1.10f., Rev. 20.11). Among these, the synoptic logion Mk 13.31 (cf. Matt. 23.35, Lk. 21.33) appears to possess especial relevance, wherein heaven and earth pass away, but the Word remains.

A third group of expressions is not so easily assigned to one of the two typologies but can be taken as independent evidence for both, depending on interpretation. Paul's discussion of the new creation (2 Cor. 5.17, Gal. 6.15) or the discussion of a new heaven and a new earth can be understood as expressions for the totality of the world in that continuity is emphasized, whereas on the other hand, it also appears to fit to Scripture that the old world will pass away and no longer be remembered (Is. 65.17, 1 Pet. 3.13, Rev. 21.1, 5).

Biblical evidence exists both for the notion of an eschatical transformation and for an eschatical annihilation of the world.

4.1.1 The transformation of the world (*renovatio*)

4.1.1.1 Transformation in the tradition

The view that the world will not be annihilated but transformed (*renovatio*) is by far the one most broadly advocated in the history of Christianity. It is also interesting that entirely different theological schools and confessions are in agreement on this point, details notwithstanding. The reason for this could possibly consist in the fact that in the early church Irenaeus of Lyon (d. 202), in a key argument against Gnosticism, had already formulated the thesis of a transformation, but not an annihilation of the world.[1] Gnosticism saw the material world as the product of an evil or at least incompetent creator, meaning that it could not fathom any redemption *of* the world, but only redemption *from* the world. Irenaeus could not let this view stand, whereby the emergence of 'orthodox' Christianity involved not only the dispute with Gnosticism, but also with the emergence of thinking about this eschatical *renovatio* of the world. The theological point to take from this is that if God is good and created the world, then God will not then destroy it. This would otherwise imply a contravention of God's faithfulness and therefore a contravention against God's own self, meaning God would not be identical with Godself.

During the Middle Ages, there was generally broad agreement on the following points as detailed: the world will be transformed as even the world's most basic features, according to the understanding of the time, earth, water and air, are infected by humanity's sin. As fire was primarily considered to be associated not with the earthly, but the sublunar sphere (the space between earth and moon), it was thought that nearly the entire cosmos would be purified and reformed by fire at the divine command.[2] The stars were normally considered to be an exception which had not been infected by sin and were to be rewarded for their faithful service in not having to be reformed by fire, but rather simply stopped when God as unmoved mover ceases movement.[3] According to Thomas Aquinas (d. 1274), worldly, bodily substances survive this process of purification, but not their present forms. The consequence of this is that there will be no more plants and animals.[4]

In Reformed theology and in parts of the Lutheran tradition, these conceptions survive and are only moderately reformed. Luther himself assumed a transformation of the world, not an annihilation, though he largely refrained from speculating about the course of the transformation, with the exception of a few statements geared towards the fact that time will no longer be measured by the heavenly bodies with hours, days and

---

[1]Irenaeus, 'Against Heresies', in Alexander Roberts and James Donaldson (eds), *The Ante-Nicene Fathers, Vol. 1: The Apostolic Fathers* (New York: Scribner's, 1899), pp. 566–7 (V.XXXVI.1).

[2]Ott, *Eschatologie in der Scholastik*, pp. 54–6.

[3]Cf. Ott, *Eschatologie in der Scholastik*, pp. 54–6.

[4]Thomas Aquinas, *Summa Contra Gentiles, Book Four: Salvation* (trans. Charles J. O'Neil: Notre Dame: Notre Dame, 1975), p. 348 (IV.97.4–5).

years.[5] Calvin also held back from making any highly explicit statements, thinking based on his interpretation of Matt. 24.29 that only the event itself could make this known; it was however surely to be powerful enough for the stars to fall from heaven.[6] Orthodox Reformed theology is once again more courageous in its expressions, though most likely in dispute with Lutheran orthodoxy, which in many parts had taken over and developed the doctrine of annihilation. Since heaven and hell were understood to be places within the created world, it was preferable to teach a transformation of the cosmos instead of its annihilation.[7] The notion of transformation was even preserved under the stipulations posed by the Enlightenment. Lutheran theologians also returned to the doctrine of transformation, as they only assumed there would be a destruction of the solar system or that humanity would be given a new place to live.[8] In the nineteenth century, Martin Kähler also falls into this group, though he only discussed 'cataclysmic changes to nature'[9] without any greater precision. The twentieth century also witnessed a series of eschatologies that can more or less be ordered to this same type as well. One quintessential example is that of Paul Althaus (d. 1966), for whom the inclusion of the world in eschatological reflections is based on the fact that 'in its autotelic character … nature [proclaims] to us that God's lordship does not open up in the beauty of his spiritual cosmos, but – speaking symbolically – also has a sensory side'.[10] How we are to conceive of the world's participation in the eschatical reality, however, remains open at this point.

4.1.1.2 Transformation in the philosophy of nature

The fact that we find the notion of the transformation of the world in both the Ptolemaic and Copernican worldviews appears to suggest that in principle this motif is neutral with respect to worldview. If this assumption is correct, then corresponding expressions would also have to be found which draw on the standard model of cosmology. This is in

[5]Cf. Luther, WA 17 II, 253, pp. 19–22; WA 10 III, 194, p. 10; WA 49, 732, pp. 9–10; WA 12, 596, p. 26.
[6]John Calvin, 'Commentarius in Harmoniam Evangelicam', in Eduard Reuss et al. (ed.) *Corpus Reformatorum*, vol. 73 (Braunschweig: Appelhans und Pfenningstorff, 1890), p. 667.
[7]Erhard Kunz, *Protestantische Eschatologie von der Reformation bis zur Aufklärung* (Freiburg: Herder, 1980), pp. 62–3.
[8]Sigmund Jacob Baumgarten, *Evangelische Glaubenslehre*, vol. 3 (ed. J.S. Semler; Halle: Gebauer, 1760), pp. 724–5; Volkmar Reinhard, *Vorlesungen über die Dogmatik* (ed. J.G.I. Berger; Amberg: Seidl, 1801), pp. 680–1.
[9]Kähler, *Die Wissenschaft der christlichen Lehre*, p. 422.
[10]Althaus, *Die letzten Dinge*, p. 135.

fact that case, even if the most comprehensive attempt to provide such a description comes not from a theologian, but a physicist: Frank Tipler's 'physics of resurrection'. Tipler binds this with the explicit claim to be able to reformulate the substance of theological *topoi* into the terminology of the natural philosophy. Before this approach can be introduced, however, it will first be necessary to review some of the basic features of prognoses for the future of the world as found in contemporary natural philosophy.

The standard model of cosmology describes the world by means of the Einstein–Friedmann equations. Here, a value, the so-called cosmological constant λ, is of particular significance. Its value is hitherto unknown but depends on the mass of the universe. If $\lambda = 1$, then we would be living in a 'flat' universe, i.e. space-time would expand from the Big Bang until the expansion comes to a standstill and levels off at a final static level. If $\lambda > 1$, then the expansion of the world will eventually slow and reverse towards a re-collapse. In this case, the end of the world would be a 'Big Crunch', corresponding to the 'Big Bang'. If $\lambda < 1$, the universe will continuously expand. In this case, the second law of thermodynamics is significant, which says that in closed systems differences in energy will even out. This would mean that the world would die of a so-called 'warm-death', though it would perhaps be better to call it a cold death: all differences in energy will even out, nuclear reactions will come to a halt and ultimately there will be nothing in the universe apart from identical matter, which continuously spreads out from itself in an infinitely lengthening duration. If the baryons as building blocks of matter were ultimately to become unstable, matter would dissipate over the course of time into cosmic radiation. Now, if one were to confer the notion of the transformation of the world to extrapolations in physics, then this only seems to allow for the improbable case of a 'flat' universe with $\lambda = 1$. Far more likely at the present time, extrapolating from the observable mass of matter, is either the warm death model or, in case one accepts the existence of the as yet unobservable 'dark' matter, the Big Crunch model. While the former appears to boil down to a kind of immanent lethargy in the world process, the later boils down to a form of annihilation. In any case, to postulate that the universe is either flat or closed, it would be necessary to presuppose that there is at least ten times more dark matter than visible matter.[11] This has not yet been proven.

Nevertheless, what is unresolved for all cosmological models is the question of why the world developed in the way that it actually developed.

[11]Cf. Evers, *Raum – Materie – Zeit*, pp. 342–6.

This is because there was obviously a multitude of conditions at the beginning of the world, constants, which influenced this development. For many scientists, it was dissatisfying not to be able to ask further questions about where these initial conditions and their so-called 'symmetry breaking' came from.[12] In the last quarter of the twentieth century, different varieties of the 'anthropic principle' were used to provide clarification about the totality of these improbable coincidences. In its weaker version, it says: because there is intelligent life in the cosmos, the universe must be so constituted that the emergence of intelligent life is possible. The stronger variant runs: the universe must be so constituted that it brings about intelligent life necessarily. The 'final' anthropic principle ultimately says: the universe is so constituted that it brings about intelligent life and that as soon as it has emerged, it will not die off but rather obtain power over all physical mechanisms in the universe.[13] The anthropic principle clearly shows to what extent cosmology stands between the natural sciences and philosophical speculation. The weak variant appears to be banal, really saying little more than: 'The world is like it is because it is like it is.' What is not to be underestimated, however, is that this weak principle can be used as a criterion of scientific cosmology: Many contemporary cosmological theories rely on the same observations and can be distinguished purely by their high amount of mathematical speculation. According to the weak anthropic principle, these theories cannot claim to be scientific ones.

Tipler has since proposed a scenario that also allows the transformation model to be explained in terms of the 'Big Crunch' model. Tipler's attempt to conceptualize a version of an enduring inhabitable and transformed world is not the only one put forward by natural scientists,[14] but his attempt might be the only one that actually allows this transformed world to design itself.

In his Omega Point Theory, the name of which is borrowed from Theilhard de Chardin (d. 1955), Tipler supposes that life and consciousness can ultimately be reduced down to information processing, meaning that although the universe brought about human consciousness according to the final anthropic principle, this consciousness is not necessarily bound to its biochemical 'hardware', but can ultimately become independent of it as

---

[12]Cf. Volker Weidemann, 'Cosmology – Science or Speculation?', in A.v. Diemer (ed.), *World Congress of Philosophy*, vol. 16 (1978) (Frankfurt am Main: Lang, 1983), pp. 173–9.

[13]Cf. John D. Barrow and Frank J. Tipler, *The Anthropic Cosmological Principle* (Oxford: Oxford, 1986).

[14]Cf. Evers, *Raum – Materie – Zeit*, pp. 338–42.

a result of increases in technology.[15] As a result, Tipler suggests that in a brief moment before the Big Crunch an infinite amount of energy will be available to this consciousness making it capable of an infinite amount of information processing. This means, however, that despite what is actually, objectively speaking, a split-second, a subjectively infinite amount of time will be available wherein the universe attains consciousness of itself as God and can therefore allow all of the occurrences that have happened within it - and thus also all the human beings that have ever lived - to exist as simulations, now creating for them a subjectively remodelled, transformed and infinite world.[16] It would also be possible, according to Tipler, for this Omega Point to inaugurate the beginning of the material creation itself.[17]

4.1.1.3 Renewal as new creation

If one compares the thinking of the theological tradition on the renewal of the world with Tipler's formulations, notwithstanding the latter's pantheistic implications, it is striking that renewal is obviously comprehensible within a broad spectrum of views that can be arranged in a polar manner: on the one side are those positions supposing such an intense purification of the world that they hardly come short of advocating *annihilatio*, with the result that the renewed world is to be understood as a new creation through God's creative power. On the other side are those positions teaching renewal as perfection of the world, in the extreme case with Tipler in such a way that this consummation is already prearranged within the order of the world. Nevertheless, we are not dealing with two different models at this point, but rather a broad spectrum with fluid transitions.

> Conceptions of an eschatical transformation of the world in the history of theology are most frequently concerned with the destiny of the world. Since the time of Irenaeus, they have been understood as a point of resistance against gnostic heresies that could endanger the goodness of the world and the faithfulness of God. Within such conceptions, there is a broad spectrum extending from emphasis

---

[15]Cf. Tipler, *The Physics of Immortality*, pp. 124–8.
[16]Tipler, *The Physics of Immortality*, pp. 138, 181, 220.
[17]Cf. Tipler, *The Physics of Immortality*, pp. 214–16.

on continuity to emphasis on discontinuity. Precluded from the Christian perspective are those conceptions emphasizing a continuity that conceive the future transformation of the world as somehow immanent to the world as it is at present. The conception of new creation that emphasizes discontinuity occasionally nearly touches the notion of the annihilation of the world.

4.1.2 The annihilation of the world (*annihilatio*)

4.1.2.1 Annihilation in the tradition

The model alternative to that of the transformation of the world is that of the eschatical annihilation of the world. It is seldom encountered in the theological tradition and nearly exclusively limited to Lutheran orthodoxy in the train of Johann Gerhard (d. 1637). We therefore only have to enquire into Gerhard's interpretation of this doctrine and the nature of his argumentation.

Gerhard's thesis about the negation of the world is nearly his only completely innovative formulation. He defines it in this way: 'The consummation of the world or the destruction of the world is an act of God, in which by using the fire of heaven he will reduce, earth, sea and all the creatures that are in them, excepting only angels and humans, into nothing for the manifestation of his truth, power and justice for the purpose of the liberation of believing humanity.'[18]

Gerhard is clearly aware that he is taking on the tradition of important medieval scholastic theologian Peter Lombard, who had defended the general meaning of the *renovatio* of the world, though certainly not against any specifically named representatives of the notion of *annihilatio*.[19] Those were ultimately to be found, as noted, in the Gnosticism present in the early church and were from that point on only treated positively

[18]Johann Gerhard, *Ioannis Gerhardi Loci Theologici cum pro adstruenda veritate tum pro destruenda quarumvis contradicentium falsitate per theses nervose solide et copiose explicati* (Lipsiae: Hinrichs, 1885), XXIX, 26: 'Consummatio seculi sive destructio mundi est Dei actio, qua per ignem coelum, terram, mare et omnes creaturas, quae in eis sunt, solis angelis et hominibus exceptis, in nihilum rediget ad veritatis, potentiae ac justitiae suae manifestationem et piorum hominum liberationem.'
[19]Konrad Stock, *Annihilatio Mundi: Johann Gerhards Eschatologie der Welt* (Munich: Kaiser, 1971), p. 9.

with extreme rarity.[20] From that point, one can ask why Gerhard, the paradigmatic Orthodox Lutheran, promoted the thesis of the annihilation of the world. According to Konrad Stock, Gerhard had four primary reasons for doing so.

First, from the doctrine of God, the Word of Scripture not only has authority, but true being belongs to it alone as God's faithful Word.[21] Scripture, however, in Mk 13.31 and parallels speaks of the passing away of the world, but not of the Word. It is therefore the case that the *faithfulness* of God requires the annihilation of the world. The *annihilatio* is possible on the basis of the *absolute* will of God. If God were to contradict God's own self-revealed will, then God would be untrue to Godself and therefore not self-identical. However, God, in God's own being and constancy, is perfect actuality (*actus purus*), not potentiality. The world, on the contrary, is essentially non-constant and finite. Thus, eternal existence cannot be attributed to the world, not even an eternal existence granted it by God. The notion of the annihilation of the world is therefore an expression of the absolute incomparability of God and world and consequently ultimately an expression of what is implicitly the impossibility of analogy between God and world.[22]

The second are reasons stemming from the character and purpose of the world itself. In all of its happenings, the world is dependent on God's preserving action as the necessary condition of its existence. Its purpose is only a mediate one: the purpose of humans and angels is the *gloria dei*, i.e. giving glory to God. The world serves humanity only for subsistence and as means of provisional knowledge of God as if through a mirror (cf. I Cor. 13.12); thus it no longer needs them in the eschatological fulfilment. Preservation of the world thus becomes superfluous. Gerhard then interprets Rom. 8.19–22, the *locus classicus* for the notion of *renovatio*, in such a way that the redemption of non-human creatures into freedom consists precisely in their annihilation.[23]

The third concerns the nature of the anticipated eschatical salvation. Vision of God is salvation: 'In annihilating the world, God becomes the world of humanity in God's own self. In abolishing (*aufheben*) the time and space of human existence, God becomes the time and space of human beings. This is the meaning of eschatological salvation, and this abolishes

[20]Cf. Stock, *Annihilatio Mundi*, pp. 11–12.
[21]Cf. Stock, *Annihilatio Mundi*, p. 60.
[22]Cf. Stock, *Annihilatio Mundi*, pp. 58–60.
[23]Cf. Stock, *Annihilatio Mundi*, pp. 77–89.

(*aufheben*) the meaning of the existing world and therefore its essence.'[24] As a result, new creation becomes superfluous.

Fourth are reasons from the Lutheran understanding of the Eucharist and the ascension of Christ: Whereas the Reformed tradition thought of corporeality from the standpoint of spatiality so that a real presence of Christ in the Eucharist was not conceivable because it is located in heaven as a place in space, the Lutheran tradition sees Christ as present in the Eucharist on the basis of the reciprocal communication of the attributes of God and humanity in the person of Christ (*communicatio idiomatum*) on account of his will (*Multivolipräsenz*). Gerhard now goes a step further and, unlike the Reformed tradition, does not derive corporeality from spatiality, but rather, on the basis of the antecedent Real Presence of Christ in the Eucharist, corporeality is for him antecedent and therefore not bound to spatial or worldly structures. However, if the Eucharist and the person of Christ together are indeed an expression of our eschatical hope, then it follows that the existence of the world as an eschatical circumstance is also indispensable for corporeality and the notion of the *annihilatio* of the world has to fall away.[25]

4.1.2.2 A modern version of annihilation

The question of whether the natural world is heading towards annihilation or renewal can also simply be rejected if one were to assume that it is not meaningful in religious terms. In the end, even Luther and Calvin exercised restraint on this point, while ultimately keeping to the classic doctrine of *renovatio*. It is also possible to find instances where the question has been dismissed altogether since the nineteenth century, e.g. in Schleiermacher and Ritschl, as well as in broad streams of the theology of the twentieth century and even up to the present day in Ulrich Barth.[26] In these cases, however, the question is not ultimately being rejected but rather answered in a way that implicitly supports Gerhard's proposal. That is, if we consider the question of a possible future for the natural world as not being relevant to humanity's eschatical hope, then we are denying relevance of the natural world for ultimate creaturely salvation. But this, however, is precisely the same point underlying Gerhard's thesis about the annihilation of the world. Furthermore, beyond the general flow of ideas this way of thinking

---

[24]Cf. Stock, *Annihilatio Mundi*, p. 123.
[25]Cf. Stock, *Annihilatio Mundi*, pp. 164–7.
[26]Cf. Barth, 'Abschied von der Kosmologie – Befreiung der Religion zu sich selbst', in *Urknall oder Schöpfung?*, pp. 14–42.

entails, there are still a number of significant points to be drawn out of the individual argumentation.

Schleiermacher (d. 1834) also failed to acknowledge the question of the destiny of the world within his treatment of the prophetic doctrines. The significant phrase is found within his treatment of the problem of the Parousia: 'For in Christ the Divine Essence is permanently united with the human nature; hence human nature cannot be so inseparably restricted to a particular planet as to be involved in that planet's destruction as resulting from cosmic laws. On the contrary, everything pertaining to it must be capable of being conceived in the light of this union and as an effect of it.'[27] While the specific issue here is the decay of the body of Christ, not of the entire world, the argumentation strongly recalls that of Gerhard: the unity of the humanity and divinity of Christ is independent from what is worldly and bodily.

Even clearer in this regard is Albrecht Ritschl (d. 1889), who entirely dispenses with having a chapter on future eschatology within the systematic arrangement of his main work.[28] For Ritschl, because the divine personality, like the human, only exists in being directed towards the goal of the kingdom of God and the function of the natural world is nothing other than being the source of the separation between aim and actuality through its restraint, then redemption essentially consists in not being obstructed by the world in the pursuit of this goal. Ritschl expresses this with the concepts of the overcoming of or of the Lordship over the world, which occurs precisely in the cross of Christ and Christian believers.[29] Materially, this overcoming and dominion over the world coincides with nothing other than the annihilation of the world: in the eternity of God, there is no difference between aim and goal and therefore also no world. The world has only medial character for the actualization of the kingdom of God and, when this comes about, it is superfluous.

The conception of an eschatical annihilation of the world appears in two variants: On the one hand, there is the classical version going back to Johann Gerhard that assumes that the non-personal world

[27]Schleiermacher, *The Christian Faith*, p. 708 (§160).

[28]Cf. Albrecht Ritschl, *The Christian Doctrine of Justification and Reconciliation: The Positive Development of the Doctrine* (Eugene: Wipf and Stock, 2004).

[29]Albrecht Ritschl, 'Die christliche Vollkommenheit', in Frank Hofman (ed.), *Kleine Schriften* (Waltrop: Spenner, 1999), pp. 41–65.

will be eschatically annihilated because it only possesses a mediate or indirect relevance for personal creation that it will no longer need, eschatically speaking, when God becomes the world for humanity. The other variant consists in the assessment of the eschatical future of the non-personal world as being religiously insignificant. Both theses are ultimately equivalent or have the same outcome.

It remains to be pointed out that a correspondingly modified position on *annihilatio* is understandably in good company when it comes to the cosmological extrapolations of present-day natural philosophy: if the world was either to slowly fizzle into the eternal lethargy of the warm death or suddenly perish in a Big Crunch, both would only confirm the modified position on *annihilatio* as the eschatical irrelevance of world.

4.1.3 Evaluative criteria

If we are now to ask which position on the fate of the world seems most appropriate, we will have to give an account of the applicable criteria. This should happen at this point.

First, we can assume that like Irenaeus resistance to Gnostic heresies could play a role. At this point, the gnostic heresy consists in the fact that ultimately the world, and indirectly also God, cannot be understood as being good. By contrast, if the basis for making eschatic statements follows on from the threefold self-disclosure of the Trinitarian persons as *eschatoi* in the spatio-temporal world, then God must very well be thought of as good and true to Godself and the world must likewise be understood to be good in some sense. Unsurprisingly, from this follows the fact that the notion of *renovatio* is preferable. This is because we have seen that both Irenaeus and Gerhard could argue their respective positions based on the faithfulness of God without becoming entangled in contradiction.

As a second criterion, we can assess the *problem of continuity*. If the eschatic reality is to be understood as genuinely *eschatic*, i.e. as good and only good, there must be a sharp difference between the here and now and the eschatical reality, because the eschatic reality cannot be thought to be afflicted with the evils of this reality. On the other hand, however, at least so much continuity is necessary that the identity of those who are in hope of salvation is preserved. The problem would thereby be deferred to the question of whether relationships in the world in their historical processuality can or must contribute something to the identity of created persons; a question we will follow up on in the next chapter. What is to be grasped here is that both positions claim to be able to resolve the problem of continuity. Most positions on *renovatio* contain sufficient discontinuity in order to be able to maintain the eschatical character of the eschatical reality. On the other hand, however, the problem of the identity of at least the personal part of creation is taken into consideration in the *annihilatio* model.

It is further possible to ask whether or not the *authorship* of God and the gratuitous nature of the world could play a role. If it is correct that in creation, reconciliation and consummation, a coherent basic structure of the distinction between creaturely effects and divine actions is to be found, which is created in such a way that divine effects on the world always mean *actio ex nihilo sola gratia*, then at least those positions not accounting for this distinction are to be excluded. This, however, is ultimately only Tipler's position, which does not take the eschatical reality into consideration since it does not stem from an eschatical horizon of expectations but rather understands the consummation of the world as being immanent to the world itself. This leads to an entire series of incompatibilities with the Christian understanding of reality. The most conspicuous of which consists in the fact that here, in following Enlightenment tradition, the world is conceived as being perfectible in itself. On the basis of the notion of the universality of sin, however, Christianity must necessarily reject the possibility of the present course of the world turning out positively in such a way that it could issue into a condition of perfection on its own. As a result, radical positions such as Tipler's are excluded, but all other positions are at least theoretically conceivable.

The conception of the *autotelic* nature (*Selbstzweckhaftigkeit*) of the world is far more promising. It is possible to give theological grounds that require conceding intrinsic value to even the non-personal creation. This was not first emphasized after the ecological crisis at the end of the 70s and the beginning of the 80s in the twentieth century but was already vocalized by Althaus (see section 4.1.1.1 above). However, even if one accepts an autotelic account of the world, this does not automatically mean a decision for the first type, but rather only perhaps against *annihilatio*. This is because even in the *renovatio* type the renewal of the world can be conceived in such a way, as became evident in Thomas Aquinas for example, that the forms of the world including non-personal life are not due any further existence.

The decisive question can therefore be reduced to the question of whether and in what way the non-personal creation could exist eschatically. This, however, presupposes a few considerations from the theology of creation as well as certain decisions in fundamental eschatology, i.e. considerations already encountered in the chapter on the eschatoi and the eschaton.

4.1.4 Guidance from the theology of creation

If we are to assume that God brings about being other than Godself out of the love which God is in Godself, that is, in love *ex nihilo*, which is a love that is not grounded in any presuppositions that derive from the world itself, then this means that we have to accept that the principle to which creation is ordered is also that of love. Such creaturely love could not thereby be identical with the love which is God on the basis of the difference between the economic and the immanent Trinity, but it is rather to be expected that the created order corresponds to the love of God. From that point, the rules by which creation as a whole is ordered are to be understood as constituting an order of love. However, this order can be further differentiated into cosmic regularities as well as social and personal structures of love, which can once again be distinguished into those having thetic character – i.e. rules that cannot be broken – and those having deontic character, i.e. rules that can be broken.[30] The following explication can be understood as a reformulation of the classical notion of the *lex naturalis* or orders of creation.[31]

4.1.4.1 Thetic structures of love

To say that God resolved to fashion a creation out of love that would correspond to his own being means that God intended creatures to be both capable of and constituted by relations of love, i.e. bringing forth persons and the conditions necessary to sustain them. This enduring divine act of creation can be understood as the establishment of structures that creatures cannot contravene. These are personal structures because they ultimately exist for the benefit of created persons. This action of God is bound up by the love that is God's own self through the faithfulness of God to God's self

---

[30]On the different concepts of rules, cf. Conte, 'Konstitutive Regeln und Deontik', in *Ethik*, pp. 82–6.
[31]On natural law, see Mühling, *Versöhnendes Handeln – Handeln in Versöhnung*, pp. 296–8.

and thus by the veracity of the divine persons. For creatures, this means a radical asymmetry in their relation to God, one in which the conditions of the constitution of their own creaturely being and becoming – their particular existence – are not completely conveyed to them but are rather largely not at their own disposal. To put it concretely, humans as personal creatures are not capable of completely abolishing the factors that personally constitute them, not even in the contradiction that is sin.[32]

4.1.4.2 Incomplete rules

The entirety of the apersonal and non-social created world falls into this category. If we are to speak about structures of love, the advantage over against the not entirely unproblematic concept of natural law consists in that the concept of structure allows one to assume an order that is dynamic, has a historical course and in some cases even allows for creaturely co-creativity. These structures are characterized by love. This is bound up with a thesis that is far stronger than the mere assessment that God's action is to be described as love. This now has to be shown. First, love presupposes that the capacities for relationship and alterity are not peripheral but rather appertain to personal being as such. Second, this concept of love includes the fact that worldly structures enable or permit freedom. In the case of the apersonal creature, a modification is certainly to be made here since the concept of freedom implies intentionality, which is *per definitionem* a hallmark of the personal creature and is therefore not attributed to the realm of the apersonal. We can speak here of contingence in analogy to freedom with Colin Gunton (d. 2003).[33] The natural order contains contingence, which is understood as a precursor to freedom. A further important indicator of the concept of love comes with the concept of devotion and consists in the fact that a lover always wants the good for the other or provides himself or herself as a means to the one who is loved. However, given the missing concept of intentionality, it is clear that this analogy cannot be fully preserved. In any case, the more significant question is whether it can be preserved at all. While the relational nature of creaturely being can hardly be denied and is widely recognized, we first have to acknowledge that in modernity this intrinsic relationality is very

[32]Cf. Luther, *Lectures on Genesis: Chapters 26–30*, in *Luther's Works*, vol. 5, p. 76.
[33]Cf. Colin E. Gunton's essay, 'Relation and Relativity: The Trinity and the Doctrine of Creation', in *The Promise of Trinitarian Theology* (Edinburgh: T&T Clark, 1991), pp. 142–61, esp. pp. 152–4.

often explicitly conceived not in terms of love, but rather with predation, as if the apersonal world was constituted by the rule of 'eat or be eaten', which is explicitly bound to the reality of suffering and force.[34] It was precisely at this point, however, that Martin Luther had the courage to define the realm of the non-personal nature as being structured by love: 'By all means no creature lives for its own sake or serves itself except humans and the devil. The sun does not shine for its own sake, water does not flow for its own sake, etc. In this way every creature serves the rule of love, and its complete essence is in the law of the Lord.'[35] Here, Luther describes the relational capacity of the *Dasein* of creatures among one another not with quality of life coming at the expense of others, but rather as being for the being of others. In the apersonal realm, the structure of nature is a good ordering of the *Dasein* of existing entities (*Seiendem*) for the being of other existing entities (*anderes Seiende*). Of course, this raises questions about phenomena in the natural world: being predated entails suffering and is not something that such species give into willingly, in so far as they generally exhibit flight behaviour. We can respond to this difficulty, however, by indicating that the apersonal creaturely order of love involves a dynamic set of rules that is *not yet* fulfilled, but first requires fulfilment. Then, the question arises about why this order was not immediately fulfilled. A classic biblical answer to this question can be found in Paul. Apersonal creatures do not suffer for their own sake, but ultimately for personal creatures, and this situation will be overcome by the Holy Spirit at the 'revealing of the children of God' (Rom. 8:18–25). A majority of interpreters understand this to mean that Paul is consciously alluding to Gen. 3.15, that the suffering of creatures exists as a result of the *sin* of humanity.[36] This line of interpretation also stands in the broader Christian and Pauline tradition that understands natural death as the 'wages of sin'. On the basis of our knowledge of the world, this interpretation is hardly possible, however, because it does not acknowledge the fact that death for apersonal creatures existed both before and apart from humanity and that death possibly even fulfils an important evolutionary function.[37] But not even this explanation is necessary. If one

[34]Cf. Michael Welker, 'Konzepte von "Leben" in Nietzsches Werk', in Wilfried Härle (ed.), *Marburger Jahrbuch Theologie IX* (Marburg: Elwert, 1997), pp. 41–52.
[35]Luther, WA 5, 38, pp. 14–17.
[36]Cf. Ulrich Wilkens, *Der Brief an die Römer* (Zürich: Brenzinger, 1980), pp. 154–5.
[37]Schleiermacher, in *The Christian Faith*, p. 321–2 (§76.2), vehemently points out the independence of evil from death as such. An exceptional conversation on the topic can be found in Pannenberg, *Systematic Theology*, vol. 2, pp. 265–75.

examines Rom. 8:18–25 more closely, it turns out that sin is not actually the topic of discussion; the suffering of apersonal creatures rather fulfils a function for personal creatures and will eventually be overcome.

This is all we can say on this for now. We have already given a possible answer to the question of why the structures of creation remain unfulfilled in section 3.3 above: this state of incompleteness means contingence and this contingence is a necessary condition of freedom. Now, we have to ask why freedom is an important aspect of creation. But, this means that we have to ask about the structures of personal love, which we will turn to first in our examination of human death.

If God, first, creates the non-personal creation in correspondence to his love and if, second, this non-personal creation remains unfulfilled according to its natural structure for the sake of the higher good of human freedom, then any eschatic total annihilation of the world would appear to be unlikely.

4.1.5 Guidance from fundamental eschatology

In the section on fundamental eschatology concerning the relation between the good, the true and the beautiful (section 3.3), we saw that the eschatic reality will be good and only good and that it will also be beautiful. We also determined that there could be multiple possible good outcomes, which could not be distinguished by their actual degree of beauty, but only by the kind of beauty they entail, and that the meaning of contingence in the world and human freedom consists precisely in contributing to the kind of beauty that is realized. God indeed remains exclusively the creator of the eschatical reality in terms of its goodness *ex nihilo*, that is, without worldly presuppositions, but not however exclusively as to its concrete aesthetic form. Here, God allows for the possibility of contribution not only from human freedom, but also for contingency in the world, without which the creation of a first unfulfilled, i.e. not eschatic, reality could not be explained. From this follows the fact that the natural apersonal world also exists for the purposes of contributing to human freedom, but not only that. It also has its own ultimate relevance, which consists in the fact that during the course of the world something will be contributed to the fulfilment of reality by chance. At the moment, though, knowledge of precisely what that might be remains beyond our grasp.

4.1.6 The consummation of the world in God

In our analysis of the problem of time and space in relation to the eternity and infinity of God, we made the diagnosis that both exhibit the same logical structure on the basis of the free creative action of God. Both God in and for Godself and the world have structures allowing eventfulness that are asymmetric, irreflexive and transitive. The simplest solution of the problem of whether the world will be annihilated or renewed consists in accepting the fact that the events occurring in the world can be eschatically incorporated by grace into the very event which is Godself. On the one hand, this would be related to the notion of annihilation, because then God becomes humanity's 'world', so to speak, as expressed by Gerhard. The world's time and space would no longer exist, but only its structure in so far as this provides for the possibility of events. In this regard, heaven and earth would actually vanish and the divine logos would remain. On the other hand, this could also be understood in terms of *renovatio*, because then the notion of being face to face with God would apply not only for personal creatures, but also for the apersonal creation on the basis of its own intrinsic eschatic value. The question of precisely which events from among the apersonal, historically contingent events of the world would be sublimated into God necessarily goes beyond the scope of our knowledge at present.

At first glance, this solution appears to be somewhat astonishing, but it is frequently encountered both in the history of modern theology and in the Eastern Christian tradition. It can be found in Pannenberg's theology as follows:

> The problem of linking the thought of an end of time with that of life, including eternal life, disappears only when we consider that *God and not nothing is the end of time*. As the finite is bounded by the infinite, so are time and the temporal by eternity. The end of the temporal, of time and history in general, thus means transition to eternity. This can mean participation in God's own eternal life.[38]

---

[38] Wolfhart Pannenberg, *Systematic Theology III* (trans. Geoffrey W. Bromiley; Grand Rapids: Eerdmans, 1998), pp. 593–4.

Here Pannenberg is not only thinking about personal creatures, but non-human creation also shares in the fulfilment of creation:

> In this way I have included nonhuman nature in my discussion of the theme.... Some degree of independence is an essential condition of the existence of the creature alongside the eternal being of God.[39]

The fact that Pannenberg is thinking not only about non-human but also about personal creation is clear on the basis of his doctrine of creation, in which the *Logos* functions as the generative principle of the particularity of created being. Differences in the particularities notwithstanding, statements by Evers,[40] Schwöbel[41] and Hans Schwarz[42] can be understood as running in the direction of the possible solution under discussion here.

> The solution here consists in the fact that both those world events in which humans are involved and those events in which no humans are involved can be eschatically transferred from the relational order of the world to the divine relational order but do not have to be. On the one hand, this would correspond to the theory of eschatical annihilation but contradict the theory of eschatical transformation on the other, because the spatial-temporal world would no longer exist. On the other hand, this conforms to the transformation theory and contradicts the annihilation theory, because not only the personal creation, but also the apersonal creation will be transformed, even if the precise extent of this transformation remains beyond our ken in the here and now.

4.1.7 Ethical relevance

Humans live in the here and now, embedded in their world. Their hopes however determine their actions. This has become clear in our handling of the question of the meaning of the pre-eschaton. This is particularly significant when we look at the non-Christian versions of annihilation or renewal of the world.

---

[39]Pannenberg, *Systematic Theology III*, p. 642.
[40]Cf. Evers, *Raum – Materie – Zeit*, pp. 371–2.
[41]Cf. Schwöbel, *Gott in Beziehung*, p. 465.
[42]Cf. Hans Schwarz, 'Eschatology', in Robert W. Jenson and Carl E. Braaten (eds), *Christian Dogmatics II* (Philadelphia: Fortress, 1984), pp. 529–37.

The annihilation of the world on the basis of its inferiority first arose in Gnosticism. This can bring about an interesting twofold ethical stance: if the world, inclusive of one's own body, is destined for destruction, one can either live entirely ascetically, in order to receive a foretaste of hope for the salvation of the world, or, on the contrary, one can treat the world and one's own body profligately, because they are irrelevant for everything that is eschatically relevant. Thus, an expectation of the annihilation of the world motivated by gnostic thinking can either lead towards radical asceticism or towards radical libertinism. Both have actually appeared historically as forms of the gnostic ethos[43] and also appear today in terms of the structures by which actions can be motivated.

Also interesting are those forms of hope that proceed from expectations of eschatical renewal that is ordered within the confines of history. Because humanity itself belongs to the world, it alone bears responsibility for the eschatical fate of the world. This is clear both for Tipler and those who have followed him. Carl Sagan (d. 1996), garnering a great deal media attention, advocated the notion that humanity's future could only lay in populating and having mastery over the cosmos,[44] with the result that research into technology and manned space travel are not only ethical imperatives, but are also urgent political and economic goals that can bring in their train solutions to other problems such as the pacification of the world. Since the solutions arising for other problems are side effects of the primary goal, less attention should be correspondingly ceded to them. We have to note in the margin here the fact that any version of this idea that entails the realization of the eschatical reality immanently within the world could possibly tend towards totalitarianism. This is certainly not directly the case with Tipler's conception of the future, because what is ultimately intended is a long-term goal, meaning that we are to deal with this specific problem in all its complexity in another place. What can have particular influence on motivating our action is the reductionistic image of life and personality that is bound up with this conception, because, going beyond the philosophical problem, it must ultimately refrain from ascribing any uniqueness and particularity to creation and can therefore

[43]On Gnosticism, see Beyschlag, *Grundriß der Dogmengeschichte I*, pp. 130–52.

[44]Cf. Carl Sagan, *Pale Blue Dot: A Vision of the Human Future in Space* (New York: Ballantine, 1997). The nearly missionary publicity surrounding Sagan's work was evident with his novel, *Contact* (New York: Pocket Books, 1997), and the later 1997 Hollywood film of the same name by Robert Zemeckis, as well as by various popular science TV series and book publications such as, *Cosmos* (New York: Ballantine, 1985).

lead to a questionable, un-distilled materialistic-naturalistic approach to human personality.[45]

The question becomes even more difficult when we turn ourselves to the Christian options of *renovatio* and *annihilatio* in the narrow sense. Gerhard's conception of *annihilatio* confers only temporary and medial value to the non-personal creation. An ethical posture conceding intrinsic value to the non-human parts of the natural world, valuing it for its own sake, is hardly possible. In any case, a wasteful stance towards natural resources is not compulsory with this view, since it concedes medial value to the world. Conversely, the conception of *renovatio* does not mean that it would not be impossible not to ascribe value to the natural world, since we saw that *eschatic* hope for a wide-reaching purification or transformation of the world does not necessarily entail an ascription of value to the creation for its own sake.

If one assumes that the entire creation has at least the possibility of finding its eschatic goal in Christ and is to be fulfilled as such, then on the one side it is not also unlikely to treat the non-personal creation with respect and deference, whereas on the other side, notwithstanding the biblical commission to dominion, it also unburdened through the motif of the realization of the eschatical reality through the grace of God, to be responsible for this titanically and completely.[46] Humanity cannot adopt 'sustaining the creation' as such as its own proper task, because this is a divine work – specifically entailed within *creatio continuata* –, but can indeed *participate* and *contribute* in the divine task of sustaining creation.

> The non-Christian gnostic conceptions of an annihilation of the world led to both problematic ascetic and libertinistic ethics, whereas non-Christian conceptions of an immanent transformation of the world have led to problematic 'titanistic' ethics. The Christian conception of the fate of the natural world, on the contrary, provides us enough leeway for perceiving various options for responsible ethical action on the one hand, whereas on the other it excludes problematic human interaction with the world.

---

[45]For an introduction to the theme, see Philip Clayton, 'Neurowissenschaft, Mensch und Gott', in Ted Peters, Gaymon Bennett and Kang Phee Seng (eds), *Brücken bauen: Neurowissenschaft und Religion* (Göttingen: Vandenhoeck & Ruprecht, 2006), pp. 169–86.

[46]Cf. Christoph Schwöbel, 'Gott, die Schöpfung und die christliche Gemeinschaft', in *Gott in Beziehung*, pp. 161–92, esp. 161–2.

4.2 Human death

Even more clearly than with the fate of the natural, apersonal world, human death does not appear to be an actual eschaton, but a penultimate, even experiencable circumstance, which is not only to be understood within the ultimate horizon of expectations given in faith, but even within the everyday horizon of expectation that everyone has to die and also have different experiences with dying and death. This view, however, is nevertheless deceptive. Epicurus of Samos (d. 270 BCE) could already write: 'So death, the most terrifying of ills, is nothing to us, since so long as we exist death is not with us; but when death comes, then we do not exist.'[47] We are certainly not able to follow Epicurus in affirming that death has nothing to do with us, but it is still clear that death itself – in contrast to dying – does not belong to the experiential reality of human subjectivity. To this extent, it is understandable if death is understood under the condition of the eschatical horizon of expectations as one of the last or penultimate things. The death of others can certainly be experienced, because death is a social fact. A dead person can no longer react to us, communicate with us and does leave a gap behind in the relational structures of communication and action, one which is often painful for those who remain.

What is clear is that talking about death presupposes talk about life, or more precisely, talk about human life, so that the question of death is indivisible from the question of humanity. As a result, a discussion about what particular anthropology is constituted within the eschatic horizon of expectations is a necessary condition for talking about death.

The difficulties indicated with speaking about death are also evident in a biological examination of human death, which in any case is also not altogether free from problems of definition. In what follows, after a brief discussion of the modern definition of scientific death (section 4.2.1), various understandings of death and humanity will be elucidated, and selected problems in the understanding of death that have played a large role in the Protestant theology of the twentieth century will be discussed. At this point, a unique solution can be proposed, which in essentials depends on the notion of humanity in terms of *imago dei* and personhood, and contains the one specific understanding of the relationship between death and sin,

---

[47]Epicurus of Samos 'Epicurus to Menoeceus' (trans. C. Bailey), in Whitney J. Oates (ed.), *The Stoic and Epicurean Philosophers: The Complete Extant Writings of Epicurus, Epictetus, Lucretius, Marcus Aurelius* (New York: Random House, 1940), p. 31.

as it is enclosed through the reconciliation of Christ on the cross (sections 4.2.6–4.2.7). The conclusion of the chapter is shaped by ethical and pastoral considerations (section 4.2.8).

4.2.1 Biological death

4.2.1.1 What is biological death?

Death appears to be the opposite of life, and dying the transition from life to death. Given this this basis, would it not be more meaningful to begin with a definition of life and only then to press onwards towards a definition of death? Surprisingly, radical problems also await the attempt to formulate a biological definition of life. It is not only the fact that 'life' can be defined variously as based on the concept of metabolism or on the concept of reproduction and the reverse,[48] it is also the fact that systems that are biologically alive can only count as living as long as they are not dead. But that would then mean that a definition of the concept of death is necessary for that of a concept of life.[49] It is for this reason that it is not possible to utilize a general definition of life. Nevertheless, if a general definition does not at first appear to be very meaningful, then one promising procedure might consist in first asking about the extension of the terms 'death and dying' while also looking at some examples. What cannot be considered at this point are forms of life that transition between living and non-living entities, such as viruses, for which the concept of death and life cannot be used in the same sense as with cellular life.

In the case of single-cell life forms under normal conditions, it is not appropriate to talk about death as the end of the material, since in cellular division the original cell is completely preserved in the cells that are subsequently produced. It does not therefore really make sense to say that the original cell has died or is alive in all subsequent cells, since neither the original cells nor the subsequent cells are *individuals* in a biological sense, but rather 'dividuals', that is divisible entities. As a result, with regard to normally developing single-cell organisms, it certainly makes sense to talk about the concept of life, but not about that of death. *Single-cell* life can however be damaged in such a way by external conditions such as the

---

[48]Cf. Peter Hucklenbroich, 'Tod und Sterben – Was ist das? Medizinische und philosophische Aspekte', in Peter Hucklenbroich and Petra Gelhaus (eds), *Tod und Sterben: Medizinische Perspektiven* (Münster: Lit, 2001), p. 4.

[49]Cf. Hucklenbroich, 'Tod und Sterben', in *Tod und Sterben*, p. 6.

removal of nutrients and poisoning that irreversible damage occurs leading to a 'point of no return' causing the cell to moulder and resulting in cellular death.[50]

Even more difficult is establishing the notion of death and dying with respect to multicellular life. On the one hand, individual cells do succumb to cellular death, but this is not identical with the death of the organism and does not have anything to do with death. As to the converse, the death of the organism ultimately also leads to the death of all its cells, but the death of the organism here is the cause, not the result of cellular death.[51] Just as much as the complete death of all the cells of an organism would also lead to the death of the organism, the decomposed body of an organism is actually dead, but this is still not identical with death. Complete cellular death would then only be something like the latest possible point of time at which death can be the diagnosis. On this basis, one can assume that particular groups of cells in a multicellular organism can set off a chain reaction that leads to the death of the entire organism. This process, called 'dying', would then begin when individual groups of cells that serve a specific function were irreversibly damaged. By finding this point, one would have identified the beginning of the process of death. In practice, however, this is not possible. There is no mono-causal group of cells that can set off an irreversible process of death, but it is rather a matter of a variable, multi-causal process, which can be delayed considerably through modern medicine and transplantation medicine.[52] This much is clear: in multicellular organisms, there is indeed a theoretical, factual and yet still not identifiable beginning of the process of death. When the process of the decay of the organism is complete, then the death of the organism can be said to be complete, although this is not identical with the conclusion of the process of decay. What we have to take on board is the fact that 'death' signifies a point or a segment of this process of dying. But, if this is right, then we have to accept the fact that death and dying signifies something different according to the different kinds of multicellular organisms in question. Further clarification can be reached if we limit ourselves to the question of the biological death of human beings.

[50]Cf. Hucklenbroich, 'Tod und Sterben', in *Tod und Sterben*, p. 7.

[51]Cellular metabolism of individual cells or groups of cells even after the death of the organism is possible. The normal example that the hair continues to grow after death cannot be used because it rests on a misunderstanding: after death the skin shrivels only giving the appearance that the hair has grown. Cf. Martin Hörning, 'Medizinische Aspekte', in Martin Hörning and Peter Leppin (eds), *Der Tod gehört zum Leben: Sterben und Sterbebegleitung aus interdisziplinärer Sicht* (Münster: Lit, 2005), pp. 5–24, esp. p. 11.

[52]Cf. Hucklenbroich, 'Tod und Sterben', in *Tod und Sterben*, pp. 8–9.

Up to the 1960s, human death was understood to be the point at which the cardiovascular system and breathing were irreversibly impaired. An altogether simple phenotypic diagnosis could be made as a result.[53] But, even these stipulations do not result in a definition of death, but rather a very practical *terminus ad quem* that appears sufficient, in order that we might avoid the all-too impractical task of determining the precise point of complete cellular decomposition. Based on progress in medicine, it is nevertheless even possible to maintain the breathing and circulatory functions of the body when a number of groups of cells have discontinued their activity. This is possible in particular when brain function is no longer evident.[54]

Since the 1960s, a particular kind of irreversible coma[55] called 'brain death' or 'cerebral death' has been accepted as the most meaningful definition for the complete death of a human being, one that is now also binding in a legal sense. According to German law, for example, this is the 'irreversible end of the functioning of the cerebrum, the cerebellum and the brain stem'.[56] This makes clear that the issue is not a definition of the point of death, but rather of a condition of the brain that has already occurred and that the point of death conceived legally pertains not to an ontological state of affairs, but rather an epistemic one, the conclusive documentation of the doctor.[57]

What is clear is that even this brain death so conceived presents a *terminus ad quem*, which really cannot be moved forward meaningfully, as the debates over brain death have shown.[58] At this point, the concept of brain death shares in the difficulties of establishing definitions for every criterion for death in the course of the process of dying. Similar to how there is no solid distinction between waking and sleeping consciousness, we have to

---

[53]For a listing, see Eberhard Jüngel, *Death: The Riddle and The Mystery* (trans. Iain and Ute Nichol; Edinburgh: Saint Andrew, 1975), pp. 22–4.

[54]Cf. Cf. Hörning, 'Medizinische Aspekte', in *Der Tod gehört zum Leben*, p. 12.

[55]Not every irreversible coma is considered to be brain death according to German law. Appalic syndrome, for example, where the functioning of the cerebral cortex ceases, is not understood to constitute death. Cf. Dag Moskopp, 'Zum Hirntod aus der Sicht eines Neurochirurgen', in Peter Hucklenbroich and Petra Gelhaus (eds), *Tod und Sterben: Medizinische Perspektiven* (Münster: Lit, 2001), pp. 21–43 (30).

[56]Cf. the laws on transplantation medicine for the Federal Republic of Germany (*Transplantationgesetz der Bundesrepublik Deutschland*) in the version from 28 February 2003, last altered by the German Medical Association (*Bundesärztekammer*) on 2 April 2004 (§16, Ab. 1, 2–5).

[57]Cf. Hörning, 'Medizinische Aspekte', in *Der Tod gehört zum Leben*, p. 13.

[58]Cf. Michael Reuter, *Abschied von Sterben und Tod? Ansprüche und Grenzen der Hirntodtheorie* (Stuttgart: Kohlhammer, 2001), pp. 154–6 and Moskopp, 'Hirntod', in *Tod und Sterben*, p. 32.

accept that in the course of the process of dying, there is no solid border between life and death, regardless of what criteria one attempts to bring to the problem.

On this basis, it is worth going into the prevailing criteria for brain death as established in the 1968 definition. Why does this push into the foreground of the question? Standing behind this is ultimately intensive care medicine, which has made it possible to recover from a nearly irreversible failure of the cardiovascular system because of improvements in medical technology since the 1960s. The series of ethical problems bound to this need not interest us at the moment. A more significant question is why *brain* death is the criterion here. The answer consists in the fact that the brain is ascribed a special role among all other human organs in so far as it is brought into relationship with the consciousness in a particular way. Determining the meaning of 'consciousness' from a biological or medical perspective is not a particularly minor problem. Biologically speaking, it appears on the one hand to be a *background consciousness* that is responsible for the feeling of personal identity and perceiving difference between reality and imagination, and on the other, an *actual consciousness*, in which thoughts, emotions and willing appear. These forms of consciousness are not, however, simply localizable in the brain. The cerebral cortex as well as the thalamus and the hippocampus appear to be coupled with the consciousness in significant ways. There is certainly also a series of brain processes that have absolutely nothing to do with the consciousness.

> These processes do not occur in a fundamentally different way as those with which the conscious is bound. Thus, how can consciousness arise from a little electrical activity with a very low current occurring throughout a few pounds of cells? How is it the case that something can happen only in the brain, but not excite the heart or the ganglion nodes in the intestines? We don't know.[59]

Apart from the fact that, according to the contemporary status of medical research, it is manifestly impossible to find a reason or the working principles of this connection between the conditions of consciousness and brain function, another problem arises from the philosophical perspective: brain death has evidently been selected as the criterion for the death of

---

[59]Hörning, 'Medizinische Aspekte', in *Der Tod gehört zum Leben*, p. 16.

the entire human being because human consciousness is bound to the brain. Human consciousness is something like the experience of oneself. However, the determination of what this experience is and why of all things this experience of self or the end of this experience or at least the end of the coupling between this experience and the conditions of the brain ought to be crucial for the definition of the human death is neither a medical, nor biological nor ultimately even a question for the natural sciences, but rather an issue of worldview. Interestingly, in analogy to the notion of brain death, there is no designation for 'brain birth', that is, the diagnosis that those brain functions, whose absence would result in the diagnosis of brain death, have now begun to operate.[60]

The diagnosis of brain death and its distinction from other clinical syndromes does cause a few problems. The criteria for brain death have not ultimately changed since the 1960s. Although the German Medical Association has had to put forward a series of revisions – also after the introduction of the German organ transplantation act of 1997 – this does not come down to the fact that new medical factors have been recognized, but solely due to the advances in hi-tech medicine and the necessarily interconnected changes in technical diagnostic procedures (which otherwise vary from country to country).[61]

After everything we can presume to have established on this point, we can hold fast to the following:

> In the course of the process of the death of a human being understood as the irreversible failure of an individual human organism as a whole, a point in time can be assessed as the *terminus ad quem* at which the functioning of the brain, on which self-conscious and self-experience can be understood to depend, is no longer perceptible and at which active actions and reactions to the environment in the sense of intentional action are likewise no longer possible.

The second relative clause already transcends the limit of what can be expressed in medical terms. The sheer limitation of what can be said about death from a medical perspective is astonishing.

---

[60]Cf. Moskopp, 'Hirntod', in *Tod und Sterben*.
[61]Cf. Moskopp, 'Hirntod', in *Tod und Sterben*, p. 26.

4.2.1.2 Near-death experiences

The difficulties of grasping biological death could disappear if death could be experienced and researched not only out of the third person perspective, but also out of the first. In this regard, we are actually confronted in almost every culture with reports of the experiences of those who have died and come back to life. From a scientific perspective, we are not dealing with death as such, but of cases where the process of death was reversed before reaching the 'point of no return'. The correct terminology for this occurrence is therefore 'near death experience', whose descriptions have produced a great deal of interest since attempts to popularize it during the last quarter of the twentieth century.[62] In so far as these reports reflect, in part, similar experiences (lights, lapses in time, contentment, discontentment, tunnels and out of body experiences as well as flying), there are still a number of basic difficulties with the phenomenon:

- The issue remains that of a *near*-death experience, i.e. experiences that occur *before* the 'point of no return'.
- Even when the experiences correspond to perceptions, this does mean that anything can be said about the truth of these perceptions.
- Proposed sources for these perceptions include displacement of the perception of reality with fantasy as a result of sensory deprivation, psychic defence reaction as a result of proximity to death, hallucinations resulting from an altered cerebral metabolism, social construction of a fantasy reality and other similar explanations.[63]

Whatever the case may be, it is a fact that very little can be said with certainty about near-death experiences from a medical perspective, making it clear that popular interest in near-death experiences needs to be reckoned with from a theological perspective. This is because it could be the case that such interest rests on attempts to extrapolate about death and the ultimate eschatic situation from provisional, non-eschatic horizons of expectation – that is, an attempt to develop statements about a situation that is not at our disposal at in the pre-eschatical present. We can only look at such extrapolations as failures in proper categorization, if not also as sinful attempts to make what is not at our disposal available to our manipulation.

---

[62]Cf. Raymond A. Moody, *Life after Life: The Investigation of a Phenomenon – Survival of Bodily Death* (New York: Mockingbird, 1975). In addition to publications by Elisabeth Kübler-Ross, the moralizing film *Flatliners* by Joel Schumacher (USA, 1990) also contributed to the popularization of this 'experience'.

[63]Cf. Hörning, 'Medizinische Aspekte', in *Der Tod gehört zum Leben*, pp. 18–24.

What can be said with certainty at this point is that:

Near-death experiences do not tell us anything about death itself.

With respect to all the possibilities for interacting with death – philosophical, cultural, liturgical, literary, sociological, psychological or the history of particular burial practices etc. – one can make a limited determination from the perspective of Christian hope and faith that these will always be uninteresting in the case that one wants to attempt to sound out what death actually means with their help. This is not to say in any way that these forms of dealing with death are of no value and cannot bring about fruitful results in many respects. We naturally only mean this in so far as these do not actually constitute attempts to provide definitions of death. It is for this reason that we can forgo a more detailed review of such practices here.[64]

4.2.1.3 Why is there biological death and aging?

If it is not meaningful to speak of death for single-cell organisms, and regeneration and growth processes are evident in multicellular organisms, then we are approaching the possibility of concluding that death and dying are not biological necessities for multicellular organisms but rather simply biological facts. But, one can certainly ask why this is the case. The biological answer to the question is aging, which occurs in a series of different processes. A few of these processes are based on genetics or are inherent to the process of cell generation itself: according to the momentarily well-supported telomere hypothesis, the chromosomes are shortened with every cellular division until the end is reached and the cell can no longer be divided.[65] The majority of these processes of aging do not express any kind of biological necessity, and in particular cases, there are also examples for the unlimited production of cells.[66] But, this means we must shift the question: We have to die because we grow older, but why do we have to grow older? From a biological perspective, one can ultimately only respond from the realm of evolutionary theory, by showing that death, dying and aging bring about certain advantages. The older

[64]For a cultural history of death, see Philippe Ariès, *Geschichte des Todes* (Munich: Dt. Taschenbuch-Verlag, 1993, 6th edn).
[65]On this, see Reimara Rössler, Peter E. Kloeden and Otto E. Rössler, *Das Thanatosprinzip: Biologische Grundlagen des Alterns* (Munich: Beck, 1997).
[66]Cf. Hucklenbroich, 'Tod und Sterben', in *Tod und Sterben*, p. 11.

answer given by evolutionary theorists ran that individual organisms that were wearing out, that is, older, have to be replaced by death in favour of younger and more vital individuals, thus providing a kind of advantage for all as a whole. The consequence of this principle is that propagation and death have the same common origin. This older answer, however, is no longer accepted. For one, gerontological studies show not only that death is not biologically necessary, but that aging is also not biologically necessary. Further, according to newer understandings of natural selection, there is no mechanism that is related to the survival or success of a species as a whole, but only mechanisms that are related to the reproductive success of individual organisms. It would certainly be possible to adjust correspondingly the evolutionary answer if it could be shown that there are mechanisms underlying the aging process that bring survival or reproductive advantage in youth but in the course of development lead to aging, dying and death. A specific gene could also bring advantage in youth, but disadvantage in longer-term development, where the advantages of youth prevail over long-term development. This would mean that aging and death are compromises for the sake of a higher reproductive process.[67] This can be illustrated by the following example:

> Let's assume that a gene changes the metabolism of calcium in the body so that bones heal more quickly. The same gene also causes a slow and steady deposit of calcium in the arteries. This gene could be thoroughly promoted by selection, because many would profit from its advantages in youth, but few would live long enough to become aware of the disadvantage of arterial calcification. Even if the gene led to everyone dying by the age of 100, then it would nonetheless still spread even if it only offered the slightest advantage in youth.[68]

It goes without saying that other, perhaps sociological, answers could be given in response to the question about the purpose or use of aging. In principle, however, the matter stands with these questions just as it does with other possible answers to questions about death which cannot yet be given on the basis of an eschatic horizon of expectations that is always bound to presuppositions grounded in particular worldviews: they cannot give us a satisfactory answer, at least not when the question of the why of aging, dying and death includes the question of the *meaning* of aging, dying and death. At this point, we can only turn to the attempt to find answers in theology.

---

[67]Cf. Hucklenbroich, 'Tod und Sterben', in *Tod und Sterben*, pp. 12–13.

[68]Randolph M. Nesse, George C. Williams and Susanne Kuhlmann-Krieg, *Warum wir krank werden: Die Antworten der Evolutionsmedizin* (Munich: Beck, 1998, 2nd edn), p. 138.

Aging does not appear to be a biological necessity, but rather a compromise that can, from the standpoint of evolutionary theory, heighten reproductive success. From the perspective non-eschatic horizons of expectation and interpretation – such as biology and medicine – the question of the why and use of aging, dying and death can indeed be answered, but not the question of the meaning of aging, dying and death.

4.2.2 Death as division of the body and soul

In order to be able to reconstruct the options of the Christian understanding of death and humanity, comprehensive historical work is needed. We shall begin with the Hellenistic tradition. There is of course no unified Hellenistic understanding of humanity and death. Since we do not need to present this material for its own sake, but rather for the sake of comparison with the Christian tradition, a few qualifications will be helpful at this point.

Plato (d. 347 BCE), in accepting Orphic and Pythagorean thinking in the mouth of Socrates, who had been sentenced to death, describes the following as the meaning of Socrates' imminent death:

> Let us reflect in this way, too, that there is good hope that death is a blessing, for it is one of two things: either the dead are nothing and have no perception of anything, or it is, as we are told, a change and a relocating for the soul from here to another place. If it is a complete lack of perception, like a dreamless sleep, then death would be a great advantage .... If on the other hand death is a change from here to another place, and what we are told is true and all who have died are there, what greater blessing could there be?[69]

Here an alternative interpretation of the meaning of death is introduced, which at any rate leads to reassurance about death:

- Death is either like an absolute sleep – then, as in the saying from Epicurus at the head of this section, it is nothing to fear, because we are no longer there when we are dead.

---

[69]Plato, 'Apology' (trans. G.M.A. Grube), in John M. Cooper (ed.), *Plato: Complete Works* (Indianapolis: Hackett, 1997), p. 35 (40c–e).

- Or, there is a hereafter that is not dependent on biological bodily death. In the passage above, Plato accepts the second possibility. How is this conceived according to the Greek tradition? It assumes that the capacities for knowing, willing and the emotions are not attributable to the body, but to the immaterial soul. The soul is the central point of human identity, that is, what makes humanity *human* and what makes a human into *this* human. This is reproduced by Aristotle with the distinction between form and matter, a differentiation that can be applied to everything. Whereas material is pure potency and possibility, it is shaped and informed by the form. As for humanity, the immaterial soul is its form, the body its material. At this point, there are two alternatives: It is possible to accept, as is the case for Aristotelian ontology, that neither the body nor the soul can exist independently of one another, because the soul and the *forma materialis*, as the formal principle of the matter, cannot exist independently of matter. In this case, the soul is not immortal but perishes with the body. On the other hand, following a more Orphic and platonizing direction, in distinction to other connections between body and soul, the body cannot exist independently of the soul. This can be expressed not only with the Greek play on words: *soma* (body) = *sema* (grave), but also illustrated with a drastic allegory Aristotle uses to describe the Orphic conception: This soul is shackled to the body like pirates shackled prisoners to corpses in order to torment them.[70] Death, then, is nothing other than the liberation of what is most actually human about humanity from its corporeal prison: The soul *is* what makes humans human, individuates them and makes them into particular human beings; it is also precisely what makes a human an *animal rationale*. As a result, bodily death is nothing other than liberation. If in the Hellenistic tradition the human is both to 'know thyself' (*gnothi sauton*) and be mindful of death, or 'remember that you will die' (*memento mori*), then this is an identical and indeed positive state of affairs in which the human knows what he is – namely, immaterial soul – and how he can be liberated in his particularity – namely, through death.[71] Death, therefore, is not the end of the human being, but the beginning of his immortality, specifically, the immortality of his soul. This view of the human as a

[70]Cf. Jüngel, *Death*, p. 42.
[71]Cf. Jüngel, *Death*, pp. 49–50.

compound composed of a body and predominant soul constitutes *de facto* a dualistic anthropology.

The Orphic–Hellenistic tradition was certainly not the only possible conception in antiquity and late-antiquity. We have already seen that the Epicurean position knew of no hope beyond death and that the Stoic conception also did not conclude with continuation of the individual soul. The notion that following on Hellenic antiquity Christian antiquity and its subsequent tradition largely adopted Orphic–Hellenistic thinking is considered to be a case of mistaken prejudice by Roman Catholic theologian Joseph Ratzinger.[72] Nevertheless, the Orphic-dualistic conception does form an exemplary conception against which to contrast the biblical understanding of death.

Similar conceptions can be found not only in the philosophy of the Orphic–Hellenistic tradition, but also in various modern philosophies. René Descartes' (d. 1650) distinction between *res extensa* and *res intelligibilis* heralded modern philosophical dualism and even Immanuel Kant (d. 1804) could construe the immortality of the soul as a postulate of practical reason that is necessary for human morality.[73] These indications of the trend are sufficient at this point.

4.2.3 Humanity and death in the biblical tradition

By contrast, the biblical tradition of the Old Testament has a completely different understanding of humanity and death. The Hebrew word *nefesh* can indeed be translated by the word 'soul', but a more accurate rendering is 'breath', 'wind' or even, especially in the phrase *nefesh haja*, 'vitality', 'breath of life' or 'living thing'. In explicit contrast to the Hellenistic conception, *nefesh* does not mean the principle of identity that makes a human being into *this* human being, i.e. the centre of one's personality, but rather a general vitality that the human, who is otherwise *basar* (flesh) or *afar* (dust), receives from God. It is breathed into the man's nose by God and loaned to him for a time, but it remains God's possession, something that the man does not have at his command (Gen. 2.7; Is. 10.18). Differently from the Greeks, this is not an

---

[72]Cf. Joseph Ratzinger, *Eschatology: Death and Eternal Life* (trans. Michael Waldstein; Washington, D.C.: Catholic University, 1988, 2nd edn), pp. 146–50.

[73]Cf. Immanuel Kant, 'Critique of practical reason', in *Practical Philosophy* (trans. and ed. Mary J. Gregor; Cambridge: Cambridge, 2005), pp. 238–9.

indication of a dualistic anthropology, but rather it refers to the human being as a whole, and indeed, both when referred to as *basar* or *afar*, as when also referred to as *nefesh* or *leb* (heart). This is not surprising because all of these bodily descriptions, taken in the strong sense, exist in an undifferentiated manner from spiritual capacities. This, nevertheless, is not the basis for a materialistic anthropology. Since humans are themselves identical to their vitality, but this vitality only exists in an asymmetrical relation to God, this also applies to humanity: humanity in general and *this* human in particular are not in command of their own vitality but are what they are in relation to God (Pss. 31.16, 139.16). To borrow from Eberhard Jüngel's expression: because human beings are self-related, they stand in relation to God, or better, it is because they are related to God that they are self-related.[74] At this point, it suggests itself to clarify what 'the image of God' means, which expresses that humanity is created (Gen. 1.26) in God's *zelem* (image, *imago*, *eikon*) and *demut* (image, *similtudo*, *homoiosis*). As to the image of God and a more precise description of Old Testament anthropology, we do not have the space to say anything more here.[75]

This conception of humanity has various effects on the understanding of death. First and foremost, when God withdraws his vitality, the human being no longer exists. The predominant writings of the Old Testament do not conceive of an individual or personal eschatic hope, but only of hope for the entire people. The individual human passes away, withers like grass (Ps. 90.5), is gathered to his fathers (Judg. 2.10) – which does not mean a kind of family reunion for the deceased, but only that the bones were deposited in the tombs cut out of the cliffs in the Iron Age for the purpose of the decomposition of the body, then taken from these tombs into caverns for the bones[76] –, goes to the grave, i.e. in the rock-cut tomb without personal inscription (1 Kgs 2.9; Pss. 28.1, 88.4 and 6, 143.7; Prov. 1.12, etc.) or leads a subterranean, shadowy, nearly void existence in *sheol* that can no longer really be described as existence but is more like annihilation since one is

---

[74]Cf. Jüngel, *Death*, p. 63.

[75]On this, cf. the still valuable work by Hans Walter Wolff, *Anthropology of the Old Testament* (Norwich: SCM, 2011) and Hans-Peter Mathys (ed.), *Ebenbild Gottes – Herrscher über die Welt* (Neukirchen-Vluyn: Neukirchener Verlag, 1998). In the Priestly account, the story of creation is bound tightly with the mandate for dominion and is the source for the ideology of kingship, originally having understood humanity as the symbolic representative of God's lordship in the world, just as ancient Near Eastern kings set up images of themselves as symbols representative of their dominion in distant areas and saw themselves as representatives of the dominion of particular gods.

[76]Cf. Elizabeth Bloch-Smith, *Judahite Burial Practices and Beliefs about the Dead* (Sheffield: JSOT Press, 1992).

now far from God. God is a God of the living, not the dead; one does not return from *sheol* and is in darkness, silence and forgotten. All distinctions between individuals are meaningless (Job 3.19, 7.9f, 10.21; 2 Sam. 12.23; Ps. 49.15, 88.13, 94.17, 115.17; Is. 38.18f., etc.). The dead and death are unclean for those who are left behind (Lev. 11.24f.) and the practice of necromancy is in the very least punishable by death (Lev. 19.31, 28; Deut. 8.10f; 2 Kgs 21.6). Broadly in the Old Testament, individual hope for the future is directed towards leading a good and long life of abundance and contentment (Gen. 25.8; Job 42.17, etc.). Early layers of the Old Testament do appear to presuppose at the very least the conceivability of an individual resurrection from the dead,[77] a hope that slowly took over in the intertestamental literature so that by the time of Jesus a few groups of Jews believed in individual eschatic hope, although others did not. The first bit of evidence drawing on God's power as creator is propounded in connection to the problem of justification (2 Macc. 7.14). In the Apocalyptic literature, not even the realm of the dead has not been divested of Yahweh's power, and in the distant future, Yahweh is to destroy death itself (Is. 25.8), although this only applies to those belonging to the community of Israel (Dan. 12.2).

In comparing the conceptions of anthropology and death in the Old Testament with those of Hellenism, it becomes evident that the two could not possibly be more different:

> In the Orphic–Hellenistic understanding, the human being is dualistically composed of body and soul, whereas in the Hebraic, human beings are understood monistically. In the Hellenistic world, the human being is an individual, understood primarily as a soul, because the body is deficient. On the contrary, in the Hebraic world, humans are not individuals, but human only in relation to God. In the Orphic–Hellenistic tradition death means the liberation of humanity for what is truly its own, whereas in the Hebraic, the withdrawal of God's life-sustaining breath means annihilation of the human individual. In correspondence to these conceptions, one can see Socrates greet his death singingly, whereas individual hope for the Hebrews is directed towards long life, prosperity and contentment.

[77]Cf. the vision of the resurrection of the dead remains in Ezek. 37. The point here is not an individual hope for salvation, but an image about the collective restoration of the people, which at the very least presupposes a specific act of God.

For Jesus and his contemporaries, the understanding of death changed little in comparison to early Jewish conceptions. It was through the events surrounding Jesus himself that both new understandings of anthropology and death came about.[78] These developments are recorded in the writings of the New Testament. Jesus died a death that was understood by Paul as a curse on the basis of the law (Rom. 5.14,17). This means that it is ultimately the law that kills, so that now death can be designated as the wages of sin (Rom. 6.23), which is not expressed in this way in the Old Testament. Yahweh's threat of death against Adam and Eve as a result of their violation of the command (Gen. 2.17) does not refer to the general mortality of humans, but only directly to Adam and Eve and is in any case not put into effect by Yahweh because they continue living.

Christ reigns over the living and the dead (Rom. 14.9). The believer is baptized into the death of Christ (Rom. 6.3), suffers death in the here and now and can therefore hope to be in Christ at death (Phil. 1.20f.). As a result, death is essentially changed: it is now no longer the relationlessness of *sheol*, but rather Christ is already present. According to John 5.24, the believer has already gone from death in life here and now, in which a presentist eschatology can be seen that is criticized by Paul: death is the last enemy over which God will have victory (1 Cor. 15.26). According to Rev. 20.6 and 14, the possibility exists in the final judgement for a second death, which is then made eschatically eternal.

In the New Testament, general mortality is brought into connection with sinfulness. God not only no longer has anything to do with death, but can suffer death himself in Christ, an act which subsequently changes the meaning of death for humanity. On the one hand, the believer can be understood to be already dead in life, and on the other hand, biological death can no longer be understood as relationlessness. In connection to the notion of the final judgement, the idea of a second death arises in some marginal texts.

[78]For a detailed analysis, see Udo Schnelle, *Neutestamentliche Anthropologie: Jesus, Paulus, Johannes* (Neukirchen-Vluyn: Neukirchener Verlag, 1991).

4.2.4 Humanity and death in the theological tradition

In the Christian theological tradition, the biblical and the Orphic-Hellenistic conceptions of death quickly merged. The twofold thesis about the Hellinization of Christianity and the Christianization of Hellenism can hardly be seen anywhere more clearly than in the realm of theological anthropology.

The significant historian of Christian doctrine, Adolf von Harnack (d. 1930), held the view that that dogma, i.e. developing Christian doctrine in the early church, was 'work of the Greek spirit on the foundation of the Gospel',[79] so that, in essentials, the history of Christianity from the beginning onwards can be evaluated as the history of the decay of the simple gospel of Jesus Christ – a decline that has only occasionally been interrupted. This thesis has both descriptive and normative aspects: descriptive, because it is actually possible to talk concretely about a Hellenization of Christianity; normative, because the notion of a 'history of decay' is clearly evaluative. Today, it is hardly possible to accept the fact that there could be a non-Hellenistic Christianity. As a result, it is necessary to balance out the Hellenization thesis. This can be seen in the work of Werner Elert (d. 1954) in the form of a Christianization of Hellenism or a de-Hellenization of the Greek spirit in the history of Christian theology.[80]

In principle, the dualistic anthropology that distinguished between body and soul was adopted, although the soul was not understood to be immortal *per se* but its immortality relied on God's gift. Augustine, as with so many other things, strongly influenced the early church's understanding of death, one that remained in place until the Middle Ages. According to Jüngel:

> Augustine developed a very differentiated doctrine of death in which he attempted to unite the biblical and Platonic views. In theory, four kinds of death are to be distinguished: the death of the soul, which is nevertheless regarded as immortal, the death of the body, the death of both body and soul understood as the death of the whole man, and the – second – death of the whole man, the man who is resurrected from the dead and who exists

[79] Adolf von Harnack, *Lehrbuch der Dogmengeschichte I* (Tübingen: Mohr Siebeck, 1909, 4th edn), p. 20.

[80] Cf. Werner Elert, *Theodor von Pharan: Der Ausgang der altkirchlichen Christologie* (Berlin: Lutherisches Verlagshaus, 1957), pp. 313–15.

> once more in the unity of body and soul. According to Augustine, the death of the soul occurs when God leaves the soul; the death of the body when the soul, as the life-principle of the body, leaves the body. And the second death occurs when the soul which God has forsaken is reunited with its soul forsaken body. Thus raised from the dead man lives only to suffer *eternal death* and to endure endless suffering.[81]

This synthesis even remained in place, in part, during the Reformation, precisely because it was held to be biblical. The intention was to turn from the theology of the Middle Ages conceived as being a falsification of the Christian message and to return to the early church as the true successor of early Christianity, but which in this particular case had actually furthered a Christian neo-Platonism. This is especially clear in Calvin (d. 1564): humans consist of the material body and the purely spiritual soul, which is not immortal *per se*, but is immortal through its relation to the Father, Son and Holy Spirit. The image of God rests exclusively on the soul. Death, as the separation of body and soul, is the punishment for sin, although for believers death is nothing other than the transition, the *transitus* into a better life, and indeed, immediately so after the separation from the body: since the soul is purely spiritual, it cannot rest or sleep but is found to be in God-contemplating activity and awaiting the final judgement to be united with its resurrected body. Accordingly, death is nothing to be feared. Calvin explicitly rejects two notions: the idea that the soul can sleep or rest until the judgement, as well as the idea that the soul is only the body's vital principle that decays with the body, therefore suffering a 'total death'.[82]

Luther's understanding is completely different. While he does retain the talk about the soul, he *de facto* redefines it. Luther no longer understands the soul as a human being's 'concrete' personal centre, constituting its *forma substantia*, but instead actually frees the concept of the soul from this Aristotelian background. Now, the soul signifies humanity in its relation to God, in distinction from humanity's relationship to other things in the world and its relationship to itself. The basics of this new understanding appear in 'On the Freedom of a Christian' and are further elaborated in *Disputatio de homine*. Here, Luther advances to a new definition of humanity that is now no longer that of the Aristotelian *animal rationale*, but the definition now

---

[81] Jüngel, *Death*, pp. 92–3.

[82] On Calvin's doctrine of the soul, see John Calvin, 'Psychopannychia; Or, Imaginary Sleep of the Soul between Death and Judgment', in *Calvin's Tracts*, vol. III (trans. Henry Beveridge; Edinburgh: Constable, 1851), pp. 413–90.

runs *homo justificare fide*: the essence of humanity consists in the fact that it is related to God in faith, that it is preserved in its existence passively by God, or in short, being human means being justified by God through faith.[83]

It is debatable whether Luther actually already left the Aristotelian ontology behind and proposed a new relational anthropology or whether he simply tendered biblical correctives to medieval anthropology. Since Luther was a biblical theologian, neither his expressions nor the materials on which he is dependent can always be rendered systematically. But, this is not altogether decisive for understanding Luther, because however one sees it his anthropology does lead to an altered understanding of death: death, like sin and devil, belongs to the powers of destruction, which have lordship over humanity. Humans fear natural death, because it can mean the end of the human being and this means the end of its relatedness to the world as well as to God. As a result, death is no natural condition, but a calamity resulting from the wrath of God. It is through this fear that death ultimately gains power over the living. While death is changed through Christ, he bore the God-forsakenness of the cross and won victory over death in the cross and resurrection from the dead. Christ's death is therefore the death of death and overcoming death seems to be a drama of God against God, since on the one hand it is God's wrath that is the origin of death and on the other hand it is Christ as the second person of the Trinity who overcomes death. The significance of natural death for humanity changes with this concept. After an encounter with the judging God, natural death becomes a form of sleep[84] for humanity until the resurrection. Here, Luther is adopting precisely that perspective which Calvin rejects. The notion of death as sleep also solves an important problem: both biblical conceptions of being with God immediately after death (Phil. 1.23 *et al.*) and a resurrection at the end of time (1 Cor. 15 *et al.*) can be compared in this way. What is decisive for Luther, likewise in contrast to Calvin, is that with this conception, death does not lose its horror for living humans: death remains punishment for humanity and even the great saints are marked by it in that they do not want to die but die in fear of death.[85]

[83]On Luther's anthropology, see Gerhard Ebeling, *Die theologische Definition des Menschen* (Tübingen: Mohr Siebeck, 1989) and Wilfried Joest, *Ontologie der Person bei Luther* (Göttingen: Vandenhoeck & Ruprecht, 1987, 2nd edn).

[84]Cf. Martin Luther, WA 17 II, *(WA = D. Martin Luthers Werke: kritische Gesamtausgabe)*, 120 vols (Böhlau: Weimar, 1883–2009), p. 235.

[85]A short summary of Luther's understanding of death can be found in Friedrich Beisser, *Hoffnung und Vollendung* (Gütersloh: Gütersloher Verlagshaus, 1993), pp. 60–8.

The history of Christian theology contains many interconnections between Hellenistic and biblical ideas. As a result, in the early church, Middle Ages and in strands of the Reformation, either the Hellenistic tradition can be predominant (Calvin) or the biblical tradition (Luther).

We can now bring our series of examples to an end, as what we have seen so far is sufficient for drafting a summary of the history of theology on this point.

4.2.5 Problems in the contemporary theological understanding of death

4.2.5.1 The total-death theory

In the twentieth century, in Protestant theology, a theory was developed that was subsequently labelled the 'theory of total death' (*Ganztodthese*) by Catholic theologians that rejected it. Numerous debates preceded the extensive acceptance of this theory: Carl Stange (d. 1959) first advocated it against Paul Althaus (d. 1966), who over the course of time was also associated with it.[86] Theologians that could hardly be counted as more opposite like Karl Barth[87] and Werner Elert[88] both held to the theory, as well as Wolfhart Pannenberg,[89] Eberhard Jüngel and many others. We will here use the most well-known presentation of the theory as given by Eberhard Jüngel: Human beings are understood monistically, not as constituted of a body and an immortal soul, but as entities in a unified sense that are alien to themselves and are therefore constituted by multiple relationships, above all to God. Death, owing to sin as human desire for freedom from God, means the abandonment of all relations and therefore relationlessness.

> Sin exerts a pressure which issues in the absence of relationships. It renders man relationless. Death thus becomes one facet of this pressure which drives towards relationlessness.... When death has actually occurred, then

[86]Cf. Beisser, *Hoffnung und Vollendung*, pp. 64, n. 162, 188–9.
[87]Cf. Karl Barth, *Church Dogmatics III/2: The Doctrine of Creation* (trans. H, Knight et al.; eds G.W. Bromiley and T.F. Torrance; London: T&T Clark, 2004), pp. 595–7.
[88]Cf. Werner Elert, *Der christliche Glaube: Grundlinien der lutherischen Dogmatik* (ed. Ernst Kinder; Hamburg: Furche-Verlag, 1960, 5th edn), pp. 502–6.
[89]Cf. Pannenberg, *Systematic Theology III*, pp. 556–7.

> man's life has become completely relationless. The dead person is then forever alienated from his God. And apart from God, everything becomes relationless.[90]

Through the event of Christ's death and resurrection, death itself is changed, but this does not alter anything about the definition of death or human relationlessness:

> However, when God's relationship to us remains unbroken even in death, when he identifies himself with the dead Jesus in order to demonstrate his gracious concern for all men through the crucified One, then out of the midst of the relationlessness of death there emerges a new relationship between God and man. And we must be careful to note that this new relationship of God to man consists in God himself bearing the relationlessness of death which alienates man from him.[91]

The total-death theory is by no means automatically bound to a relational ontology. It is also compatible with a substance ontology of Aristotelian provenance: If the soul is understood to be the formal principle of the body that exists nominally or conceptually only in concrete human beings, then bodily death would also mean the death of the soul and therefore the human being's total death.[92]

The advantages of this understanding of death are readily apparent:

> Understanding human death in terms of 'total death', i.e. as total relationlessness, appears to approximate to biblical understandings of death, its relational terminology is well matched to the positions taken here to this point, it is compatible with sociological, historical and also biological understandings of human being and it takes very seriously what we have said above about biological death.

The conception of death as a separation of the soul from the body must always construe the observable process of death in such a way that it only actually refers to the body. It is also necessary to give a precise time of death, which then would be used to designate the separation between the soul and the body. Under contemporary medical understanding that

---

[90] Jüngel, *Death*, p. 78.
[91] Jüngel, *Death*, p. 109.
[92] Cf. Beisser, *Hoffnung und Vollendung*, p. 307.

sees death as a process and correspondingly no precise point of time for death, this, however, appears to be inconceivable. To be sure, there have been curious medical experiments that wanted to prove the release of the soul from the body by measuring a supposed loss of body weight.[93] On the other hand, the biological criterion of death as brain death is relativized against the background of death as relationlessness, because the preference for brain death rests on an ontological presupposition, according to which it is precisely those capacities attributed to a dualistic anthropology of the soul that have now been taken on as being decisive for human death. It is precisely this that does not allow it to hold its ground against the background of the understanding of death as relationlessness, because brain death does not present any such lack of relationality.

Although the total-death theory appears to have won over Protestant theology in the twentieth century and although it does possess indisputable advantages, it has not remained uncontroversial. While the mainstream of Roman Catholic theology could never accept the theory in principle, at the turn of the last century dissent also arose out of the ranks of Protestant theologians, particularly Wilfried Härle, Freidrich Beißer[94] and Kirsten Huxel. Grounds for rejecting the total-death theory vary as much as the positive conceptions that have been proposed as replacements. For Huxel, ecumenicity, the actual beliefs of church members, as well as issues arising in pastoral care and systematic theology are all occasion for not only giving up the total-death theory, but also to return to the view of the existence of a soul.[95]

Härle, by contrast, does not return to a dualistic anthropology but rather modifies Jüngel's total-death theory at several decisive points, incidentally, in such a way that Jüngel himself was able to understand

---

[93]See Duncan McDougall, 'Hypothesis Concerning Soul Substance together with Experimental Evidence of the Existence of Such Substance', *Journal of the American Society for Psychical Research* 1.5 (1907), pp. 237–64. This idea was recently popularized in the film *21 Grams* by Alejandro González Iñárritu (USA, 2003). The experiment was apparently not repeated since the lost of weight could lie with countless other factors, of which the actuality of a material soul would seem to be the most unlikely of all.

[94]Beisser, *Hoffnung und Vollendung*, p. 308–9, indicates that the element of truth in the total-death theory is that not only the body, but the spiritual existence of the human being suffers death as well, so that there can be no simple discussion of continuity between here and there. On the other hand, it also cannot be a matter of sheer discontinuity in such a way that would entail a fully new creation at the resurrection.

[95]Cf. Kirsten Huxel, 'Untersterblichkeit der Seele versus Ganztodthese? – Ein Grundproblem christlicher Eschatologie in ökumenischer Perspektive', *Neue Zeitschrift für Systematische Theologie* 48 (2006), pp. 342–66.

them as not contradicting his position.[96] Härle's critique proceeds from a theological, anthropological and empirical observation, which leads to the same modification: if God created humanity, can it then be consistent with God's faithfulness if these humans are annihilated? Since Härle answers this question in the negative on the basis of the coherence of the doctrine of God, he is not able to completely accept the understanding of death as relationlessness. If the human being were to be completely annihilated at death, including all his or her relations, then it appears that the person's identity has been lost. But, then, it could not be re-awoken by God at a theoretically posited final judgement. The notion, however, that a new creation of the person could come about on this day is also not satisfactory, because nothing could guarantee the identity between these two persons apart from the will of God. But, this, however, would mean that will would be God's most significant predicate, not God's love. Apart from the fact that this causes difficulties in the doctrine of God by postulating an arbitrary God, it would also violate the principle of the logicality of God[97]: This is because if the divine will is the only thing that is decisive for human identity, then it would not only be possible for one person who is now living to be annihilated and created anew, but it would also be possible for two persons living at the same time to be declared identical by an act of divine will. But, this is self-evidentially absurd.

In the same way, one can already grasp the fact empirically that creaturely relations to someone who has died are not entirely discontinuous: even after death those affiliated with the deceased still relate to that person, and in particular cases, such as with significant historical events, this occurs over the course of centuries. This also speaks against the conception of death as total relationlessness. Härle's solution consists in understanding death as the end of the possibility of active relationality, whereas one's passive relationality is preserved: partially within human relations, under all circumstances on God's part to the deceased person. However, the problem both of God's faithfulness and the problem of the identity of the deceased person remains.[98]

---

[96]Cf. Eberhard Jüngel, 'Death: History of Dogma and Dogmatics', in Hans Dieter Betz et al. (ed.), *RPP*, vol. 3 (Leiden: Brill, 2006–2013), pp. 697–9.

[97]On the logicality of God, see Markus Mühling, 'Logic', in Hans Dieter Betz et al. (ed.), *RPP*, vol. 7 (Leiden: Brill, 2006–2013), pp. 583–6.

[98]Cf. Härle, *Dogmatik*, pp. 629–33.

This revocation of the total-death theory is not completely satisfying. Here, Luther's famous saying can be brought in, that 'where and with whomever God speaks, whether in anger or in grace, that person is surely immortal',[99] but problems concerning relational anthropology and the relationship between God and the world also arise: If humans are actually constituted by their relations, then their worldly relations, i.e. what someone experiences and does, cannot be external to their identity. But, in that case, sin would not be external to one's identity and God could not simply distinguish between sinner and sin and would then not have the possibility of wiping out their sin if God could not also annihilate the person. Moreover, it appears as if every human being, once created, is immortal, therefore pertaining to God's eternity. Apart from the fact that in this case creation would have to be understood pantheistically, it would then also inaugurate a new anthropological problem because one would then have to ask how human immortality is now supposed to look: does the person remain purely passive, in relation to God, but without the future possibility of reactualized relationality so that he or she is preserved at the same time in the divine memory, to use the terminology of process thought? And, would this mean the necessity of an *apokatastasis panton*, universal salvation, or rather on the other hand an immortalization of the suffering of personal creatures endowed with consciousness?

With these questions we have reached a point at which not only a solution to the problem in question impedes a clarification of death, but also would lead to the handling of other eschata. We will therefore have to postpone our search for a solution momentarily. At this point, however, we can say:

> The understanding of death as total relationlessness can be questioned from the standpoint of the faithfulness of God, the identity of the human person, as well as for empirical reasons and can be modified in such a way that death is understood as the end of the capacity for active relationality, whereas passive relationality, according to Härle, is preserved primarily in the relationship to God. Even this modified understanding of the total-death theory is not without problems vis-à-vis the Christian doctrine of grace.

[99]Cf. Luther, *Lectures on Genesis: Chapters 26–30*, in *Luther's Works*, vol. 5, p. 76.

The debate as detailed here suggests that the question of whether some conception of total death is to be accepted or not is primarily a problem in Protestant theology, as the overall trend has been a slow movement away from body–soul dualism in favour of a relational anthropology. Equivalents existing under other language regimes are certainly to be found in Roman Catholic theology. It has always held to the notion of the soul, but not always in the Orphic-dualistic sense, but rather interpreted relationally in a way that comes very close to Härle's relational formulations and the conception of death as the end of the capacity for active relationality. For example, Joseph Ratzinger maintains that, though adopting Aristotelian ideas, Thomas Aquinas' conception of the soul as the form of the body (*forma corporalis*) actually signifies a complete alteration of Aristotelian anthropology that is genuinely Christian and tantamount to the same definition of the soul that we have already encountered in Luther. Here, the soul is the principle of continuity in human identity, even in death, but it is ultimately nothing other than the communicative reality of being addressed by God and is therefore to be understood in neither a substantialist nor a dualistic sense:

> Firstly, the determinative starting point of the Christian understanding of immortality is the concept of God, and from this it draws its dialogical character ... God too possesses immortality, or, more correctly, he *is* immortality, being that actuality of relationship which is Trinitarian love. God is not 'atomic': he is relationship, since he is love. It is for this reason that he is life .... The signal we derive from this view of being tells us: relation makes immortal .... Matter as such cannot provide the underpinning for man's continuing identity. Even during our life on earth it is changing constantly .... Hence the indispensability of the body-soul distinction. Nevertheless, the Christian tradition, with an ever increasing consistency of purpose ... has conceived this duality in such a way that it is not dualistic but rather brings to light the worth and unity of the human being as a whole.[100]

4.2.5.2 Death and finitude, sin and creatureliness

A further important problem existing independently of the *Zeitgeist*, that is a theological problem in its own right, but has been considerably sharpened through debates with the natural sciences in the twentieth

[100]Ratzinger, *Eschatology*, pp. 157–9.

century, is the question of how death and finitude, and sin and creatureliness are to be ordered (see section 4.1). This problem arises in its essentials through two propositions, generally expressed in a positive sense:

- [A] If the human is a creature and not the creator, and creator and creature are distinguished by the fact that the creator is infinite, but the creature is finite, then the human as creature must be 'finite' according to essence.
- [B] If sin means a breach in relationship and death means relationlessness, then the consequence of sin is 'death'. Or, expressed differently: death is the wages of sin (Rom. 6.23). This presupposes that sin as original sin (*peccatum originale*) applies universally to every human being and affects humanity as a whole, but that it does not constitute the essence of humanity, but rather signifies the lapse or mutilation of this essence.

The theological problem consists in the fact that both propositions do not have to be compatible with one another: if 'finitude' in proposition A is replaced with 'death' from proposition B, then A and B contradict each other. In order to avoid this problem, there is a series of possible solutions:

- [C] Proposition A is rejected, i.e. 'finitude' is rejected as an attribute of human nature.
- [D] Proposition B is rejected, i.e. the notion that death is a consequence of sin is rejected.
- [E] An attempt to distinguish between 'death' and 'finitude' is made in such a way that humans are understood to be finite by nature, but not mortal. This means that when biological death is drawn in, there is a choice between two possibilities:
- [E1] Biological death belongs to the goodness of the creatureliness of humanity and therefore to its finitude and is no longer identical with death as a result of sin, which consists in a special spiritual death. This can either be identified with an eternal, 'second' death, or with a particular attitude of the living to biological death.
- [E2] Biological death is identified with the death that is the wages of sin, not with the human finitude. In this case, human finitude has to be seen as inherent to other empirical phenomena, and further, the reason why biological death also affects non-human creatures also has to be clarified.

The dialogue between theology and the natural sciences aggravates this problem but does not initiate it. The aggravation consists in the fact that biological death can be understood as the motor of evolution, which could be seen theologically as an instrument for God's creativity. In any case, the classification of death as a motor of evolution is strongly imbued by a particular worldview. We saw above in this chapter that according to the contemporary understanding of evolution, the death of individuals is understood not as a kind of motor, i.e. a necessary principle of evolution, but only as a necessary evil, as a compromise, that can facilitate reproductive success in individual cases. This would once again reduce the pressure of having to bind biological death with creatureliness. The problem that is attached to that is nevertheless a secondary one, but it is ultimately, as said above, a purely theological problem. We can now review the individual possibilities for a solution and their meaning.

- As to [C]: The problem does not arise when one denies that finitude belongs to humanity as such. This would only mean that one must retract the creator–creature distinction. This occurs *de facto* in every understanding of reality that immortalizes the world in some form or another, be it panentheistic, pantheistic or materialist. This can be seen clearly in the Hegelian, Ludwig Feuerbach (d. 1972), in so far as the nature of humanity as a species is designated as God, so that 'the divine being is nothing else than the human being'.[101] If this solution is chosen, then reasons for the biological death of individuals have to be given. This ultimately only falls under the premise that one sees 'biological death' naturalistically as not belonging to human finitude in any way. This could happen if one accepts with the Platonic tradition that biological death is only the separation of the immortal and infinite soul from its finite body or if, like Frank Tipler,[102] one assumes that personal individuals are resurrected as a result of a law inherent to the world, so that biological death would only be an apparent end. It is obvious that option C collides with the many of the basic assumptions of Christian theology, so that it is hardly acceptable from this standpoint but indeed presents possibilities that are to be rejected as incompatible with an eschatical horizon of expectations.

---

[101]Ludwig Feuerbach, *The Essence of Christianity* (trans. George Eliot; Amherst: Prometheus, 1989), p. 14.

[102]Cf. Tipler, *The Physics of Immortality*.

- As to [D]: Death has nothing to do with sin in any sense whatsoever. This is a thoroughly conceivable possibility. It does contradict the biblical witness to some degree, but it is neither inconceivable nor entirely unbiblical. In the Old Testament, death as such is not yet understood as the wages of sin, but only an early or quick death. This is the position that is maintained in parts of the Jewish tradition. With regard to Christianity, it does not appear that any tradition has adopted this position. First and foremost, this solution clashes with a relational anthropology, because if human being is brought into relationship with being in some way, then the phenomenon of death and sin have to be brought into connection in some way with the damage to relationships, so that this solution is out of the question.
- As to [E]: The identification of biological death with creation's finitude positively conceived is the solution to the problem that is preferred by most at present. It calls for us to see the 'death', previously known as the wages of sin, differently. It is generally assumed that sin changes biological death or that this finitude causes a different experience. For Karl Barth, human mortality and finitude is a condition for the fact that the redemption occurring once and for all in Jesus Christ can be real at all.[103] As a result, distinctions can be drawn between good and bad death, between death as finitude and death as judgement, and between death as natural and death as unnatural.[104] These things, however, do not allow us to make such distinctions, for as sinners we are encountered by both in the unity of the fact of death (that will then be changed in Christ).[105] The formulation of the creative Barthian Eberhard Jüngel is very similar:

> That is the meaning of death and that is what makes it so bitter: we cannot die and yet we must. In reality, death is something different from what it could be: in reality death is unnatural. In reality it is a curse .... The significance of this may be expressed quite pointedly: in the course of our lives it is what we make of life that causes death to become the uncanny power which threatens not only the individual, but whole communities and even nations .... It does not necessarily have to imply a sudden break with everything, for in the true sense it can be a genuine ending.[106]

---

[103]See Barth, *Church Dogmatics III/2*, pp. 631–2.
[104]See Barth, *Church Dogmatics III/2*, pp. 599–600.
[105]See Barth, *Church Dogmatics III/2*, p. 632ff.
[106]Jüngel, *Death*, pp. 74–5.

Interestingly, the solutions given by Barth and Jüngel are prefigured by Schleiermacher, who distinguishes between the fact of death and our relation to it as follows: the first belongs to the good finitude of humanity, and the last stands under the opposition between sin and grace.[107] This solution also has problematic aspects, because 'death' as the wages of sin, i.e. death as the judgement over or as a consequence of sin, whether it is personally imposed by God or is a consequence inherent to sin itself, is first of all not objective, but rather only subjective and as a result, second, does not actually concern sin itself, but only the living and not yet dead person. If, however, the consequence of sin is only subjective and not also objective, then sin is also not objective but only subjective, meaning Christ's act of reconciliation on the cross would then be devoid of any objectivity. But this cannot ultimately be accepted.

Pannenberg sought to escape this trap. Against Martin Heidegger (d. 1976) and Karl Rahner (d. 1984), who saw in death either a positive or negative closure to the identity of our life and with Jean Paul Sartre (d. 1980), who construed death as the discontinuation of life, Pannenberg concluded that our identity did not appear complete but broken and fragmentary.[108] Pannenberg assumed that the sin of sinners consisted precisely in not accepting the finitude consistent with creatureliness. The punishment of death consists precisely in the fact that it traps humans in their finitude. As a result, death appears to be a breaking apart of human identity. Sin understood as *amor sui*, as a refusal to accept one's finitude, is effectuated in that our experience of time splits in two with the result that past is always what is not being experienced now, that is, the what has been. If we were not to live in *amor sui* but were excentrically corrected in God's direction, this would mean:[109]

> For this I … the end of this process of our life means death. But it does not have to be this way. If we could as ourselves exist as the finite whole of our Dasein, then the end as a moment in the identity of our Dasein would be integrated into it and would therefore not pose an end for it. But the I in its I-relatedeness that structures its self-consciousness always has its end beyond itself.[110]

Pannenberg's argument appears to be elegant, but it is not without problems. It takes very strongly after that of Albrecht Ritschl, for whom the human

[107]Cf. Schleiermacher, *The Christian Faith*, pp. 319–20 (§76,2).
[108]Cf. Wolfhart Pannenberg, *Systematic Theology III* (trans. Geoffery Bromiley; Grand Rapids: Eerdman, 1997), pp. 559–60.
[109]Cf. Pannenberg, *Systematic Theology III*, pp. 560–3.
[110]Pannenberg, *Grundfragen systematischer Theologie II*, p. 154.

experience of time arises only through the hindrance of its goals by evil and conflicting aims. This leads to the fact that humanity according to Ritschl is then immortal if it is not hindered in its goals, since the immortality of personhood draws neither on the material capacities of humanity nor on a potentially spiritual soul, but alone on the goal of humanity understood as existence in the Kingdom of God. This is precisely the reason why Christ on the cross, in which he holds fast to his aim of founding the Kingdom of God, is immortal and therefore Christians are perfect and reign immortally over the world in suffering.[111] The difference between Ritschl and Pannenberg – apart from the fact that the concept of identity is in control for Pannenberg and the concept of goal is in control for Ritschl – consists solely in the fact that Pannenberg postulates that there could contra-factually be another experience of identity, whereas for Ritschl, the human that holds fast to his goal is already immortal, only is not yet aware of it because of the experience of time in death. But, this ultimately means that the same problem that appeared for Barth, Jüngel and Schleiermacher also appears for Pannenberg and Ritschl: the difference between death as finitude and death as the wages of sin can be objectively identified but no longer be objectively experienced.

There remains a final possibility: relating death as the wages of sin not to biological death but instead to a 'second death' after the resurrection affecting those that do not endure the judgement. This solution naturally presupposes the notion of a resurrection, a judgement and ultimately the notion of a twofold outcome in a specific form that does not assume eternal punishment, but rather complete annihilation. Although significantly determined by its highly specific presuppositions, this solution is not impossible and at the very least – if coherence were the singular criterion of theological thinking – extremely elegant. In actual fact, this possibility has only rarely been adopted, or at least not within the ranks of what is more or less orthodox Christianity, but by the Socinians.[112] Since this solution presupposes a decision about the other eschata yet to be dealt with, we are not able to say any more on the topic at this point.

- To [E2]: The final possibility would be to identify 'death' understood as the wages of sin with biological death and then creaturely finitude not with death, but with other created realities such as finitude of

[111]Cf. Ritschl, 'Instruction in the Christian Religion', in *Three Essays*, p. 230 (§23).
[112]Cf. Johanna C. Janowski, *Allerlösung: Annäherung an eine entdualisierte Eschatologie*, vol. 2 (Neukirchen-Vluyn: Neukirchener Verlag, 2000), pp. 514–18.

knowledge, love, the spatial expansion of humanity etc. Although a broad swath of the theological tradition is able to move in this direction, since biological death is simply equated with the wages of sin, there is no concept in present day Lutheran or Reformed theology that selects this approach to the problem with consistency and without contradiction. Friedrich Beißer, perhaps a bit too faithfully to the Scriptures, holds that biological death is an evil and punishment of God and does not belong to the nature and essence of humanity, but at the same time, perhaps a bit too inattentive to the spirit of the times, he is of the view that 'it is not debatable that in the world the death of the living creature is necessary'.[113] Thus, the problems remain unresolved for the time being.

The problem of seeing human finitude on the one hand as a good aspect of its createdness and on the other hand death as the wages of sin and therefore as not belonging to the essence of humanity, in so far as 'finitude' and 'death' are presumed to be identical with one another, is a theological problem that is nonetheless intensified by the dialogue with the natural sciences about the role of death. The different answers to the problem might contain *particula veri* of a reasonable solution, but they are restrained by deficits that cannot be underestimated.

4.2.5.3 Excursus: Reincarnation and absorption

The notion that death involves a transition of one's self or 'soul' to other individuals in the world, i.e. the idea of reincarnation or the transmigration of the soul, is found in many cultures, though not in the Christian and Jewish. One of the most well-known forms is recounted by Plato in *The Republic*: After death, the soul enters a place of cleansing and can choose a new fate for its new life on earth from an infinite number of possibilities. The order of choice is determined by lot. This, however, does not mean that those who are able to choose first will necessarily live better lives, because their success may lead them into pride and a bad choice. At the end of the

[113]Beisser, *Hoffnung und Vollendung*, p. 311.

process, the souls are made to forget their choice and their former life by drinking water from the River of Unheeding and are then reborn into their newly chosen life.[114] A variety of different conceptions of transmigration and incarnation also appear in Vedantic and Buddhist teaching. Buddhist teachings are interesting in this regard since they do not presuppose the subsistence of an individual soul, but rather that the individual actions of a living person constitute the karma, a system of dispositions of character that understands re-embodiment according to the various dispositions. This does not inevitably occur on the same or higher step, but also on a lower one. As a result, these conceptions of reincarnation, regardless of what particular step they imply, are all considered negatively, whereas positive hope for the future consists in the absorption of the individual into the universal and nothingness, since at any rate, human individuality is conceived as an appearance.[115] The vulgar modern Western esoteric reception of these teachings does not generally acknowledge these aspects of the traditional Buddhist understanding of reincarnation.

The primary problem with this teaching consists in the philosophical problem of the continuity of identity that appears here in an intensified form. It is already the case that in everyday life personal identity over time is a presupposition of the ontology of identity that is neither provable nor necessary. This can be shown with a simple example suggested in the writing of Stanisław Lem (d. 2006). It is possible to conceive of the manufacture of my doppelgänger, then killing me at night and without me knowing it replacing me with the doppelgänger, who then takes itself to be me according to its experience of self-consciousness.[116] This fictitious scenario is not falsifiable, i.e. it actually *could* take place, and it shows that the identity of a subject over time is not an *apriori* fact, but rather a presupposition about the ontology of personal identity that is more or less plausible through social and empirical perception in interaction. In the case of accounts of reincarnation, the supports are nevertheless completely missing, so that an actual reincarnation of an individual soul would not be distinguishable in anyway from an imaginary reincarnation therefore

---

[114]Plato, 'The Republic', in John M. Cooper (ed.), *Plato: The Complete Works*, (Indianapolis: Hackett, 1997) pp. 121–3 (Book X, 617d–621d).

[115]John Hick, *Death and Eternal Life* (London: Collins, 1976), pp. 297–396.

[116]Cf. the short story, Stanisław Lem, 'Die Auferstehungsmaschine' in *Die phantastischen Erzählungen*, (Frankfurt am Main: Insel, 1980). The substance of the argument goes back to Anthony Flew, *Body, Mind and Death* (New York: Macmillan, 1964), p. 6 and Anthony Flew, *The Logic of Mortality* (Oxford: Blackwell, 1987), pp. 9–12.

presenting a semantically meaningless concept. In the words of the great Protestant Wilhelm Busch (d. 1908):

> 'The doctrine of return is of total doubt,
> since it's not then possible "tis I" to shout.'[117]

This objection does not count against the Platonic myth and the doctrine of karma, because neither present conceptions of reincarnation in the sense used here: according to Plato, it is a myth that shows one particular aspect of justice, and karma does not presuppose anything like an extension of identical individual existence. All of the evidence that is used for esoteric purposes to justify the biblical nature of reincarnation is a radical misinterpretation of the text because the biblical terminology of 'born-again' means something completely different from reincarnation: the sanctification of one who has died to sin with Christ and is therefore justified. In this sense, there are no Christians who have not been 'born-again'.

Another idea is the absorption of the individual into the universal in death. This idea is found in various forms in a number of different cultures. Here, we can think of the Buddhist version of nirvana or even medieval mysticism, according to which the soul can be absorbed into God like a drop of wine in an ocean of water, so Heinrich Seuse (d. 1366).[118] In principle, the ideas are equivalent, since the universal, if it really encompasses all of reality – even a concept and its negation – is identical with the nothing, if the nominal notion is held to be admissible. In every case, this notion excludes personality and subjectivity. Although there are sophisticated concepts in the neo-Platonic tradition, we at this point do not need to attend to them any further, because:

> Depictions of death as absorption of personal experience into the universal are ultimately identical with the annihilation of the person and as a result possess similarities to the total-death theory.

---

[117]Wilhelm Busch, *Schein und Sein: Nachgelassene Gedichte* (Munich: Joachim, 1909): 'Die Lehre von der Wiederkehr ist zweifelhaften Sinns, es fragt sich sehr, ob man nachher sagen kann: ich bin's'.
[118]Cf. Seuse, *Das Buch der Wahrheit*, cited in Vincent Brümmer, *The Model of Love* (New York: Cambridge, 1993), p. 69.

4.2.6 Human being as *imago dei*

In order to resolve the problem at hand and attain a responsible Christian perspective on death, death will have to be conceived only against the backdrop of a Christian anthropology and as such can only be outlined at the outset under the eschatic horizon of expectations. But, since this is essentially constituted by the life, death and resurrection of Christ, who as true God and true human is not only the epistemological principle of divinity but of humanity as well, it will not be possible to give a description of humanity without reference to Christ.

4.2.6.1 Human being as person in relation

If we take this point seriously, the image of God in humanity according to Gen. 1.26 consists in the relational capacity of the human being as a person: just as God is an uncreated event of three divine persons in relation, it is also to be expected that human beings are relational as well. This means that the concept of personhood would then be applied epistemologically and univocally both to God and to humanity. But what, then, is a person? There are several possibilities.

According to Boethius (d. 524), a person is an 'individual substance of a rational nature'.[119] This definition emphasizes on the one hand the rationality and on the other the individuality of the person. It is immediately evident that this definition, if applied to the triune God, is problematic, because three individual substances would jeopardize the unity of the Trinity. However, since a univocal conception of personhood is demanded, the Boethian concept cannot now be applied to humans. The Boethian version of personhood is problematic precisely because of the fact that it attaches personhood to a predicate, such as intelligibility or the capacity for reason, because a person, be it angel, human or God, can only be a person as long as it possesses these attributes or at least has the potential to possess them. However, since the Boethian definition of personhood can be taken as paradigmatic for a related series of other similar definitions, such as that of John Locke (d. 1704) or more recently of Peter Singer,[120] our rejection of the Boethius' concept as unsuitable for God and humanity can be applied to the entire series.

---

[119]Boethius, 'A Treatise against Eutyches and Nestorius' (trans. H.F. Stewart et al.) in *The Theological Tractates and The Consolation of Philosophy*, pp. 84–5 (III, lines 4–5): 'naturae rationalibus individua substantia'.

[120]Cf. Peter Singer, *Practical Ethics* (Cambridge: Cambridge University press, 2006), pp. 87, 100.

Another possibility would be to define personhood along with Kant and Alexander of Hales (d. 1245) by means of the concept of dignity. For Alexander of Hales, a person is distinct by possession of individual dignity.[121] Whereas Boethius delineated the difference between persons and non-persons by virtue of reason but cannot give an account of the individuality of individuals, Alexander was devoted to precisely this problem: the individuality of persons consists in the fact that they are differentiated with respect to their dignity, whereas non-persons are assigned no dignity. The concept of dignity serves both to provide the specific difference between persons and non-persons and the principle of individuation. We are acquainted with the first through concepts like human dignity or the dignity of human life, and the second we are less familiar with but is completely comprehensible if one uses the concept of human dignity in analogy to the concept of the dignity of an office or position (e.g. in a hierarchy or an organization), which varies according to the particular kind of office or position. Nevertheless, this definition as expressed in a purely formal sense would fall under the same verdict as that of Boethius. But, this is only superficially the case, because it is possible to ask what particular attribute of dignity is there anyway. Alexander of Hales does not explore the question any further on this point, but it is perhaps possible to apply for help by means of Kant's famous third form of the categorical imperative: 'So act that you use humanity, whether in your own person or in the person of any other, always at the same time as an end, never merely as a means.'[122] If this is taken as an attempt to clarify the concept of dignity, then it would have been defined by an autotelic account of an action and not exclusively by reference to the means of that action. Now, the concept of dignity can indeed provide the specific difference between persons and non-persons, but it can no longer speak to the individuality of the person. Further, the reason why a person is due this dignity also remains an open question. By orienting ourselves with Kant's other definitions, it is clear that rationality once again plays a decisive role.[123] All in all, one can say that these definitions are also inadequate for expressing the image of God in humanity as personhood.

---

[121]Cf. Alexander von Hales, *Glossa in quattuor libros Sententiarum Petri Lombardi* (Quaracchi: Collegii S. Bonaventurae, 1960), pp. 49–50 (Book I, 3, 27).

[122]Kant, *Groundwork of the Metaphysics of Moral*, in *Practical Philosophy*, p. 80.

[123]On the various forms of the categorical imperative in Kant, cf. Wilfried Härle, 'Die weltanschaulichen Voraussetzungen jeder normativen Ethik', in Wilfried Härle (ed.), *Marburger Jahrbuch Theologie XIII* (Marburg: Elwert, 2001), pp. 15–38, 22–5.

Richard of St Victor (d. 1173) gives a third definition of a person as an 'incommunicable existence' (*incommunicabilis existentia*),[124] which can be broken down further into an 'incommunicable from-another-and-to-another-becoming' or as an 'incommunicable whence-and-whither-becoming'. This concept of personhood is specifically designed to be applicable to divine and human persons, as well as angels.[125] What does it mean? As an *ex-sistentia*, a from-another-and-for-another-becoming, personhood is distinguished by relationality. This applies to each of the three divine persons of the Trinity, in so far as each one is always related to the other two, and for humans, in so far as they are always related to God, their neighbours and to the non-personal world around them. As a result, humans are by no means individuals; they are not autarchic, meaning a truly individual human person is not conceivable. On the contrary, the entirety of humanity forms an organism. Nevertheless, the individual human being (or better 'human becoming', since the relationships at stake are not static but dynamic and narrative) is a particular person, whose particularity is formed in terms of its becoming-in-relation in such a way that in these relations an incommunicable, partially untouchable remainder is likewise constituted. Particularity is not something prevalent to relationships but is constituted in personal relationships: incommunicability (= particularity) emerges in communication. Put briefly, Richard's definition stands beyond both collectivism and individualism and is applicable to our problem. A human being, in bearing the image of God and being a person, is an 'incommunicable-from-another-and-to-another-becoming' in three relational structures: to God, to other humans and to the non-personal creation.

The image of God in humanity consists in human personhood. The three different attempts to define personhood in this section have been essential: 1. Boethius sees personhood as constituted by possession of reason. 2. Alexander of Hales and Kant variously see personhood as constituted by one's individual dignity. 3. Richard of St Victor understands personhood as reciprocal being in relation. Richard's notion is fruitful but still as yet under-determined.

---

[124]Richard of St. Victor, *On the Trinity*, p. 157 (4,XVIII).
[125]Richard of St. Victor, *On the Trinity*, pp. 151–6 (4,XII–XVI).

4.2.6.2 Human being as creaturely love

Richard's expression 'from-another-and-to-another-becoming' is still quite indeterminate. He actually only indicates that *relata* stand in relations and relations always exist between *relata*. However, if we remember that God brought about creation in correspondence to his own being as love, then it is evident that these relations are nothing other than love. In sections 3.3 and 4.1, we saw that God's entire creation can be understood in terms of a basic set of rules about love. In section 4.1, we discussed the cosmic regularities of love, which still remain unfulfilled in the here and now. We also saw that there are personal roles of love, and indeed such that cannot be broken by the creation and are therefore personal thetic rules of love and thus are deontic rules.[126] Both kinds of rules can be summarized in terms of the double rule of love, so that the human being is an entity constituted by love to God and neighbour. But this still needs further clarification.

If God's intention in creation is to bring forth a created love that corresponds to his personal creation, then it aims at bringing about personal creation and that means positing deontic-constitutive rules of love. Conditioned by the creator–creature distinction and by the diversity of creation in the constitutive relationality of its being, the content of the rules of relationality is to be understood in a twofold way: first, in relation to the creator, the content of the rules of relationality in the Christian tradition is designated as love to God, i.e. with a filially asymmetric but nevertheless reciprocal relationship of love, and second, between the personal creatures among one another with rules based on the love of one's neighbour, i.e. the demand for brotherly and sisterly love. The double rule of love provides the material content of the rule. It is the result of the thetic-constitutive, ordered and loving action of God, and it therefore cannot be revoked by his personal creatures. The double rule of love is therefore a part of the *lex naturalis* (natural law).

The content of the rule is thus paradigmatically filial love in relation to God (i.e. from the human perspective, an unconditional trust that is determinative for one's existence) and brotherly and sisterly love among creation itself. These relationships of love are certainly also to be understood as interaction, but interaction in such a way that the internal structure of human-personal intentionality is involved in a particular way, to which human affectivity also belongs.

---

126 For distinctions in the concept of rules, cf. Conte, 'Konstitutive Regeln und Deontik', in *Ethik*, pp. 82–6.

What is important now is that most social rules possess a content that regulates behaviour and action, but not the internal structure of human intentionality itself. This leads to the fact that these rules, similar to traffic laws, once they are known, concern those relations which exist between intellectual capacities and capacities of the will: we ought to obey traffic laws even when we don't want to. The double rule of love does not belong to these rules because it contains not only rules for relations of actual action, but it is also related to the capacity for intentionality in such a way that the rules are only actually being observed when the object of the will explicitly includes motivation by pleasure in its affectivity: that is, the aim is 'love and delight' for God's commandments.[127] One could also say that the twofold rule of love is also doubled in a second sense because it demands concordance between human wishes of the first and second orders (see section 1.3.3). This has two immediate consequences: First, not observing the rule cannot likewise be linked to another social rule which imposes forced sensations of displeasure. Second, the pure intellectual knowledge of the twofold rule of love is insufficient for following the rule because the affectivity is always dependant on external *relata*, either directly through passive relations (drive) or indirectly through the real experience of intellectual capacities. All in all, this means that the actual and real, passive directedness of humanity by external relations (events) increasingly appears with the implication of affectivity in the material content of the rules.

The twofold rule of love, however, is not only to be understood as a deontic rule, but also as constitutive and regulative. If it was only a regulative rule, it would not be constitutive for the being of the personal creation. If it is not constitutive for the being of the creation, then God's intention to bring forth creaturely love corresponding to God's own love would not be fulfilled and would therefore mean accepting the notion of a self-contradiction in God: God has the freedom to bring forth a creation or not to, precisely because God is love in and of Godself. By choosing to bring about a creation in correspondence with God's own love, the deontic rules of creaturely love must be understood as being constitutive for creation. This constitutive character of the rule of love of the personal creation itself indeed only has the character of a necessary condition, which is first sufficient by inclusion of God's differentiating action. Nevertheless, it has to do with a character constitutive of the being of creation and this has significant implications.

[127]Cf. Luther, 'The Large Catechism', *Book of Concord*, p. 441; line 69; Luther, WA 5, pp. 18–20 et al.

First, we can take from this, against a broad tradition of Christian theology, that not only can God's being and action not be divided, but that this also applies for created persons on the basis of the constitutive nature of the double rule of love. To express it even more clearly: the actions undertaken by created persons cannot be separated from their being and identity. Human being is what it does and experiences. This applies first and foremost to the divine perspective. If it is perhaps necessary to comfort the disconcerted reader, we can point out that this is not the last word on this topic and that there will still be something to say about this from a soteriological perspective. First of all, however, we have to lock onto the fundamental anthropological advantage of this state of affairs: in so far as the personal creatures in question are humans, theological anthropology proves to be compatible at this point with anthropologies from other academic fields such as the social psychology of George Herbert Meade (d. 1931), the symbolic interactionism of Erving Goffman (d. 1982) and Tamotsu (Tom) Shibutani, the biological anthropology of Agustín Fuentes or the social anthropology of Tim Ingold. While we cannot go further into these theories at this point and can therefore only point to external literature,[128] we can highlight several significant implications: the human self is formed by interactive connectivity and there is no hidden personal substance behind the various roles that persons play and beyond the stories

---

[128]Cf. George Herbert Mead, *Mind, Self and Society* (Chicago: University of Chicago, 1934), pp. 135–226; Pannenberg, *Systematic Theology I*, pp. 431–2; Wolfhart Pannenberg, *Anthropologie in theologischer Perspektive* (Göttingen: Vandenhoeck & Ruprecht 1983), pp. 151–235; Wolfhart Pannenberg, 'Person und Subjekt', in *Grundfragen Systematischer Theologie I* (Göttingen: Vandenhoeck & Ruprecht, 1980), pp. 80–95; Elisabeth Dieckmann, *Personalität Gottes – Personalität des Menschen: Ihre Deutung im theologischen Denken Wolfhart Pannenbergs* (Altenberge: Oros-Verlag, 1995), pp. 66–104; Jan Rohls, 'Person und Selbstbewußtsein', *Neue Zeitschrift für Systematische Theologie und Religionsphilosophie* 21 (1979), pp. 54–70; Erving Goffman, *Stigma: Notes on the Management of Spoiled Identity* (New York: Simon and Schuster, 1963), esp. pp. 2ff., 51–62; Dwight Van de Vate Jr., *Romantic Love: A Philosophical Inquiry* (University Park: Pennsylvania State, 1981); Markus Mühling, *Gott ist Liebe: Studien zum Verständnis der Liebe als Modell des trinitarischen Redens von Gott* (Marburg: Elwert, 2005, 2nd edn), pp. 269–3; Volkmann, *Der Zorn Gottes* pp. 30–4; cf. Tamotsu Shibutani, 'Reference Groups as Perspectives', *American Journal of Sociology* 60 (1995), pp. 562–9; Tamotsu Shibutani, 'Human Agency from the Standpoint of Pragmatism', in Horst Jürgen Helle (ed.), *Verstehen and Pragmatism: Essays in Interpretive Sociology* (Frankfurt am Main: Lang, 1991), pp. 183–94; Tim Ingold, 'Becoming Persons: Consciousness and Sociality in Human Evolution', *Cultural Dynamics* 4.3 (1991), pp. 355–78 and Tim Ingold, 'To Human is a Verb', in Agustín Fuentes and Aku Visala (eds), *Verbs, Bones and Brains: Interdisciplinary Perspectives on Human Nature* (Notre Dame: Notre Dame, forthcoming); Tim Ingold and Gisli Palsson (eds), *Biosocial Becomings: Integrating Social and Biological Anthropology* (Cambridge: Cambridge, 2013); Agustín Fuentes, *Biological Anthropology: Concepts and Connections* (New York: McGraw Hill, 2011); Agustín Fuentes', 'Evolutionary Perspectives and Transdisciplinary Intersections: A Roadmap to Generative Areas of Overlap in Discussing Human Nature', *Theology and Science* 11 (2013), pp. 106–29.

persons are involved in. We can therefore say quite concretely that the self's identity is composed of the interactively connected identity-claims and identity-expectations on the one hand as well as by the acceptance and rejection of these claims. The second implication consists in the fact that sociality and personality have to be understood as being reciprocally constitutive. Persons are not solitary individuals, but just as actions cannot be separated from the being of persons, created persons, by which we concretely mean humans, are also reciprocally constitutive of each other. Since this is an implication of the constitutive twofold rule of love, this also means that the actions of particular persons cannot be seen as a purely private matter. And, this further means responsibility and therefore guilt as well are neither exclusively individual phenomena nor are they non-transferable, but guilt is rather highly transferable. There will be more on this in our reckoning with sin.

The being of humanity so understood also consists in the fact that the person can be construed as the intersection of storied relations in such a way that the person's relationship to God determines its relations in the world. Since all of these relations can be characterized by love, but love in the present is actually damaged as a result of the fall, then the concept of personhood is an eschatical concept, which means that what a human being is as such biologically speaking in the here and now is now what he or she ought to be. Therefore human beings are always human becomings.

It is on this point that the results of our enquiry into personhood more or less match up with the concept of personhood as rendered by the Metropolitan of Pergamon, John D. Zizioulas, which is influenced by philosophical distinctions employed in the early church. Zizioulas also understands personhood as relationally constituted but distinguishes a human biological hypostasis from an ecclesial hypostasis: humans first receive their true personal being in those relations of the church that have been restored, and the biological hypostasis is only a shadow of this.[129]

We can specify at this point that the ecclesial hypostasis is actually to be defined as an eschatic hypostasis, i.e. it is not the restored relational structure of the church in the here and now that constitutes the person, but rather the human being at present in the church, which is also *simul*

---

[129]Cf. John D. Zizioulas, *Being as Communion* (Crestwood: St Vladimir's Seminary Press, 1985), pp. 50–2; John D. Zizioulas, 'Human Capacity and Human Incapacity', *Scottish Journal of Theology* 28 (1975), pp. 401–8; John D. Zizioulas, 'On Being a Person: Towards an Ontology of Personhood', in Christoph Schwöbel and Colin E. Gunton (eds), *Persons, Divine and Human* (Edinburgh: T&T Clark, 1991), pp. 33–46.

justus et peccatrix, can only live in the hope of its eschatical identity. Properly speaking, human beings *are not* yet persons but *will be* persons. In the present, human beings have their personal being and becoming and therefore their identities only in the mode of promise. If this is indeed the case, then we shall have to ask in the next section what it is about human being that is damaged.

The human being and becoming is a person in reciprocal but differentiated loving relations to God, to fellow humanity and to the non-personal environment. Since these relations can be understood as constitutive rules, they define the being and becoming of humans. Since human beings and becomings do not conform to this rule in the present, their personal being is eschatic, promised to them in the present, and thus remains an object of Christian hope.

4.2.7 Sin and death

4.2.7.1 Sin as misplaced love

With regard to the formal side of our model of rules, sin can be understood pre-eminently as damage to the twofold rule of love. This is expressed not only in the fact that sin would be lovelessness, but also in the fact that sin (understood objectively) is a kind of 'unregulated' love or (subjectively) a kind of love that wants to make its own rules.[130] In so far as this implicates the rule of love for God, this means that many other entities or situations could come into God's place, i.e. that on which the humans hang their hearts.[131] This is the fundamental form of sin as superstition or *false trust*, which then becomes expressed with respect to the relation to God with either absolutely no trust at all or as mistrust.

[130]This can be seen in Gen. 2.4–3, 24. In succumbing to the serpent's temptation of *eritis sicut deus* the man attempts to make himself the standard of good and evil (Gen. 3.5), a move which can by no means altogether displace the actual standard of good and evil constituted by God's rule giving but does hinder its recognition. This story explains the factual uncertainty in human instinct and the *difference* between humans and animals, though against the excellent introduction in Jan Christian Geertz et al. (eds), *T&T Clark Handbook of the Old Testament: An Introduction to the Literature, Religion and History of the Old Testament* (London: T&T Clark, 2012), pp. 327–9.

[131]Luther, 'The Large Catechism', *Book of Concord*, p. 386; line 3.

This form of sin will be observable for humans, among other things, by the fact that first-order desires will no longer correspond to second-order desires (see section 1.3.3). This is because the twofold rule of love is not only doubled by the fact that it refers to both God and humanity, but also because it demands in love the accord between first- and second-order desires. We generally only become aware of our ability to have second-order desires for the first time when they do not correspond to first-order desires. Conversely, our ability to have second-order desires is then a necessary condition for knowledge of sin through the character of the command as law. Paul trades on this situation in Rom. 7.19: 'For I do not do the good that I want, but the evil I do not want is what I do.'

But, sin also expresses itself within the demand for sibling love among humans, and indeed primarily in three further basic forms: first is the functionalization of persons, in which persons maintain relations with another person, which do not primarily correspond to personal relations of love, but a mercantile or trade relationship. Personal relationships are distinguished from mercantile relationships by the fact that the good exchanged and 'communicated' in the personal relationship is the identity of the person ('I am the one who loves you'), whereas in mercantile relationships one person primarily (but not exclusively) fulfils a function for the other person as provider of a non-personal good. This comprises a dangerous temptation for the problematic of death: because if I do not really love the person of the other, but only see this person as bearer of a function, then I can seemingly come to grips with death. As caricatured in one of Stanisław Lem's short stories:

> You yourself are an individual.
>
> Not at all .... You have noticed, surely, that there is no difference among us in our faces. In the same way we have achieved the highest degree of social interchangeability .... At any given moment there exists in a society a certain number of functions or, as we say, roles .... One has the occupational roles, namely those of rulers, gardeners, mechanics, physicians; there are also family roles – fathers, brothers, sisters and so on. Now in each role a Pantan [i.e., one of the members of this fictional society] serves for 24 hours only .... Who I shall be tomorrow I do not know today .... The exchange of roles takes place at midnight on the basis of a general lottery, over which none of us has any control. Now do you begin to understand the great wisdom of our system?
>
> Can one really love a different person everyday? ...

> Affection, respect, love were at one time gnawed by constant anxiety, by the fear of losing the person held dear. This dread we have conquered. For in point of fact whatever upheavals, diseases or calamities may be visited on us, we shall always have a father, a mother, a spouse and children. But this is not all. That which does not change will soon begin to pall, regardless of whether it brings us happiness or sorrow. Yet we also crave stability, we wish deliverance from vicissitudes and tragedy. We wish to live, but not to be fleeting, to change, yet remain, to experience all – and risk nothing. These contradictions, unreconcilable it would seem, are with *us* a reality …
>
> What do you do about death? …
>
> Death? It is an obsolete idea. There can be no death where there are no individuals. We do not die …. Consider for a moment, what means death? A loss, tragic since irrevocable. The one who dies, whom does he lose? Himself? No, for once dead, he has ceased to exist, and the one who exists not, there is nothing he can lose. Death is the province of the living – it is the loss of someone near …
>
> Have your ever heard of Master Oh? …
>
> Yes. It was he who created our state. In so doing, he produced his masterpiece – the Simulation of Eternity.[132]

The second fundamental form of sin is the mirror image of the other, or *pseudo-personalization*, in which a quasi-personal relation to non-personal entities and situations is maintained.

The third fundamental form of sin consists in denying any contingency to human becomings and therefore in the attempt to define humans as mechanistic beings instead of as becomings. This is the mistake of denying the eschatical dimension of human personhood and therefore the mistake of attributing eschatic character to present experience.

Since humanity as a whole can be said to form an organism constituted by the deontic-constitutive twofold rule of love, sin is first and foremost something that affects the entire framework of human persons and is not limited to the *relata* alone. In principle then, sin is not conceivable in such a way that it only concerns a single *relatum*. On the contrary, if a single *relatum* is affected, regardless of which it is, then the entire relational structure is affected. This is why sin and guilt are transferable. This state of affairs finds expression in the disturbance of human sociality but cannot be empirically limited to this alone. Since the deontic-constitutive

---

[132] Stanisław Lem, 'The Thirteenth Voyage', in *The Star Diaries* (trans. Michael Kandel; New York: Harcourt, 1985), pp. 97–101.

twofold rule of love is co-constitutive for the being of the human relational organism, it will not only be damaged morally, but in its very storied being as well. Since human personality and sociality is a reciprocally constitutive state of affairs, damage to the organism as a whole also means damage to the individual *relata*.

> Sin is damage to love, affects the entirety of humanity as an organism of persons in relations and is therefore transferable from person to person. Sin expresses itself with respect to relation to God in terms of false trust, in relation to other humans in the functionalization of other humans and in relation to the non-personal environment as pseudo-personalization, in which non-personal things are ascribed a significance that only properly belongs to persons. Another expression of sin is the attempt to exclude contingency and openness in conceiving oneself, i.e the attempt to understand human persons not as human becomings but as human beings.

4.2.7.2 Chaotic suffering and the confirmation of justification

We saw that sin is a violation against the twofold rule of love that is expressed in the attempt to establish one's own deontic-constitutive rules, an attempt which is doomed to failure. In this regard, i.e. by virtue of the fact that such rules are impossible for humans to put in place, the twofold rule of love remains in power. Since on the other hand, however, punitive consequences are excluded, the single possible result of this particular violation of the rules is that the human attempt to transgress the twofold rule of love is quite simply successful, precisely in the fact that both the social and the personal consequence is that one is now abandoned to the attempt to live without rules. Since, however, we are dealing with a deontic-constitutive rule for the ontic being of humans, it would be now expected for one to instantaneously lapse into non-being – and indeed, this would be expected with respect to both personal and social existence. But this is not the case. On the contrary, it ought to be noted here that the deontic-constitutive twofold rule of love is not God's only kind of regulatory act, so to speak, but there are also thetic-constitutive rules, i.e. natural regularities, which cannot be broken by human activity. Since these are necessary conditions of human becoming, human beings cannot revoke the constitutive factors of their own being and becoming. This is also necessary because God's regulatory and rule-establishing action in the world would be damaged if humans were to be allowed to carry out their own self-destruction in a way that would also repudiate God's loving intention for creation, a circumstance that would immediately imply a self-contradiction in the very essence of God, a possibility that has to be excluded from the outset.

The consequences of sin can therefore only consist in a partial loss of rules, that is, only up to point where the thetic-constitutive rules continue to regulate particular human existence despite the reality of sin. But, this has two aspects: first it proves to be the existence of mere regularities, and second it also consists in contingence, passion and death being consonant with the fragmentary nature of this set of rules. The consequences of sin are therefore to be identified in such a way that this aspect of divine action in creation only has an ontically unchecked affect on humanity in two ways, one epistemically from the human perspective and the other ontically.

Epistemically, from the human perspective, one consequence of sin is *orientationlessness* or *misorientation*. On the one hand this is ethical, with regard to human attempts to create their own deontic-constitutive set of rules in the formation of an ethos, because the twofold rule of love can now no longer be accessed and experienced. But, this also applies to the capacity of human intellectual activity as a whole and comes to expression in that humans are now tempted to absolutize the two aspects of the thetic-constitutive regularities. This can occur inasmuch as the aspect of regularity is emphasized, such as with deterministic-naturalistic anthropologies. This can also occur inasmuch as incomplete, contingent aspects of the thetic-constitutive structure of rules are emphasized, such as with constructivist or sceptical anthropologies.

Ontically, however, the lack of any set of rules expresses itself in chaotic suffering. The entire human organism and its individual personal *relata* now experience contingence in an unchecked, chaotic condition and this implies the experience of chaotic suffering. The consequence of sin thus consists not in the experience of an unbroken sequence of deeds and consequences that impacts the sinner poorly, but the righteous well. Rather, it is the very construction of such a sequence of actions and consequences itself that as a human attempt to establish its own rules is destined to failure. Suffering and death now encounter humanity, as allowed by God, in a chaotic and purely arbitrary form. But, this means biological death now becomes a burden for humanity. This is because death can indeed no longer be understood as the wages of sin, but rather as the mark of sin: in death, the loss of rules is fulfilled to the highest degree, for in death the individual human being is completely alone, forsaken by God and humanity. It is only in death under the conditions of sin that the human being is an individual in a radical sense.

> The consequence of sin as a violation of the rule of love is that humans are partially relinquished or given over to their wills, i.e. they fall prey to the lack of rules and the questionable attempt to reign in this partial chaos by establishing rules according to their own power. In an epistemic sense, we can say that one is misoriented. Ontically speaking, however, one is impacted by the incompleteness of the natural rules of creation and experiences chaotic suffering, including death as total death.

Total death as the consequence of sin applies only *etsi Christus non daretur*, as if there were no Christ. But, Christ is the second person of the Trinity, who in his devotion on the cross suffered the death of absolute relationlessness, in that he devoted himself to humanity and was resurrected by the Spirit's devotion to him. But, this event has changed the nature of human death as such.

In one way, death, and indeed even biological death, has been overcome by the self-sacrifice of the Son and the Spirit. In this regard, the restoration is primarily the unique, particular spatial-temporal fulfilment of the thetic-constitutive order of rules and on the basis of the self-sacrifice of the Spirit to the creation is also at the same time the anticipation of the eschatical fulfilment of these rules, especially the eschatical overcoming of death. This state of affairs is significant because the thetic-constitutive set of created rules requires fulfilment independently of sin. As a result, in this regard, the restoration is not only a cosmic event of the continuous creative activity of God, but one will also come to the conclusion that even without sin the world needs the restorative activity of the Son and the Spirit. As to the precise form of such a hypothetical restorative divine action, there is certainly nothing that we are able to say.

However, the person of Christ, as the person of the divine incarnate *logos*, to whom as brother of humanity all relations to all particular humans belong, dies this death of abandonment changing thereby death for all other humans: The consequence is that in death for human persons, Christ is present as God the Son, so that the sinful human being no longer has to endure death alone. But, now the Son dies in his devotion to humanity, while he – even despite an overdue response by the Father – trusts in the Father and Spirit and relies on them, but not in vain, as becomes clear with the self-sacrifice of the Spirit. Death therefore means exposure to abandonment and the discontinuation of all potential action to pure passivity. However, human death in conformity to the dead Christ means confirmation of faith in God's justification.

Humans are in the image of God as persons in loving and constitutive relations to God, other humans and the rest of the non-personal creation.

- As a result of the damage caused by sin, personhood itself has to be understood as an eschatological concept. Human beings are only persons according to God's promise.
- Sin as the attempted self-regulation of its own being relinquishes humanity to the sphere of cosmically established rules that is unfulfilled and therefore to chaotic suffering and death as sheer relationlessness – *etsi Christus non daretur*.
- But since Christ has died and been resurrected through the Spirit, our death changes: we do not die in relationlessness, but rather in Christ. As a result, death now only consists of the relinquishment of human beings in so far as they actively attempt to constitute themselves, others and the apersonal environment by establishing their own rules and is therefore likewise confirmation of justification: now one is dependent on God in sheer passivity.
- This presupposes a relational anthropology, in which there is no place for the notion of an immaterial soul.
- Nevertheless, humans do not suffer a 'total death' of relationlessness; this has been transformed by Christ's act of reconciliation: The relational structure which all human beings share with the Triune God, the personal and the non-personal parts of creation in life, consists in death exclusively of their relation to Christ as the second person of the Trinity: humans die in Christ.

- Biological death rests on the unfulfilled nature of cosmic rules and is for humanity effectively a consequence of sin and its restoration. As such, it belongs not to finite creation as such, but only in so far as it remains unfulfilled due to sin. Human finitude is attached to all other particularly human attributes, which along with its life are bound together in a world as a finite structure of ordered relations.
- Since the non-personal co-creation belongs in a partially constitutive way to human being, it is clear that it is of eschatical relevance, even if it is not clear to what extent this is true.

4.2.8 Ethical, pastoral and liturgical aspects

The ethical, pastoral and liturgical problems bound to the theme of death are so diverse and weighty that they cannot possibly be discussed in this book adequately. It is also important to see in particular that the pre-eschatical character of death ought not to be discussed in this regard without other *eschata* such as resurrection, judgement, etc. As a result, the enumeration of problems and a few pointers should be sufficient at this point:

- *Problems in pastoral care*: With some illnesses, there is the problem of whether patients ought to be consecrated for death and whether they can or should be given less care or a different kind of care (e.g. hospice).
- *Dealing with coma patients*: In a similar way, the question can be raised as to how the comatose are to be handled, especially in cases concerning an irreversible coma.
- *Ethical problems in transplantation medicine*: Here, the operative understanding of death also plays a significant role (even if, in Germany at least, the laws governing transplant medicine introduced in 1997 can be used to resolve many of the legal problems).
- *The elimination of death from society*: Today, most do not die with their family at home, but in the hospital. Something like an 'outsourcing' of death from the general lifeworld has occurred. The problem of death has seemingly also been lightened or overcome by the problem

of the functionalization of persons, i.e. in that personal relationships are reduced to mercantile relations that are exchangeable, because persons who primarily serve the purpose of fulfilling a function are easier to replace.

- *The lifeworld of the aging*: Dying leads to death, and aging often to dying. The lifeworld of the aging in its significance for the future of society in the northern hemisphere in particular has not yet been researched satisfactorily in either sociology or in theology and pastoral care. A number of prejudices often predominate at this point that likely hinder conversation with older people and lead to the establishment of unrealistic perceptions about aging. On the one hand, there is the *infantilization* of the aging, and on the other hand, the notion that one can become 'old and wise' as well as the notion that old age effectively means the conclusion of someone's life history. By comparison, it is necessary to point out that old age offers specific problems that ultimately are nothing other than exemplary for the problems of human-being-in-the-world, which are naturally also basic theological problems.[133] In this regard, it is necessary to remember that finitude and exhaustion[134] also belong to the notion of creatureliness and are of particular pertinence in old age. In the Christian perspective, one does not die 'old and full of years' – even if this is a worthy dream – but in most cases, death and old age will be experienced as a kind of breaking-off, and the fragmentary character of life reminds us that we are not the authors of our own life stories and identities. Further, death in old age has increasingly become death from cancer, which brings an altogether particular set of problems in tow.[135] All of this reminds us that it is precisely its understanding as a breaking-off and not as a fulfilment of life that death, for Christians, can be nothing other than a confirmation of God's justification.
- *Pastoral care for the dying*: Pastoral care for the dying also poses a particular problem. It is not to be done without serious knowledge of a systematic theological approach to death. Further, it also requires

---

[133]Cf. Wolfgang Drechsel, 'Das Schweigen der Hirten? Altenseelsorge als (kein) Thema poimenischer Theoriebildung', in Susanne Kobler-von-Komorowski and Heinz Schmidt (eds), *Seelsorge im Alltag* (Heidelberg: Winter, 2005), pp. 45–64.

[134]Cf. Christoph Schwöbel, 'Verdrängte Geschöpflichkeit: Die Flucht vom Tod', *Pharmazeutische Zeitung* 44 (1997), pp. 11–17.

[135]Cf. Wolfgang Drechsel, 'Der bittere Geschmack des Unendlichen: Annäherungen an eine Seelsorge im Bedeutungshorizont des Themas Krebs', *Wege zum Menschen* 57 (2005), pp. 459–81.

knowledge of the certainty provided by the Christian understanding of resurrection, which we will turn to explicitly in a later chapter. Decisive here is the fact that the pastoral carer does not play the role of 'lecturer', which already inhibits personal respect, but it is decisive that the carer has reflected on all possible and perhaps not even explicitly enunciated questions about death from someone who is dying and has found responsible answers and strategies for finding answers, even if these themes never actually arise in pastoral care situations.

- *Pastoral care with the aggrieved*: Another problem not to be underestimated concerns pastoral care for those in mourning. At this point, there are many prejudices to circumvent, not only in practice, but also in theoretical investigation of the past. The first thing to deal with is that without a reflective and systematic theology of death and resurrection, pastoral care with the aggrieved is simply not easy to do. Furthermore, if the relational understanding of humanity as given here is correct, then the Epicurean perspective that death does not actually concern the living is quite simply false: death is an empirical situation that we can experience, specifically in the deaths of others. But, since the other is ontically a part of me, the death of others is also my death, or at least causes an injury to my person. If our relational anthropology is correct, then the attempt to establish distinct periods of mourning would simply have to be abandoned. This is because the construction of individual schematic phases of mourning corresponds to our view of the functionalization of persons, i.e. the reduction of persons to functional roles, and passes by reality, as recent investigations can confirm. In certain cases, such as with the myth of a 'shock-phase' in mourning, a pastoral carer's actions could have dangerous consequences, for example, if he or she were to assume that effective care is not possible at such an early stage in the process of personal grief. Models that depict distinct stages in the morning process are also highly problematic because they implicitly understand grief as a crisis or a sickness in a way that contradicts a properly Christian conception of humanity and therefore contributes to the problem of the 'outsourcing' of death, as mentioned above. By contrast, modern grief counselling occurs around the time of death and will have to be mindful of the variety and the impossibility of schematizing the grieving processes, without letting the specific tasks that have to be performed in the situation slip from view (realization of the death, giving space for reaction, recognizing the loss, support in transitioning, memories and stories for the purpose of identity reconstruction and the evaluation of resources as well as of the risks and their prevention).[136]

- *Prayer for the dead*? There are also a whole series of problems concerning the relationships between *praxis pietatis*, liturgical procedures and death, to which naturally belongs the problem of whether one ought to pray for the dead. Calvin explicitly affirmed the act of mutual intercessory prayer among the living but explicitly excluded the practice of praying for the dead.[137] The basis for this among the Reformers consisted in the fact that in principle the dead are in God's hands and no more evil could befall them. Prayers for the deceased are now under suspicion of presupposing some kind of meritorious effect, in that some influence could be exercised on God's acceptance of the dead. But, this would naturally contradict justification and is therefore to be rejected. However, there is still a good reason that speaks for prayer – both private and public – and other liturgical practices relating to the dead. In accepting the anthropology and understanding of death that has been presented in the argument to this point, then we can see that death is not an individual phenomenon, because humans are not merely individuals but rather persons in relation. In this case, then, death affects those who remain behind in the same way as it does those who have died: even death itself is an occurrence characterized by its relationality. As a result, the living can do nothing better than casting their grief and troubles on God the Creator, Reconciler and Consummator, and this means nothing less the praying for the dead. This does not in anyway involve prayer presupposing a meritorious effect but rather ought to be understood in the sense of a normal intercessory prayer.
- *Who should be buried*? In view of the steady loss of membership in the German *Landeskirchen*, i.e. the regional churches that maintain an official tax contract with the state – as well as in view of decreasing church membership in other industrialized counties, there is discussion at the moment about who ought to receive a church funeral. These are various possible criteria:

  [A] That the deceased and closest relatives are members of the church.

[136]Cf. Kerstin Lammer, *Den Tod begreifen: Neue Wege in der Trauerbegleitung* (Neukirchen-Vluyn: Neukirchener Verlag, 2006, 4th edn).

[137]Cf. Calvin, *Institutes*, vol. 1, pp. 681–4 (III,V,10).

[B] That the deceased was not a member of the church, but the closest relatives are.

[C] That the deceased was a member of the church, but the closest relatives are not.

[D] That neither the deceased nor closest relatives were members of the church.

In case [A], when a request for interment is imposed upon a pastor, there is in generally no problem. In case [B], problems and uncertainties arise because the intention is most often to honour the wishes of the deceased and not the wishes of relatives who do want a church funeral. As to [C], it is conceivable that relatives might or might not express desire for a church funeral. At first glance, case [D] does not appear to be relevant. If it is right that humans are not individuals, but rather particular persons in relation, then this problem is also easily resolvable. Death is just as little a private phenomenon as love. Analogously, grief is also not a private phenomenon, but rather an open one, and indeed as an open phenomenon grief is not only a kind of working through the experience of loss. Thus, there is no basis for refusing funeral wishes in any of the cases [A] through [D]. Even in cases [C] and [D], it is possible and meaningful to conduct a public funeral (without a burial service). The Christian duty of caring for the dead does not depend on baptism and the order of salvation but instead on love as an order of creation and therefore applies to all human beings.

–*Burial practices*: In itself, the question of burial practice is not an eschatological, dogmatic or ethical one, but rather one of tradition. However, traditions are not constituted without the input of faith, intentional action and hope. Further, faith and hope are reflected in them and therefore they become essential in the communication of this faith and hope. As there is a great deal to say about present day burial practices as well as their organization by professional undertakers, we shall limit ourselves to the most significant points: due to the relational understanding of anthropology and death developed here, a number of forms of burial can be positively evaluated, including traditional forms of burial in the ground, as long as they do not included anonymous interment, which as a practice is problematic in itself. What is not acceptable is cremation, as it descends from the Orphic–Hellenistic tradition where it symbolizes an understanding of death as a separation of the soul from the body, in which the soul is freed from the body that is destroyed by the fire. If, nevertheless, Christian cremations are to be performed, the liturgy should be supplemented or changed so that this anthropological misunderstanding is unequivocally excluded. With regard to relational anthropology, there must also be questions about the psychic effect that the decision by the relatives for a cremation of the body of the dead person in relation then left with them. Naturally, the deceased does not accrue any disadvantage from this practice, whatever the case may be.

–*Baptism as practice of assurance of death in Christ*: Of completely different liturgical significance is the bond between baptism and death. This is because the circumstances that are experienced in death, that in death the believer does not fall into relationlessness because of Christ's restorative work on the cross but rather dies in Christ so that through the death of Christ as the event of salvation our death can also become an event of salvation made present through the Word and Sacrament, especially in baptism, in which the Christian dies with Christ (Rom. 6.8).

As to the many ethical, pastoral and liturgical problems that arise with the understanding of death, there are numerous problems, such as when to stop medical care, dealing with the comatose, transplantation medicine, public procedures related to death and dying, the lifeworld of the aging, pastoral care for the dying and grieving, the question of public or private prayer for the dead, the question of who ought to be provided with church burials and funerals, as well as about the various practices of interment. Believers, however, do have genuine assurance in their lives in these matters because of the linkage, in baptism, of their own death with the death of Christ.

4.3 The apocalyptic revelation of the future of history

As the last of the '*pre-eschata*' – i.e. those things that concern not what is properly eschatic, but only the final notions of our present life in the here and now – we have to take into consideration in this section the social world, as we have already dealt with the natural and personal world. It only appears to be the case at first, however, that this question stands in analogy to the question of the future of the non-personal natural world as a question of whether the social world can be of eschatic relevance or not. This is because, apart from some forms of radical mysticism, the eschatic relevance of the social world is not denied, for instance, on the basis of the centrality of the concept of the kingdom of God. In any case, human sociality does not only consist in the spatio-temporal togetherness of personal creatures, but also in the communication and interaction that is necessary for their identity. Communication, however, is never ahistorical: it depends on what is already known and is directed towards what is expected and formative. But, this does make it clear that the question of a possible pre-eschatic future of sociality is synonymous with the question of the role of history and its course. Various kinds of human interaction can be distinguished within history such as religion, the sciences, economics and politics[138] that define a society and develop historically. And, as a matter of fact, this kind of historical development has a broad tradition – especially in modernity. With regard to the question of how human sociality will develop historically, there are at least three primary options that have also been taken on in the course of the history of Christian theology: first is the assumption that by and large things in the world will improve over the course of history (section 4.3.2), second is the assumption that things will by and large worsen over the course of history (section 4.3.3), and third, it is possible to remain fundamentally sceptical about the notion of an evaluative assessment of the course of history altogether (section 4.3.4). Before these particular options are described, it is necessary to discuss the pre-modern notion of an end of history or a revealed course of history as such (section 4.3.1).

4.3.1 Pre-modern and modern millennialism

In the later years of the Old Testament, a special kind of literature emerged with new attributes that took on a new perspective on history in contrast to that of prophetic literature, mixing Hebraic with Hellenistic thinking: Apocalyptic. In the following, we will use this term in a systematic sense that stands quite closely to this original genre of literature but is not limited exclusively to it. In Greek, *apokalyptein* actually means 'revelation'. However, apocalyptic is not simply identifiable with a theology of revelation. At least since the philosophies of Schelling and Hegel, theology has generally used

[138]Cf. e.g. Eilert Herms, 'Grundlinien eines theologischen Begriffs sozialer Ordnung', in *Gesellschaft gestalten* (Tübingen: Mohr Siebeck, 1991), pp. 56–94.

the concept of revelation in the strong sense as referring to the self-revelation of God: it is God who reveals God's own self.[139] Apocalyptic, however, uses the concept of revelation in another sense: God is not what is revealed, but rather the course of history, the future of history is revealed, uncovered and laid open in various forms. We can thus define this genre as follows:

> Apocalyptic denotes a spiritual or intellectual stance that reckons primarily with an insight into the *course* of history.

With regard to the Bible, only a small amount of such material can be found. To be sure, there is one passage that at least for modernity has become the *locus classicus* of apocalyptic: Rev. 20.1–7, a passage that speaks about the 'millennium'. At the end of history, a 1000-year time of salvation awaits the earth, in which Satan is bound and the righteous will rule with Christ after a first resurrection. Subsequently, Satan is to be let free for a short time and the world will reach its final end. This is indeed found at one place in the Bible, and there is a series of early Jewish apocalyptic literature that likewise maintains this interim kingdom of a time of salvation at the end of history.[140] This idea likely demonstrates the intention to draw parallels between the course of the world and the course of the week, so that there would be one week for the world consisting of seven days lasting 7,000 years, taking from Ps. 90.4 that one day for God is equal to 1,000 years. The notion of a time of salvation at the end of history then binds Hellenistic–Roman conceptions of a golden age with the conception of a world Sabbath, a time of salvation at the end of time. In the particularities, however, these two conceptions diverge sharply. The image from Rev. 20.1–7 does not easily allow for an actually coherent course of events. It is heavily reliant on a new interpretation of Ez. 37–48 and there are similar parallels in Jewish literature such as 4 Esdras 7.28–33 and 2 Baruch 24–32.

Contrary to the current preponderance of this notion, faith in a 1,000-year reign, often called millennialism or chiliasmus, has not played an important role throughout most of the history of Christianity. There have indeed always been expectations of the imminence of the end of time, but this can be conceived without millennialism. Before pre-modern times,

---

[139]Cf. Pannenberg, *Systematic Theology I*, pp. 222–3.
[140]Cf. 1 Enoch 91.12–17; 2 Enoch 32.1–33; 4 Esdras 7.26–30 etc.

millennialism can only be found occasionally in the early church, such as in Papias (d. ca. 130) and Justin (d. ca. 165), in Tertullian's monastic phase (d. ca. 230), Hippolytus of Rome (d. ca. 235) and Irenaeus of Lyon (d. ca. 202). In the East, particularly in Alexandrian theology, hardly any millennialism developed, whereas in the West, it disappeared at the latest with Augustine (d. 430).[141] In the Middle Ages, one can find in Joachim of Fiore's (d. 1202) writings a new interpretation of the course of world history that is independent of older millennialism and, strictly speaking, also does not present any millennialism because it does not use the normal schema of 1,000 years and does not rest primarily on Rev. 20.1–7, but rather presents a Trinitarian theology dependent on a philosophy of history: after the age of the Father and the age of the Son, the age of the Spirit begins. These individual stages are divided into different generations and compared with the notion of a world week but not formally synchronized.

> The mysteries of Holy Scripture point us to three orders (states or conditions) of the world: to the first, in which we were under the Law; to the second, in which we are under grace; to the third, which we already imminently expect, and in which we shall be under a yet more abundant grace .... The first condition is in the bondage of slaves, the second in the bondage of sons, the third in liberty .... The first condition is related to the Father, the second to the Son, the third to the Holy Spirit.[142]

Joachim not only intended to contribute to a theology of history, but to the early scholastic debate on God. Since Joachim here runs afoul of Peter Lombard (d. 1160), who was understood to be *the* theological authority in the Middle Ages, his treatise on the Trinity was declared heretical – likely unjustly – by the fourth Lateran Council of 1215. Joachim did not mean that the divine Trinity had evolved in history, but only that the various stages of history are appropriated to the Trinitarian persons – i.e. could be attributed to them – but on the whole remain works of the Trinity as a whole. Joachim's theology is also not millennialist to the extent that he assumes that the millennium as the final 1,000 years of history is the inner historical time of the church. The final seventh age is not the millennium. Joachim actually still expected the eschatical breaking in of the kingdom of God after the third age of the Spirit. However, it is possible that it was his discussion

[141]Cf. G.G. Blum, 'Chiliasmus II', in Müller, Gehard et al. (eds), *Theologische Realenzyklopädie*, vol. 7 (Berlin: De Gruyter, 1981), pp. 729–33.

[142]Joachim von Fiore, *Liber Concordia Novi ac Veteris Testamenti* (Venice: 1519), Book V, 84,112, cited in Moltman, *The Trinity and the Kingdom*, pp. 204–5.

about the kingdom of Christ being overtaken by the kingdom of the Spirit that was most troublesome, be it either for his 'orthodox' opponents or his 'heterodox' disciples, that later labelled him millennialist.[143]

Nevertheless, Joachim's theology always gives occasion for the development of independent apocalyptic views of history, such as in the fourteenth century with the Franciscan spiritualists, the Taboriten and Müntzer's (d. 1525) purely apocalyptically motivated participation in the Peasant's War, not to mention the catastrophic Anabaptist kingdom in Münster (1534–1535).[144]

This makes clear that millennialism in the history of Christianity – and especially in the history of the early church and the Middle Ages – actually constitutes an exception to the rule. The popular notion that it is precisely these times that have been impregnated with millennialistic expectations perhaps appear with an imprecise synthesis of millennialism with the expectations of the end times: such expectations have frequently appeared, but they are not as we will see identical with apocalypticism and millennialism:

> Expectation about the end times means an awareness of living close to the end of history. Apocalyptic on the other hand means an awareness of the hidden course of history.

The situation changed dramatically at the beginning of modern era: modernity has seen an explosion of millennialism and chiliasm that continues into the present. This trend also includes the observation that a broad stream of the philosophy of history is more or less a secularized form of chiliasm.[145] However, we have to reject that notion at this point: if there are structural similarities between modern chiliasm and non-specific Christian accounts of history, then the thesis that the relation between the two is a case of the secularization or de-christianization of what were previously Christian ideas is highly unlikely since millennialism was not a

---

[143]For a systematic account of Joachim's thought, cf. Jürgen Moltmann, 'Christian Hope: Messianic or Transcendent? A Theological Discussion with Joachim of Fiore and Thomas Aquinas', *Horizons* 12.2 (1985), pp. 328–48 and Moltmann, *The Trinity and the Kingdom*, pp. 203–9.

[144]Cf. Reinhard Schwarz, *Die apokalyptische Theologie Thomas Müntzers und der Taboriten* (Tübingen: Mohr Siebeck, 1977).

[145]Cf. Volker Leppin, 'Millenarianism/Chiliasm: III. Church History, 3. Reformation and Modern Times', in Hans Dieter Betz et al. (ed.), *RPP* vol. 8, (Leiden: Brill, 2006–2013), p. 360.

significant factor in pre-modern theology. What is far more likely is this thesis in the reverse: Christian millennialism that arose during modernity rather presents a case of Christianity's reception of modern, non-explicitly Christian thought – in other words, a Christianization of Enlightenment thinking. In order to develop this thesis, which is not only historical but also has significant systematic implications, it is first necessary to give a description of the history of millennialism. At this point, we can say:

> Millennialism, that is, the view that there will be a period of salvation at the end of history, was only a peripheral phenomenon up to the onset of the modern period but then expanded greatly.

In order to be able to give a history of millennialism, we shall have to introduce a twofold distinction in what follows.

On the one hand, there is a distinction between postmillennialism and premillennialism. Historically speaking, this definition has to be introduced primarily in order to be able to discuss the development of millennialism in America in the eighteenth and nineteenth centuries.[146] Here, postmillennialism literally means the idea that the Parousia of Christ, the return of Christ, follows after the 1,000-year interim reign, whereas premillennialism teaches that the return of Christ comes before the interim reign. This does not result in a pointless debate about what precisely is to happen at the end of history, but rather it coalesces in America in the late nineteenth century into two main options: If the return of Christ occurs after the interim reign, then the present can either be understood as the realization of or at least as a period of working towards the realization of the interim reign:

> As a result, postmillennialism means – and this is the only meaning that it will be given here – that the development of history will be judged by and large positively and as part of a period of salvation.

On the other hand, *premillennialism* means that the return of Christ has to occur *before* the millennium and that there is no period of salvation within history – since the return of Christ has not yet occurred – but present and

[146]Cf. Hans Schwarz, *Jenseits von Utopie und Resignation* (Wuppertal: Brockhaus, 1990), pp. 203–9.

future history takes place before the return of Christ and the millennium. This is connected to a pessimistic view of both history in general and of the present, which are interpreted in terms of decline.[147]

> We have also separated the historical use of the term premillennialism from its systematic usage in such a way that premillennialism means every conception of history that – more or less – diagnoses the history of human society before the millennium as a history of decline.

Furthermore, we can make a distinction that allows us to subdivide our thesis about postmillennialism and premillennialism into secular (i.e. not specifically Christian) and Christianized versions.

After a description of what we are limiting our analysis to, we will evaluate our options, relate them to one other and then advance the thesis that under the conditions of the eschatic horizon of expectations none of the four forms are satisfactory and that a non-millennialist Christianity is preferable.

> In conclusion, we can say that these distinctions are bound together with the thesis that Christian millennialism is a christianized form of a secular, Enlightenment millennialism and not, conversely, a modern secularized and ideologically progressive variant of antecedent Christian ideas.[148]

4.3.2 Postmillennialism

4.3.2.1 Secular postmillennialism

Here, the paradigm is composed of the fundamental aspects of the Enlightenment worldview. In order to render this in outline, it makes sense to select a work paradigmatic for the Enlightenment. For this reason, we shall examine Lessing's (d. 1781) 'The Education of the Human Race.'

[147] Cf. Schwarz, *Jenseits von Utopie*, pp. 205–9.

[148] Cf. the precise opposite interpretation in Ernest Lee Tuveson, *Redeemer Nation* (Chicago: University of Chicago, 1968), p. 39.

Here, Lessing describes how he views religion from an Enlightenment perspective: in religion, revelations relate to human social forms in the same way that the education of an individual child relates to the fully grown adult.[149] This has as its consequence a rationalistic understanding of revelation according to which revelation – regardless of the particular religion – cannot actually make anything new known:

> Education gives to man nothing that he could not evolve from himself, but gives it to him more swiftly and less arduously. Similarly, revelation gives to the race no things which the un-aided human reason would not come upon by itself; but revelation has bestowed and is still bestowing, somewhat earlier, the most important of these things.[150]

However, this accelerated effect of revelation only works in specifically adolescent forms of human intellectuality: 'Revelation had conducted their reason; and now reason suddenly illuminated their revelation.'[151] The most decisive point, however, is not that the capacity for reason is being set over-against revelation, but rather the kind of content that is being attributed to reason and revelation, respectively. What accords with reason is only the universality and natural character of this content, but which can also be made known by revelation for humanity at the lower stages of development:

> And this at least Christ taught now for the first time. For, although among many nations the belief had already been introduced before him, that evil actions would yet be punished in that life, they were, nevertheless, only such actions as wrought injury to the civil community, and therefore already had their punishment in the civil community. To recommend an inner purity of heart with regard to another life was reserved alone to him.[152]

The generally accessible content of reason and revelation is thus nothing other than morality, i.e. the moral law or the good for its own sake. The general accessibility by reason is still supported by the rejection of the doctrine of original sin: 'And the doctrine of original sin. What if everything finally persuaded us that man, when on the *first and lowest* round of his humanity, is by no means such master of his actions as to be able to follow

---

[149]Cf. Gotthold Ephraim Lessing, *The Education of the Human Race* (trans. John Dearling Haney; New York: Columbia, 1908), p. 33 (§§1–2).
[150]Lessing, *Education*, p. 34 (§4).
[151]Lessing, *Education*, p. 44 (§36).
[152]Lessing, *Education*, p. 49 (§61).

moral laws?'[153] This means that everything negative about humanity, everything evil, imprudent etc., ultimately goes back to an insufficient stage of development and an inadequate amount of enlightenment. What is being rejected then is that humans are sinners by necessity. Humanity rather develops and strives towards perfect enlightenment:

> For, moreover, in this selfish state of the human heart, to incline to exercise the understanding only on those things which concern corporeal needs, would blunt it rather than whet it. It positively will be exercised on spiritual concerns if it is to attain to complete clarification and bring out that purity of heart which qualifies us to love virtue for its own sake.[154]

This perfected condition, however, is not a limit-concept but is historically realizable and will indeed be realized in history:

> Or shall the human race never reach this acme of clarification and purity? Never? Never? Let me not, All-Bountiful, think such blasphemy! Education has its *goal*, not less for the race than for the individual. What is to be educated, is to be educated for *something*.... No! It will come, it will surely come, the time of perfection, when man – the more convinced his understanding feels of an ever better future – will not, however, have to borrow from this future, motives for his actions; when he will do the good because it is the good and not because there were imposed upon it arbitrary re-wards which were earlier intended merely to steady his inconstant vision and strengthen it to recognize the inner, better rewards.[155]

What is striking here is the passion with which Lessing designates any possible denial of the historical realization of a true moral social form as a 'blasphemy' (*Lästerung*). Here, we can see five of the significant characteristics of Enlightenment thinking:

- Humans are not bad according to their nature.
- Humans are first located on morally lower stages.
- Knowledge of what is morally good is universally accessible.
- Humans are therefore morally perfectible.
- In the future, the perfect human social form will be realized within history.

---

[153]Lessing, *Education*, p. 52 (§74).
[154]Lessing, *Education*, pp. 53–4 (§80).
[155]Lessing, *Education*, pp. 54, 55 (§§81, 85).

What is clear is that in these hallmarks seemingly diverse Enlightenment ideologies and conceptions of history find their least common denominators, be it that of the French Revolution, Hegel (d. 1831) and F.C. Baur's (d. 1860) dialectically reconstituted version of history that culminates in the Prussian state,[156] the Marxian futuristic discussion of a classless society[157] as well as Ernst Bloch's (d. 1977) utopia of hope[158] or even more recently of Francis Fukuyama's discussion of the end of history in view of the end of the 'Cold War'.[159] It is also clear that the first hallmarks aim towards the final ones and the last presupposes the first four and summarizes them as well. The fact that these hallmarks of Enlightenment ideologies are being labelled as millennialist rests not only on similarities in their structures, but on the fact that Lessing – in alluding to Joachim of Fiore or those who refer to him – points out this connection themselves:

> It will surely come, the time of a *new, eternal gospel* which is promised, in the primers of the New Covenant, to us. It may be that even certain visionaries of the thirteenth and fourteenth century had caught the gleam of this new, eternal gospel and erred only in announcing its dawn as so near. Perhaps their threefold age of the world was no mere empty vagary, and certainly they had no evil aim when they taught that the New Covenant must become just as antiquated as the Old. There remained even with them always the same economy of the same God, always – to let them use my phrase – the same plan for the universal education of the human race.[160]

> The secular millennialism of the Enlightenment taught that humanity is first found to be at a morally basic level, but that it is moving towards the historical realization of a perfect social form because the good is universally evident.

---

[156]This interpretation is certainly disputed and relates to the famous saying, Georg Wilhelm Friedrich Hegel, 'The State is the Actuality of the Ethical Idea', in *Elements of the Philosophy of Right* (ed. Allen Wood; trans. H.B. Nisbet; Cambridge: Cambridge, 2012), p. 275 (§257).

[157]Cf. e.g. Friedrich Engels, 'Schelling und die Offenbarung', in Karl Marx and Friedrich Engels, *Gesamtausgabe I/3* (Berlin: Dietz, 1985), p. 313: 'The self-consciousness of humanity, the new grail, about whose throne the peoples joyfully gather … this is our calling, that we gird the sword around our loins and happily risk our lives in the final, holy war, after which the 1,000 year kingdom of freedom will follow.'

[158]Cf. Ernst Bloch, *Das Prinzip Hoffnung* (Frankfurt am Main: Suhrkamp, 1990, 3rd edn).

[159]Cf. Francis Fukuyama, *The End of History and the Last Man* (London: Hamilton, 1992).

[160]Lessing, *Education*, p. 55 (§§86–88).

4.3.2.2 Christianized postmillennialism

Christian forms of millennialism developed concurrently in the Enlightenment's modern twin brother, pietism, which arose in England and then coloured Christianity on the continent. Spener (d. 1705), Francke (d. 1727) and Bengel (d. 1752) were not free of millennialist tendencies.[161] A rather strong postmillennialist, i.e. culturally optimistic, attitude first appeared in Germany along with Enlightenment theology in the nineteenth century with the theology of mediation and culture Protestantism. Among the numerous names rightly or wrongly associated with ascribing the historical realization of the Kingdom of God understood in moral terms, Richard Rothe (d. 1867) is an outstanding example. He could already write in the middle of the nineteenth century: 'In the relation in which the organism of the state develops, the church recedes more and more .... In the general organism of the state the moral task is realized in the appropriate ways.'[162] Rothe is accordingly of the opinion that the moral task of the realization of the universal community is a task of the piety of the visible church, but whose success is apparent in culture and the state to the extent that with cultural and political progress, the church ultimately dissolves into the state. What one has to observe here is the fact that it turns on the actual realization of this process within history, the signs of which are already now clearly evident:

> Seen from the historical standpoint the organism of the state constituted in this way is nothing less than a fantastic dream. On the contrary after myriads of centuries the specific preambles to their future realization show themselves to already be very clear .... The current trend in history is evidently to let the State increase, and the church (which is not to be confused with true living Christianity) decrease.[163]

In German Protestant theology of the twentieth century, postmillennialism assumed moral progress and an ethical impetus in their theology and eschatology even when they did not make explicit recourse to the original meaning of the word. This is especially apparent in Jürgen Moltmann and contextual streams of the theology of the fall that were influenced by him.

---

[161]Cf. Erhard Kunz, *Protestantische Eschatologie von der Reformzeit bis zur Aufklärung* (Freiburg: Herder, 1980), pp. 73–84.

[162]Richard Rothe, *Theologische Ethik II* (Wittenberg: Zimmerman, 1869, 2nd edn), p. 473.

[163]Rothe, *Theologische Ethik II*, pp. 472–3. For another interpretation cf. Matthias Heesch, *Transzendentale Theorie und religiöse Erfahrung: Ihre Vermittlung als erkenntnistheoretische Grundintention in Richard Rothes Theologischer Ethik* (Frankfurt am Main: Lang, 1990), pp. 109–10.

In his *Theology of Hope*, this occurs for the most part without reference to historical strands of millennialism. First, Moltmann defines humans themselves as eschatical lifeforms.

> Man has no subsistence in himself, but is always on the way towards something and realizes himself in the light of some expected future whole.... In other words, the *natura hominis* first emerges from the *forma futurae vitae*.[164]

Human nature does not simply find its fulfilment in the future revelation of God, but in the sending of God to humanity and that means in its eschatically grounded ethical motivation:

> The call to obedient moulding of the world would have no object, if this world were immutable.... Thus the transforming mission requires in practice a certain *Weltanschauung*, a confidence in the world and a hope for the world. It seeks for that which is really, objectively possible in this world, in order to grasp it and realize it in the direction of the promised future of the righteousness, the life and the kingdom of God. Hence it regards the world as an open process in which the salvation and destruction, the righteousness and annihilation of the world are at stake.... The obedience that comes of hope and mission forms the bridge between that which is promised and hoped for and the real possibilities of the reality of the world.... This horizon fills him [man] with hopeful expectation, and at the same time requires of him responsibility and decision for the world of history.[165]

Although here Moltmann sees humans as responsibly forming history and changing it in a positive direction, he is aware that this activity is still due to the inspiration of the Spirit of God:

> [Human] experience of reality as history in all its possibilities of change is not, on the other hand, conditioned by whether history can be made at the whim of the human subject.... The subject of the transformation of the world is for him therefore the Spirit of the divine hope.... Rather, he adjusts being to the universal, rectifying future of God.[166]

Moltmann is clear about the fact that the modern impetus aiming towards the alteration of history presents a millennialist ideology that can only hold with both positive and critical considerations. Positive, because humanity is actually called upon for the formation of history, critically, because this

---

[164]Moltmann, *Theology of Hope*, p. 287.
[165]Moltmann, *Theology of Hope*, pp. 288–9.
[166]Moltmann, *Theology of Hope*, pp. 289–90.

impetus cannot be separated from its eschatical horizon of expectations that relativizes it at the same time:

> The emancipation of reason and society from their historic past is upheld in modern times by a millenarian enthusiasm…. We cannot turn our backs on the open horizons of modern history and return to perpetual orders and everlasting traditions, but we must take these horizons up into the eschatological horizon of the resurrection and thereby disclose to modern history its true historic character.[167]

If in the earlier Moltmann the connection between his position and the millennialist one still appears stereotypical, then in the later Moltmann it is done explicitly and with reference to Joachim of Fiore:

> Do the *parousia* and the kingdom of Christ fall within history or do they lie beyond it? Is an 'earthly future' or a heavenly one intended? These are questions pertaining to the symbolically-named 'thousand-year' reign, to *chiliasm*…. Chiliasm is the immanent side of eschatology. Eschatology is the transcendent side of chiliasm. Thus, there can be no chiliasm without eschatology – this leads to the political chiliasm which has had disastrous effects in European history. And there can also be no eschatology without chiliasm – this leads to the dissolution of the Christian hope into transcendental yearning, a condition which has led to no less disastrous results in the ecclesiastical history of Europe. [168]

Historically speaking, postmillennialism does not get its name from any of the previously discussed characteristics, but from its manifestation in American intellectual history. Representatives of the Great Awakening in America, especially Jonathan Edwards in the eighteenth century (d. 1758),[169] saw the movement as the beginning of a new era of salvation that would spread across the whole world and slowly disseminate through

---

[167]Moltmann, *Theology of Hope*, p. 303.

[168]Moltmann, 'Christian Hope: Messianic Or Transcendent?', pp. 347–8. Cf. also Moltmann, *The Trinity and the Kingdom*, pp. 203–9.

[169]On Edward's notion that the Christianization of the New World can be seen as the conversion of the last corners of the earth and therefore as the beginning of the millennium, see Robert Jewett and John Shelton Lawrence, *Captain America and the Crusade against Evil* (Grand Rapids: Eerdmans, 2003), pp. 57, 136. The description of America as the 'New World' is therefore invariably regarded as being ambiguous. This is symptomatically portrayed in the poem 'America' by Timothy Dwight from 1771: *'Hail Land of light and joy! Thy power shall grow/Far as the seas, which round thy regions flow;/Through earth's wide realms thy glory shall extend,/And savage nations at thy scepter bend […]/Then, then an heavenly kingdom shall descend,/And every region smile in endless peace;/Till the last trump the slumbering dead inspire,/Shake the wide heavens, and set the world on fire.'* Cited in Tuveson, *Redeemer Nation*, pp. 105–6.

evangelization. The source of this thinking can be found in Puritan immigration to America and postmillennialist thinking unfolds as the American War of Independence was conceived as the final eschatological battle against Satan from which America would ultimately emerge as the 'redeemer nation' of the world.[170] The social gospel movement was even more 'ethicistically' oriented, which gripped Methodists, Presbyterians and Congregationalists in the nineteenth century, who believed that poverty and social conflict could be overcome within history.[171] Postmillennialism ultimately resulted in the American conception of a 'civil religion', that is, the notion that there is an unexpressed, worldview-oriented explicit Christian consensus that forms the fundament of society and is responsible for the Western ethos as a minimal consensus.[172]

Christian postmillennialism appeared in Germany in the optimistic stances of both mediating theology and culture Protestantism of the late nineteenth century, which conceived of the realization of the Kingdom of God within history, in many strands of American theology since Jonathan Edwards up to the conception of America as a redeemer nation as well as in a weaker form in those twentieth-century theologies influenced by Jürgen Moltmann's *Theology of Hope*.

4.3.3 Premillennialism

4.3.3.1 Secular premillennialism

There are certainly not only historical interpretations that are apocalyptic in that they believe to have recognized a positive development of history, but there are also interpretations that assume that history takes a negative course and is characterized by decline. Interestingly, these often-pessimistic versions of premillennialism occur far less often both in their secular as in their Christian variants. Differently from the optimistic

---

[170] Cf. Jewett and Lawrence, *Captain America*, pp. 55–61.
[171] Cf. Jewett and Lawrence, *Captain America*, pp. 136–8.
[172] This terminology goes back to Robert N. Bellah, 'Civil Religion in America', *Dædalus* 96.1 (Winter 1967), pp. 1–21. For a theological interpretation cf. Eilert Herms, 'Pluralismus aus Prinzip', in *Kirche für die Welt* (Tübingen: Mohr Siebeck, 1995), pp. 467–85, esp. 472–5.

postmillennialist apocalyptic interpretation of history, we are not dealing here with a simple case of an antecedent but more in the sense of the two running adjacently.

The most popular among such secular premillennialist interpretations of history could be the famous model developed by Oswald Spengler (d. 1936), which enjoyed especial popularity after the First World War in Europe. Spengler interprets world history in terms of various high cultures, which, similar to that of human development, run through various stages. Spengler expressly rejects there being one single goal for the development of the human biological organism as such, as well as for the history of the world: 'As for humanity, I am a thoroughgoing and decided pessimist. Humanity for me is a zoological concept. I can see no progress, no goal, no pathway for humanity.'[173] This expression only refers to a goal understood positively. Individual cultures experience stages of growth and decline similar to spring, summer, autumn and winter: to begin, a culture experiences a pre-historical stage, then its early stage time, its later stage and finally civilization.[174] Although the model is not simply a model of the decline of the entirety of world history since this is ultimately an abstract concept, it is also not simply a cyclical model since one civilization dissolves into another through its death. According to Spengler in his time, Western civilization was in an interim stage, that is, the final stage marked by decline. This was evident in a materialistic worldview, the acquisition of mathematical theories, the development of philosophy as a scientific discipline, the sovereignty of money and thus democracy and various other factors. At the end, private and family politics of individual rulers predominate, pre-historic conditions intrude into the highly civilized way of life and the world will be divided like plunder and conquered successively by newer peoples.[175] Spengler saw his own time – i.e. the early twentieth century – as the beginning of this epoch of civilization and estimated its end would come around the year 2200.[176] Spengler received a great deal of approval, even theological. The Erlangen Lutheran theologian Werner Elert adopted Spengler's language but did not himself develop a

[173]Oswald Spengler, *Pessimismus?* (Schriftenreihe der Preußischen Jahrbücher 4; Berlin: Stilke, 1921), p. 14. Cf. also Oswald Spengler, *The Decline of the West I: Form and Actuality* (New York: Knopf, 1928), p. 21: '"Mankind," however, has no aim, no idea, no plan, any more than the family of butterflies or orchids. "Mankind" is a zoological expression, or an empty word.'

[174]Cf. Ulrich H.J. Körtner, *Weltangst und Weltende: Eine theologische Interpretation der Apokalyptik* (Göttingen: Vandenhoeck & Ruprecht, 1988), p. 217.

[175]Cf. Körtner, *Weltangst*, pp. 217–18.

[176]Cf. Körtner, *Weltangst*, p. 218.

premillennialist theology, rather arguing for a separation of Christianity from a doomed culture:

> Whoever at present considers Christianity to be like a companion saving decadent power is binding Christianity's barque to a sinking ship. Therefore there is ... only a single great commandment: loosing Christianity from the web of a declining culture .... The more one is convinced of the liberating, clarifying majestic power of Christianity the more impartially one will witness the rupture of false buttressing.[177]

For Elert, Christianity, similar to revelation for Barth, does not belong to culture and can even develop independently of these cultural factors.

In the present, Samuel Huntington's discussion of a new world order that could lead to a 'clash of civilizations' can be interpreted as having a negative perspective on historical development. Huntington's claim is thereby not primarily informed by a normative pessimism, but he rather understands his analysis as being simply descriptive.

Huntington's famous article from 1993 entitled, 'The Clash of Civilizations', spawned a number of discussions and several books dedicated to debating the original thesis. The discussion to follow, however, will rely exclusively on the original article. Huntington's thesis is that modern conflicts from Westphalia up to the French Revolution were wars between princes, up to the First World War wars between nations and up to the end of the Cold War conflicts between ideologies and since then conflicts between cultures or civilizations that can be divided by objective facts such as religion, language, history, values and customs.[178] According to Huntington, seven to eight world cultures are emerging,[179]

---

[177]Cf. Werner Elert, *Der Kampf um das Christentum: Geschichte der Beziehungen zwischen dem evangelischen Christentum in Deutschland und dem allgemeinen Denken seit Schleiermacher und Hegel* (Munich: Beck, 1921), p. 489.

[178]Cf. Samuel P. Huntington, 'The Clash of Civilizations', *Foreign Affairs* 72.3 (1993), pp. 22–8: 'A civilization is thus the highest cultural grouping of people and the broadest level of cultural identity people have short of that which distinguishes humans from other species. It is defined both by common objective elements, such as language, history, religion, customs, institutions, and by the subjective self-identification of people.'

[179]Cf. Huntington, 'The Clash of Civilizations', p. 25: 'Civilization identity will be increasingly important in the future, and the world will be shaped in large measure by the interactions among seven or eight major civilizations. These include Western, Confucian, Japanese, Islamic, Hindu, Slavic-Orthodox, Latin American and possibly African civilization. The most important conflicts of the future will occur along the cultural fault lines separating these civilizations from one another.'

among which several kinds of conflicts could develop. Huntington thinks that a conflict between the West and the rest will emerge, primarily against the Islamic–Confucian alliance.[180] However, Huntington's theses are understood to be descriptive and therefore not dependent on historical theories of cycle or decline, so that it cannot explicitly be labelled a form of premillennialism.

One can see that similarly to voices in Europe after the First World War that – especially after 11 September 2001 – there is a new consciousness of a decline of Western civilization that can be bound entirely to premillennial thinking.

Also interesting are postmodern variants of premillennialism in which premillennialist thinking is virtually overcome by a kind of amillennialism. For postmodern thinking, it has been Jacques Derrida (d. 2004) in particular who has been conscious of the similarity between Enlightenment and Apocalyptic literature: the point of literature in the apocalyptic genre, like that of the Enlightenment, is to uncover something and make it known. Modernity is thoroughly apocalyptic and apocalypticism is a transcendental condition of the possibility of this discourse itself.[181] There are however better and worse forms of apocalyptic and respectively better and worse forms of enlightenment: whereas the Enlightenment largely holds fast to one single truth and rejects others, it is its own principles that are not fully transparent and obvious, whereas postmodernity is the better form of Enlightenment and therefore corresponds better to the apocalyptic structure, because there is no truth in the singular but only truths in the plural. As a result, postmodernity can be said to be an 'apocalypse without vision, without truth, without revelation'.[182] It appears to Ulrich Körtner that the term 'postmodernity' itself is 'a variation on the theme of the decline of the West'.[183] However, in comparison to these notions, there are decisive marks of postmillennialism and true apocalyptic thinking that consist precisely in the possibility of recognizing and schematizing the course of history. If the apocalyptic uncovering of the course of history is to consist precisely in this, then apocalyptic premillennialism is already overcome in favour of amillennialism.

---

180 Cf. Huntington, 'The Clash of Civilizations'.

181 Cf. Jacques Derrida, 'Of an Apocalyptic Tone Recently Adopted in Philosophy', *Oxford Literary Review* 6.2 (1984), pp. 3–37.

182 Derrida, 'Of an Apocalyptic Tone', p. 34.

183 Körtner, *Weltangst*, p. 239.

Secular premillennialism can be found where the course of history as a whole is interpreted in terms of decline. Prominent examples can be seen in Oswald Spengler's interpretation of history, in interpretations of the present day that view contemporary history in terms of decline and at least somewhat nominally in a few postmodern conceptions of history.

4.3.3.2 Christianized premillennialism

In the nineteenth century in America, there were not only optimistic postmillennialist streams of thought, but also pessimistic premillennialist currents that did not in any way assume that a time of salvation had already broken out or would break out in the near future. On the contrary, these premillennial currents assume that present state of world history is negative and consequently that the end of history will soon break out in the form of the final judgement.

Religious movements that have gone beyond Christianity and belong in part to this grouping are those of the Mormons in the 1830s by Joseph Smith (d. 1844), William Miller's (d. 1849) reckoning of the beginning of the end in the 1840s that triggered the establishment of various new religious groups such as the Adventists and the founding of the Jehovah's Witnesses by Charles T. Russell (d. 1916) at the end of the nineteenth century.[184] However, pessimistic premillennialist movements emerged not only in America but also from the English Awakening such as by Edward Irving (d. 1834) from which the New Apostolic Church arose.

Within Christianity in nineteenth-century America, premillennialism was most operative in dispensationalism, which experienced new impetus in the 1970s. Historically speaking, dispensationalism can be said to derive from Reformed Federal Theology. This theology assumes that God deals with humanity in different historical periods through varying *foedera*, i.e. pacts, contracts or covenants.

According to recent studies, Federal Calvinism has more than one root and possesses predecessors in the theology of one of Calvin's students, Kaspar Olevianus (1536–1587) and Melanchthon's student Zacharias Ursinus (1534–1583), though it hardly appeared in the Heidelberg Catechism. An

[184]Cf. Jewett and Lawrence, *Captain America*, p. 137.

explicit federal schema can be found in Johannes Cocceius (1603–1669) and independently also in the Scottish theologians John Cameron (1579–1625), Thomas Cartwright (1535–1603), Robert Rollock (1555–1599), William Perkins (1558–1602), William Ames (1576–1633) and finally in the 'Westminster Confession'.[185] In Cameron's three-fold scheme, the concept of the covenant was used for introducing a conditioned, hypothetical gift of grace (*foedus hypotheticum*). In the *foedus naturale*, the Covenant of Works or Covenant of Law, God concludes a covenant or contract with Adam as federal head of humanity, in which the gift of salvation is conditional on fulfilment of the law. But, since in eternity the Father and Son had seen that Adam would break this covenant, they made a *foedus gratiae* (covenant of grace) in eternity, a covenant of salvation in which the Son agreed to pay for the sin of humanity in the form of penal atonement in order to merit grace for the elect. A third covenant, the *foedus gratiae subserviens*, is dependent on this second covenant. Aided by this, the elect enter into the gift of salvation guaranteed by the *foedus gratiae* on the condition that they attain salvation if they demonstrate repentance and faith.[186]

Dispensationalism goes back to the Plymouth Brethren, founded in the 1830s in England by John Nelson Darby (d. 1882), also spread to America by means of the Scofield Reference Bible and experienced a revival in the 1970s as a result of Hal Lindsey's book, *The Late Great Planet Earth*, and even plays a role in contemporary global politics.[187] Dispensationalism expands Federal Theology to such an extent that not only the three *foedera* or pacts of God are adopted, but rather seven stages of the world and seven different pacts and corresponding ages (dispensations) of God with humanity are also adopted. 'The seven dispensations are: innocence (in the Garden); consciousness (until the flood); the human regiment (from the Tower of Babel); the promise (from Abraham); the law (from Moses); grace (from Christ); the Kingdom (the coming millennium).'[188] All the dispensations are marked by the fact that humanity falls short and breaks the corresponding pact. At present, history is understood to be at the end of the penultimate dispensation, after which the return of Christ is imminent and the millennium breaks in, wherein humanity will but once again fall

---

[185]Cf. David Alexander Weir, *Foedus natural: The Origin of Federal Theology in 16th Century Reformation Thought* (Unpublished doctoral dissertation, St Andrew's University, 1984); Michael Jinkins, *A Comparative Study in the Theology of Atonement on Jonathan Edwards and John McLeod Campbell* (San Francisco: Mellen, 1993), pp. 422, 403–7.

[186]Cf. James B. Torrance, 'Covenant or Contract?', *Scottish Journal of Theology* 23 (1979), pp. 55–7.

[187]Cf. Jewett and Lawrence, *Captain America*, pp. 138–47.

[188]Schwarz, *Die christliche Hoffnung*, p. 91.

short followed by the freeing of Satan. Ultimately, the course of the world is to end entirely negatively, whence the real *eschata* are to begin.[189]

In continental Germany, virtually no independent premillennialism developed in the nineteenth and twentieth centuries. It has indeed blossomed among the various free churches (i.e. Christian groups that do not belong to the *Landeskirchen*), though as a result of Anglo-American influence. In the middle of the nineteenth century, it was only the conservative Lutheran Wilhelm Löhe who developed a kind of premillennialism that could scarcely be called paradigmatic, though which ironically led to his separation from the American Lutheran Missouri Synod that had been supporting him and had insisted on keeping explicitly to traditional confessional writings that were non-millennialist. Löhe wrote:

> Once the hope for a second coming, and notions of Antichrist and decline have receded to the background and it is nearly impossible not to see that love instantly becomes cold ... 1800 years have gone by and what has happened .... What has happened? The church stands, the decline in it always increases, the masses give themselves blatantly over to the working of the world, evil wins more and more ears and hearts .... The cock's cry even penetrates to you, my cries of loneliness and silence; I cry from out of the depths to you and witness to the decline, of the possible proximity of the Antichrist, of the first return of the Lord and the first resurrection .... We stand there and see the red sky of the dawning of the future lighting, and the coming of the end and the Lord and with his Resurrection, and we are smeared over and over with the grime and wickedness of our common life.[190]

It is clear that we are dealing with a form of premillennialism at this point: Löhe paints a picture of a history of decline that had reached its peak in the middle of the nineteenth century, in which the pessimism typical of premillennialism is readily identifiable. His mention of the 'first resurrection' means that Löhe first expected the end and that the millennium would follow afterwards.

What is perhaps even more premillennialist in form can be seen in the theology of Isaak August Dorner (d. 1884). Dorner formally rejected millennialism[191] but nonetheless conceptualized an increasing dissemination

---

[189]Cf. Schwarz, *Die christliche Hoffnung*, p. 92.

[190]Wilhelm Löhe, 'Das Entgegenkommen zur Auferstehung der Toten. Predigt über Phil 3, 7–11. 1857', in Klaus Ganzert (ed.), *Gesammelte Werke*, vol. 6.1 (Neuendettelsau: Freimund-Verlag, 1957), pp. 695–706, esp. 703–5.

[191]Cf. Isaak August Dorner, See Isaak August Dorner, *The Future State: The Doctrine of the Last Things* (trans. Newman Smyth; New York: Scribner's, 1883), pp. 78–82 (§152.II).

of Christianity along with an account of the decline of the world. This conception is notable to the extent that it offers an answer to the question of why the world as a whole has not become better since the death and resurrection of Christ if we are to understand justification as really being effective. At this point, it is anyone's guess as to whether Dorner is posting a good answer:

> It follows directly from the growing influence of Christianity in the world, that those who nevertheless persevere in resistance will be impelled and hardened by the stronger revelation of Christ to more and more malignant, especially to more spiritual forms of wickedness, in order to hold their ground against it. In this way, then, the apostasy, supported by lying and the semblance of spiritual being, is the more seductive and contagious, and to it even outward apostasy, in increasing expansion, may attach itself in further development and revelation of the inner state. But the transition to this is formed by the inner apostasy through falsification of Christianity.[192]

Christian premillennialism, i.e. the thesis that history can be accounted for in terms of a continual process of decline, can be found in the Anglo-American sphere among various groups influenced by Christianity, in dispensationalism, which teaches that history takes place in seven ages or dispensations, and more or less by way of exception in German Protestantism in Wilhelm Löhe and Isaak August Dorner.

4.3.4 Amillennialist Christianity and the ethical consequences

The mainstream of Christianity is neither millennialist nor apocalyptic. In the Christian East, millennialism has hardly any adherents in the wake of the Origenist tradition. Eusebius of Caesarea (d. 339) sought to refute millennialist beliefs. In the West, Augustine sounded the death knell for every form of millennialism. Although Augustine had first toyed with millennialist thinking, this was radically excluded in four chapters of *The*

---

[192]Dorner, *The Future State*, vol. 2, p. 85 (§152.III).

City of God,[193] in which the thousand-year reign of Rev. 20.1–7 was applied to the present age of the church:

> But while the devil is bound for a thousand years, the saints reign with Christ also for a thousand years, which are without doubt to be understood in the same way: that is, as the period beginning with Christ's first coming.... Then [Christ] proceeds to give a short account of what the Church does, or of what is done in the Church, during those thousand years. 'And I saw thrones', he says, 'and they sat upon them, and judgment was given'. We are not to suppose that this is a reference to the last judgment. Rather, it is to be understood as a reference to the thrones of the rulers, and to the rulers themselves, by whom the Church is now governed.[194]

In the subsequent period, both the early church as well as the church in Middle Ages held to this interpretation and rejected millennialism as being heretical.[195] The Reformation not only reaffirmed this judgement, when millennialism was rejected in the seventeenth article of the *Confessio Augustana*,[196] but in a certain sense even augmented this interpretation. This is because if the 1,000-year reign was the reign of the church and at the end of time the devil will once again be unbound, then it was easy to relate the present to this time after the 1,000 years: the devil has now been loosed and is identical with the pope or the papacy. This interpretation meant that the Reformers could be both amillennialist and nevertheless conceive of themselves as living in proximity to the end times. In the mainstream of both later Roman Catholic and Protestant theology, millennialism did not subsequently arise, with the exception of the cases mentioned above.

> The Christian mainstream in both in the East and the West were amillennial from the time of Augustine onwards in relating the 1,000 years mentioned in Rev. 20.1–7 to the time of the church and therefore to the present.

---

[193]Augustine, *The City of God against the Pagans* (trans. and ed. R. W. Dyson: Cambridge: Cambridge University Press, 2013, 10th edn), pp. 975–91 (XX,6–9).
[194]Augustine, *The City of God*, pp. 987–9 (XX,9).
[195]Cf. Aquinas, *Summa Contra Gentiles IV*, p. 319 (IV,83,22).
[196]Cf. Melanchthon, 'The Augsburg Confession (1530)', in *The Book of Concord*, pp. 50–1 (XVIII: Concerning the Return of Christ to Judgment): 'Likewise rejected are some Jewish teachings, which have also appeared in the present, that before the resurrection of the dead(,) saints and righteous people alone will possess a secular kingdom and will annihilate all the ungodly.'

Systematically, this means amillennialism assumes that there is no revelation of a particular course of history, either good or bad. It draws off a historical consciousness that presumes that in its historical condition, the world is not perfectible. Present day historical order is not categorically improvable, and the time of the church cannot be overcome within history. Amillennial Christianity therefore renounces every utopia that assumes any kind of state of salvation within history.

The ethical consequences of this position are enormous: postmillennialism inevitably tends towards totalitarianism, because it holds to the necessity of the realization of the hope for redemption in the historical future. In so far as one obtains enlightenment and insight in the course of history, be it through reason or through some other means, one will have to seek to convince those that are not convinced about this disclosure or enlightenment of the same interpretation or, in the case that this is not possible, to eliminate these views or their representatives. History since the Enlightenment is filled with such obvious examples of cruelty that we need not recount them here in further detail.

In contrast to every form of optimistic postmillennialism, pessimistic premillennialism appears at least not to be burdened by this form of ethical danger – the inevitability of the onset of totalitarianism. At most, the danger arises of a kind of stillness or of a kind of doubt-driven self-fulfilling prophesy with respect to human action in history. These dangers are always less harmful than those of postmillennialism.

Nevertheless, from a systematic standpoint, one has to say that ultimately both forms of millennialism cannot be united with a Christian understanding of reality. Apocalyptic thinking as such, the fact that it is generally a matter of the revelation of rules in religion, after which the course of history is fulfilled, is wrong: under the condition of the eschatical horizon of expectations intrinsic to the Christian faith, there is in fact a kind of disclosure, uncovering or revelation of the last or ultimate things. But, its object is not future historical facts but Godself. Both the origin and content of revelation are consequently identical with the Triune God. Millennialism reduces the notion of a personal God and this God's living action to that of an ultimately deistic God, that is, a God that has only seemingly endued history with contingence, but in reality has history run according to a natural regularity be it for good or for bad. Ultimately, the attempt to formulate an apocalyptic interpretation of history proves to be a faulty attempt to grasp hold of the future under what are only provisional horizons of experience. It is therefore possible to understand millennial forms of Christianity as the attempt of making what is not at human disposal calculable and manipulable and therefore as an attempt to deny the eschatic and ultimate character of the ultimate future. Similar to the way that drawing out connections between actions and consequences in life histories of specific persons is an expression of sin, millennialism in the social sphere is a likewise an expression of sin, i.e. in terms of humans attempting to establish their own rules.

All of this does not mean of course that the older apocalyptic literature was without any value. It can still be taken on in other ways. Wolfhart Pannenberg gives an outstanding example of this calling on both the extra-canonical early Jewish literature and on the postmillennial Hegel and his thoughts about the unity of the truth, without himself being postmillennialist.[197]

What is interesting is the fact that amillennialism, as in the case of the Reformation, can exist side by side with an expectation of the imminence of the end. The systematic significance of non-millennialist expectation consists in the fact that present-day history is radically relativized and those who act and live in it are conscious of its provisional nature in particular ways. Luther gave a famous anecdote that could have taken place in the middle of the twentieth century, though it nevertheless demonstrates that an amillennialist conception of history indeed results in the appropriate forms of action within history: When asked what he would do if the world was going to end tomorrow, Luther answered that he would plant an apple tree. When then asked why he wanted to do this, he answered simply because he wanted to, demonstrating that he always acted and would continue to act as if the end could come tomorrow.

However, it is also possible to describe the public and social action of non-millennialist Christians even more definitely: the primary public task of Christians is communication of the gospel and, in this way, participation in divine action, which is saving action because it constitutes faith, and whose complete success in the world is not possible. However, this participation in the divine activity that creates faith in humanity still has to be distinguished from another kind of participation in God's activity. This is because in order to be able to proclaim the gospel of cross and resurrection, certain

[197]Cf. e.g. Pannenberg, 'Der Gott der Geschichte', in *Grundfragen systematischer Theologie II*, pp. 112–28.

minimal conditions must be fulfilled in the historical condition of a society: material needs for the provision of the living body have to be stilled, non-material goods such as peace or an order of civic laws[198] are necessary in any case. Further, proclamation can only occur where it is certain that the proclaimer and the hearer will not be killed. The divine action preparing these non-material goods is labelled God's preserving action. It does not have an eschatical quality in and of itself, but only a medial character, as long as the world exists. But, even in this preserving divine action, humans can and must participate in all their sociality. Such participation has just as little of its own salvific quality as the corresponding action of God: it is not directed towards salvation, but only to opposing evil. Economics and politics as well as Christian participation in them are indeed for commanded activities for Christians, but only provisional ones: on the basis of the medial character of this preserving action for divine saving action, economic and political activities do not possess eschatic relevance. The distinction between both of these kinds of divine action like human participation in them can among other things be grasped conceptually with the help from the so-called doctrine of the two realms.[199]

An amillennialist Christianity attains its societal relevance on behalf of the distinction between God's preserving action and God's salvific action, meaning that the last things bring salvation, whereas the first things only bring the necessary conditions for the last things. God's preserving action is indeed only identifiable in the eschatic horizon of expectations and divine action, but unidentifiable in provisional horizons of expectation. In contrast to this, God's saving action genuinely belongs in opposition to the eschatic horizon. Human action in politics and economics can be characterized as participation in God's preserving action and has the task of opposing evil, but not bringing about salvation. The proclamation of the church, which nevertheless remains not at the church's disposal, is, on the contrary, to be understood as a task of participation in God's saving action.

---

[198]Cf. Eilert Herms, 'Theologische Ethik und Rechtsbegründung', in Wilfried Härle (ed.), *Marburger Jahrbuch Theologie XIV* (Marburg: Elwert, 2002), pp. 13–40.

[199]Cf. Wilfried Härle, 'Luthers Zwei-Regimenten-Lehre als Lehre vom Handeln Gottes', in Wilfried Härle (ed.), *Marburger Jahrbuch Theologie I* (Marburg: Elwert, 1987), pp. 37–77; Eilert Herms, 'Theologie und Politik. Die Zwei-Reiche-Lehre als theologisches Programm einer Politik des weltanschaulichen Pluralismus', in *Gesellschaft gestalten* (Tübingen: Mohr Siebeck, 1991), pp. 95–124.

4.3.5 Excursus: Omens of the end

In the history of Christianity, perceptible signs of the final judgement and the return of Christ have been continually sought based on the great New Testament apocalyptic depictions in Mk 13, Lk. 21, Matt. 24f., 1 Thess. 4.13–18; 1 Thess. 5.1–11 as well as in the book of Revelation. Corresponding to their apocalyptic role models, these signs concern or show both the personal and the social and cosmic world. In the Middle Ages, there was a broad debate over the question of how far this doctrine could actually be systematized. Thus, in the twelfth century, one can find a doctrine of mostly fifteen signs that are not identical. Among them were, for example: the rising or sinking of the ocean, the demise of marine life, the burning of bodies of water, the emergence of a bloody dew on plants, collapsing buildings and cliffs, earthquakes and the levelling of the earth, humans acting manically or losing the ability to speak, the opening of graves, stars falling from heaven, the death of everything living and new resurrection, the burning of heaven and earth, and general resurrection.

Also mentioned are significant independent events such as the appearance of false prophets and anti-Christs – either individual or institutional – whose identity would provide much speculation, a great battle on the day of God against evil at a place called Armageddon (according to Rev. 16.16), the appearance of the sign of the Son of Man in the heavens (according to Matt. 24.30) often thought to be a fiery cross, the appearance of Enoch (who had been enraptured, but not Elijah, since he was supposed to have already returned in the person of John the Baptist) as well as the conversion of Jews to Christ. To some extent, there was an attempt to arrange these events into a temporal succession. The great theologians of the Middle Ages were highly opposed to these rather popular ideas. Thomas Aquinas, for example, saw the appearance of the fifteen signs as extremely unlikely and only dealt with the Anti-Christ once in his work.[200] Calculations about the end were instead excluded on biblical grounds (Mk 13.21 and 32, 1 Thess. 5.2) and were rightly held to be heretical whenever they were nonetheless asserted. All in all, these interpretations pervert the intention of the various biblical meanings of the signs in question to the extent that they attempt to make what was intended to be inaccessible to us both accessible and predictable.

In asking about the conceptual value of all these signs, one will come across little as to their individual content, but a great deal as to their totality:

---

[200]Cf. Ott, *Eschatologie in der Scholastik*, pp. 29–32, 107–111.

(1) All told, these signs do not demonstrate any historically perfected final condition of humanity, world or society, but rather a hopelessly anarchic state of calamity.
(2) As a result, every hope for a state of salvation to be attained within history from the perspective of the Christian faith is rejected.
(3) Such rejection of the predictability of the end ought to promote consciousness that we live preliminarily in the historical world and emphasize the ethical exhortation of wakefulness.
(4) In effect, these signs of the end describe nothing other than catastrophes experienced in various historical situations, be they natural catastrophes, the emergence of corrupt leaders or wars. Such signs can and have indeed conveyed consciousness of life at the end of time in many different ages and eras, meaning that they therefore fall indirectly under the ethical effect of wakefulness named just above in point 3, including its bearing to the here and now.
(5) The Anti-Christ consistently receives especial interest. What is clear at this point is that both the dissolution of the notion of the Anti-Christ into general opposition to Christ and the concrete identification of the Anti-Christ with a historical individual in the past, present or future are ultimately amiss. Identification of the Anti-Christ with forms of political leadership, systems or institutions downplays the significance of the notion and run against its intended meaning: 'It would constitute an undue attenuation were one to understand this as a political power striking out to persecute Christians. Persecution has often decimated the church, but never seriously jeopardized its existence. The satanic character of this final great danger can rather occur in what the church does inwardly to adjust to it, for, as to proclamation of God's rule and lordship in the human realm, the presence of Christ – who can resist that?'[201]

In the history of Christianity, various attempts have been made, primarily using the book of Revelation, to combine and systematize various signs of the end of the world or to calculate the end of the world. These attempts prove to be unbiblical and contradict the convention of eschatology to develop statements on the basis of the horizon of Christian hope, because they in fact proceed on the basis of our present horizon of experience by means of extrapolation.

[201] Elert, *Der christliche Glaube*, p. 523.

5
The Eschata

Chapter Outline

The Parousia of Christ 252
The resurrection of the living body 276
The judgement 302
The consummation of the Kingdom of God as the eschatical reality 338

After our treatment of the pre-eschata, we now come to the actual eschata, or the 'last things'. It is still also the case here that we are not simply dealing with a juxtaposition of various events that the Christian faith anticipates as happening in the future. On the contrary, the concern here is a structured state of affairs, an event that can be segmented into various aspects that are related to each other in specific ways.[1] If we are correct in saying that the basis of Christian hope is the self-disclosure of the Triune God in the centre of the Christian faith in the cross and resurrection of Jesus Christ, then no more can be said about those events anticipated individually than can be said by the constitution of the horizon of expectations of ultimate hope in the redemption of humanity by the Triune God in the person and work of Jesus Christ. But, then, it immediately suggests itself that *we look upon the appearance of Jesus Christ* – the Parousia – *as the constitution, efficient cause or intentional-personal source of the eschatic reality* and then *the kingdom of God* as the form of implementation, *telos* or goal of the eschatic reality – *and that means as nothing less than the eschatic reality itself*, *whereas the*

[1]Cf. Robert W. Jenson, *Systematic Theology II: The Works of God* (New York: Oxford, 1999), p. 314.

resurrection of the dead and the judgement together with their outcomes are the means by which this will be reached. This makes it feasible to deal with the Parousia and the Kingdom of God as the first and last of the eschata (see sections 5.1 and 5.4), thereby also framing the question of the means of the resurrection (see section 5.2) and the final judgement (see section 5.3).

5.1 The Parousia of Christ

5.1.1 The problem of the Parousia

A number of problems are wrapped up in the Parousia. First is the problem of marginalization. As things go, the Parousia has received precisely the opposite treatment to that of the millennium. Whereas the millennium is mentioned only one time in the Bible and nevertheless exploded as a theme in modern times, things are the exact opposite with the Parousia. The Parousia is one of the central themes of the New Testament but has received very little attention in systematic theology from the onset of modernity to the present day. This inability to deal with the Parousia in systematic terms can be seen in Schleiermacher (d. 1834), who gave the doctrine of the 'Return of Christ' a particular weight by placing it at the beginning of his treatment of the 'prophetic doctrines'.[2] Schleiermacher nevertheless hardly capitalizes on this. On the one hand, the entirety of eschatology as 'prophetic doctrine' indicates that it is not an integral part of dogmatics, and on the other hand, the content of the theme of the Parousia is restricted: it has nothing to do with the return of the person of Christ, but only Christ's effect on the church. Christ is not to return *in person*, it is rather the church, according to Schleiermacher, that will be consummated:

> Thus all that might go to form a definite picture falls asunder; and, as the essential content of our paragraph, there remains simply this – that (if we substitute the efficacious activity of Christ for his bodily presence) the consummation of the Church, regarded as the cessation of its wavering growth and development, is possible only through a sudden leap to perfection ... and that, therefore, this leap to perfection must be regarded as an act of Christ's kingly power .... So that in this doctrine everything that is figurative and necessarily uncertain in quality flows from our interest in

[2]Schleiermacher, *The Christian Faith*, pp. 707–9 (§160).

personal survival, whereas everything that can be stated with assurance relates to the consummation of the Church.[3]

The problem of marginalization thus ultimately reveals a further problem, that of functionalization: even if the central role of the Parousia for eschatology is recognized, that is, if it is recognized that absolutely nothing can be said about the eschatical reality other than what has happened in Jesus Christ, then this still indicates that is taken from the work of Christ, but not his person. The Parousia suggests that nothing can happen in the eschatical reality other than what has already happened soteriologically in Jesus Christ.[4] This is by no means wrong, but it is not the entire truth of the matter. This is because the function, that is the work of Christ, is christologically speaking not independent of the person of Christ. It is even more astounding when both are still decoupled from the doctrine of the Parousia. Also of interest is the inner-disciplinary imbalance with Christian theology itself: whereas there are a number of historical-exegetical studies on the Parousia, this appears to be rather murky in terms of its systematic reconstruction.

In New Testament studies, the question of the meaning, origin and transformation of the conception of the Parousia, often held to be the motor of the entire history of early Christianity, is a significant and disputed field. The controversy in the research as to *whether* there was a problem concerning the delay of the Parousia, and if yes, *what* role it actually played, cannot be resolved here.[5] It is possible, however, to formulate a cautious outcome of this debate. In the second and third generations of early Christianity, the delay of the Parousia had become a sustained irritation by 60 to 70 CE A number of different ways of dealing with this delay were adopted and were variously reflected in early Christian writing. First, the imminence of the Parousia could be retained under the condition that the presence was seen as an extended time of ethical probation or testing (1 Pet. 1.3–12, 4.7; Rev. 1.3, 3.11). Second, the imminence of the Parousia was almost replaced by an individual experience of salvation in the present – especially in the sacramental transformation of humanity (1 Cor. 10.4, 15.29; Col. 3.1–4; Eph.

---

[3]Schleiermacher, *The Christian Faith*, pp. 708–9 (§160).

[4]Cf. Härle, *Dogmatik*, p. 609, who writes explicitly 'that Christian eschatology is well advised when it seeks its point of contact not primarily in the doctrine of God or in anthropology, but in soteriology'. Härle appropriately entitles section 15.3.3 'Christ's arrival and judgment' (cf. Härle, *Dogmatik*, p. 639), but then only deals with his judging function (pp. 642–3).

[5]Cf. Erich Grässer, *Das Problem der Parusieverzögerung in den synoptischen Evangelien und in der Apostelgeschichte* (Berlin: De Gruyter, 1977, 3rd edn);Kurt Erlemann, *Naherwartung und Parusieverzögerung im Neuen Testament. Ein Beitrag zur Frage religiöser Zeiterfahrung* (Tübingen: Francke, 1995).

2.4ff et al.). Third, one could completely eschew expectation of the Parousia by adopting the Johannine identification of the Parousia with the sending of the Son into the world, which draws this in with the individual death of a believer (John 3.17f, 5.24f).[6]

By comparison, the dogmatic problem of marginalization has consequences that have to be taken seriously. According to Moltmann, this negligence leads to the 'wildly proliferating fantasies surrounding the expectation of the Parousia which we come across in many Christian sects'.[7]

Marginalization thus reflects an ontological problem: if eschatic hope includes the appearance of Christ, it is possible to ask the correct ontological question of *what* then is actually the content of hope, i.e. what kind of degree of reality is the object of hope. This problem will be handled in the dealing with questions about other eschata, but hardly at all in relation to the question of the Parousia itself. It is apparent that one can expect that what is hoped for in the Parousia depends on what decisions are made about fundamental eschatological issues, especially as to how to relate time and eternity as well as space and infinity (see sections 3.1 and 3.2).

A first approach to such problems can often simply consist in attaining terminological clarity. However, in the case of the Parousia, not even this is particularly promising. In both English and German, the discussion mostly centres on the 'return' (*Wiederkehr*) of Christ. But, this is at best misleading, because 'return' can only be used in a meaningful way assuming that Christ was once present and is now absent. In other words, this is seemingly only possible presupposing a strongly Calvinistic Christology, which assumes that, after the ascension, Christ is to be found at the right hand of the Father as a place in space understood as a container, if this term 'return' is to be accepted – if at all.[8] Assuming a Lutheran Christology of unity, Christ is present at present. However, it is also possible to conceive this presence under premises that are not specifically Lutheran, such as if one calls on the *Christus praesens* of Matt. 28.20b ('I am with you always, to the end of the age') or if one is mindful of the fact that the action of the Spirit means nothing other than a realization of Christ. In both English and German, it is also possible to speak not of the 'return' of Christ, but rather of the appearance (*Erscheinen*) or the coming (*Kommen* or *Kunft*) of Christ. All of

[6]Cf. Becker, *Das Urchristentum als gegliederte Epoche*, pp. 97–101.

[7]Jürgen Moltmann, *The Way of Jesus Christ: Christology in Messianic Dimensions* (trans. Margaret Kohl; Minneapolis: Fortress, 1993), p. 313.

[8]This qualification is necessary since according to the Reformed understanding, Christ's divine nature is present in the present, making it incorrect to speak of his 'return'.

these solutions are at least not burdened with the aforementioned problem, but they also fail to resolve it. This is due to the fact that it is clear that various forms of the presence of Christ in the world can be conceived and are also real, so that it is not only necessary to name the status of the reality of the Parousia, but also the distinction between the status of the reality of the Parousia and other forms of the presence of Christ.

However, before we become occupied with these basic questions, it is necessary to give a brief historical overview of the topic.

The notion of the Parousia of Christ, which is preferable to the usual English and German expressions of Christ's 'return' (*Wiederkehr*), appears in an extremely limited manner in the modern theology compared to its importance for biblical exegesis and its central place in the New Testament. This betrays a functionalization that divorces the Parousia from the person of Christ by putting nearly exclusive emphasis on its effects, similar to the ever-persistent ontological problem about what kind of reality the Parousia actually concerns.

5.1.2 Biblical conceptions of the Parousia

The Parousia of Christ in the New Testament draws upon ideas taken from throughout the early Jewish horizon of expectations, i.e. from ideas extending from the Old Testament as much from Hellenistic thinking. Consequently, it is necessary to mention at least the most important of these motifs.

One significant background motif for the Parousia stems from the Old Testament prophets: the notion of the *yom Yahweh* or the 'Day of Yahweh'.

Early prophecy appearing in the book of Amos appears to assume that the Day of Yahweh was known to the people of Israel as a future event to be awaited positively, possibly including the expectation that Yahweh himself would lead his people to military victory. Amos, however, proclaimed the Day of Yahweh to be the day of God's wrathful judgement over Israel in which any and all attempts to flee would be doomed to failure.[9] In

[9]Cf. Amos 5.18–20: 'Alas for you who desire the day of the LORD! Why do you want the day of the LORD? It is darkness, not light; as if someone fled from a lion, and was met by a bear; or went into the house and rested a hand against the wall and was bitten by a snake. Is not the day of the LORD darkness, not light, and gloom with no brightness in it?'

Zeph. 1.7, 14–18, it is a judgement of total annihilation that no one can escape. According to Is. 2.12–17, it is a day of equality that is to even out all differences and make the high to be low. In contrast to Amos, the judgement of the Day of Yahweh in Is. 13.9 only concerns sinners. This day is also broadly construed in Joel 2.1–12 as one of fearful judgement, whereas in Joel 4.14–15 a cosmic and social expansion takes place in which the judgement of all nations and nature has been drawn in. The following context of Joel 4.16–17 makes clear that the people of Israel will survive and will reside in a purified Jerusalem.[10]

The New Testament takes up this tradition. Since in the Greek version of the Old Testament, the Septuagint, Yahweh is translated as Lord (*kurios*), there is no problem transferring the notion of 'the Day of Yahweh' to 'the day of the Lord' as the day of the Parousia of Christ. According to 1 Thess. 5.11, the Day of the Lord is to come as a surprise, like a thief in the night: Christians and children of the light will make it through this, but Paul then still uses the passage for exhortation about 'spiritual armour' (1 Thess. 5.8). The Day of the Lord is taken up in Matt. 24.42–44, 2 Pet. 3.10 and Rev. 3.3, 16.15, especially with regard to the moment of surprise about the Lord's entry. The first Christians could also interpret the hope of the arrival of their Lord with the Old Testament image of the Day of the Yahweh as one of wrathful judgement. The surprising entrance was now bound up with conception of a judgement, but now became hopeful.

The idea of the coming of the 'Son of Man' emerged earlier out of the Apocalyptic literature.

The Son of Man appears in Dan 7.13f, 1 Enoch 37–71, 2 Enoch 25.16 and 4 Esdras 13.3. In Dan 7.13–14 it runs: 'As I watched in the night visions, I saw one like a human being coming with the clouds of heaven. And he came to the Ancient One and was presented before him. To him was given dominion and glory and kingship, that all peoples, nations, and languages should serve him. His dominion is an everlasting dominion that shall not pass away, and his kingship is one that shall never be destroyed.' A form of Messianic expectation, already partially mixed in with this passage, is bound up with the idea of the Son of Man at this point.

In the New Testament synoptic Gospels, 'Son of Man' is widespread and used in over 80 instances, frequently in the mouth of Jesus as a statement

[10]Cf. Jörg Jeremias, 'Der "Tag Jahwes" in Jes 13 und Joel 2', in Reinhard Gregor Kratz, Thomas Krüger and Konrad Schmid (eds), *Festschrift für Odil Hannes Steck* (Beihefte zur Zeitschrift für die alttestamentliche Wissenschaft 300; Berlin: De Gruyter, 2000), pp. 129–38.

about himself. Since, however, there are actually no direct expressions of self-identification among these ('I am the Son of Man'), it is suggested that Jesus could have expected a future Son of Man different from himself to be ruler of the end times. But, this would mean taking the words of the suffering Son of Man as being secondary formulations of the early Christian community – which is certainly not the most likely solution.[11] These historical questions cannot be conclusively resolved here, though this is also not important for our present purposes, since what is crucial at this point is that the community can express its hope in the Parousia of Christ with motif of the Son of Man that was quickly bound up together with the idea of the coming of a Messiah, a future ruler of the end times, who would bring a time of salvation with him. However, the tradition of Messianic expectation is so broad that it is not possible for us to go any further into it at this point.[12]

What is certain is that the expectation of the Parousia belongs to the oldest New Testament witnesses and was anchored fast in the *praxis pietatis* of the time. The only Aramaic call to prayer in the New Testament that has come down to us, the *marana-tha* ('Our Lord, come') in 1 Cor. 16.22 and Rev. 22.20, makes clear that the Parousia was nothing to fear, but something on which one was to hope and for whose quick arrival one was to pray.

However, if we are to ask how early Christianity conceived the Parousia of the Lord, then we inevitably bump up against material that can only be understood on the basis of familiarity with Greek concepts.

The Greek term *parousia* is a technical term for the advent or arrival of a God or ruler who had previously been absent. This arrival was patterned according to a definite ritual in which an escort came to meet the ruler and accompany him along the way.[13]

Among the numerous New Testament attestations that describe the Parousia itself,[14] two stand out in particular: one from Paul and the other from the synoptic tradition.

---

[11]On the historical question of the Son of Man, cf. Delbert Royce Burkett, *The Son of Man Debate: A History and Evaluation* (Cambridge: Cambridge, 1999); Ulrich B. Müller, 'Parusie und Menschensohn', *Zeitschrift für die Neutestamentliche Wissenschaft* 92 (2001), pp. 1–19.

[12]On the connection between the ideas of the Son of Man and the messiah, cf. Becker, *Urchristentum*, p. 60.

[13]Cf. Christoph Auffarth, 'Parousia I. Classic Antiquity', in *RPP*, vol. 9, p. 555.

[14]Cf. 1.Thess. 4.13–18, 5.1–11, 5.23; 1 Cor. 1.7, 15.23–28, 16.22; 2 Thess. 2.2–8; 1 Pet. 1.7; 2 Pet. 1.16; 1 Jn 2.28; Jas 5.7; Mk 1, 14.62; Matt. 10.23, 24–25; Lk. 21; Rev. 1.7, 6, 8f., 16, 19.11–16, 22.20; and many others.

According to 1 Thess. 4.13–18, Christ will come down from heaven through the air with a battle cry, the trumpet's blow and the voice of the angel, the dead will rise and together with the living will rise through the air to the Lord, to meet and escort him according to the pattern of the ritual. Interestingly, judgement plays no role at this point, whereas the eschatical reality itself is given as the goal of the Parousia and is understood as being personally together with Christ in eternity. 1 Thess. 5.1–11 comprises indications of the surprising and sudden entrance of the final judgement bound together with ethical exhortation. In 1 Cor. 15 Paul takes up these conceptions and partially modifies them, but no longer describing the Parousia of the Lord.

According to Mark 13.24–27, after the stars have fallen from heaven, the Son of Man will descend from the clouds of heaven in 'power and glory' and send out his angels to gather those who belong to him, whereas Mark 13.32–37 emphasizes the fact that this Last Day will come as a surprise and is unpredictable (even the Son does not know!), thus concluding with a parenetic section. Matt. 24.27 indicates that the Parousia will occur suddenly but also universally on such a scale, like a lightning flash running across the sky, that any other prior announcement of the Parousia would not only be superfluous, but also a direct proof of its own falsity (Matt. 24.23).

The New Testament conception of the Parousia takes up traditional elements from the 'Day of Yahweh' as day of judgement from the Old Testament tradition, the notion of the coming of the Son of Man from early Jewish traditions and the arrival of a ruler from the Hellenistic tradition and correlates them to Christian hope in the future appearance of Christ. According to the New Testament witness, it will occur suddenly, usher in final judgement and, in Paul's understanding, will make it possible for the faithful to be with their Lord forever. The Parousia of Christ formed a central component of early Christian faith and practice, as exemplified in the Aramaic call to prayer, *marana-tha* (*Our Lord, come!*).

5.1.3 Parousia in the tradition

If we compare present-day reluctance about the Parousia with the concreteness of its imagery and its overall biblical significance, it is not possible to avoid diagnosing the presence of a lacuna. In light of this gap, the question arises of how the broader, post-biblical tradition has dealt with the Parousia. There are naturally a wide variety of conceptions that cannot easily be ordered because they depend on countless other preliminary decisions about fundamental eschatology, so that a systematic typology of various doctrines of the Parousia would be extremely complicated.

The early church and the medieval Christianity did not generally distinguish between the occurrence of the Parousia of Christ and the signs that are to indicate it (see the excursus in section 4.3), i.e. there was no categorical distinction between the eschata and the pre-eschata. This can likely be attributed to an attempt to keep to the biblical material. In part, however, there was an attempt to draw conclusions about the appearance of Jesus Christ at the judgement in glory from the specification of the function of his Parousia. Thus, there was a broad debate in the Middle Ages over how Christ would appear to those being judged: in the form of a servant, or in glory, or whether he would appear to the rejected in the same way as to the saved, i.e. whether or not the rejected can also see his glory as this would seem to constitute an unjustified reward etc.[15]

In order to simplify the presentation somewhat, we can group what follows into three positions: first, positions advocating a non-historical understanding of the Parousia that also takes leave from a temporal and inner-historical conception of the final judgement in not connecting the Parousia to either time or eternity; second, those conceptions that keep to a supra-historical conception of the Parousia in some form and therefore simultaneously in relation to history, and third, positions holding to a historical meaning of the Parousia in one form or another. In order to be able to disencumber the presentation and quickly move from the stage of identifying problems bound up with the Parousia to the point where we can work on solutions for them, we shall limit ourselves in what follows to the nineteenth and twentieth centuries.

5.1.3.1 Ahistorical versions of the Parousia

It could be Paul Tillich (d. 1965) who pushed the dehistoricization of the notion of the Parousia the furthest and thus an atemporal understanding of the Parousia, forgoing the usage of temporal concepts altogether. For Tillich, the Parousia belongs to symbolic speech. This is not, however, meant to devalue the theme, because apart from the designation 'being itself', one

---

[15]Cf. Ott, *Eschatologie in der Scholastik*, pp. 48, 144–50.

can only speak symbolically about God. According to Tillich, a symbol is to be distinguished from what it signifies, though it is also understood to participate in its being.[16] Since symbolic speech cannot therefore be confused with verbal speech, it is then necessary to balance it out through polar speech. If one speaks about God as the living one, then this contains the fact that the symbol of the individuality or personality of God has to be counterbalanced by the participation of God in all being and vice versa. The polar symbol of participation is therefore, according to Tillich, connected to the Parousia:

> Certainly such statements ... have the unfortunate logical implication that there is something alongside God in which he participates from the outside. But the divine participation creates that in which it participates. Plato uses the word Parousia for the presence of the essences in temporal existence. This word later becomes the name for the preliminary and final presence of the transcendent Christ in the church and in the world. *Par-ousia* means 'being-by', 'being with' – but on the basis of being absent, of being separated. In the same way God's participation is not a spatial or a temporal presence. It is meant not categorically but symbolically. It is the parousia, the 'being with' of that which is neither here nor there. If applied to God, participation and community are not less symbolic than individualization and personality. While active religious communication between God and man depends on the symbol of the personal God, the symbol of universal participation expresses the passive experience of the divine parousia in terms of the divine omnipresence.[17]

Tillich does not primarily connect the doctrine of the Parousia to Christ but rather to the doctrine of God. Nevertheless, there is still a Christological impulse in this move because Tillich points out the fact that the 'being-with' is significant against the backdrop of being-separated, which is concrete human being in alienated existence, or sin. However, under the condition of existence in Jesus as the Christ as the New Being, this is overcome and it is in this sense, according to Tillich, that speaking of the Parousia is also correct:

> According to eschatological symbolism, the Christ is the one who brings the new eon. When Peter called Jesus "the Christ", he expected the coming of a new state of things through him .... But it was not fulfilled in accordance with the expectation of the disciples. The state of things ... remained

[16]Cf. Paul Tillich, *Symbol und Wirklichkeit* (Göttingen: Vandenhoeck & Ruprecht, 1962).
[17]Tillich, *Systematic Theology I*, p. 245.

> unchanged.... One approach to the solution of the problem was to state the distinction between the first and the second coming of the Christ. The new state of things will be created with the second coming, the return of the Christ in glory. In the period between the first and second coming the New Being is present in him. He *is* the Kingdom of God.... In terms of the eschatological symbolism it can also be said that Christ is the end of existence. He is the end of existence lived in estrangements, conflicts and self-destruction.... This oscillation between "already" and "not yet" is the experience which is symbolized in the tension between the first and second comings of Christ; it belongs inseparably to the Christian existence.[18]

Tillich not only connects the Parousia to the notion of the omnipotence of God, but also to the fact that human existence – even where it has been healed and is no longer alienated and 'essentified' – always stands in a fundamental tension that cannot be eliminated. For Tillich, then, the Parousia can only be meaningfully discussed in terms of a first and a second Parousia, where the second Parousia cannot be understood in isolation from the first. In the course of the history of theology, there are a number of theories of multiple parousias of Christ (see below), although this does not always mean the same thing. In Tillich's case, the first Parousia simply refers to the historical appearance of the New Being in Jesus as the Christ, i.e. what is traditionally referred to as the incarnation. The second Parousia refers to the being of Christ as *simul justus et peccator*, i.e. the tension of Christian life on the one hand as alienated being that is bound in its existence and to sin on the one hand, whereas on the other, it is healed and capable of participation in the New Being. This essentially means that Tillich has removed the notion of the Parousia from eschatology and transferred it to the doctrines of God and reconciliation, though this is also proven by the fact that a doctrine of the Parousia is not to be found in his eschatology.

In his atemporal understanding of the Parousia, Tillich relates the notion of the Parousia to God's being with created being, thereby approximating to the notion of God's omnipresence, but it does have its christological specificity in the fact that it deals with the presence of the unalienated being under the conditions of alienation. This clarifies the fact that even redeemed humans are always *simul justus et peccator*.

[18]Tillich, *Systematic Theology II*, pp. 118–20.

5.1.3.2 Trans-historical versions of the Parousia

One twentieth-century theologian exemplifying this view is Paul Althaus (d. 1966). The Parousia is an event that can be explained against the backdrop of the second model of time and eternity – the Boethian model – of eternity as absolute simultaneity to all times: the Parousia is not historical, but equally near to all times. Astonishingly, for Althaus, the problem of the Parousia cannot be distinguished from the problem of the Millennium.

> Furthermore ... accepting the Parousia is ... a self-contradiction .... Everyone experiences the Parousia; its supra-temporal character is proven by the fact that history is only the location of particular revelation. What is the meaning of accepting the 1000 year reign as an interim epoch? .... It does not have a basis with any religious or theological weight .... As a supra-temporal event the Parousia is equally close to every generation and will not be prepared by one end age in particular, but in every age .... It is with total seriousness that we are keeping ... to the expectation of a Parousia even if we regard it as a supra-temporal event instead of a temporal one. The simple mind tends to locate it at the end of history – actually it really means the sublation (*Aufhebung*) of all history, and this form of the idea is credible as long as at the same time it is held that every time stands in an immediate relation to the Parousia. The Parousia does not in any way lead to the dissipation of our certainty that in death all of us will be consecutively placed before God and come to Jesus. On the contrary, it is a universal fact, a common and simultaneous experience that everyone has .... Everything vertical that we erect along the line of time to bump up against eternity, the Parousia, meets the consummation at one point in the supra-temporality .... We can say: the Fathers are already with Christ, have experienced the Parousia and judgement, we will experience the Parousia and after us the other generations up to the final one – but in this we are only expressing a supra-temporal simultaneity from our standpoint. This corresponds completely to God's relationship to time.[19]

It is at this point that Althaus explicitly develops a necessary clarification about the placement of the notion of the Parousia in relation to the temporality of the world, one which we found to be missing in Tillich's thought. For Althaus, the Parousia cannot be discussed within the same framework as eternity, because the Parousia concerns the *coming* of Christ, but the Boethian model for time and eternity Althaus is using at this point is not explicitly bound to Christian thinking. The specific difference between the two is clear at this point:

---

[19]Althaus, *Die letzten Dinge*, pp. 95–8.

> The Parousia consists in the fact that God's self-disclosure in Christ, which has passed through history to this point as a kind of reality that entreats us, is now a kind of reality that brings about conviction for everyone. After everything we have said so far we cannot like many theologians speak of a 'sensory', 'visible' phenomenon for 'this visible world' – that the Parousia is unthinkable as a historical act has long since become clear –, but this expression is correct in that it is meant to distinguish sharply the supra-historical revelation of Jesus from the historical, inner kind of revelation that is meant to attract us in the Word through the Spirit.[20]

With this distinction between a historical, *entreating* revelation of Christ and a *convicting* revelation, Althaus does make progress beyond Tillich's concept of the Parousia because it is no longer simply a matter of fixing the experience of *simul justus et peccator*. Althaus has therefore penetrated into regions that – by adopting the Boethian model of time and eternity – indeed make it possible to envisage the particular status of the presence of Christ in the Parousia.

The model developed by Althaus is not however without its problems: to the extent that the Parousia and eternity are conceptually paralleled, everything that applies to eternity will also apply to the Parousia. Consequently, if the Parousia does not take place in history but is understood to be a supra-historical *event*, the structure of the ordered relation that makes events possible as such now has to come into play. This, however, is explicitly excluded in the Boethian model of eternity. A further issue consists in the fact that in both Althaus and Tillich, the problem of the fuctionalization of the Parousia or the person of Christ that was diagnosed at the beginning of the chapter once again appears: the meaning of the Parousia for the person of Christ never actually comes into question. The only important thing is its function in that this convicting revelation leads to understanding of the judgement. Althaus is certainly not the only one who presents a supra-historical understanding of the Parousia but rather is representative of a broad range of similar conceptions. In this regard, we could mention both Rudolf Bultmann and the earlier Karl Barth.

By means of another set of philosophical tools, but to the same effect, Rudolf Bultmann (d. 1976) sought to modernize the Parousia by indicating that 'the future Kingdom of God . . . is not something which is to come in the course of time . . . . Rather, the Kingdom of God is a power *which, although it is entirely future, wholly determines the present*'.[21]

---

[20] Althaus, *Die letzten Dinge*, p. 99.

[21] Rudolf Bultmann, *Jesus and the Word* (New York: Scribner's, 1934), p. 51.

In the earlier theology of Karl Barth (d. 1968), there is a detemporalization and dehistoricization of the Parousia in that every time is the end time, with every age being immediately before God and the eternal, divine moment standing equally over against all moments in time.[22]

> In terms of a supra-historical understanding, the Parousia of Christ is equally near to every time. This presupposes a Boethian understanding of eternity (see section 3.1). For Paul Althaus, the reality of the Parousia consists in its function as revelation, which differs in comparison to historical revelation in that it is not merely a form of revelation that entreats us but is rather revelation that brings about conviction.

5.1.3.3 Historical versions of the Parousia

5.1.3.3.1 Multiple parousias?

One can occasionally find in the history of theology the view that there are multiple parousias, for example in Ignatius (d. 110) and Justin (d. 167).[23] In this case, there is often emphasis on either a historical, a history concluding or a strongly temporal but post-historical Parousia.

The most elaborate form of a doctrine of multiple parousias can be found in the theology of Isaak August Dorner (d. 1844), who rightly identified the doctrine of the Parousia as the central point of the entirety of Christian eschatology and as a necessary element in the Christian understanding of reconciliation.[24] On the one hand, Dorner uses the expression Parousia in terms of a sense of Christ's presence, but on the other in terms of Christ's Second Coming, thus distinguishing between two different parousias. The first Parousia as the presence of Christ is, according to Dorner,

---

[22]Barth, *Epistle of the Romans*, p. 498.

[23]Cf. Thomas D. Lea, 'A Survey of the Doctrine of the Return of Christ in the Ante-Nicene Fathers', *Journal of the Evangelical Theological Society* 29.2 (1986), pp. 163–77.

[24]See Dorner, *The Future State*, p. 63 (§152.1): 'Individuals, as well as the Church and the kingdom of God, await their consummation from the second coming of Christ, which forms the centre of the whole eschatology of the New Testament, and serves not only for the overcoming of all hostile powers, but also for the realization of the idea both of the individual and the Whole. This second coming is not made dispensable or superfluous by any previous development of the individual and the Whole in this world or the next, since it alone brings the complete conquest of sin and death – to the individual in the resurrection, and to the Whole by the transfiguration of the world, by the exclusion of evil, and the consummation of the church of God'; cf. Dorner, *The Future State*, p. 65.

> in part invisible, but always as real – the former, when he says: 'Where two or three are gathered, there am I in the midst of them;' .... The whole doctrine of his word and the means of grace is only understood in its real divine-human import when these means of grace are regarded as the outward media, through which, in virtue of his heavenly, regal office, he efficaciously continues his presence with believers. But he also promised his *visible* second advent. Here come in his reappearances after his resurrection, which as a fulfilment of his prediction, on the one hand, seal the certainty of his enduring visible communion with them, and on the other were to be a real foretype of his visible, universally discernible, second coming at the judgement and consummation of the world.[25]

The first Parousia is therefore partially visible, partially invisible and relates to Christ's appearance at Easter and the *Christus praesens*, but not, as in Tillich, to the incarnation itself. The first Parousia relates to the second in the sense of preparation but is itself indeed real.[26] The balanced mutual relatedness of the first and second Parousia of Christ is important on soteriological grounds and, when this is not observed, can lead to serious heresies, which according to Dorner can be reconstructed as polar opposites of the correct version:

> In respect to the earthly history of Christianity... two opposite modes of thought present themselves. The one thinks the chief thing is still wanting ever after Christ's manifestation, salvation being a matter first of the world, eternal life not a present reality. This undervaluing of Christ's first manifestation, of the worth of the atonement, and the gift of the Holy Spirit, is a false doctrine of the future of the world (Jeseitigkeitslehre) or Ebionitic eschatology. To it approximates the Romish doctrine in relation to individuals, so far as it does not properly admit an assurance of salvation in the temporal life.... Conversely, faith and the inner possession of eternal life in this world may be so emphasized in a spiritualistic manner, and with indifference to the confirmation of the whole, as though nothing further were needed.... Hence the evangelical eschatology maintains the pure Christian character, since it keeps the mean between those two extremes, and, on the basis of God's kingdom having come, preserves the hope of a full coming in visible power in behalf of individuals and the whole.[27]

But, the interconnectedness of the first and second Parousia is not only necessary on soteriological grounds for defence against heresy, but also

---

[25]Dorner, *The Future State*, pp. 66–7 (§152.I).
[26]Cf. Dorner, *The Future State*, p. 67 (§152.I).
[27]Dorner, *The Future State*, pp. 82–4 (§152.III).

on the basis of salvation itself: salvation consists in the healed personal relationship of the faithful to Christ, which is to be understood in the sense of a loving relation or 'personal inter-communion with Christ'. The first Parousia and its idiom (Eucharist etc.) effects human desire to be visibly and really together with him. But, on the other hand, what applies for Christ: 'For it is also his loving desire to be seen, and by this means share his glory with them .... It is an essential trait of Christian piety not to imagine blessedness by itself outside communion with Christ.'[28]

Dorner attempts to ground the doctrine of the twofold Parousia on notions extending from the doctrines of the person and work of Christ, which ought to be conceived in concert with the resurrection, the appropriation of Christ's reconciling work and the Spirit's 'presencing' of Christ as well as the eschatic Parousia including its meaning for Christ himself. For the moment, we will defer any estimation about the extent to which this can be judged successful.

Karl Barth (d. 1968), without referring to Dorner, appears to adopt his predecessor's doctrine of the twofold Parousia of Christ materially but rebrands it in speaking of a threefold Parousia conceived in direct analogy to the doctrine of the Trinity: The first Parousia is the appearance of the Lord at Easter, the second Parousia the presence of Christ through the Holy Spirit in the church and the third Parousia is that to occur in the eschatical reality. Barth divides Dorner's doctrine of the first Parousia into two resulting in the three in total. Similar to the doctrine of the Trinity, the three elements have to be distinguished from one another in one way, but not in another and instead be understood as related in a perichoretic sense: all three belong together and are 'forms of the one and same event'.[29] Their unity consists in the fact that the Easter event is not only constitutive of the end time but is also the first eschatological event, the communication of the Holy Spirit and the eschatic coming of Christ, so that: 'The happening of the parousia is thus eschatological throughout its course.'[30] The particularity of the third Parousia must remain open, however, since in the aforementioned context Barth is occupied with the first Parousia as Easter, and the other passages that mention the Parousia do not shed any further light on this question. Within the *Church Dogmatics* as a whole, Barth's conception of the threefold Parousia is of primary significance in that it assigns an eschatical meaning

[28]Dorner, *The Future State*, p. 88 (§152.III).
[29]Barth, *Church Dogmatics IV/3.1: The Doctrine of Reconciliation* (trans. Geoffrey Bromiley; London: T&T Clark, 2004), p. 294.
[30]Barth, *Church Dogmatics IV/3.1*, p. 296.

to the Easter event in that the 'first' Parousia is to be clarified by means of the 'third' Parousia, though the meaning of latter remains unclear.

The *particular veri* of a doctrine of multiple parousias, regardless in which form, is that it concerns the unity of several actual events. Wolfhart Pannenberg brings this clearly to expression. He also advocates what one could call a threefold Parousia but nonetheless avoids this expression itself by speaking of the fact that incarnation, resurrection and return[31] together form the unity of a single differentiated event, so that the truth of the incarnation is first visible only from the perspective of Easter, but that contentiousness over Christian claims about Easter only then cease with the return of Christ.[32] This not only emphasizes the necessary interconnectivity of the events, but also the specific difference of the Parousia of Christ: it is the form of the presence of Christ in such a way that there can no longer be any contention about his presence. This can be seen to parallel the discussion by Althaus about convicting revelation (see above). Pannenberg, however, goes a step further in suggesting that the return of Christ is to be understood not as the 'appearing of a single individual', but of the 'making manifest of a vital nexus originating in the crucified Jesus of Nazareth in the light of the glory of God'.[33] This vital nexus consists in the fact that Pannenberg rightly takes Paul's discussion of the body of Christ explicitly and not only symbolically:

> The community is linked to Christ in the unity of the *one* body, of *his* body .... But if we take what Paul says about the church as the body of Christ just as it stands, it follows that we must understand the new life of the resurrection, the life of the risen Christ, as a removal of the individual autonomy and separation that are part of the corporeality of earthly life, though with no simple erasure of individual particularity.[34]

The Parousia of Christ is therefore an event that is also of immediate significance for the creation, and the event of the Parousia of Christ binds collective eschatic hope – represented by the notion of the Kingdom of God – and individual eschatic hope – represented by the notion of the resurrection of the dead – into one event.[35] As a result, humans become in the Parousia

---

[31]Pannenberg deals with the notion of the threefold character of the Parousia differently than Barth in not counting the action of the Holy Spirit which makes Christ present as part of the Parousia, but rather, more similar to Tillich than to Barth at this point, to the incarnation.

[32]Cf. Pannenberg, *Systematic Theology III*, p. 627.

[33]Pannenberg, *Systematic Theology III*, p. 630.

[34]Pannenberg, *Systematic Theology III*, pp. 628–9.

[35]Cf. Pannenberg, *Systematic Theology III*, pp. 627–8.

of Christ precisely what they are anthropologically: particular becomings in perfected relations of love, so that the Parousia can also be seen as the fulfilment of the world.

Historical versions of the Parousia of Christ concern an event of the presence of Christ in or at the end of history that must be interpreted in terms of its connection and distinction from other forms of the presence of Christ. They can occasionally also be expressed in terms of multiple parousias. For Dorner, these are the presence of Christ in the Easter witnesses and in the Eucharist as the first Parousia and the eschatic Parousia as the second. Barth divided Dorner's first Parousia into two parts. Neither recognizes the incarnation as a form of the Parousia. Pannenberg views the interconnection between the incarnation, life and eschatic appearance of Jesus as a reciprocally self-interpreting event.

5.1.3.3.2 Cyclical Parousia?

Jürgen Moltmann belongs among the few recent theologians who have attempted a conceptual clarification of the Parousia. A roughly thirty-page treatment of the Parousia forms the conclusion to Moltmann's christology.[36] To begin, Moltmann's doctrine of the Parousia turns on what it delimits. Whereas he does not take into account any entirely atemporal understandings of the Parousia as exemplified by Tillich, Moltmann does critique both supra-historical and historical understandings of the Parousia. The problem with supra-historical understandings of the Parousia consists in the fact that this type 'puts an end to all the real and futurist expectation of the Parousia which echoes in the early Christian "maranatha – come soon!", and transforms eschatology into mysticism. "I myself am eternity when I forsake time and gather myself together in God and He in me", wrote Angelus Silesius'.[37] The problem of the historical understanding of the Parousia as found in Karl Barth's doctrine of the threefold Parousia consists in the fact that the structure of temporality is transferred directly to the eschatical reality.[38] Moltmann now believes himself able to speak of both the Parousia and eternity by having found a further possibility beyond these

[36]Cf. Moltmann, *The Way of Jesus Christ*, pp. 313–41.
[37]Moltmann, *The Way of Jesus Christ*, p. 318.
[38]Cf. Moltmann, *The Way of Jesus Christ*, p. 318.

two types and beyond any abstract atemporality. The Parousia, according to Moltmann, occurs in 'aeonic time':

> 'Aeon' is not the absolute eternity of God. It is the relative eternity of those he has created who partake of his eternal being, first of all the angels in heaven .... It is part of the nature of created time to be experienced by way of irreversible changes. In the 'before' and the 'after', future and past become distinguishable .... But the movement from which aeonic time, or relative eternity, is perceived is different: this movement is circular .... Heaven is the sphere of creation which already totally corresponds to God because it is totally pervaded by his glory .... What the son of man brings to earth therefore has its archetype and beginning in heaven .... The time of heaven is different from the earthly time of transience, since it is the cyclical time of the aeon.[39]

At this point we can set aside the question of whether his discussion of cyclical, circular time and therefore the idea of a constant repetition of events stands beyond the two models of the Parousia that Moltmann critiques. What is most problematic is that in using the notion of cyclical time, the complementary structures of both eternity and time as ordered relations which make relationality, particularity and eventfulness possible have to be nullified. What Moltmann takes from both models of the Parousia and his claim to have justification for a new type of aeonic time concerns only the Parousia's relation to time and eternity but does not yet reckon with the question of what actually occurs in the Parousia. In order to answer this important question, Moltmann draws on his doctrine of creation. There, touching on Isaac Luria's (d. 1572) idea of Zim-Zum – i.e. the notion of creation as a self-limitation of God – Moltmann suggested that God limited God's own omnipotence and made room for the creation. As a result, time itself came about along with creation. For Moltmann, the Parousia and the final judgement are the reverse of this process:

> If we transfer these conceptual possibilities to 'the end of the world', we can then say that the world does not end *in time* (so that there continues to be time afterwards) but that it ends *together with* time, time ending with the world .... In both cases it would seem helpful to differentiate between the *primordial moment* and the *moment of inception*, and also between the *last* and the *eschatological* moment .... The *eschatological* moment corresponds to the *primordial* moment. It is to be found in God's own ending of his self-restriction. God de-restricts himself and manifests his glory so that in the transfigured creation he may be 'all in all'. Created time ends and 'the time

[39]Moltmann, *The Way of Jesus Christ*, pp. 330–3.

> of creation' passes away. The created spaces will be dissolved and 'the space of creation' passes away. Heaven and earth find their final, transfigured form in God's unrestricted omnipresence itself. The original divine self-limitation which made the time and space of creation possible gives away to God's all-embracing, all pervading derestriction of himself.... The eschatological moment, then, has these two sides: God derestricts his glory, and creation enters into the kingdom of glory.[40]

The advantage of this consists in the fact that Moltmann was one of the few who did not totally disregard the question of the final judgement, i.e. the question of the transition from the pre-eschatic to the eschatic reality and indeed attempted to answer it. The disadvantage comes in that – although it is actually an issue arising in his doctrine of the Parousia at the end of his christology, Christ astonishingly only appears to be functional. A further disadvantage consists in the fact that Moltmann's doctrine of the Parousia is dependent on *his* doctrine of creation: in order to adopt his understanding of the Parousia, it is also necessary to adopt his doctrine of creation as well. Moltmann's understanding of the Parousia appears to raise more questions than it can answer. In any case, Moltmann has provided a great service by having posed these questions.

In order to escape the aporia of historical understandings of the Parousia that consist in the fact that the end of history itself cannot be a historical event, Moltmann attempts to develop a *cyclical* understanding of the Parousia grounded in the notion of cyclical or aeonic time and reverses the movement of creation understood as the self-limitation of God in the form of a re-expansion.

5.1.4. The eschatical assembly with the Lord

The Parousia is about the presence of Christ. However, not all conceptions of the presence of Christ are the same. The Christian tradition has employed at least five:

- the presence of the logos of creation in the world since creation
- the incarnation of the logos of creation in Jesus Christ

[40] Moltmann, *The Way of Jesus Christ*, pp. 328–9.

- the presence of Christ at Easter
- the presence of Christ now in the Spirit
- the return of Christ at the final judgement

Normally, the Parousia refers to the final form of the presence of Christ given above, nevertheless the various attempts to talk about multiple parousias of Christ appear to be variations on a single theme. In the tradition, the first form of Christ's presence as the logos of creation has not rightly been designated to be a form of the Parousia, because it does not concern the presence of the incarnate logos that took on a human nature in Jesus Christ. The third and fourth forms of the presence of Christ, i.e. the Easter appearances and the presence of Christ in the Spirit, were rightly considered by Dorner to be one form. It is not only exegetical findings that show that the outpouring of the Spirit and the accounts of Easter are of the same source historically.[41] Systematic clarification also demonstrates that certainty about the resurrection of Christ and the experience of Easter are to be ascribed to the work of the Spirit (see above). This allows us to produce a christological interrelationship between the following aspects:

- the presence of the logos of creation
- the incarnation
- the resurrection of Christ and the presence of Christ in the Spirit
- the return of Christ on judgement day

Given the background rendered by our fundamental eschatological decisions (see Chapters 2 and 3), descriptions of the first three kinds of presence are not difficult.

As eternal logos and second person of the Trinity, the Son is related to creation as a whole, but in an unmediated way only to the Father and the Spirit. The incarnation is a change in perspective for the Son, and he enters into the concrete spatio-temporal structure of creation and is concretely and spatio-temporally individuated and identifiable in Jesus Christ. With his resurrection and presence in the Spirit, it is clear that the entirety of humanity now belongs permanently to the identity of Christ (in biblical terms: to the body of Christ) and is therefore also incorporated in God's Trinitarian being by grace. The Parousia of Christ now means the immediate presence of the person of Christ for every creaturely person, which is only possible under the condition that the creation – in a movement opposite

[41]Cf. Becker, *Urchristentum*, pp. 29–38.

to that of the incarnation – will now be incorporated into the Trinitarian framework of individuation. The Parousia also means nothing other than *theosis* by grace. Taken in the strong sense, this means not only an immediate relation to Christ, but also to the Father and the Spirit. Nevertheless, it is still right to speak about the Parousia of Christ, because being in the immediate presence of the three divine persons cannot mean anything other than what has already occurred in the incarnation, resurrection and presence of the Spirit. The incarnation and the resurrection further generate the gospel as the promise of salvation. Salvation in the Christian sense is nothing other than a personal relationship of love to Jesus Christ. The presence of the Spirit now only partially fulfils this *promissio*, because in the reality of salvation, the relationship of love to Christ is to be unmediated, that is, no longer mediated by the presence of the Spirit. This also applies to the relationship between Christ and personal creatures, who place their hope on his immediate presence as the one who they love, but this also implies the immediate presence of all other personal creatures, since they now belong to Christ's identity as a result of the resurrection. With Pannenberg, we also want to point out that despite being in an *unmediated* relationship to Christ, this indeed remains a real relationship and does not mean any kind of dissolution of the creaturely person into Christ. The personal transcendence between the Father, Son and Spirit remains intact.

This also settles the question of whether the Parousia is an ahistorical, supra-historical or a historical event. The Parousia is first and foremost a personal event, namely, our immediate being together with Christ and therefore also the Father and the Spirit. This is nothing other than the eschatical reality itself. We have seen that time and space are not important for the world in and of themselves, but rather only their logical structure as an ordered relation that makes particularity within creation possible as well as its event-like character. It is precisely this structure that shows God's triunity. As a result, the Parousia can be understood as the merging of the creation into the spatio-temporal structure of the event – or into the framework of individuation – that is Godself, that is, the asymmetrical fusion of the worldly and divine frameworks of individuation.

Consequently, we can say on the one hand the Parousia is timeless, because it no longer makes sense to talk about space-time once the Parousia occurs. Expressions that refer to Parousia as the final judgement are therefore not amiss, because this is indeed what the Parousia symbolizes.

On the other hand, however, the Parousia is also a supra-historical event because it means the realization of an immediateness of *all* personal creatures to Christ, regardless of the spatio-temporal location in which it can be found. In this respect, it cannot be a historical or temporal event, precisely because this would exclude universal immediacy. However, this aspect of immediacy can directly be expressed by means of temporal metaphors to the extent that what is being said is that the Parousia can occur like a thief in the night, suddenly and apparently unexpectedly, at any time. Yet, the Christian knows that the Parousia is not unexpected at all and rather hopes for it with longing.

Ultimately, however, the view that the Parousia is a historical event is also not incorrect, since the structure of the sequence of events is not abolished by the Parousia but is rather newly ordered, directed and transformed.

These statements directly bear out the idea that the Parousia will occur through death and resurrection[42] for every created person independent of their spatio-temporal location, and the 'beloved final judgement' (Luther) will be experienced. Nevertheless, the Parousia is not a purely personal event that occurs between individual human beings and the Son, Father and Holy Spirit, but is also a social and cosmic event. This follows necessarily from the notion of the Parousia as a social event, because the immediacy applies equally to all persons, so that their relationships among one another are also objects of the Parousia. The Parousia is also a cosmic event because we have assumed that non-personal creation is to share in the eschatical reality in so far as it represents an end in itself for God. As personal creatures, we certainly cannot know in what measure and in what form. To the extent that this does occur, Christ will also be present to the non-personal creation.[43] These cosmic and social aspects of the Parousia can be meaningfully drawn out later in our account of the final judgement.

The new form of personal relationality that enters in with the Parousia can be described in terms of its immediacy along with Althaus as a 'convicting' presence. It is the fact that the Parousia as the immediate presence of Christ is just as real as the presence of Christ, like the real presence of Christ in the Spirit in the here and now in Word and Sacrament, which justifies the notion of the multiple parousias. As Dorner was able to demonstrate, this could rule out certain problematic forms of salvation. We will cover this in greater detail in the section on the ethical implications of the Parousia.

---

[42]So Pannenberg in *Systematic Theology III*, pp. 577–80. This conception also plays a role in Roman Catholic dogmatics; cf. Gisbert Greshake, *Auferstehung der Toten* (Essen: Ludgerus, 1969), p. 387.

[43]This is the *particula veri* of Teilhard de Chardin's notion of the sudden Christogenesis of the entire creation; see section 4.1.

It can be said in summary that the Parousia is ultimately nothing other than the eschatic reality itself with regard to its eventuation. This means that Christ, the second person of the Trinity who became human, enters into an immediate personal relation to all human persons, who by grace enter into an immediate relationship to Father, Son and Spirit (*theosis*). This means that all hope is contained in the hope for the coming of Christ. In this regard, it has to be distinguished from the notion of the Kingdom of God as a designation for the eschatical reality in terms of its fulfilment, as well as from the resurrection of the dead as the final judgement including its outcomes as mediate forms of the realization of the eschatical reality.

5.1.5 Ethical implications

The Parousia is the immediate presence of Christ in the personal filial relationship of love between him and us and therefore, with regard to its constitution, is itself the eschatical reality. As a result, the Parousia has consequences for our action in the here and now:

1. Even at present, personal relationships of love appear exceptional in comparison to both manipulative and mercantile relationships. If in the Parousia every personal creature stands in an immediate loving relationship to Christ, the relationships of persons among one another will also be characterized primarily by their share in this eschatical love. As a result of the present cohesion between the Parousia and the presence of Christ in the Spirit, Christians are accordingly inspired and motivated to perform ethical action in love. This includes a careful distinction: mercantile relationships, or relationships in which the good being exchanged is not essential to the identity of the transaction partner, and manipulative relations in which only one of the partners makes decisions about the identity of both, can both have their provisional justification at present, but they do not have any eschatic relevance. Christians will therefore not hang their hearts on these manipulative and mercantile relationships, regardless of how important they are at present and how much time they command within the totality of our life histories.

2. This applies even more to the fact that the immediacy of the Parousia includes the fact that it comes like a thief in the night. This means that the distinction between what can be experienced of the eschatic and of the past not only drops out, but the believer knows about the possibility of the

instantaneous onset of the Parousia. This instantaneousness as a temporal expression is only a euphemism for the social and cosmic immediacy of the Parousia, but this temporal conception of a possible end of history at any time has nothing theologically and ethically false about it, even if it is only a necessary postulate of the trusting reason.

The first two ethical aspects also come to expression in parenetic material in the New Testament, which generally follows a discussion of the Parousia or the final judgement: the temporal immediacy is expressed and therefore 'wakefulness' is urged, but also 'sobriety' as the capability of the trusting reason to make the right distinctions between what is important, i.e. what is eschatically relevant, from what is unimportant, i.e. what is not eschatically relevant.

3. The Parousia and the presence of Christ in the Spirit both belong together and are distinct from each other. They belong together because both deal with the presence of the person of Christ. They are distinct from each other because only the Parousia is the immediate presence, whereas the presence of Christ in the Spirit is a mediated presence. This leads to the critical exclusion of particular possible attitudes of faith and their ethical implications: the here and now is already determined by the presence of Christ and therefore actually salvation, which is taken on in the assurance of faith and in trust. Contrary to all the pretences of the pre-eschatic world, Rom. 8.38 describes the whole of reality in light of the Parousia: 'For I am convinced that neither death, nor life, nor angels, nor rulers, nor things present, nor things to come, nor powers, nor height, nor depth, nor anything else in all creation will be able to separate us from the love of God in Jesus Christ our Lord.' Also belonging to the proclamation of the gospel is the fact that there is no other proclamation of judgement to be expected with the Parousia, as it occurs through the proclamation of the gospel on the basis of the cross and resurrection. Faith in the Parousia brings about assurance of salvation in the present and therefore free action in accordance with justification, thus excluding the notion of the subjective necessity of both individual and collective forms of self-constitution. Hope for the Parousia is just as much hope on the fact that what is now experienced in a mediated way will then be experienced in an unmediated way, so that there is also space to maintain our understanding of the not-yet aspect of what is now: the Christian is accordingly aware of the fact that there is no expectation of an end to death, suffering and guilt prior to the Parousia. There is therefore no 'enthusiastic' (*schwärmerische*) disposition with regard to the world and there is an exercise of restraint with respect to all implicit attempts to bring about the realization of salvation within history.

4. The liturgical location for reassurance about the Parousia in the life of the faithful is to be found where there is a real presence of Christ, even if it is not the real unmediated presence of Christ but the presence of Christ in the Spirit on the basis of human proclamation of the Word and Sacrament, especially in the presence of Christ in the Eucharist in which the church proclaims Christ 'until he comes'.

In summary we can say that the meaning of hope in the Parousia of Christ as being together with the person of Christ and the Father and the Spirit consists in that those who posses this hope:

- are aware of the permanent distinction between personal relationships of love and mercantile or manipulative relationships and therefore act accordingly;
- know that the graphic description of the suddenness of the Parousia enables the trusting reason of those who possess this hope to the extent that they are gifted with wakefulness (attention) and sobriety (a sense of reality);
- are assured of their salvation because nothing can happen in the Parousia other than what happens in other forms of the presence of Christ, and that they now have cause to undertake free and patient action;
- know that the proclamation of the Word and the community of the sacrament are related to the Parousia, but also different and that they can experience the eschatical reality under provisional conditions of these forms of the presence of Christ.

5.2 The resurrection of the living body

If the connection of the eschata as explained here is correct, then the doctrine of the resurrection of the dead has no eschatological weight: it is a medium for the Parousia and Kingdom of God, which as the form of the constitution and life of the eschatical reality itself are the explicit content of Christian hope. The resurrection of the dead is then only the object of

Christian hope in an indirect sense, at least to the extent that it is necessary for the Parousia and Kingdom of God to be able to come about. The resurrection of the body is more precisely a condition for that continuity that makes it possible for the creaturely person to live through the Parousia. At this point, it has to be distinguished from the notion of the judgement that likewise presents a means for the realization of the eschatical reality, but explicitly emphasizing discontinuity. Since the Christian understanding of resurrection is dependent on the understanding of the Parousia, Christian hope is already judged and corrected: it can indeed take on the general human longing for life beyond death in an unlimited future,[44] but it is no longer identical to this. Likewise, the critical discussion about the resurrection of the dead is, like the other eschata, only meaningful under the eschatic horizon of expectations, not in the horizon of penultimate experience of the world. On the contrary, however, the eschatic horizon of expectations will change and fix the penultimate horizon of the experiences of Christians in the world, so that it is also meaningful to ask about the ethical consequences (see section 5.2.4). This bit of doctrine itself begins with a description of the biblical discussion of the resurrection of the dead and its early tradition (see section 5.2.1), then presenting the tradition of Christian thinking about it by means of a typology (see section 5.2.2). This will show that one type above all has played a prominent role in the history of theology, possessing a great deal of potential both for solving existing problems and creating new ones. Belonging to this among other things are the doctrines of the interim states – resting places between death and resurrection for different kinds of persons, such as Purgatory, the *limbus patrorum* (the interim location of the righteous of the Old Testament) and the *limbus infantium* (the interim location of children who died unbaptized) – that will be dealt with in a separate excursus (see section 5.2.3). This comparison will show the persistence of a specific problem: How is personal continuity between the present and the eschatical reality to be conceived in relation to the resurrection of the living body? A separate section suggests a possible solution (see section 5.2.4) before we characterize the ethical considerations as usual at the end of the section (see section 5.2.5).

---

[44]On the notion of humans as *ex*centric beings open to the word and the future, who demonstrate a hope for life beyond death as an anthropological constant, cf. Wolfhart Pannenberg, *Was ist der Mensch? Die Anthropologie der Gegenwart im Lichte der Theologie* (Göttingen: Vandenhoeck & Ruprecht, 1962), pp. 31–40.

5.2.1 Bodily resurrection in the early Christian tradition

The notion of the resurrection of the dead slowly began to emerge in a few likely later Old Testament passages and in the extra-canonical early Jewish literature. In Dan. 12.2, traces of this notion are perceptible, although only with respect to Israel's dead. In any case, it is a matter of a 'general' resurrection of the dead, that is, a resurrection not dependent on the person's moral worth. 2 Macc. 7.14 and 23 is an extremely important text because it presents a theological ground for the possibility of the resurrection on the basis of God's power as creator. In this case, the resurrection applies either only to martyrs or only to the righteous and is therefore still not a general resurrection. In the apocalyptic tradition, the notion of the resurrection was slowly established, but not to the extent that it attained widespread prevalence. It was only adopted by a few Jewish groups prior to the destruction of the temple (70 BCE).

The idea of the resurrection of the dead did not play a large role in the first generation of the early church, but rather the opposite. It does not appear in either the teaching of John the Baptist or Jesus. The judgement or end-time salvation only concerned the generation alive at the time.[45] Even the earliest forms of Christian proclamation, which always presupposed Jesus' resurrection, did not mention any other kind of resurrection. They expected rather salvation to come in the Parousia of Christ, understood to include the judgement. Paul could therefore also tap into this proclamation and specifically change it, as can be seen in 1 Thess. 1.9f. – a passage where Paul deals with a traditional notion and that also demonstrates the purpose of his mission,without referring back to the resurrection of the dead. On the contrary, the first gentile Christians converted from a multiplicity of gods to the one God, in order to escape God's wrathful judgement by means of the Parousia of the resurrected Christ.[46]

The first hint of the resurrection of the dead positively understood can be found in 1 Thess. 4.13–18. Apparently, as members of the Christian community had begun to die, the question had arisen about whether and in what way they would be able to share in the expected salvation of the Parousia. Paul responded to this with the 'word of the Lord'. Whether

---

[45]Cf. Jürgen Becker, *Auferstehung der Toten im Urchristentum* (Stuttgart: Katholisches Bibelwerk, 1976), pp. 11–13.
[46]Cf. Becker, *Auferstehung der Toten*, pp. 32–45.

this actually meant something said by the so-called historical Jesus or the resurrected Lord does not play any role for us at this point. Under all circumstances, this is indicative of an existing tradition, that is, Paul is referring them back to something they already knew. This makes our reconstruction of the earliest tradition no longer very difficult: it relates to the statements of 1 Thess. 4.15–17 that only deal with the Parousia, but not with the general resurrection of the dead.[47] Paul now reaches his solution by associating the saving event of the Parousia with the problem of the death of Christian brothers and sisters: the dead will arise before the Parousia and then go to meet the Lord along with the living. Paul is not particularly interested at this point about the details of the resurrection, its cause or its possibility. It is therefore possible to suggest that the resurrection is understood by Paul in terms of what we have called a pre-eschatical event: in order to resolve the problem about the death of individuals in the community, Paul suggests they will quite simply be revived and will be preserved in life (1 Thess. 4.17) until the Parousia including himself and those in the community to whom he is writing, when they are to meet the Lord together. Paul's argumentation here is quite simple and evidently born out of need: the fact that members of the community would die before the Parousia had not previously been considered. As this did begin to happen, it was apparently no major problem for Paul to suppose an earthly revival. If we also do not know why this was not a problem for him, then we can also suppose that Paul could take God's power as creator as his starting point, at least according to later Pauline statements.

In the time to follow, however, the problem became increasingly acute. Deaths of members of the Christian community were no longer the exception, but the rule, and it became increasingly necessary for Paul to deal with the problem from the ground up. Also intensifying the problem was the fact that the Christian community in Corinth had either developed a conception of the resurrection on their own or received one from missionaries that Paul was not responsible for. In 1 Cor. 15.12, Paul mentioned the fact that there were members of the Corinthian community that did not accept the resurrection of the dead. However, since it hardly seems possible to suppose that this meant that they had no hope for the dead at all, but only accepted the significance of the Parousia for those living, one can assume that there were two different attempts to resolve the problem at the time: one arguing against Paul and then Paul's own solution.

---

[47]For a reconstruction, cf. Becker, *Auferstehung der Toten*, p. 51.

The understanding of the resurrection by those who denied it comes to us only indirectly, and in the course of the history of New Testament research, various differing conceptions have been reconstructed. It is most likely that the Corinthian Christians were thinking in terms of the Orphic–Hellenistic tradition that the body (*soma*) was an 'undesirable vessel for the (spiritual) soul'.[48] But, then, the corporeality of the resurrection would have been criticized by the Corinthians and death would be 'nothing more than a shedding of the undesirable body on behalf of the salvation of the immortal soul'.[49] In accordance with this idea, salvation in Christ would take effect in that the soul would be immortal until death and consequently a strong, if also one-sided continuity affecting only the soul would persist between the present time and the eschatical reality 'after which one's earthly life would only appear to exist'.[50] This idea could have arisen in the tradition of Jewish–Christian Hellenism. On the one hand, we are aware of the Orphic–Hellenistic content of several early Jewish ideas from Philo of Alexandria, and on the other hand, we can take from 1 Cor. 3.5 that this tradition could have become known from a missionary, perhaps Apollos.

Paul's own solution to the problem looks entirely different: holding fast to the corporeality of salvation, he developed a theology of resurrection in 1 Cor. 15. The basis for the resurrection of the dead is the resurrection of Jesus Christ, whose fate will be ours as well. The death and resurrection of Christ are therefore bound up in a reciprocal relation with our death and resurrection. When one of these two is denied, regardless of which one, then the other must also necessarily be denied. However, denying the resurrection of Christ robs the entire Christian understanding of reality of its meaning (1 Cor. 15.14–19). Paul ultimately constructs this solution in Rom. 6, and it is bound with liturgical implications. In contrast to 1 Thess. 4.13–18, Paul not only employs thoughts about a christological, or better, a holistic foundation of the resurrection of the dead, but he also develops thinking about the reality of the resurrection, which leads to a change in the view of what will happen with the Parousia: now, the dead will also be resurrected and Paul also supposes that his contemporaries will experience the Parousia, but the resurrection of the dead no longer simply means revival or reanimation and therefore the passing of the dead back into life. On the contrary, Paul's notion centres on the transformation of the corporeal body into a spiritual

[48]Gerhard Sellin, *Der Streit um die Auferstehung der Toten: Eine religionsgeschichtliche und exegetische Untersuchung von 1. Korinther 15* (Göttingen: Vandenhoeck & Ruprecht, 1986), p. 290.
[49]Sellin, *Auferstehung der Toten*, p. 290.
[50]Sellin, *Auferstehung der Toten*, p. 292.

body, which will also happen for the living (1 Cor. 15.51). Now, Paul has to fit the fate of the living in the Parousia to that of the dead. Paul teaches that there will be a bodily resurrection in the eschatical reality and that persons will receive a *soma pneumatikon*, a spiritual body (1 Cor. 15.44), regardless of whether they are alive at present or already dead.[51]

But, what is a *soma pneumatikon*? It is clear that is some kind of living *body* [*Leib*], because Paul argues explicitly against the Corinthian's rejection of the corporeality of the resurrection. It is also clear that corporeality in this sense is not determined by materiality, because flesh and blood cannot inherit the Kingdom of God (1 Cor. 15.50). Although Paul undertakes several deliberations about created bodies as well as about the transformation of bodies, he indeed answers some questions, but also raises others. Belonging to the questions that he answered is his notion of the difference between the body at present and the body in the eschatical reality: the eschatical body will be imperishable and incorruptible, in short, what the tradition has called *incorruptibilitas*. The spiritual nature of the body can also be characterized. This does not mean that the resurrection body is somehow more ephemeral, opaque, radiant and immaterial than the corporeal body, even if the allusion to *doxa* (radiance, glory) in 1 Cor. 15.40f seems to allow this conclusion. On the contrary, a material body according to Paul is a body that is completely determined by its relations in the world, and a spiritual body is one that is completely determined by the action of the person of the Holy Spirit.[52] Paul did not, however, provide an answer to the question of what the body actually is in general or as such.

What is interesting is that at the earliest stages in Christianity, there is already such a broad range of understandings of the resurrection marked off by polar opposites, according to which later conceptions of the resurrection up to the third generation of early Christianity could still be classified.

On the one hand, Paul in Phil. 1.23 and Lk. 23.43 assumes an immediate experience of the Parousia after individual death. How this was actually to be understood – whether as the exclusive fate of martyrs, as 'resurrection in death' or as a Parousia on the basis of an interim state of 'sleep' – does not play a role at this point. What is decisive instead is the fact that these ideas are to be classified more under the Pauline rubric than that of his opponents in Corinth. They are certainly not identical with Paul's thinking,

---

[51]Cf. Becker, *Auferstehung der Toten*, pp. 66–105.

[52]Cf. Peter Lampe, 'Paul's Concept of a Spiritual Body', in Ted Peters, Robert John Russell and Michael Welker (eds), *Resurrection: Theological and Scientific Assessments* (Cambridge: Cambridge, 2002), pp. 102–14, 108–10.

so that they appear as a result of systematic questions whether and how they can be reconciled with Paul's statements in 1 Cor. 15. In any case, the contradiction between 1 Cor. 15 and 1 Thess. 4.13–18 on the one hand to Phil. 1.23 and Luke 23.43 on the other aided the development of the notion of an interim state in the history of theology.

On the other hand, however, a sacramental tendency can be made out in the Gospel of John (cf. John 3.5) which understands eternal life as the gift of salvation in the present through the sacrament, possibly waiving the notion of a future resurrection.[53] This stream would then rather be located among the Corinthian pole of those denying the bodily resurrection. Since this conception does not remain uncontested in the Gospel of John, it is possible to suggest that the evangelist that dealt with and criticized this tradition could have meant the following: John 3.17f and John 5.24ff indicate that the Parousia presently appears in the first coming of Christ as well as in the presence of the Holy Spirit as Paraclete, so that the believer has already moved beyond death in life without having more closely defined the ideas or conceptual content bound to this notion.

Also interesting is the development in the history of the early church in which the spectrum is virtually expanded beyond both of its margins: the rather speedy development of the clause that was built into the Apostle's Creed (but not translated into the official German version) about the 'resurrection of the flesh'. Whether this is to be understood as a reaction to excessive speculation coming from the school of Origen in Alexandria with regard to the Pauline spiritual body as a mathematically ideal body in the form of a sphere,[54] or simply as a more precise statement about what a body actually ought to be, can remain undecided at this point. On the other hand, in the gnostic realm, the earlier Corinthian position was radicalized in the adoption of the Orphic–Hellenistic conception of liberation in death of a good or even divine soul from the evil or corrupted body of creation.[55]

Between the Corinthian version of a denial of the bodily resurrection in favour of a soul that has become immortal through the saving work of Christ and the Pauline conception of a resurrection of a 'body' that has been transformed by the work of the Holy Spirit, early Christianity

[53]Cf. Becker, *Auferstehung der Toten*, p. 137.
[54]Cf. the examples given in Ratzinger, *Eschatology*, p. 177.
[55]Cf. Brian Daley, *Eschatologie in der Schrift und Patristik* (Freiburg: Herder, 1986), pp. 103–6.

had a broad variety of attempts to mediate the eschatically ultimate hope of salvation together in the presence of Jesus Christ (Parousia) with the pre-eschatic experience of the continuation of death, even of Christians. In the second century, the spectrum increased on both sides through acceptance of orphic notion of immortality through gnosis, and on the other side through the emphasis on the resurrection, not of the body, but of the flesh.

5.2.2 Bodily resurrection in the history of theology

The typology to follow arises from the reduction of our conceptual field to two criteria, one being a basic description of the eschaton, namely, the concrete conception of eternity, and the other being a description of a pre-eschatic condition, namely, the understanding of death and the anthropology implicitly contained therein (see Chapter 3 and section 4.2). With regard to the conception of eternity, it was possible to draw up models for three types of eternity: eternity as timelessness, eternity as partial or complete simultaneity and eternity as infinity. As to conceptions of death, it was possible to discern two types representing ideally opposite perspectives: those that in following the Orphic–Hellenistic tradition radically distinguish between body and soul in devaluing the body, and those that emphasize the unity of the person, whether in a relational sense or in the old substantialist paradigm. The following theoretical possibilities now arise.

	A dualistic anthropology	B monistic anthropology
A eternity as timelessness	AA	AB
B eternity as simultaneity	BA	BB
C eternity as endlessness	CA	CB

Despite the theoretical possibility of all the various combinations, they have actually played extremely differing roles, and only some of them are meaningful in a systematic sense.

AA 'timeless-dualistic' versions of the resurrection

This category covers conceptions that accept the priority of a soul and therefore hold to a timeless (and spaceless) understanding of resurrection. At first glance, this does not appear to be very meaningful for two reasons: on the one hand, the notion of the *resurrection* of a soul that is already immortal either *per se* or *per gratia* does not appear to be very meaningful. On the other hand, the reunion of the soul with the body also does not appear to be very meaningful, since the body in any case cannot be conceived atemporally. Nevertheless, there are a number of versions of the resurrection in the history of theology that do fall under this category. They are predominantly neo-Platonic and mystical. Since Christian neo-Platonism was of considerable importance in the past, it is not surprising that the biblical terminology of 'resurrection' is assigned to personal mystical hope for the future.

It was John Scotus Eriugena who may have had the most coherent and widest reaching understanding of the resurrection under this rubric. This is what happens: the soul lives on beyond death and, in the resurrection to follow, the body is transformed into soul, the soul into spirit, the spirit into intellect and this finally is taken up into God, who is beyond all being and infinitely one.[56] A literalistic echo of the biblical conception of the resurrection is evident here in so far as 1 Cor. 15 employs the terminology of transformation. For Eriugena, however, this step- or stage-like transformation is not a means for the Parousia – understood as the immediate presence of Christ to creatures that preserves their personal transcendence. On the contrary, it runs according to the neo-Platonic understanding of creation according to which what exists overflows and unfolds in various stages[57] from the One that is beyond being,[58] into an ontic counter-movement and therefore a return to its origin or source. John Eriugena's doctrine of the resurrection was rejected by the church in 1210

---

[56]Cf. Johannes Scotus Eriugena, *De divisione naturae*, PL 122, pp. 986C–987C.
[57]Cf. Arthur Oncken Lovejoy, *The Great Chain of Being* (Cambridge: Harvard, 1961).
[58]Cf. Ott, *Scholastische Eschatologie*, p. 33.

and in 1225 as heretical, even though one can already find its forerunners in theologies such as that of Clement of Alexandria (d. ca. 215), who was influenced by Middle-Platonism.[59]

There is no need for a more detailed critique of these versions of the resurrection at this point, since they only really deal with resurrection in the verbal sense, but not actually. All that we have already said about the model of eternity as timelessness also applies at this point.

A doctrine of resurrection according to which only the incorporeally conceived soul participates in a timeless eternity can be found in the thought of the Christian neo-Platonist John Scotus Eriugena, who taught the transformation of the body into the soul.

AB 'timeless-monistic' versions of the resurrection

This category would formally include those versions that conceive of the non-temporal resurrection of human beings that are not divided into body and soul. Since, however, a monistic conception of humanity can only be understood on the one hand either relationally or on the other reductionistically in such a way that humans are reduced to their materiality, this version of the resurrection is logically contradictory. Materiality first and foremost presupposes temporality. However, a relational understanding – be it of humanity, God or something else – presupposes, if not temporality itself, at least its structure (see section 3.1). To the best of my knowledge, this corresponding understanding of eternity has not appeared anywhere in the history of theology.

Conceptions of the resurrection depicting human persons as timeless and relationless material bodies in eternity are incoherent and do not appear anywhere in the history of theology.

---

[59]Cf. Reinhard Staats, 'Auferstehung 1/4', in Gehard Müller et al. (eds), *Theologische Realenzyklopädie*, vol. 4 (Berlin: De Gruyter, 1979), pp. 467–77, 475.

BA 'simultaneous-dualistic' versions of the resurrection

In this category belong versions of the resurrection that assume only spiritual beings or souls participate in eternity, understood as the simultaneity of all worldly events. The notion of resurrection also appears to possess little meaning in this category as well; since this version of eternity supposes that all events are equally co-present, it does not make sense to conceive of a resurrection that is somehow separate. There are further difficulties as to how we are to understand an exclusively spiritual co-presence of temporal events in eternity without bodily occurrences. It is possible to suggest that the bodily occurrence of the world is co-present not to a bodily, but an only spiritually understood divine eternity. This would accord with process philosophy's idea 'of a tender care that nothing be lost'.[60] This loving care relates to the so-called consequent nature of God that takes all worldly events up into itself and can also be referred to as God's memory. The question as to what extent Alfred North Whitehead's philosophy presupposes a pure spirituality can be put to the side for now. This corresponds to the attempt to anchor pure spirituality on the side of eternity. Conversely, one could suppose that only the spiritual experience of the course of the world can be component to eternity understood as simultaneity. However, since this kind of spiritual experience is hardly identifiable without recourse to events that occur in time and space, such conceptions do not to my knowledge appear in the history of theology. What we can take from this is that these ideas ultimately have very little to do with resurrection in the sense of being together with Christ in a completely unmediated way. Here, co-presence with Christ is indeed given, but only indirectly.

The notion that only spiritual realities participate in an eternity understood as the co-presence of everything temporal, and that this would be identified with the resurrection, can only be depicted with great conceptual difficulty and thus plays no role in the history of Christian thought.

[60]Whitehead, *Process and Reality*, p. 346.

BB 'simultaneous-monistic' versions of the resurrection

A similar analysis also applies to the category of resurrection as the co-presence of bodily [*leiblich-körperlichen*] occurrences in eternity, which themselves take on aspects of corporeality. This is slightly more coherent than closely related type BA, but the objection that this conception is also incompatible with the notion of resurrection as defined here also applies. Interestingly, this idea of a personal hope for eternity appeared in the first half of the twentieth century in eschatologies as different as that of Rudolf Bultmann, Paul Tillich and Karl Barth.[61] Significant in their eschatological formulations is the fact that it does not really deal with resurrection in the strongest sense. This is especially evident in the fact that extreme caution ruled with respect to the conceptual meaning of 'resurrection of the dead', which is not to be understood as an erroneous hesitancy but goes factually with the corresponding model of eternity. As a result, the conceptualization of the Parousia among these theologians has an entirely different meaning, one which was especially radical in Tillich's case (see section 5.1).

> The idea that all temporal events participate in an eternal spiritual-material unity – understood as the simultaneity of all events – can be found in the twentieth century among theologians as diverse as Tillich, Barth and Bultmann. Since this idea consists in the immortalization of personal being, but not the notion of a bodily resurrection, the aforementioned theologians are also cautious on this point.

CA 'infinite-dualistic' versions of the resurrection

This version takes the resurrection as a presupposition of the Parousia given that there is a dichotomy between body and soul and preservation of a (spatio-temporal) interrelation between events. At first glance it would appear that this option only appears infrequently, but this is actually not the case. This is because if the soul is immortal either as such or *per gratia*, then the notion of a resurrection already appears to have been settled. This

[61]Cf. Barth, *Church Dogmatics III/2*, pp. 624–5; Tillich, *Systematic Theology III*, pp. 412–23; Rudolf Bultmann, *Geschichten und Eschatologie* (Tübingen: Mohr Siebeck, 1958), p. 161.

version is by far the most common to be found in the Christian tradition as a whole since it has a number of advantages.

- This conception is represented by a broad spectrum: on the one hand, strongly Hellenistic future expectations can be integrated into it that place all their weight on the immortality of the soul, as with Origen (d. 253/254) or Augustine (d. 430). Even the strongly platonist Origen rejects the gnostic notion that the body will not be resurrected,[62] taking the line that it will be transformed into a spiritual body – though only first after the soul, having been judged, is purified and refined.[63] For Augustine, the resurrection of the soul occurs already in this life, so that they are immortal and only the resurrection of bodies occurs at the final judgement. Augustine waivers with respect to the question of whether materiality in the sense of flesh and blood belongs to these types of bodies or whether this is to be rejected.[64]

What kind of potential does this version of the resurrection possess?

- At the very least, it appears to solve the problem contained in the biblical texts in that there are on the one hand pericopes maintaining the notion of an immediate state of togetherness with Christ after death (Phil. 1.23, Luke 23.43) or an altogether presentist eschatology as in Johannine theology, or on the other hand those where a future resurrection is apparent (1 Thess. 4.13, 1 Cor. 15). The first kind relate to the soul, whereas the latter relate to the resurrection and reunification of the soul with the body.
- In essentials, the problem of the continuity of personal existence is resolved: the continuity of humans in the here and now does not ultimately reside in their materiality, but with the soul, which endures beyond death. This solution, which actually derives from the Orphic–Hellenistic tradition, is difficult to maintain. This is because it would also be possible to ascribe an aspect of continuity to the body, especially if one were to speak of the resurrection of the flesh. But, then, does the identity of the person also reside in the identity of the material parts of which it consists? This problem was discussed in the early church and the middle ages by means of a

[62]Cf. Origen, *On First Principles* (trans. G.W. Butterworth; ed. Tania M. Geist; Notre Dame: Ave Maria Press, 2013), pp. 173–82 (II,10).
[63]Cf. Origen, *On First Principles*, pp. 140–2 (II,VI,5–6).
[64]Cf. Staats, 'Auferstehung 1/4', p. 477; Daley, *Eschatologie in Schrift und Patristik*, pp. 201–2.

question that was taken with all due seriousness: What can be said of resurrection in cases where someone was eaten by wild animals or even cannibals? Would their resurrection not then be jeopardized because their materiality would now belong to the materiality of the cannibals that would also be resurrected? A variety of different solutions were put forth. On the one hand, numerical identity can be retained by means of the material. Augustine argued that the material of the cannibalized person could not be assimilated into the cannibal, so that a separation is possible in the case of the resurrection in which the original proprietor of the material regains it.[65] The other position, taken by Thomas Aquinas (d. 1274) and Durandus of San Porcino (d. 1334), consists in the fact that the materiality of the body at present is always characterized by continuous metabolic processes and therefore cannot be decisive for personal identity. Both Thomas and Durandus suggest understanding the soul as the sole principle of human identity.[66] Whether this solution sees Thomas standing more explicitly than normal in the Aristotelian tradition, or he transcends[67] it in favour of a relational and constitutively embodied understanding of identity is anyone's guess.

- A variety of different versions of how to understand the resurrection body are possible within this model. A hodgepodge of varying conceptions of the resurrection body has appeared in the history of Christian theology:
- The body, according Origen and his school, is spherical, as this is the ideal bodily form.[68]
- The body is like a human body, but, at least for those surviving the final judgement, furnished with a bright lustre (*doxa* = glory) or, per Augustine, with a wondrous levity.[69]
- According to Augustine and Wilhelm of Auxerre (d. 1231), mass is either added to or taken away from the body according to whether the body of a human being is over- or underweight in the here and now.[70]

---

[65]Cf. Daley, *Eschatologie in Schrift und Patristik*, p. 202.

[66]Cf. Ott, *Scholastische Eschatologie*, pp. 130–1; Ratzinger, *Eschatology*, pp. 178–81.

[67]Cf. Ratzinger, *Eschatology*, pp. 148–50. Ratzinger emphasizes that Aquinas's definition *anima forma corporis* has to be seen in the light of the council of Vienne's (1312) declaration that the substance of the rational soul is the form of the human body.

[68]Cf. Ratzinger, *Eschatology*, p. 177.

[69]Cf. Daley, *Eschatologie in Schrift und Patristik*, p. 202.

[70]Cf. Ott, *Scholastische Eschatologie*, pp. 37, 39.

- According to Augustine and Peter Lombard, the resurrection body has an age of 32 years, modelled on the resurrected Lord, regardless of what age the person died.[71]
- As a spiritual body, the body according to John Scotus Eriugena is complete without materiality and is tantamount to the immaterial soul.[72]

This incomplete list nonetheless makes the point: despite its great potential for solving problems, this model for understanding the resurrection also raises important new questions and further issues. Among these, two stand out:

- What happens to the immortal soul between death and the resurrection of the body? This question will be dealt with separately in the next section in an excursus on the doctrines of the interim state, since this has captured a great deal of attention in the history of theology.
- If the personal identity of a human being is located in an immortal soul, is the notion of justification even still possible? If human personal identity is now understood to possess this autonomy and is not entirely dependent on God, this changes the entire conception of how God and humanity are related to one another and, even more basically, of what God and humanity actually are.

The broadest part of the Christian tradition has understood resurrection to entail the unification of the immortal soul with either a newly created body or a reawakened body at the final judgement, understood to be the beginning of eternity in the form of timelessness. However, this understanding is not without its problems and leads necessarily to questions about what happens to the soul between death and resurrection.

CB 'infinite-monistic' versions of the resurrection

It is possible to conceive of a resurrection without the use of a dualistic anthropology and an immaterial soul. This can go in two ways: one, a

---

[71]Cf. Ott, *Scholastische Eschatologie*, p. 40.
[72]Cf. Ott, *Scholastische Eschatologie*, p. 33.

reductionistic version that sees human personality as a function of the body, and the other conceives of the resurrection in relational terms.

The reductionistic version of the resurrection is, as a rule, rarely advocated. It has recently appeared in the physicalistic reduction of Frank Tipler, who suggests that a reductionistic and functionalistic personal continuity is indeed possible. In Tipler's view, what will actually be resurrected are simulations of ourselves and the structures of our personal and natural relationality, which are nonetheless identical with us.[73] Tipler goes as far as to suggest that it would be possible in the post-resurrection reality for two men to interact sexually with the same beautiful woman at the same time, because in this understanding of resurrection double simulations can be resurrected and yet still be identical.[74] While Tipler is responding to a question often posed by his male students, it nonetheless speaks to his otherwise good theological background in that he seems to have turned the 'Sadducees' question to Jesus' (Mark 12.18–27 and parallels) into the 'male students' question to Tipler'.

The issue at stake here is not that of identity, as this remains unanswered. Jesus' answer, that God is the God of the living, not the dead, is ambiguous for his audience since it is possible to take from it both that there is a resurrection and that there is not, since the phrase 'God of the living' comes from the Old Testament at a time where there was no operative conception of resurrection. This pericope's function in the context of the passion is something else: the Sadducees are not actually interested in the theological question but rather want to see on which side of the issue Jesus stands. Jesus, however, evades answering the question, which appears to be what specifically provoked offence.

Tipler himself is aware of what philosophical problems stand over against his notion but cannot resolve them. The problem of identity belongs to the so-called philosophical riddles that cannot be solved by either empirical or reductionistic means. Anthony Flew has tackled the philosophical problem of identity in particular and we have already seen in the reference in section 4.2 that Stanisław Lem (d. 2006) raises the question of whether it would be possible to produce an exact copy of someone with all their memories after their death. Would this then be the same person? Not at all, because this scenario is the same as if one were to produce this copy including all memories to that point in the life

[73]Cf. Tipler, *Physik der Unsterblichkeit*, pp. 219–20.
[74]Cf. Tipler, *Physik der Unsterblichkeit*, pp. 256–7.

of the same person. This would mean having two persons with the same memories but nevertheless two different identities.[75] Tipler is aware of this argument and attempts to counter it with the proof that it is the physical exemplar that ultimately determines identity,[76] but his thesis of identity is purely declarative: he simply asserts that there is the identity between the dead and the resurrected person, and this is simply not sufficient to rebut Flew and Lem's objection. This objection applies not only to Tipler, but to all monistic-reductionistic versions of the resurrection, so that it no longer appears to be a suitable option but has to be excluded as incoherent.

The idea that resurrection means that only the material body is created anew is a monistic, but also materialist-reductionistic solution. This view is presently maintained by the physicist Frank Tipler as part of a series of theological claims. However, for fundamental philosophical reasons, this version of resurrection cannot resolve the problem of the continuity of the personal identity of the human being between now and later.

After all this, a relational-monistic version of the resurrection is still possible. We have already seen in the understanding of death that Luther approximates to such a position (see section 4.2). In this paradigm, the soul is simply God's relationship to particular human beings. The soul then sleeps in death, according to Luther,[77] which can also be characterized following Härle as the end of one's active relational potentiality, but not of one's passive relatedness that is borne by God.[78] In this case, the resurrection body would be a new body originating from God by new creation, which then has nothing more to do with worldly materiality but actually could be a *soma pneumatikon*, a spiritual body, whatever this might mean. This new creation would occur in analogy to *creatio ex nihilo*, that is, to creation without any pre-existing worldly conditions, in so far as it is based on God's power as creator. However, it is different at one decisive point as well: in this new creation, God remembers something of one's lived human life that God incorporates into the new creation of the body. This notion

[75] Cf. section 4.2.5.3.
[76] Cf. Tipler, *Physik der Unsterblichkeit*, pp. 227–40.
[77] Cf. Beisser, *Hoffnung und Vollendung*, p. 60.
[78] Cf. Härle, *Dogmatik*, pp. 629–33.

is also not without its problems in so far as it appears to anchor human identity solely to the absolute will of God, whose primary attribute would then be will, not love. Thus, two problems arise at the same time: on the one hand, it resembles a solution to the problem of identity appearing in the reductionistic models, which at the same time cuts through the Gordian knot of identity with the sword of the divine will. On the other hand, serious problems emerge in the doctrine of God, which now has to be understood as voluntaristic, meaning that the saving work of Christ on the cross would be either incomprehensible or otherwise rest solely on the arbitrary will of God. An arbitrary God, however, does not offer a basis for a proper distinction between *actio dei* and *actio hominum* in accordance with the doctrine of justification. One could also say, and this is not all that different from Tipler's solution, that in both cases, the identity of the person is primarily the result of a declaration: in Tipler's versions, by the person himself or herself, but in the relational version, by God.

> The idea that the person conceived as a unity will be created anew on the last day by the fact that God remembers the person and their identity resolves the problem of the continuity of personal identity, putting this not in the hands of human but divine will. This, however, results in the necessity of understanding the divine will as the primary divine attribute and not love, which then leads to problems in the doctrine of God.

5.2.3 Excursus: Intermediary states?

The various doctrines of the interim state have two direct and two indirect presuppositions.

The first direct presupposition is that in accepting a finite-dualistic resurrection, the question arises as to what happens to the soul between death and resurrection. Since the question of the resurrection is about personal continuity, it must also be resolved for a possible interim state. In itself, this presupposition would only justify speaking of *one* intermediate state in the singular.

The other direct presupposition of the doctrine of the intermediate state does not involve the continuity problem of resurrection, but the problem of the transformation or discontinuity entailed in the doctrine of the judgement (see section 5.3). Since the eschatical reality cannot be conceived as a re-duplication of the pre-eschatical world, transformations are necessary that affect sin, death and suffering. The traditional outcome of the final judgement, understood to affect the entirety of humanity i.e. those whose souls have been reunited with their bodies in resurrection, are therefore provisionally kept for the spiritual soul more or less in an isolated manner after their deaths but pre-eschatically. The soul experiences this in the way that the entire human being, after resurrection and judgement, will experience it. On this basis, the language of *multiple* intermediate states in the plural arises. Since its development in the early church, this doctrine cannot be understood as being strictly unified. In the Middle Ages, it is possible to find the following versions of the various doctrines[79] of the intermediate state:

- The souls of the just of the Old Testament are to be found in the *limbus patrorum* and the souls of children that died unbaptized in the *limbus infantium*.
- Souls that will later be damned feel the agony of separation from God.
- The souls of those who will later survive the judgement already enjoy the pleasure of God.
- The souls of those who are already saved but not yet pure have the possibility of purification in an intermediate state. This is the doctrine of purgatory (*purgatorium*).

The indirect presuppositions consist in the fact that these conceptions of the intermediate state are not spatially conceived, since the soul itself is not spatial. However, with the pre-figuration of the verdict of the judgement that concerns the whole person reunited with the body, a spatial conception in the sense of space as an enclosed container within the world is necessary or is brought in here once again through the backdoor.

The other indirect presupposition touches on purgatory. Purgatory itself is unbiblical, though Paul's comparison of the final judgement with fire is erroneously brought in as evidence for this doctrine. Plato's influence on the development of the doctrine cannot be ruled out.[80] 2 Macc. 12.42–45 can

[79]Cf. Ott, *Scholastische Eschatologie*, pp. 19–29, 70–85, 95–107, 169–217.
[80]Cf. Plato, 'The Republic', in *Plato: The Complete Works*, pp. 121–3 (Book X, 617d–621d).

be used as an indirect proof for purgatory, since it presents an intercessory prayer for the dead. The doctrine of purgatory was finally made canonical for Roman Catholicism in 1136 by Pope Benedict XII.[81] The Reformers rejected the doctrine of purgatory because they had the impression that it meant humans could still merit blessedness through their works after death, so that human contribution to salvation was evident in a virtually unendingly increasing synergism of salvation, making the reconciling work of Christ either unnecessary or at the very least minimizing it.[82] The source of the doctrine of purgatory is in any case often located in the theology of Origen, who for another reason had to accept an endlessly continuing process of the purification of souls.[83] This is one of the problems of grace that does have to be taken seriously, the paradox of grace, that also appears independently of Origen in Protestant theology with Thomas Erskine of Linlathen (d. 1870), a nineteenth-century Scottish theologian: How can the notions of omnipotent divine grace and human freedom be reconciled? If the notion of divine grace is really taken seriously, does God not then work all in all, or does one not have to accept the notion of double predestination? Can one still speak of grace if rejection also resides with God? If, on the other hand, the rejection of universal grace, which is directed as an offer to all humanity through the cross of Christ, can be rejected for a few humans on the basis of human will, is grace then not already too weak and human participation in salvation, or synergism, being taught? There is a satisfactory, if not speculative solution to this problem. Erskine adopts the notion of a pre-eschatic but post-mortem kind of process of education under changed conditions in which humans, in an endlessly long period, can always still accept grace, and thereby finally reach their goal.[84] Structurally, this theory is similar to Origen's version of the doctrine of universal salvation, which requires the possibility of the purification of all souls given an infinite amount of time in which this can be accomplished.[85]

Despite the elegance of this solution, it still has to be rejected. An intermediate state that still offered possibilities of development, if it were to include sociality and corporeality, would simply mean a duplication of this social world or at least the constitution of a new, natural and social

---

[81]Cf. Herbert Vorgrimler, 'Das Fegefeuer', in Franz Böckle et al. (eds), *Zwischenzeit und Vollendung der Heilsgeschichte Mysterium Salutis*, vol. 5 (Zurich: Benzinger, 1976), pp. 453–7.

[82]Cf. Luther, WA 7, p. 453; WA 39I, pp. 352; 409f.; 'The Smalcald Articles' (1537), in *The Book of Concord*, pp. 303–4 (lines 12–15); Calvin, *Institutes*, vol. 1, pp. 675–84 (III,V,6).

[83]Cf. Staats, 'Auferstehung 1/4', p. 476.

[84]Cf. Markus Mühling, *Versöhnendes Handeln – Handeln in Versöhnung*, p. 226.

[85]Cf. Origen, *On First Principles*, pp. 326–8 (III,VI,5–6).

world, but which would not also be the eschatic world. Such a doctrine, however, would be an exception within Christianity and would also pose profound problems for the relationship of the present world to that of the eschatical reality.

Apart from the problem of grace, both purgatory and all other doctrines of an intermediate state meet with the verdict of incoherence: they are necessarily intensely individualistically conceived, at least as far as they pertain to the fate of individual souls. Incorporeal souls, however, are inconceivable, if we are mindful of the following argument rendered by Peter F. Strawson (d. 2006):

> When I was discussing the concept of a pure individual consciousness, I said that though it could not exist as a primary concept to be used in the explanation of the concept of a person ... yet it might have a logically secondary existence .... Each of us can quite intelligibly conceive of his or her individual survival of bodily death .... One has simply to think of oneself as having thoughts and memories as at present ... whilst (a) having no perceptions of a body related to one's experience as one's own body is, and (b) having no power of initiating changes in the physical condition of the world, such as one at present does with one's hands, shoulders, feet and vocal chords .... Then two consequences follow .... The first is that the strictly *dis*embodied individual is strictly solitary .... The other ... is that in order to retain his idea of himself as an individual, he must always think of himself as disembodied, as a *former* person .... Since then he has, as it were, no personal life of his own to lead, he must live much in the memories of the personal life he did lead .... In proportion as the memories fade, ... to that degree his concept of himself as an individual becomes attenuated. At the limit of attenuation there is, *from the point of view of his survival as an individual*, no difference between the continuance of experience and its cessation. Disembodied survival, on such terms as these, may well seem unattractive. No doubt it is for this reason that the orthodox have wisely insisted on the resurrection of the body.[86]

If one, as I think is the case, holds this argument to be valid, then every possible doctrine of an intermediate state is immediately invalidated, because it generally prohibits any form of dualistic anthropology. The human being as person is a unity; body and soul are actually secondary concepts that cannot be assigned any ontologically independent reality and are derived from the concept of the person, which is primary. 'Body' and

---

[86]Strawson, *Individuals*, pp. 115–16.

'soul' are therefore purely conceptual distinctions. If this is right, then all understandings of the resurrection that presuppose a dualistic anthropology (AA, BA, CA) are incoherent. With this, the question of how one is to conceive or understand the resurrection as a medium of the Parousia still appears to be unresolved.

The doctrine of various intermediate states arose, among other reasons, through the question of what happens with the immortal soul until its reunification with the body. This is problematic because it is individualistic and because it introduces a dualistic anthropology.

The doctrine of purgatory is a special problem. The Reformers rejected it as unbiblical and synonymous with the notion of merit.

Similar to purgatory, in Protestant theology, conceptions about the possibility of the post-mortem but pre-eschatical development of the person have arisen for the purposes of reconciling the notion of divine grace with human freedom.

The doctrine of the intermediate state can be rejected along all dualistic anthropologies, if body and soul are only understood as abstractions from a personal reality to the extent that an incorporeal soul ultimately turns out to be a meaningless concept.

5.2.4 The living body as the medium of communicative relationality

The passage from Strawson cited in the last section not only critiques the concept of the soul, but can also help us clarify the concept of the resurrection body. We could see in Paul that he attempted to specify the specific difference between our present and our future body but did not actually say what a body itself actually is. This question can be treated first in asking about the reality of the eschatical resurrection. According to Strawson, body and soul are secondary concepts that are purely conceptual abstractions from the ontically primary concept of personhood. The passage cited in the last section ultimately does clarify the meaning of the body positively in that it critiques what a soul conceived as being independent would lack. This is the possibility for communication, the possibility for relational interexchange. The concept of the living body as *Leib*, therefore, in contrast to the concept of an exclusively corporeal or material body as *Körper*, is not characterized by materiality but is rather defined as *the medium of our personal and communicative being-in-relation*. If we now remember the results from the earlier section on death, then we can suggest that according to the reconciling work of Christ, humans die into Christ in such a way that death would no longer be absolute relationlessness and therefore non-being, but that the passive relationship to Christ remains. Since, however, being and personality are always being in relation, the necessary factor of continuity is also preserved in death. Humans do not have their identities in themselves, but in passive relationship to Christ. If personhood is now characterized by becoming-in-relation and if the concept of the body constitutes the medium of human becoming-in-relation, then the concept of bodily resurrection means that God revives the relational structure of the dead person to the extent that this does not contradict the person's identity. Belonging to this is the fact that the person receives active relational possibility and stands in relation not only to Christ and the other Trinitarian persons, but also those with whom they have mutually co-formed their identities through the course of their life histories in the here and now, as well as with non-personal entities. This resurrection body cannot be a spatio-temporal body since the world's spatio-temporal frameworks of individuation have no eschatic valence. On the contrary, the body in the framework of the Trinitarian relational structure that is God's self will be resurrected as the medium of a communicative becoming-in-relation. This means the resurrected human participates in God or is deified. This version of the resurrection can be traced primarily back to the Eastern Orthodox Church.

Athanasius of Alexandria (d. 373) had already recognized that Christ became man, so that we would become like God.[87] Although the church in the Latin West was also aware of this notion, with a few exceptions it only played a role in the neo-Platonic mystical tradition. One example is the eschatic hope depicted by Heinrich Seuse (d. 1366), which entails being like a drop of wine in the unending ocean of God.[88] Although the Reformers were known to be anxious about a careful distinction between God and humanity, Luther could accept the doctrine of deification and give it his own specific character, as Finnish Luther research following[89] Tuomo

---

[87]Cf. Athanasius, *On the Incarnation of the Word* (trans. Archibald Robertson; London: Nutt, 1891), p. 93 (LIV,3).

[88]Cf. Seuse, *Das Buch der Wahrheit*, pp. 27–62.

[89]Cf. Simon Peura and Antti Raunio, *Luther und Theosis: Vergöttlichung als Thema der abendländischen Theologie* (Erlangen: Luther-Agricola-Gesellschaft, 1990).

Mannermaa[90] has been able to show, even if their findings rightly remain debated on individual points.[91]

It is primarily the Western association with the aforementioned mystical tradition that is responsible for the fact that deification or *theosis* in the West is often misunderstood even up to present. Thus, it will be useful at this point to review once more the characteristics of bodily resurrection within the framework of the Trinitarian relational structure:

- The alterity or otherness of persons is preserved; there is no process of amalgamation.
- The distinction between God and humanity, or creator and creature also remains in place. Anastasius from Sinai (d. around 700) understood deification to be elevation to higher condition, but not a broadening or transformation of nature.[92] Even in the eschatical reality, direct participation in God as incorporation into the inner-Trinitarian relational structure always remains characterized by grace, not nature: the creation is fulfilled by its participation in God in grace. Participating in God through grace, wherein humans are in direct communication with the Trinitarian persons, the vision of God is shifted but is only possible through the action of the Holy Spirit and remains the abiding condition of this participation. If only the body is a condition for reciprocal communication and a human creature can only participate in God through the action of the Holy Spirit, then the resurrection body will be a body that is completely determined by the action of the person of the Holy Spirit, i.e. a *soma pneumatikon*, a spiritual body.

In the West, the eschatical reality was rendered less in terms of the notion of *theosis* and more in terms of the *visio beatifica* or *visio dei*. It is possible to draw on 2 Cor. 5.7, where Paul outlines the difference between the present time and the eschatical reality by means of the difference between faith and sight. Thomas Aquinas (d. 1274) describes this *visio dei* in connection to Augustine as seeing God in God's essence.[93] Melanchthon taps into this tradition in forming his own position, which can be taken

---

[90]Cf. Tuomo Mannermaa, *Der im Glauben gegenwärtige Christus: Rechtfertigung und Vergottung; zum ökumenischen Dialog* (Hannover: Lutherisches Verlagshaus, 1989).

[91]On this discussion cf. in Carl E. Braaten and Robert W. Jenson, *Union with Christ: The New Finnish Interpretation of Luther* (Grand Rapids: Eerdmans, 1998); Luther Digest, *An Annual Abridgment of Luther Studies* (Shorewood, Minnesota: Luther Academy, 1995).

[92]Cf. Anastasius vom Sinai, *Wegweiser* (ed. J.P. Migne; Patrologiae Graeca 89; Paris: Imprimerie Catholique, 1865), p. 36.

[93]Cf. Aquinas, *Summa Theologica*, vol. 5, pp. 2945–56 (III Suppl. Q.92).

as largely representative for that of the Reformers.[94] We can see that with regard to content; however, it is not in conceptual competition with the idea of deification because all of the trademarks of the latter – unmediated presence, alterity and the inter-communication of human persons in God – are present. Within the frame of Thomas's view that the divine essence is nothing other than God's Trinitarian relational structure, it becomes clear that seeing God directly in God's essence is only possible given deification. The metaphor of *visio beatifica* or *visio dei* is ultimately only meaningful if there is a medium by means of which one can actually 'see'. 'Seeing' can likewise be understood as a form of direct communication in relation. It is for this reason that the *visio beatifica* also leads into the notion of bodily resurrection.

It now becomes clear why the resurrection of the body is taken as a means for the realization of the Parousia: if the Parousia means the unmediated presence of Christ as one of the three divine persons, and if bodiliness is nothing other than the medium of human communicative being-in-relation, then the resurrection of the bodies of those who have died is a necessary condition for their experience of the Parousia. Different to the notion of the immortality of the soul, the notion of the resurrection of the body inherently implies sociality and partial relatedness, even to the non-personal part of creation.

The question of when and where the dead are raised, whether material will be integrated, what age or weight one will be, are, however, of no relevance for the notion of the resurrection of the body, since this state of affairs stands at best in an indirect relationship to bodiliness. Nevertheless, the corresponding speculations in the history of theology also fulfil an important function: they show that the eschatic bodiliness of the resurrection is not to be understood simply as a reduplication of the world at present. The notion of the bodily resurrection secures the element of continuity between the present and the eschatical reality, but it does not provide for the idea of the necessary transformations and the necessary element of discontinuity. The notion of discontinuity on the contrary is exemplified by the notion of the final judgement and its outcomes. For this reason, we now have to turn to the notion of judgement. Before that, however, we still have to give a few indicators pointing to the ethical implications of the resurrection of the body. For the moment, we can say:

---

[94] Cf. Phillipp Melanchthon and Robert Stupperich, *Loci praecipui theologici von 1559 (2. Teil) und Definitiones* (Gütersloh: Gütersloher Verlagshaus, 1980, 2nd edn), p. 927.

The bodily resurrection of the dead has a medial character in that it is an instrument used to join respect for the reality of human death with the experience of the Parousia of Jesus Christ. The body is the medium of creaturely communicative and reciprocal relationality. The resurrection body as *soma pneumatikon* is no longer individuated within the frame of the world's space-time, but in the relational structure of the Trinity that is God in God's self. Bodily resurrection therefore means *theosis* (deification) in grace by means of the action of the Holy Spirit, so that the resurrection body can be understood as a body or *soma pneumatikon* that is entirely determined by the Holy Spirit, enabling immediate communication with the three Trinitarian persons in the beatific vision (*visio beatifica, visio dei*).

5.2.5 Ethical implications

Bodily resurrection indeed forms an object of hope in Christianity, but not directly, only indirectly to the extent that the eschatical Parousia as the unmediated presence of Christ for the faithful presupposes the body as the communicative medium of personal being. On the basis of this derivative and medial character, one will also be able to expect that the ethical implications of the resurrection are less strongly distinctive as with the other doctrinal *loci* in eschatology. We can once again point out that as far as the resurrection goes, it is not simply about a form of hope in the continuance of personal existence in contrast to the end of the person. While there certainly are ethical implications that move forth from the basis of the specific Christian hope in this ideal, here Parousia, judgement and the Kingdom of God play vastly important roles. As far as the resurrection goes, there is only one remaining issue to point out: the fact that the significance of bodiliness in the present is actually enhanced based on the eschatic relevance of bodiliness, as much as it also has to be distinguished from eschatic bodiliness as well. Christianity is therefore not a *somatophobic* religion; it is not antibody. It rather forbids both libertinism and harsh ascetic dealing with the human body. Since it understands the body as the medium of human relationality, which is constitutive for creaturely personal being, it will also not be able to accept the notion that how we deal with our own bodies can be an exclusively personal matter. Since the body does have eschatical, but nevertheless still only medial character, it does not itself independently constitute a highest good in and of itself. Ultimately, one has to be mindful in ethical deliberations of the fact that not only the soul, but also the body is a concept that has arisen in abstraction from the concept of the person, which concretely describes the reality of the being of humanity. All this naturally has influence on all spheres of action that have to do with the body: health, sports, sexuality and much more. In all these spheres, other theological aspects certainly also play an important role. The meaning of the resurrection is rather limited to the notion of the eschatical valence of the living body. It is for this reason that we are going to forego an explication of these ethical aspects at this point, whose material considerations we could not rightly deal with in the present framework.

The resurrection of the body does not have direct implications for ethics, but rather serves a regulative function for material ethics everywhere bodiliness and corporeality play a role. Whereas bodiliness as such is to be assessed positively because of the body's eschatical valence, to be rejected are purely private notions of control over the body on the basis of its character as a medium of communication, as well as overestimations of human bodiliness through the notion of the medial character of the resurrection body for the Parousia.

5.3 The judgement

The doctrine of the final judgement and its outcome, like the doctrine of the resurrection, does not possess any direct, but only indirect eschatical relevance: like the resurrection of the dead, it is a means for reaching the eschatical goal of the fulfilment of the Kingdom of God. Whereas with the resurrection it is essentially a matter of the *continuity* of the here and now with the eschatical reality, the judgement emphasizes the element of *discontinuity* between the unfulfilled creation at present and the eschatical reality. The primary question is as to what transformations of reality in which ways have to be reached in order to be able to speak about an eschatical fulfilment of the Kingdom of God. We will now tackle this question by first examining the biblical bases of the judgement and mentioning the particular questions arising in the history of theology (see section 5.3.1). Then, we will discuss the various problems involved in forming an understanding of the judgement, in which first the potential outcomes of the judgement will be reviewed and then the process of the judgement itself (see sections 5.3.2 and 5.3.3).

5.3.1 The judgement in history

5.3.1.1 The judgement in the Bible

The Old Testament account of God's judgement is burdened with the prejudice of presenting a picture of God as a wrathful judge who doles out rewards and punishments. There is indeed an element of this schema of reward and punishment in the Old Testament – i.e. that things go either well or poorly for humans in the here and now based on their actions, and yet, on the one hand, this is generally an Eastern notion, and on the other hand, it is not attached to a notion of judgement that assumes things will be apportioned as the result of a particular act but rather rests on a principle of causality.[95] The notion that in the Old Testament there is primarily a God who as guard or judge over *justitia distributiva*, or justice, who brings about compensation for action is more likely evoked by the Greek and especially Latin translations of the Bible in connection with various representations found in the visual arts.[96]

The presentations of judgement in the Old Testament are actually far more comprehensive. Yahweh's judging action can also be understood as his saving action, since *schaphath* in Hebrew can mean both 'judge' and 'save'. We can refer at this point to the fact that Yahweh not only saves after he has judged, or saves instead of judging, but that, especially in the Psalms, God judges in his saving.[97]

The notions arise in the prophetic literature in particular that Yahweh judges through his action in history and it is thereby able to understand enemy nations and their leaders as instruments of God's judgement that effects all of the people collectively.[98] The idea of a final judgement or judgement of those already dead, which many religions in history have

---

[95]Cf. Klaus Koch, 'Gibt es ein Vergeltungsdogma im AT?', *Zeitschrift für Theologie und Kirche* 52 (1955), pp. 1–42.

[96]Cf. Bernd Janowski, 'Divine Judgment II. Old Testament', in *RPP*, vol. 4, pp. 110–111.

[97]Cf. Bernd Janowski, 'Der barmherzige Richter', in R. Scoralick (ed.), *Das Drama der Barmherzigkeit Gottes: Studien zur biblischen Gottesrede und ihrer Wirkungsgeschichte in Judentum und Christentum* (Stuttgart: Katholisches Bibelwerk, 2000), pp. 33–91.

[98]On the prophecies of judgement, cf. Jörg Jeremias, *Kultprophetie und Gerichtsverkündigung in der späten Königszeit Israels* (Göttingen: Neukirchener Verlag, 1970).

affirmed,[99] within the Old Testament presupposes the notion of resurrection and is to be found first in the later writings of the Old Testament and in the extra-canonical Apocalyptic literature (1 Enoch 91.5; Dan. 7.9, 26f.; Is. 24.21; Joel 4.14; etc.). Important for the Christian tradition from among these is Is. 66.15–24 (cf. Sir. 7.17; Mark 9.48 + Rev. 20.14 and 21.8). This passage mentions judgement by fire and second death, which is not actually death but consists in the rejected being delivered over for eternity to the fire and the worms.

At the time of the New Testament,[100] the message of John the Baptist is of primary significance as a prophecy of judgement: everyone without distinction, i.e. all those who are called Israel from the ancestry of Abraham (Matt. 3.9 par) will soon meet with the annihilating judgement (Matt. 3.7 and par) accomplished by fire (Matt. 3.1 par). Escape from this judgement is only individually possible through John's baptism and the subsequent rigorous ethical practice of repentance (Luke 3.8 par).

As far as we know it, judgement does not stand at the centre of the proclamation of the historical Jesus, but rather the Kingdom of God, understood to be breaking in through his own work. This, in part, has led to the role of the judgement in Jesus' proclamation being downplayed. We have to be mindful, however, of the fact that Jesus had himself been baptized by John, indicating a basic agreement with his proclamation. Careful exegesis of the biblical materials (Luke 13.1–5, 12.16–20 and 16.1–7) indicates that Jesus is of the opinion that the whole of Israel has been rejected unless it repents. This repentance, however, takes another form from that of the Baptist, because it centres on grace of God, who lets the sun shine on good and evil alike.[101] Should texts such as Luke 17.34f and Mark 9.43–48 prove to lead back to Jesus, then it is possible to see that Jesus reckoned on a double outcome of the final judgement, one that is again dependent on how one relates to the rule of God which is breaking in through his person.[102] Jesus shares with John the Baptist the notion that not only all of those alive in his time are lost, but also that there will be a judgement. In distinction to the Baptist, however, he assumes that God will forestall this judgement with saving action and that this has broken in through his preaching the Kingdom of God.

---

[99] Cf. Sigurd Hjelde, 'Divine Judgement I. Religious Studies', in *RPP*, vol. 4, pp. 109–10.

[100] On judgement in the NT as a whole, cf. Egon Brandenburger, 'Gerichtskonzeptionen im Urchristentum und ihre Voraussetzungen', in Egon Brandenburger (ed.), *Studien zur Geschichte und Theologie des Urchristentums* (Stuttgart: Katholisches Bibelwerk, 1993), pp. 289–338.

[101] Cf. Jürgen Becker, *Jesus of Nazareth* (trans. James E. Crouch; New York: De Gruyter, 1998), pp. 53–8.

[102] Cf. Becker, *Jesus of Nazareth*, pp. 58–60.

Why does the Baptist belong to the old order? It is because he still measures human life in terms of behaviour and its consequences, and thus because of the coming judgement he can offer Israel no hope for the future. Jesus, on the other hand, measures human reality in terms of the Kingdom of God – a kingdom characterized by the gracious nearness with which God wants to abolish the human misery caused, in part, by the system of works and rewards. In the light of this kingdom the entire system of works and rewards is declared to be obsolete and inappropriate.[103]

Paul also assumes that all Jews and pagans are to fall to God's wrathful judgement at the end of time (Rom. 1.18). The reason for this lies in the fact that God's law is in principle known to both (Rom. 2.1–3.20), but sin is of such strength (Rom. 3.9) that ethically fulfilling the law is impossible (Gal. 3.22; Rom. 3.20). Nevertheless, there is a possibility of salvation in the final judgement, since Christ has died for humanity on the cross (1 Thess. 5.9f; Rom. 3.24f. etc.). For those who have come to faith through the Holy Spirit, there is therefore the possibility of salvation in the judgement, which will test by fire whether or not one's work is built on the solid ground that is Christ (1 Cor. 3.11–15).

The notion that there is a final judgement to follow in which Christ appears as judge and criterion of the judgement subsequently develops broadly in the synoptic literature. In Matt. 25.31–46 in particular, the coming Son of Man as judge is identified with Christ and faith in the person of Christ as criterion of the judgement is elaborately bound with the evaluation of the ethical work of human beings, whereby the dual outcome of the judgement consists in eternal pain and eternal life.[104]

By comparison, in the Johannine literature, in most layers, one finds a completely different picture. Here, the dominant idea is that the one who believes in Jesus as the eternal Logos and Son in the present has eternal life, where as the non-believer is already judged, so that a final judgement is expendable (John 3.18–20, 3.36, 5.24, 12.46). That the Logos has come in the flesh means he is the judge (John 9.39).

Finally, we can point out that in the deutero-Pauline realm, the notion appears that through Christ's redeeming action on the cross, the entire creation without exception is reconciled with the result that the judgement bears the simpler outcome if salvation alone is to occur (Col. 1.20).[105]

---

[103]Becker, *Jesus of Nazareth*, p. 79.

[104]Cf. Hartmut Rosenau, *Allversöhnung: Ein transzendentaltheologischer Grundlegungsversuch* (Berlin: De Gruyter, 1993), pp. 82–103.

[105]Cf. Rosenau, *Allversöhnung*, pp. 56–81.

A range of different conceptions of the judgement appear in the Bible that cannot easily be harmonized.

- In the Old Testament, one can find the notion of a collective judgement.
- John the Baptist in particular emphasizes the notion of only the individual being saved from the judgement.
- Most of the New Testament theologies conceive of a future course of judgement. The Johannine literature constitutes the exception, in that it assumes a judgement that is experienced in the present.
- The criterion of the judgement could be human deeds, standing towards the kingdom of God, the law, faith in the person of Christ or even combinations of these elements.
- The notion of a dual outcome with eternal pain on the one hand and eternal life on the other appears.
- A dual outcome with eternal life and, in some cases, annihilation, a dissolution of the damned person appears (1 Cor. 3.11–15).
- A single outcome of universal salvation (*apokatastasis panton*) also arises (Col. 1.20).
- The judge is often the Son of Man, who is generally identified with the person of Christ or is this person himself.

5.3.1.2 The judgement in tradition

The divergent conceptions of the judgement in the Bible have demanded theological treatment throughout intellectual history. In contrast to many other theological problems that have arisen in relation to the Biblical witness, neither a clarification nor a minimization of the problem has emerged, but all in all a diversification. This can possibly be clarified through the existential meaning of the judgement and its outcomes for believers. Since the judgement and its results were often found to be threatening and since threats often appear to occupy the human imagination more than things that are not threatening, this diversification can be easily accounted for. The task of systematic theology in this case is not simply tracing the diversification,[106]

[106]It is not the task of systematic theology to draw up a detailed account of the possible negative outcomes. At this point, we have point towards works of historical theology such as that of Herbert Vorgrimler, *Geschichte der Hölle* (Munich: Fink, 1993).

but rather checking various understandings of judgement over against their theological contents and organizing them according to the different criteria. We will therefore forgo providing a chronological account of the material and go directly into a systematic presentation in what is to follow.

5.3.2 The outcome of the judgement

In everyday life, a judgement in the context of criminal law has a verdict and the corresponding punishment as its outcome. This would suggest that one first has to describe the proceedings of the court and then turn to what follows. With regard to the final judgement, however, this procedure does not appear to be appropriate. The kernel of the judgement does not consist in an image of the judgement itself, but rather in the fact that the image of the judgement is a metaphor for the transformation that is necessary in order to bring the present and eschatic realities into alignment. Understood in the strong sense, this can only mean a single outcome: the consummation of the kingdom of God as the salvation and fulfilment of creation. We cannot therefore as a first step evaluate the traditionally conceived outcomes of the judgement as to whether they follow consistently from the proceedings, but we rather have primarily to ask in effect whether and in what way they can serve the necessary process of transformation. It is therefore appropriate to thematize the outcomes of the judgement before treating the doctrine of the judgement as a process of transformation itself.

In principle at least, it is possible to conceive of more possible outcomes for the judgement than have played actually a role in the history of theology: the possibility of total reprobation and an entirely negative verdict naturally do not play any role in Christianity as a religion centred on the notion of salvation. In addition, the option of an appeal – a possibility meaningful in everyday life – is also impossible due to the ultimate character inherent to the concept of the final judgement. The possibilities remaining as found in the history of theology are: a dual outcome in the form of eternal life and *annihilatio* (annihilation of the rejected); a dual outcome in the form of eternal life and eternal pain, often arranged hierarchically; as well as a single positive outcome. We will now deal with these possibilities sequentially in order to be able to determine whether we can use them to make more precise statements about the judgement as a process of transformation.

It appears to be appropriate to consider the judgement first in terms of its outcomes. They are to be measured by the extent to which they facilitate an answer to the question of the transformation from reality at present to the eschatical reality. The possible outcomes are: 1. a dual outcome in the form of salvation and annihilation, 2. a dual outcome in the form of salvation and eternal pain and 3. a single outcome in the form of universal salvation (*apokatastasis panton*).

5.3.2.1 Dual outcome: Eternal life and annihilation

One theoretical model consists in understanding the judgement in such a way that it takes place in created persons and leads to a dual outcome in that some will be saved and receive eternal life, but others will be completely destroyed and made into nothingness. The idea of a total annihilation of those who are not compatible with the eschatic reality rarely arises in the history of Christianity. It is possible to derive this option from the biblical witness, since the notion of the fire of judgement in 1 Cor. 3.11–15 could be understood as corresponding to the idea that some will be completely annihilated. 2 Macc. 7.14, an early witness to the idea of the resurrection of the dead, presupposes that only the righteous will arise, but not the unrighteous, making it an indirect witness to the notion of annihilation. It is also possible to interpret the Johannine presentistic notion of judgement in this way. In the history of theology, the idea of annihilation was more likely to be advocated by persons and groups considered to be heretical by the church, particularly the Socinians and the later theology of the Enlightement which they also influenced.[107] In the twentieth century, a rare exception with the Protestant mainstream came in the theology of Lutheran Carl Stange (d. 1959), who taught that in the event of death, those who were not in Christ did not endure beyond death.[108] Those who had been made righteous 'received confirmation on the last day that they have chosen life, whereas those without God have fallen into death'.[109]

The idea of annihilation can be conceived systematically in a variety of different forms:[110]

---

[107]Cf. Janowski, *Allerlösung*, pp. 514–18.
[108]Cf. Carl Stange, *Das Ende aller Dinge* (Gütersloh: Bertelsmann, 1930), p. 158.
[109]Stange, *Das Ende aller Dinge*, p. 193
[110]Cf. Janowski, *Allerlösung*, pp. 523–4.

- Only the righteous experience the resurrection, whereas the unrighteous remain in total death and are even lost to the memory of God.
- Everyone is resurrected, but the unrighteous receive the judgement of annihilation.
- Everyone is resurrected, the unrighteous first undergo a time of relatively limited punishment and then will be annihilated.
- Annihilation either rests with divine judgement or is understood as self-annihilation based on one's own choice.

The advantages of this model as a whole,[111] regardless of which particular instance, are obvious: the eschatical reality is limited to what is good and good alone. Further, as with the next model, there is no eternal perpetuation of evil, not even evil being punished. Finally, it appears to satisfy the divine attribute of justice.

The disadvantages of this model, ultimately leading to its widespread rejection, are just as clear and begin with the final, only apparent advantage: if everyone is not resurrected, but only those who survive the criterion of judgement or even if some are annihilated after the resurrection, then, even if only in a negative form, humans become partially responsible for their own salvation, which would contradict justification in a semi-pelagian direction. Then, however, the redeeming work of Christ and the Spirit would have to be understood differently, ultimately affecting the doctrine of God: the eschatical reality would indeed be good, but not exclusively dependent on God for its redeemed character, which we came to see in the section on the eschaton (see section 3.3) as an important criterion.

This could only be avoided if one were to teach an antecedent doctrine of dual predestination by God to salvation and damnation. This conception, however, has its own problems, which we will examine below.

Both cases, be it the fact that annihilation ultimately rests on the cooperation of personal creatures or that it rests on a rejection before creation, would put question marks on God's intentions for creation. On the basis of God's *potentia absoluta*, God's absolute omnipotence to effect everything that God wills, this would indeed be a conceptual possibility, but one that demands an extremely high price: God would not be faithful to Godself and God's own decisions. Given the premise that God is love, God's faithfulness to Godself, and accordingly, God's veracity, is a principle

---

[111]For a discussion of the advantages and disadvantages of this model, cf. Janowski, *Allerlösung*, pp. 524–32.

of God's own being, so that the annihilation of personal creatures would stand in contradiction to God's own being and would therefore come down to an annihilation of Godself. This consequence can be avoided, but only at the price that neither justice, nor love, but God's arbitrary will alone would be God's highest attribute. This, however, would be incompatible with what we are able to say based on God's Trinitarian self-disclosure, even to the extent that to adopt this course would mean leaving the limits of the Christian faith in God behind us.

All in all, the only conclusion that we can draw from this is that the total annihilation of personal creatures, regardless of which form, is not an acceptable outcome for the final judgement.

> The dual outcome of the judgement in the form of an annihilation of personal creatures has to be rejected for various reasons. The most important is that this would result in a contradiction of God's intention to bring about personal creatures. Such a self-contradiction, however, is excluded if God, who is love, is faithful to God's own self. According to Luther,[112] when God speaks, whether in wrath or in grace, then annihilation is impossible.

5.3.2.2 Dual outcome: Eternal life and eternal punishment

In its history, Christianity has kept mostly to the notion of a dual outcome of the judgement such that for some there is eternal life and for others there is eternal pain. This doctrine was widespread, extending from Augustine (d. 430), who laid the essential groundwork of the doctrine, through Gregory the Great (d. 604), who catered to the imaginative depiction of the dual outcome, up to Thomas Aquinas, (d. 1274), who offered a comprehensive systemization of the doctrine. This form of the doctrine was not assaulted during the Reformation. Through the upheaval of the Enlightenment and the search for an appropriate hermeneutic for biblical texts, descriptions of the dual outcome in modernity gradually receded with regard to their plasticity, certainly without having resolved the fundamental theological problem at stake.

---

[112]Cf. Luther, *Lectures on Genesis: Chapters 26–30*, in *Luther's Works*, vol. 5, p. 76.

One can say in particular that since Augustine the opinion has prevailed that those who receive the negative verdict in the judgement are subject to second death, which is not annihilation, but eternal pain through fire and the pangs of conscience in the form of the biting of worms. The punishment of hell can therefore be conceived in terms of levels, from which a model of the levels of hell emerges parallel to that of the intermediate state (see section 5.2.3). Distinctions have to be made between those who are completely lost and also cannot be prayed for, those who are lost but can be prayed for even if the prayer only eases the pangs of conscience of the living, and those who through the prayer of the living can receive some relief from their punishment. Whereas Augustine still assumed that unbaptized children that had died would receive the full penalty, the later tradition made reference to a neutral place of rest, the *limbus infantium* (see section 5.2.3). The upper levels of hell, to which the *limbus patrorum*, the resting place for the righteous of the Old Testament was found, were ultimately understood to have been empty since Christ's harrowing of hell on Holy Saturday.[113]

The notion of the dual outcome ultimately only changed in one way through the Reformation: the hierarchical structure was abolished so that there were no longer any intermediate levels, effectively putting an end to all such speculation for Protestants. Melanchthon (d. 1560) rejected a single positive outcome and retained the dual outcome in the confessional writings, as found in the *Confessio Augustana*: 'It is also taught that our Lord Jesus Christ will return on the Last Day to judge, to raise all the dead, to give eternal life and eternal joy to those who believe and are elect, but to condemn the ungodly and the devils to hell and eternal punishment.'[114] However, Melanchthon not only retains the dual outcome, but eternal pain is depicted explicitly in the Latin version of the 'Apology of the Augsburg Confession' with words that are hardly to be surpassed in terms of their gruesomeness, that 'the ungodly will be crucified without end', though both the English and German versions soften the language: 'We confess that Christ will appear at the consummation of the world and will raise up all the dead, giving eternal life and eternal joys to the godly, but condemning

[113]On the diverse individual conceptions of the hierarchical dual outcome in Augustine, Gregory and Thomas, cf. Vorgrimler, *Geschichte der Hölle*, pp. 117–27, 136–46, 200–07. On the popular presentation of the harrowing of hell as found in Dante's *Divine Comedy*, cf. Vorgrimler, *Geschichte der Hölle*, pp. 175–90.

[114]'The Augsburg Confession', in *The Book of Concord*, pp. 50–1 (XVIII: Concerning the Return of Christ to Judgment).

the ungodly to *endless torment with the devil*.'[115] The dual outcome is highly problematic for a number of theological reasons, although the tradition has been aware of these problems and has also maintained a number of responses to them.

The problem that those saved to eternal life have to have compassion for the rejected on the basis of their capacity for love has been variously resolved, sometimes in ways that are astonishing for modern ears: the most radical notion is found in Tertullian (d. ca. 220) in that seeing the rejected eternally suffering an experience like never-ending death, more horrible than being murdered, actually belongs to the peace of eternal life.[116] Christian antiquity's answer came out a bit more carefully. Compassion for the dammed is impossible, since according to Thomas compassion relates to a condition that could still be changed,[117] whereas the outcome of the final judgement constitutes the definitive end of every possibility for additional change, that is, if he does not want to contradict the very notion of a final judgement.[118] It is not that the blessed will enjoy the torments of the damned in hell as such, but only to the extent that they see in this the order of divine justice and their own deliverance.[119]

Thomas responds to the theological problem of how eternal punishment could be fitting for temporal sins by answering that eternal punishment is not unjust because sin is not imputed with regard to the severity of its temporal outcome, but rather according to its nature as transgression against the law of the eternal God.[120]

At this point, we shall leave off our account of the questions and answers raised by the dual outcome from its proponents and push on towards making some basic evaluations of the problems.

The theory of the dual outcome shares a few problems with the model of annihilation, which can also be understood as a variation of the theory of the dual outcome.[121]

---

[115]'Apology of Augsburg Confession' in *The Book of Concord*, p. 233 (XVII: Christ's Return for Judgment). For the Latin and German, see Ernst Wolf (ed), *Die Bekenntnisschriften der evangelisch-lutherischen Kirchen* (Göttingen: Vandenhoek & Ruprecht, 1967), p. 310 (§66): 'confitemur ... impios vero condemnaturum esse, ut cum diabolo sine fine crucientur.'

[116]Cf. Daley, *Eschatologie in Schrift und Patristik*, p. 113.

[117]Cf. Aquinas, *Summa Theologica*, vol. 5, pp. 2960–1 (III Suppl., Q.94, Art.2).

[118]Cf. Aquinas, *Summa Theologica*, vol. 5, pp. 2993–4 (III Suppl., Q.98, Art.6).

[119]Cf. Aquinas, *Summa Theologica*, vol. 5, pp. 2961 (III Suppl., Q.94, Art.3).

[120]Cf. Aquinas, *Summa Theologica*, vol. 5, pp. 2995–8 (III Suppl., Q.99, Art.1).

[121]Cf. Rosenau, *Allversöhnung*, p. 9.

If the dual outcome is the infliction of punishment on the basis of the fact that humans have not attained to a specific criterion in their life in the here and now – be it acting justly, having faith or rejecting the gift of the Holy Spirit – then the dual outcome would be attributing a soteriological relevance to human action that it cannot have according to the Reformation distinction between divine action and human action. Grace would not be irresistible and a structure far beyond that of semi-pelagianism would have been adopted. Ultimately, humans would be pronouncing judgement over themselves and the final judgement would only be an immortalization of this human judgement. The danger of this kind of soteriological self-contradiction was not entirely clear to the Reformation tradition. One example of such a dual outcome, in which God's pronunciation of judgement is ultimately only the fixing of individual humans' own self-judgements, can be seen in C.S. Lewis (d. 1963), who has his paragon George McDonald say in a book: 'There are only two kinds of people in the end: those who say to God, "Thy will be done," and those to whom God says, in the end, "Thy will be done".'[122] Such an approach is only a highly cautious relativizing of the notion of the dual outcome: it is not that a form of punishment will be independently imposed on human beings, rather the punishment consists precisely in the fact that they receive in eternity what they ask for without the possibility of changing whatever this might be. With this, Lewis had indeed seen – against the profane view that humanity makes its own bed and therefore has to lie in it – that the sinful human will is incapable of any good. In addition, the problem of the contradiction of how a God who is absolutely good can impose an eternal punishment does not arise at this point. However, this still does not change the fundamental soteriological problem of eschatical semi-pelagianism.

It is certainly possible to work around this fundamental soteriological problem by teaching in protology that before the beginning of the creation, God had already decided on the rejection of the reprobate in the form of double predestination. This makes it possible to view the offer of grace through the death of Christ in its universal, biblical sense (John 3.16), but it is nonetheless still possible to distinguish the universality of the *offer* of grace from its *realization*, the latter not being universal. This can be seen in Augustine, who can therefore identify the recipients of this grace as "all", and yet limit it at the same time: 'What does "all" mean? All those of the Gentiles and also all those of the Jews whom he has predestined, called,

---

[122]C.S. Lewis, *The Great Divorce* (London: Collins, 1946), p. 75.

justified and glorified. He will not spare all men; but none of these will be condemned by him.'[123] This notion of double predestination was taken up by John Calvin (d. 1564) and developed into a broad doctrine, which then culminated in nineteenth-century Scottish federal Calvinism in saying that the offer of grace and therefore the death of Christ as a saving event could not be understood as providing universal coverage as such. Christ did not die for the world, but for the 'church', meaning that community of the faithful who have also received the gift of perseverance in faith (*donum perseverantiae*).[124] Although the Synod of Dort in 1618 attempted to maintain Calvin's double predestination against the Arminians in a moderate form that did not hold the object of rejection to be the fall into sin itself, but rather only fallen humanity, now, another problem appeared: whereas grace is indeed great and God is the only agent of soteriology, this now even applies negatively. But, this only magnifies the problem touching the theory of the dual outcome in all of its forms: regardless of whether one understands the dual outcome in a semi-pelagian manner in terms of human contribution or generated on the basis of a double predestination, sin and evil are made eternal in both cases, even if as evil that is being punished, and therefore resulting in an eschatical dualism. In other words, the eschatical reality is not exclusively good in this case.

If one accepts the dual outcome on the basis of a doctrine of predestination, the problem is only protologically and theologically intensified: now, there is not only an eschatical dualism, but also a protological dualism and ultimately even a theological dualism: God is not exclusively good.

If we are to hold that every kind of eschatical dualism is incompatible with the criteria of eschatology as is given in God's Trinitarian self-disclosure, then it is necessary to reject the notion of a dual outcome.

A dual outcome of the judgement in the form of eternal life for the one and eternal pain for the other is confronted by various problems. Accepting the notion of an efficacious self-rejection on the part of the damned means admitting that the human will has eschatical relevance and teaching a kind of synergism in salvation that has to be rejected on behalf of the theology of the Reformation. If one assumes

[123]Augustine, *The City of God*, p. 1090 (XXI,24).
[124]Cf. Mühling, *Versöhnendes Handeln – Handeln in Versöhnung*, pp. 185–6, 230.

a protological double predestination, God is then made responsible for the dual outcome, thereby compromising God's good. Under all circumstances, an immortalization of evil arises through this form of the doctrine and therefore an eschatical dualism. If the eschatical reality is to be good and nothing other than good, then this version of the dual outcome also has to be rejected.

5.3.2.3 Universal salvation

The last remaining option regarding the final judgement is the possibility that all personal creatures without exception are to experience eschatical salvation. This is the possibility of the final reconciliation of everything or universal salvation (*apokatastasis panton*). Like the foregoing possibilities, this also presents the alternative that humanity is either a participant in this outcome or it is a matter of God's sole eschatical-soteriological action.

Although universal salvation has been rejected a number of times by the church as heretical, as in the confessional writings of the Lutheran church in Germany (*Confessio Augustana* 17), it has nonetheless remained nearly continually in currency, even among eminent theologians.

It was Origen (d. 254) who established the authoritative standard for a doctrine of universal salvation also designed to maintain human soteriological freedom and developed an approach, as far as it can be reconstructed, towards which the Fathers of the Eastern Orthodox churches have tended. The goal that Origen wanted to reach runs in his own words:

> We believe, however, that the goodness of God through Christ will restore his entire creation to one end, even his enemies being conquered and subdued.... For the word subjection, when used of our subjection to Christ, implies the salvation, proceeding from Christ, of those who are subject.[125] God...has so ordered everything that each spirit or soul...should not be completed by force against its free choice to any except that to which the motions of its own mind lead it.[126]

The two principles universal salvation is to effect are the goodness or grace of God and the created will. Goodness and grace also imply God's justice, whereas the created will is the freedom of choice, not just for good or evil, but also regarding the self-constitution of rational creatures such as humans,

---

[125]Origen, *On First Principles*, p. 70 (I,VI,1).
[126]Origen, *On First Principles*, pp. 94–5 (II,I,2).

angels and demons. This involves the fact that there is no actual doctrine of original sin that presupposes the necessity of human sin after the fall. What is to be overcome is evil, which as a middle-Platonist Origen understood as being fully real, and not only – as in the neo-Platonic tradition – as a deprivation of the good. Assuming that there can be an endless amount of time, then it necessarily follows that at some point in time the wills of all rational creatures will be positively orientated towards God. This is the moment of universal salvation.

Here, however, Origen assumes that creation's freedom of will is preserved. But, the same logic also means that in an unending course of history, a new fall will have to come about. Origen only wants to accept this as a logical possibility, but not the facticity of such a second fall, though his rejection of the notion at this point can only be understood as pure assertion. Thus, when the church tradition rejected Origen's formulation by claiming that he was teaching an eternal return of the same, this accusation is correct in principle, even though Origen himself explicitly rejected this notion.

However, the logical problems with Origen's teaching have not yet been taken care of. Because, following the same line of thought used to conceptually introduce universal salvation on the basis of freedom of the will, it is also possible to suggest, as Rosenau does, the necessity of everyone turning away from God at some point in the course of history or some turning to God while others turn away from God. That the course of history either does not break apart at this point or that there is an eschatical reality of total damnation or a dual outcome is, according to the logic of the argument, purely arbitrary.[127]

It is apparent that the core of the argument as it has been reconstructed here constitutes a complete abandonment of Christian ideas. Origen incorporates Christian ideas into his theory at two points: one being the notion of salvation through Christ and the other being the notion of the judgement.

The redemptive work of Christ is understood by Origen in such a way that Christ as doctor or teacher makes it possible for creatures to have their wills oriented rightly.[128] However, this is not a sufficient, but at most a necessary condition for salvation, though Rosenau disputes even this way of reading Origen.[129]

---

[127]For Rosenau's reconstruction, cf., *Allversöhnung*, pp. 113–50.
[128]Cf. Rosenau, *Allversöhnung*, pp. 139–43.
[129]Cf. Rosenau, *Allversöhnung*, p. 142.

The judgement, however, appears differently. It has a practical, rather than eschatical relevance, to some extent serving the role of a catalyst that accelerates the process by which creatures orient their wills to God. Rosenau describes it as follows: 'The judgement for Origen is an "obliteration and extinction of all sinners and those who are unworthy (*ablatis atque extinctis peccatoribus et indignis*)".'[130] This, however, is not an annihilation of all creatures whose wills are orientated towards evil,

> but a *reversion*.... Here, annihilation is "understood in such a way that nothing of the divinely created substance ceases to be, but rather its hostile orientation of will, which does not originate with God but in itself. It will be annihilated, not in order not to exist (in the future), but in order not to be hostile (any longer)".... In this way the evil wanted by rational creatures can be detached and divorced from the one's willing it.... If God is called a consuming fire, then this fire of judgement does not have us for its fuel, but rather "the evil of our deeds". They are the hay, the wood and the straw. Thus the judgement of God brings about a *catharsis*.[131]

If this reconstruction of Origen's thought is correct, then we cannot simply agree with Rosenau's assessment that Origen's position implies that either dual outcome or the total rejection are also just as likely to occur as universal salvation.[132] Instead, the judgement is rather an expression of the grace-filled action of God's goodness. Without the element of judgement, the eschatic outcome would not come about, and according to Origen's notion, it would also not be a matter of cooperation between divine grace and human action, but exclusively an accomplishment of human will. Without the judgement, personal creatures would be sufficient on their own and autarchic. The judgement is what at the very least makes Origen's position synergistic. In any case, this means that the same criterion that we also applied to the two other possibilities of outcome also has to be applied here: from the standpoint of the Reformation, the distinction between divine action and human action that is gained by the doctrine of justification is violated, bringing along with it all the necessary consequences for our understanding of Christ's redeeming action and of God; it is for this reason that we cannot accept Origen's formulation.

A similar notion about human participation can also be found in the early Christian notion of the *Refrigerium*, which was bound to the notion

---

[130] Rosenau, *Allversöhnung*, p. 130.
[131] Rosenau, *Allversöhnung*, pp. 131–2.
[132] Cf. Rosenau, *Allversöhnung*, p. 146.

of a sabbath from hell, an idea stemming from early Rabbinic tradition. It was Tertullian (d. 220) who seems to have used the term first, for whom it essentially still referred to the 'bosom of Abraham', i.e. the *limbus patrorum* (see above), as a place between heaven and earth.[133] Prudentius Aurelius Clemens (d. ca. 413) developed the notion of a place of refreshment or cooling, to where the occupants of hell could go permanently or take rest in regular intervals from their torments.[134] In the twentieth century, C.S. Lewis adopted this notion and understood it in such a way that the cyclically recurring *Refrigerium* as an intermediate state offers the occupants of hell the opportunity to make their own decision about heaven.[135] Lewis thus approximates himself somewhat to Origen's version of the eternal coexistence of human and divine freedom. He has not, therefore, developed a doctrine of *apokatastasis panton*, but the payoff is rather a form of dual outcome: the damned are only damned in so far as they have damned themselves by not choosing salvation in the *Refrigerium*. But, since neither universal salvation nor the dual outcome in itself are logical consequences of this conception, it would make more sense to formulate it in terms of a model of a judgement that lasts infinitely.

Universal salvation can also be understood without human participation. Early stages of this form of the doctrine can be found in the theology of Schleiermacher (d. 1834), which have been continued by Rosenau in the present. According to Schleiermacher, human beings are absolutely dependent on God, so that in their relationship with one another, humans are understood as being absolutely passive, whereas God is absolutely active. This is nothing other than a description of the omnipotence of God. Regardless of what one thinks about this starting point, it has the advantage of largely being able to exclude synergistic, semi-Pelagian tendencies from the outset. This only leaves the alternatives of either double predestination or universal salvation. Double predestination, however, would contradict the simplicity of God, because God cannot be thought as being divided into contradictory attributes. A dual outcome in the judgement is thus tantamount to a dualistic understanding of reality. Double predestination or a dual outcome would further contradict the

[133]Cf. Heinz Finé, *Die Terminologie der Jenseitsvorstellungen bei Tertullian* (Bonn: Hanstein, 1957).
[134]Cf. Alfred Stuiber, *Refrigerium interim: Die Vorstellungen vom Zwischenzustand und die frühchristliche Grabeskunst* (Bonn: Hanstein, 1957); Pierre de Labriolle, 'Refrigerium', *Bulletin D'ancienne Littérature et D'archéologie Chrétiennes* 2 (1912), pp. 214–9; Andre Parrot, *Le 'Refrigerium' dans l'au-dela* (Paris: Librairie Leroux, 1937).
[135]Cf. Lewis, *The Great Divorce*, pp. 67–8.

organic unity of all of humanity. This is because salvation consists in the fact that through the common spirit of the church, the constant power of the consciousness of God is disclosed. If humanity forms an organic whole, then the possibility that some are eschatically redeemed and some are not is excluded. This is because 'the compassion for those who have been definitively excluded from blessedness would diminish the blessedness of the blessed and ultimately overrule it'.[136] This means that the only outcome remaining is that of universal salvation, which Schleiermacher himself describes as follows: 'If we consider the contrast between the Kingdom of God and the world at this point to be temporary, so that everyone who is now outside of the church will at some point be within it, then this discrepancy between both elements of self-consciousness is instantly removed.'[137] More recently, Rosenau has tapped into this argumentation and made it more precise by means of modal logic and reflections on the relationship between *actio dei* and *actio hominum*, which we do not need to elaborate at this point.[138]

How, then, are we to assess Schleiermacher's idea? The thesis I want to maintain here is that Schleiermacher's argumentation is correct and yet cannot be adopted as compatible to a theory of universal salvation because it is not a soteriological theory about an eschatical universal salvation, but only a meta-theory about material theories of the eschatic outcome of the judgement, or concretely, of the dual outcome. Schleiermacher does not ultimately give an account of how or in what way this universal salvation can be reached. He 'only' demonstrates with high acuity that the notions of annihilation and the dual outcome are not compatible with Christian thinking and are even irreligious.[139] In our critique of these possible outcomes of the judgement, we have also essentially made use of Schleiermacher's argumentation ourselves. However, does this mean that we need to accept his notion of universal salvation? Both Schleiermacher's and Rosenau's arguments draw on the principle of the excluded middle and the use of *reductio ad absurdum* to negate the possibility of a dual outcome, so that only the simple outcome remains, by means of the premise that a dual outcome and universal salvation constitute a total disjunction. But, even if this premise were valid, it does not lose its status as a meta-theory.

---

[136]Rosenau, *Allversöhnung*, pp. 183–4.
[137]Friedrich Schleiermacher, *Der christliche Glaube (1821–1822)* (ed. Hermann Peiter; 2 vols; Berlin: De Gruyter, 1984), p. 169 (§137).
[138]Cf. Rosenau, *Allversöhnung*, pp. 402–27.
[139]Cf. Rosenau, *Allversöhnung*, p. 189.

It is therefore possible to ask about further possibilities along two different pathways:

- Are there indications in Schleiermacher's work that clarify materially in what way universal salvation is possible?
- Does the alternative between a dual outcome and universal salvation actually constitute a *complete* disjunction, so that other possibilities are excluded?

A positive answer to the first question would provide support for the notion of universal salvation. Counter to this is the observable fact that there are humans who are either not saved at the time of their death or at least have not come to faith. Rosenau indicates that for Schleiermacher, human development has not come to an end even after the death of the person.[140] At the very least, this would be a necessary condition of such a theory's compatibility. This would be similar to the idea suggested by Thomas Erskine of Linlathen (d. 1870), that death is not an eschatical matter at all, necessitating the adoption of the notion that humans experience a post-mortal but pre-eschatic life. We already discussed this idea in the last section on the intermediate state (see section 5.2.3) but ultimately had to reject it, so that no positive answer remains available to us here as well.

The second question, of whether there is a third way beyond the notion of the dual outcome (to which the notion of annihilation also necessarily belongs) and universal salvation, has been variously answered in the affirmative by the theological tradition. It is to the attempts to develop this alternative that we shall now turn.

The notion of universal salvation (*apokatastasis panton*) can be understood in such a way that the course of the world can last until the eschatical reality at least as long as it takes for all the damned to choose for God or to find their way to God after death via the notion of the *Refrigerium*, a place of rest from the torments of hell. These notions, however, presuppose the synergistic contribution of humans to their own salvation, meaning both are to be rejected. Following Schleiermacher, it is possible to understand the notion of universal salvation in such a way that God alone is responsible for

[140]Cf. Rosenau, *Allversöhnung*, p. 179.

it, though it is not positively developed. In any case, this possibility would presuppose post-mortal but pre-eschatical action of God on some humans. This has to be rejected since it implies a necessary reduplication of the world in such a way that things in the here and now would be robbed of their eschatical relevance. This means that an attempt to find a third way beyond the polarities of the dual outcome and universal salvation is appropriate.

5.3.2.4 Election and selective judgement

On the hunt for a third way, one inevitably bumps into Karl Barth's (d. 1968) theory, though it certainly is the case that his position cannot be easily characterized. Some theologians believe he represents a third way out of the dilemma, whereas others do not. Some see him as a representative of a doctrine of universal salvation, whereas others strongly dispute this claim.[141]

Barth's starting point is the doctrine of election, but his version only resembles the classical Calvinist form of the doctrine with regard to the linguistic forms it employs. According to Barth, the eternal decision about election, understood in Reformed orthodoxy as the *decretum absolutum*, has the great disadvantage of leaving open the actual extent of divine election: in other words, the classic version of the doctrine is unclear about who is and is not elect. Responding to this deficiency, Barth posits the *dectrum concretum*, understood as God's concrete decision about election bearing upon the concrete person of Jesus Christ as true God and true human. It is in Jesus Christ that the electing God and the electing human are concretely united, and indeed, to the extent that the human being in Jesus Christ is elect, but God chooses rejection for God's self.[142] Although Barth himself does not explicitly derive a doctrine of universal salvation from this,[143] some theologians are of the view that such a universalism

---

[141]A third way can be seen in Otto Weber, 'Die Lehre von der Erwählung und die Verkündigung', in Otto Weber, Walter Kreck and Ernst Wolf (eds), *Die Predigt von der Gnadenwahl* (Munich: Kaiser-Verlag, 1951), pp. 9–36, 12, whereas Rosenau, *Allversöhnung*, p. 200, rejects this formulation and on pp. 191–222 attributes a doctrine of universal salvation to Barth. Gregor Etzelmüller, "*… zu richten die Lebendigen und die Toten*". *Zur Rede vom jüngsten Gericht im Anschluß an Karl Barth* (Neukirchen-Vluyn: Neukirchener Verlag, 2001), pp. 316–17, 326–7, however, rejects Rosenau's claim about Barth.

[142]Cf. Barth, *Church Dogmatics II/2*, p. 94 (§33).

[143]Cf. Barth, *Church Dogmatics II/2*, pp. 417–18.

can be derived from Barth's treatment of election.[144] The election of the 'multitude' ensues from the concrete human being elected to salvation in Jesus Christ, which indeed does remain open but, according to Rosenau, does not leave any room for individually lost humans because in the unity of the electing God and the elected human, humanity is only elected to salvation, not to damnation. Here, Rosenau observes that the doctrine of universal salvation Barth actually intended cannot be arrived at by direct deduction from the notion of election in reference to Christ, because this opens up the possibility of the damnation of some humans and therefore a dual outcome.[145] This objection is correct, but only in connection with the assumption that Barth actually intended to develop a doctrine of universal salvation. This, however, is highly questionable, because the subject matter of Barth's doctrine of election is Christ and humanity, but not – or at least not only – the open number of the elect. This makes it clear that Barth is no longer focusing on the sum of elect human individuals and that his approach can be regarded as a 'third way'.

When one has a look at the judgement in Barth, a significant shift occurs: it is a matter of course that the nothing (*das Nichtige*), i.e. evil and all that is not compatible with the Kingdom of God, must be excluded. However, a new model[146] can be found at this point in Barth's thought, as well as with other twentieth-century theologians such as Tillich (d. 1965) or Pannenberg:[147] Human individuals will not be saved or annihilated in the judgement, but, according to the image of the fire used in 1 Cor. 3.11–15, it is understood in such a way that the nothing, or everything that is not compatible with the Kingdom of God, will be annihilated, but everything else will remain. As a result, the judgement is always painful, but it also offers the possibility of continued existence equally to all individual humans in that what was formerly evil has been separated out. In its various forms, this can be called the model of selective judgement over personal biography. This model, however, is also not without its problems.

[144]Cf. Emil Brunner, *The Christian Doctrine of God: Dogmatics I* (trans. Olive Wyon; Philadelphia: Westminster Press, 1949), pp. 346–52; Heinz Zahrnt, *Die Sache mit Gott* (Munich: Piper, 1966), p. 137; Rosenau, *Allversöhnung*, p. 194.

[145]Cf. Rosenau, *Allversöhnung*, pp. 194–5, 199–202.

[146]In all actuality, the notion of a selective judgement for the purposes of purification is nothing new, as a similar model can be found in Origen as noted above. The idea of purgatory is also related. What is new here is only the fact that we are dealing with an independent model for interpreting the judgement including its outcome.

[147]Cf. Tillich, *Systematic Theology III*, pp. 398–401, 415–19; Pannenberg, *Systematic Theology III*, pp. 608–30.

- Does this mean that various things remain over from the personal biographies of individual human beings, qualitative as well as quantitative, that are of eschatical valence? In borderline cases, would this mean that only the infancy and youth of a particular person would be of eschatical valance, whereas in another case, an adult human renders an eschatically enduring contribution? This would then appear to be a case of an immortalization of the soteriological capacity of individual human works in their various amounts and thus a dangerous eschatical semi-Pelagianism.
- Does this model also not cut out the fact that negatives also belong to human identity in the here and now, and do these things somehow appear positively in the judgement?
- This model also sees human beings and becomings individualistically and not relationally. However, assuming a relational understanding of humans as we have here, this model runs into difficulties. For example, if some negative aspect of Person A is involved in a situation that contributes something positively to Person B, what would it mean for both persons if the negative aspect of Person A were to be removed? In other words, this model ignores the relational constitution of human becomings and wrongly claims that humans are atomisticly compounded.
- Is this model of an atomistic individual enclosed within itself not also false to the extent that personal unity is not already given in it, but also the person has to be seen as a relata of relationships to other persons and considered to be in itself as a relational-narrative process? It would be more appropriate to talk about human becomings than about human beings.[148] This brings in the criticism that starting with the various outcomes of the judgement is one-sided and misleading in that it does not draw in the social and natural world.
- Another reproach that one could make against this model – as well as against all the other models that we have examined – consists in the fact that it remains centred on those who commit offenses and hardly considers the victims of those offenses: if negative events are removed from the identity of the perpetrator of a harmful act, does that not

---

[148] This genuine insight of theological anthropology meets the present state of biological and social anthropology, cf. Tim Ingold and Gisli Palsson (eds), *Biosocial Becomings: Integrating Social and Biological Anthropology* and especially Agustín Fuentes, 'Blurring the Biological and Social in Human Becomings', in ibid., pp. 42–58.

then mean that there also has to be an eschatical compensation with respect to the victim of that act as well?[149]

A passable third way is therefore neither to be found in the Barthian doctrine of election, nor in the notion of selective judgement of personal biographies. Nevertheless, these theories can be appraised positively for their efforts to escape all forms of strict eschatological dualism.[150] This allows us to identify wherein the progress lies. The view that there is a strict disjunction between a twofold eschatical outcome (including the model of annihilation) and universal salvation depends on the fact that particular human becomings are seen as individuals instead of as persons. In other words, this notion at the very least implicitly presupposes an individualistic concept of created personhood, which was previously regarded as highly questionable (see section 4.2). The proposal for a putative 'third way' as reviewed here abandons this classification in part and at least points in the right direction: the first step is to make the appropriate classification of what is actually to be judged. But, here, a contradiction appears: At the beginning of our enquiry into the doctrine of the judgement, we said it is necessary to start with the outcome of the judgement. But, at the end of this enquiry, we see that its object is fundamentally unclear. However, this apparent contradiction can be resolved by looking at the judgement in strongly relational terms, construed as a relational process within which both the goal of the judgement and the objects of the judgement appear as particular relata – next to which there are then still other relata of this process that are to be discussed. We shall now turn to this reflection.

Potential third ways between a dual outcome and universal salvation can be seen in Karl Barth's doctrine of election, as well as in the notion of a selective judgement about particular events in the individual biographies of created persons. This disproves the notion that the dual outcome and universal salvation constitute mutually exclusive alternatives beyond which there are no other possibilities. This

[149]Cf. the discussion by Etzelmüller, *Zu richten die Lebendigen und die Toten*, pp. 327–8. On the contrary, it is certainly the case that victims would not be able to blank out the offender and should not let their reflection degenerate into a thirst for revenge, but both have to be considered relationally. It appears that much Christian theology does not pay adequate attention to the offenders in such cases.

[150]This is the programmatic approach of Janowski, *Allerlösung*.

alternative itself only appeared to be plausible because it conceived individual created persons to be the objects of the judgement. To the contrary, Barth's doctrine of election has the person of Jesus Christ as its object, whereas the notion of selective judgement takes as its object events from the biographies of individual persons. Neither of these, however, is satisfactory: the notion of election in Christ is not a solution to the problem and the notion of the selective judgement remains chained to an individualistic atomistic-additive concept of personhood in so far as it assumes that the biographies of individual persons can be separated out from one another. Positively, however, these positions do reflect the possibility of looking for a third way.

Since all the attempts we have analysed up to this point that argue for necessary transformations to the eschatical reality have failed, the premise adopted at the beginning, that the judgement as transformation is best clarified from the standpoint of the outcome of the judgement, appears to have been proven an illusion. Instead, we can now move into an examination of a doctrine of the final judgement as a process.

5.3.3 The judgement as a process

5.3.3.1 The judgement as transformation and constitution of personal identity

In recalling section 3.3, we know that we can identify the goal of the judgement. With respect to the relationship between the good, the true and the beautiful, we suggested that the good and the true coincide and that the eschatical reality can only be good and nothing other than good, and that there can be many equally good events that are different in terms of their beauty, though not in the sense of more or less beauty, but rather in the sense of different beauty. This also applies to the eschatical reality: It can only be good and nothing but good. If, however, the world in its course through the present is to make a contribution to the eschatical reality, this cannot consist in a contribution to its goodness, as this would contradict the doctrine of justification. The contribution can, however, consist in a particular instantiation of beauty. It is possible to conceive of multiple eschatical realities that are equally good, but also different as to their aesthetic form. The judgement can then be understood as God's final action in the world, which translates all remaining ethical difference – that is, variations consisting in more or less good – into goodness without remainder to the extent that ethical differences have no further influence on the eschatical identity since they have been transformed by divine action into aesthetic differences. The goal of the final judgement is therefore precisely this transformation of ethical differences into aesthetic differences. This also means believing that the divine action of judgement is that evil will not merely be eliminated, annihilated or immortalized through a form of eternal punishment, but that it can be transformed into good to the extent that it is capable of making a contribution to the non-foreseeable aesthetic form of the eschatical reality.

> The goal of the judgement is the eschatical reality, which must be conceived as being exclusively good. At the same time, the present world, the world of the here and now, must be of eschatical relevance if the eschatical reality is to be the fulfilment of creation. But, this means that negative events cannot simply fall out of the relational structure of the process of world events. On the contrary, they will be transformed into events with aesthetic differences.

5.3.3.2 Objects and criteria of the judgement

Within the framework of our assessment of the problematic doctrine of the classical outcomes of the judgement in the form of a development of a thoroughgoing disjunction between a dual outcome and universal salvation, we determined that the error in this version of the doctrine consists in the fact that it presupposes an individualistic and atomistic understanding of the person as the object of the judgement. This means that a person's individual biography, particularly their actions, constitutes their personhood, and that this is the object of the judgement. But, this approach failed and the decisive question remains: What, then, can we see as the positive object of the judgement?

In the Bible, the works or deeds of a person are explicitly named as the criterion of judgement (Matt. 24f). The wrath of judgement to come at the end as a result of the fact that the law has not been fulfilled is occasion for Paul in Rom. 1.18f not to excuse either the pagans, for whom the standard of measurement is written on their hearts, nor for Jews, to whom the law was revealed. This criterion was practically taken for granted during the entirety of the Middle Ages.[151] While the Reformation did not deny this viewpoint, it did assume that faith was ultimately the determinative criterion. This, however, did pose a few problems for the biblicistic versions of the older Protestant theology.[152] Even if contemporary Protestant theology were to reject the manner of speaking about judgement according to works as prone to misunderstanding,[153] the actual issue of the relationship between faith, person and works nonetheless remains to be resolved.

Since we have already discussed the future and transformation of the non-personal world elsewhere (see section 4.2), it is clear that the object of the judgement is the personal and social world, the world of created persons. We also saw that a created person as an image of the Triune God who is love is constituted by the relational structures in which he or she is involved. These are relationships to non-personal and personal creatures, as well as to God. The relational structure of a created person consists of the events in which the person is actively and passively involved. Persons are not substances, but narrative processes or becomings. Further, persons, in so far as they can pursue specific aims and intentions, also establish specific claims about themselves, who they want to be with their actions, which are either accepted or rejected in their interaction with other persons. In addition, we also saw that this relational structure, were it to be undamaged by sin, could be characterized by the twofold love command. This shows, taken in the strong sense, the claims that created persons make about themselves have to be taken seriously by God so that *prima facie* in the judgement a person would also have to be identical with their particular narrative biography, what they do and experience (see section 4.2). This furthermore shows that taking God's claim over created persons seriously leads to our understanding of God's wrath about the state of the sinner, which, however, brings about not the annihilation of the sinner, but God's redeeming work in the Son and the Holy Spirit on the cross and in the resurrection. This means that a new judgement of God over the sinner is possible, with the consequence that the concept of personhood is not only strongly relational, but is also to be understood eschatologically: because God can distinguish between the sinner and the sin in that the person of the sinner is what God

[151]Cf. Ott, *Scholastische Eschatologie*, pp. 48–54, 157–60.
[152]Cf. Gerhard, *Ioannis Gerhardi Loci Theologici*, pp. 22–3 (XXVIII).
[153]Cf. Konrad Stock, 'Gott der Richter. Der Gerichtsgedanke als Horizont der Rechtfertigungslehre', *Evangelische Theologie* 40 (1980), pp. 240–56 (253).

will make out of him or her eschatically (including the judgement), the person can no longer be identified with his or her works and with what he or she experiences in relationship with others persons, but is primarily what he or she experiences in the eschatical eternity with God. As a result, the deeds and consequences of the person in his or her relational structure in the world are considered positively, and indeed so also in the judgement. The judgement is therefore not some kind of event that would conflict with the concept of the personhood, but rather it is the process of transformation inherent to the judgement that is actually *constitutive* for personhood: for the eschatical person, but also for the person in the present, because the person at present *is* nothing other than the *promise* of what he or she *will* become. The eschatical process of judgement is therefore nothing other than the process constituting created personhood. The *final judgement is therefore creation*, but not new creation in the strict sense of the word.

From all of this, it follows that nothing can happen in the judgement other than what happened on the cross and in the resurrection of Jesus Christ. The judgement can be effected by means of works, without any semi-Pelagian tendency being taught, because the judgement occurs primarily on the cross of Christ.

Konrad Stock understands the wrath of God as 'the indignation and wounding of God by this . . . experience of human history',[154] i.e. that God is wounded in light of the reality of the interweaving of human personal biographies not in accord with the twofold rule of love. The cross can then be understood as God's devotion to humanity, in which the scale of the consequence of sin is made manifest: sin is not only violence inflicted on one's self, but also an attempt to kill God. Consequently, God is actually injured, but the resurrection of Christ through the devotion of the Spirit shows humanity that the love that is God is stronger. With Konrad Stock, we can therefore define the judgement from out of the middle of the event of reconciliation: '"Judgement" is the expression for the human experience of this experience that God had while suspended [on the cross].'[155] Stock continues:

> The "judgement" correspondingly consists in that God brings about and has brought about the entire extent and the full depth of the suffering of others that has been caused by humans in the active realization of their goals – that God reveals the anguished cry of the history of human suffering and

[154] Stock, 'Gott der Richter', pp. 251–2.
[155] Stock, 'Gott der Richter', p. 152.

> brings it to mind and consciousness. The judgement is the metaphor for the definitive situation in which God confronts humanity with its own history, definitively spelling out its results and then identifying humanity with its own history … I understand the judgement as the metaphor for the revivification of the history of human life in God's eschatological present, that, in being confronted with themselves and the results of their works in God, they become aware of how they have wounded God and caused the suffering of others. God anticipates this situation in the death of Jesus Christ…. The cross of Christ… is that form of divine resistance and repulsion against the power of evil, which creatively distinguishes human life history from that of their own verdict and acquits them of their own verdict.[156]

We can take from this that both created persons and their works can be objects of the judgement in unproblematic ways, to the extent that relational events are the objects of the judgement since both persons and their actions are variations on relationally constituted events. Persons are the intersection of the events that constitute them, but within the manifold relational structures of a person, it is the relationship to God that has a determinative function, and this is always the relationship to God who took on sin on the cross. In section 3.3, we saw that the good and the true coincide, so that we could speak of an ethical theory of truth in which the true is the accordance of divine action and its effects with creaturely action and its effects. The judgement is nothing other than the application of these criteria of truth. As a result, created persons cannot be annihilated, because they are only first created eschatically by the cross, resurrection and judgement, and this verdict is retro-causally attributed to the human persons living in the here and now, wherein their complete personhood is promised to them.

The objects of the judgement as a transformative and constitutive process are nothing other than the relations of the unfulfilled world, from which persons and their actions and consequences are derived, because persons are the points of intersection of relations, and actions and consequences themselves are relations. The criterion of the judgement is the double surrender of God to humanity in the cross and resurrection of Christ through the Spirit.

---

[156]Stock, 'Gott der Richter', pp. 252–3, 255–6.

Since the judgement is itself constitutive for personal identity, there is to some extent something like a universal salvation in this perspective: if it is the eschatic confrontation between creaturely and divine action that first brings about the fulfilment of creaturely personhood, then God does not annihilate any created person. However, from the non-eschatical perspective at present, the judgement does not mean universal salvation for the individual human being: individual human persons do not know which of their identity claims will endure beyond the judgement, that is, in the actual process of the constitution of the person, and which elements in the relational structures in which they live will be translated into aesthetic differences. And, this process of transformation itself is to be understood as painful: for the person who is judged, for the persons who relate to them in one way or another and for God as judge as well.

5.3.3.3 The judge and the process of judgement

We just implied that God is the one who judges, but that is by no means self-evident. In the biblical material both God (2 Thess. 1.5; 1 Cor. 5.13; Rom. 2.3, 3.6 and 14.10; Matt. 10.28 par and 6.4–18) and Christ (Matt. 25.31–46, 7.22f and 13.46–43; Luke 13.25–27; 1 Thess. 4.6; 1 Cor. 4.4f, 11.32; 2 Cor. 5.10), but also according to Matt. 19.28, the 12 Apostles are named judges over the 12 tribes of Israel. In 1 Cor. 6.2f, all the saints, that is, all sanctified human persons, are ultimately named as judges, though not only over other humans, but also over everything, including the angels.

The divergent biblical resources have led to various attempts at systematization and reconstruction throughout the history of theology, generally centring on the effort to harmonize the various subjects of the judgement with one another.

God and Christ do not cancel each other out as agents of the judgement, since on the basis of the doctrine of the two natures, Christ is also true God. For Bonaventure (d. 1274), the saints attain the office on the basis of their position of honour more or less as assistant judges to Christ.[157] In his treatise on the judgement that was significant in the Middle Ages, Richard of St. Victor, following the lead of Gregory the Great (d. 604), focuses on Matt. 19.28 in particular and therefore hardly goes into the notion of Christ as judge. He recognizes five groups of humans:

[157] Cf. Ott, *Scholastische Eschatologie*, p. 153.

1. Those who will judge but will not be judged themselves and nevertheless saved, i.e. those who surpass the commands of the law through perfect virtue;
2. Those who will be judged and therefore saved, because they repent of their missteps;
3. Those who will be judged and damned, i.e. those who confess faith but do not do the works of the law;
4. Those who will not be judged and nevertheless damned, i.e. those who are unbelievers;
5. Those who will not be judged and nevertheless saved, i.e. children who died after baptism.[158]

Richard's schema is only superficially interested in the question of the agent of the judgement. The scheme outlined above goes into a classification of humanity into various gradations of holiness and their rewards. We have already seen, however, that such a schema cannot ultimately be taken into consideration by a perspective intentionally orientated around the theology of the Reformation.

It is possible, however, to take from this that any clarification about the subject responsible for the judgement cannot simply be a clarification about the unity of various passages in the Bible. On the contrary, the first thing is the specific question about the subject who is responsible for the judgement. In addition, it is also necessary to make clear that the term judgement is a metaphor for the process of the transformation of the provisional reality into the eschatical one. Accordingly, the judgement itself is an event-like and processual occurrence in which multiple relata can actively participate. In modern court proceedings, there is not only a judge, but also witnesses, attorneys, enforcement officers etc., i.e. the various functions of subjects within the event. The question about the judge is a question about the entity making the decision, and this presupposes that it is not simply about the independent and automatic enforcement of an abstract criterion, but rather that the judgement depends on a *personal* decision. The question of whether we ought to model the process of eschatical transformation based on these details remains questionable, since there are no qualifiers that could tell us whether these elements of the process of the eschatical transformation of created persons possess

[158]Cf. Ott, *Scholastische Eschatologie*, pp. 53–4.

neutral, positive or negative analogies to the model of judgement as found in modern court proceedings. As a result, we are only able to question the level of subjectivity and its function in this process.

The acting agent is ultimately God, because the process of eschatical transformation can only be carried out by God, who, in the form of the *eschatoi*, is the ultimate thing. Since the unity of God is not attributed to any personality independently of the divine persons, it suggests itself to designate Christ as the incarnate second person of the Trinity as subject of the judgement, since the events of his human life, especially his death and resurrection, form the standard of measurement for the judgement. The biblical tradition also teaches that humans, the Twelve Apostles or the 'Saints' can be agents of the judgement. However, in contrast to Richard of St. Victor's example mentioned above, this does not have to mean that they are also not to be judged as well. There are also examples of this from the tradition. Bonaventure assumes that even the hidden sins of the elect will be revealed and named in the judgement in order to demonstrate the greatness of God's grace.[159] This is significant because it can occasion the following consideration: if on the one hand certain humans are designated to be judges, but their sins are nevertheless also uncovered, then the office of judge, i.e. the possibility of pronouncing judgement, is not based on sinlessness. But this would mean that it is not only possible for Christ and a few saints to serve as judges, but rather that every created person who is to be judged will also serve as judge. This is certainly not to be conceived in the sense that they pronounce a verdict at their own discretion, but only that they acknowledge the soteriological-christological criterion of judgement. Self-judgement is inevitable under the condition of recognition of a criterion of judgement only if the notion of eschatically created persons is to include freedom in some way. Martin Kähler (d. 1912) went as far as to postulate that in the ideal of modern procedures of judgement, a guilty defendant *claims punishment as his or her own right*, and therefore more or less pronouncing the verdict of judgement on himself or herself.[160] This aspect is important for us because it can resolve the dilemma between grace and freedom. The question of how grace and human freedom can be compatible was resolved by Origen, Thomas Erskine and Schleiermacher among others in the postulation of a post-mortal but pre-eschatic life of created persons that offers entirely different potentiality for development and makes it possible – at least if this

[159] Cf. Ott, *Scholastische Eschatologie*, p. 158.
[160] Cf. Kähler, *Zur Lehre von der Versöhnung*, p. 409.

'intermediate state' is conceived as being fitted out with endless duration – to conceive the compatibility of grace and creaturely freedom without any semi-Pelagianism. We saw, however, that this is *de facto* tantamount to a reduplication of the world that must be rejected because it eschatically devalues the present world. However, if the judgement itself is this process and those that are to be judged also participate in Christ's pronouncement of the verdict, then these concerns fall away: there is no doubling of the world that results in a devaluation of the present life and nothing like an infinite duration has to be accepted.

The judgement is the process of transformation in which the apparent contradiction between grace and freedom is resolved, in that those that are themselves to be judged also appear as judges next to Christ, the primary judge. The judgement would then be understood as a perfect revelation in such a way that it discloses the truth about the world and one's own life with a certainty according to the twofold command as the criterion of judgement in that the one to be judged, with the help of the Holy Spirit, can do nothing other than pronounce the judgement as to its significance in relation to Christ, however it may turn out.

However, since we do not live in the eschatical situation ourselves, the particularities of this occurrence necessarily remain abstract.

5.3.3.4 The timing of the judgement

The biblical tradition speaks of the judgement in terms of various points of time. In addition to the conclusive final judgement, Johannine theology also suggests that the judgement has already occurred in the world at present (see above). The notion of a temporal localization of the judgement is naturally also dependent on which model of correlation between time and eternity is being used (see section 3.1). In the model of kairotic or punctiliar eternity, the judgement can only be understood as an isolated incursion of eternity into time. In the model of eternity as absolute or partial simultaneity, the judgement is to be thought of as occurring simultaneously with all points in time. In the linear model of time, there is the difficulty of coordinating the various points of time of the judgement with one another.

This can be seen in Richard of St. Victor's tractate on the judgement. He distinguishes three forms of judgement:

- A present judgement that occurs *uniforme* or uniformly, because it only concerns the qualitative character of the pronouncement, either damnation or salvation. It takes place on in the spirit of the person, not in the completion of works.
- A judgement on the individual person immediately after death, that occurs *multiforme* or in multiple forms. It relates to the entire life but is only carried out with regard to the soul, since Richard presupposes a dualistic body-soul anthropology. It already includes the quantity of the judgement, i.e. the amount of punishment or reward.
- A judgement at the Parousia, the last or final judgement, that occurs *omniforme* or in all forms, because it pertains to the whole life of the human and to the whole human, body and soul, and, as a social judgement, it occurs with all and for all.[161]

In contrast to Richard's three-part judgement, during the Reformation, Martin Luther spoke of two parts:

- At present, humanity constantly undergoes judgement in terms of the experience of spiritual torment (*Anfechtung*). Here, the verdict is always that of damnation, because the person is *simul justus et peccator*. One's own works cannot contribute to blessedness but are themselves deadly sins. The present phenomena in which this present form of judgement appears are fear of death, doubt sown by the devil, and brooding over whether one belongs to the elect. This is how the eschatical judgement is already real at present and affects human life in the now.[162]
- Distinct from this, however, is the final judgement, which, according to Luther's understanding of the future of individual human beings after death (see section 4.2), occurs immediately after death, so that the person goes immediately to this judgement. Now, however, the *simul* is removed, in that in the judgement faith alone gives life: *fides sola dat vitam*.[163] Nevertheless, the biblical discussion of judgement according to works does not pose a problem for Luther, since good

---

[161]Cf. Ott, *Scholastische Eschatologie*, pp. 53–4.
[162]Cf. Albrecht Peters, *Glaube und Werk: Luthers Rechtfertigungslehre im Lichte der Heiligen Schrift* (Berlin: Lutherisches Verlagshaus, 1967, 2nd edn), pp. 40–7.
[163]Luther, WA 39 I, 96, pp. 7f.

works necessarily follow on from faith and therefore in the final judgement the works bear witness to the faith.[164]

If the question of the timing of the judgement were only to rest on the question of the compatibility of various theologies in the Bible or depend exclusively on the model of the relationship between time and eternity being presupposed, then the question would be virtually meaningless in a systematic-theological sense. This is because the first aspect of the compatibility of various biblical expressions remains within the framework of an ahistorical biblicism, and the question of the model of time and eternity does not have only theological, but philosophical premises as well. However, there is one specific systematic-theological aspect that makes this question appear significant: we saw that the judgement is to be understood as a process of transformation or constitution in which nothing other than what has already happened on the cross and in the resurrection occurs. The final judgement, on the other hand, we said, must be understood as an unambiguous revelation of this state of affairs applied to the life of human being and therefore as what constitutes human personhood. From this, we can distinguish two distinct aspects of the judgement understood as a process of transformation:

- A judgement takes place wherever Christ is present and is known as the who one he is. Accordingly, the events of the cross and the resurrection, the constitution of faith in individual humans just as much as assurance and strengthening of faith in word and sacrament are experiences of the judgement sharing the same origin as the promise of human eschatical personal being.
- However, we have to distinguish this from the process of transformation that necessarily occurs when someone shifts from the provisional spatio-temporal framework of individuation in the present world to the eschatical framework of individuation that consists in being drawn into the structure of the Trinitarian relationship that is God. By contrast to the provisional phenomena of the judgement in the present, this does not leave any further room for doubt but is definitive, whereas the judgement in the here and now has to be understood as a kind of proleptic shadow of the final judgement. The question as to the precise point of time of the final judgement is no longer necessary if we adopt the solution to the problem of time

[164]Cf. Luther, WA 12, 289, 34–290, 1.

and eternity proposed in section 4.2: it is not temporal and spatial relations that individuate persons in the here and now, but the logical properties of time and space that make this possible. However, they do find the condition of their possibility in the inner Trinitarian relations of the divine life itself. The final judgement is therefore the process of transformation necessary for *theosis*, which is ultimately the same thing as the eschatical constitution of the human person in God.

The judgement takes place in the present in so far as the presence of Christ is given but remains disputed. The judgement as final judgement means the process of transformation and constitution that created persons experience when they are transferred from the spatio-temporally individuating framework into the eschatically individuating framework that is God. This dispenses with the need to determine the location of the judgement either temporally or spatially.

5.3.4 Ethical implications

It is indisputable that the idea of the judgement bears ethical implications. The fear that countless generations have felt before the final judgement immediately comes to mind. This fear itself could be misused as a motivation for certain kinds of moral conduct. For example, during the Inquisition, heretics were executed precisely for the supposed purpose of securing their rescue for the final judgement. There are also liturgical implications: the idea that unworthy participation in the Eucharist effected the final judgement for the undeserving communicant led to the fact that the Eucharist was rarely celebrated in Lutheran churches at certain times in history.

The decisive question therefore is not whether the idea of the final judgement possesses ethical implications or not, but which ones are meaningful and in accord with the gospel and which are not. Here, it appears that we can maintain the following: If the judgement is ultimately identical with the eschatical constitution of the person, it is not something to be feared, but rather to be hoped for. We determined in the section on human language (see section 1.3) that humans relate to the future with various means of speech, thereby distinguishing whether one is dealing with an immanent future resting entirely on inner-worldly horizons of expectation based on extrapolation or whether one is dealing with an eschatical horizon of expectations that is constituted by the self-disclosure of the Triune God. Section 1.3.2 showed that humans refer to this future also under an emotional component mediated by the distinction between 'hoping for' and 'fearful of'. This shows that the judgement is not an object of fear, but exclusively of hope. As a result, the linguistic distinction between 'expectation' and 'fear' is not an eschatical distinction as supposed, but only a provisional and linguistic one belonging to inner-worldly horizons of expectation. With regard to eschatology, fear can only be used positively in terms of personal 'fear' of God in the sense of awe, reverence or veneration, not in the sense of a terrifying eschatological event. In faith and trust, Christians long for and experience the unmediated personal presence of Christ. This is because the judgement means nothing less than the definitive constitution of one's person and identity. Since at present humans also make sinful identity claims, the judgement proves these to be provisional and incompatible with eschatical life. Liturgically, this means that doctrine of *manducatio indignorum* leading to judgement is to be taught, yet not as means to produce terror, but rather for consolation. Judgement as consolation should therefore be a basic theme of pastoral care. The theme of consolation is therefore the character disposition for the present, which ought to inaugurate the judgement. It releases humanity from the notion that the identity claims that they inevitably have to make in the course of their activity would also actually have to constitute their identities. Accordingly, the judgement becomes understood as consolation for the conflicting actions of both the offender and the victim. As such, it can only be experienced in the here and now *sub contrario specie* under the light of the grace of the cross and resurrection. In this light, the verdict of damnation will no longer be feared as we have mentioned several times in this book in connection to Luther's saying that whoever God speaks to, be it in wrath or in grace, is immortal, so that we can say: even if God were to send us to hell, we could go cheerfully, because it was God that had sent us and therefore hell, understood as being without relation to God, would no longer be hell. It would be transformed into life.[165]

---

[165]Cf. Luther, *Lectures on Genesis: Chapters 26–30*, in *Luther's Works*, p. 76.

All conceivable ethical implications of the judgement must satisfy one criterion (1 John 4.17F): 'Love has been perfected among us in this: that we may have boldness on the day of judgment, because as he is, so are we in this world. There is no fear in love, but perfect love casts out fear; for fear has to do with punishment, and whoever fears has not reached perfection in love.'

5.4 The consummation of the Kingdom of God as the eschatical reality

There is only one thing remaining: a discussion of the goal of eschatical hope, a discussion about the object of this hope – the eschatical reality itself. But, a number of inevitable difficulties seem to arise at this point: the eschatical reality itself only exists presently in the mode of hope on the basis of faith – it is not yet a reality that we can experience. This means that there are limits as to what we can say. On the other hand, something can only be the object hope leading to action, about what can be spoken of in any way and about what must be said, since Christian faith and Christian hope essentially exist in a communicative social form.

If one examines the images in the Bible that are used to describe the eschatical reality, it is evident that they are highly diverse and derive from a number of different contexts. The following list includes some of the most important of such images but is not exhaustive: paradise (Luke 23.43; Rev. 2.7), the new or heavenly Jerusalem (Rev. 21.10–27), the Kingdom of heaven (Matt. 5.20, 7.21, 8.11, 13.11, 18.1 and 4 etc.), seeing God 'face to face' (1 Cor. 13.12), the eschatical grapevine (Micah 4.4), the peace of the animals (Is. 11.6–9), deification (Rom. 8.14; Acts 17.28f; 2 Pet. 1.4), being with the Lord (1 Thess. 4.17), God is 'all in all' (1 Cor. 15.28), a new heaven and a new earth (Rev. 21.1), eternal life (Matt. 25.46; Mark 10.30; John 3.16; Rom. 6.22) and the consummation of the Kingdom of God (see below).

It is not the task of a systematic theology to depict the development of these images in the course of the history of theology. It also cannot be the task of this section to exhaust the metaphorical content of this imagery and relate it to present-day language. The first would have to be directed towards the history of culture.[166] The latter is not the task of academic theology but of the proclamation of the church and therefore the task of the personal witness of ultimately every Christian. However, the actualization of this imagery in the proclamation of the church has to take the conceptual criteria of systematic theology into account in order to prevent the danger of the perversion of the gospel. The conceptual standard that can be set down for this and has to give an account of the proclamation is ultimately nothing other than the entirety of the Christian understanding of reality in the perspective of hope, and, therefore, nothing other than what we have attempted to say in this book at its most basic level. It is in this regard that this concluding section has the character of a summary and will not be able to do anything else other than taking up what has been said in the preceding chapters. However, in order to avoid the impression that the eschatical reality is something that cannot be spoken about and therefore, like mystical matters, requires silence, to borrow from Wittgenstein (d. 1951),[167] it appears meaningful to describe the eschatical reality by means of a central model in which one of the previously mentioned images is taken as possessing the most possible central or organizing character for the portrayal of the Christian understanding of reality. Thus, it is the concept of the Kingdom of God, or more precisely, the fulfilment of the Kingdom of God that appears most suitable for this purpose (see section 5.4.2). We can then examine the other images from this standpoint (see section 5.4.3). Finally, there also needs to be a brief word about the relevance of all this for our action (see section 5.4.4). The notion of the Kingdom of God has such a prominent place in Christian theology that here it cannot simply concern the meaning of the idea of the Kingdom of God in and of itself, but there also has to be emphasis on the form of the fulfilment of the Kingdom of God. However, before a thematization of the fulfilment of the Kingdom of God can be undertaken, it is necessary to elucidate in rough outline the prominence of its place in the framework of Christian thinking before its biblical background (see section 5.4.1).

---

[166]Cf. e.g. Bernhard Lang and Colleen McDannell, *Der Himmel. Eine Kulturgeschichte des ewigen Lebens* (Frankfurt am Main: Suhrkamp, 1990).
[167]Cf. Wittgenstein, *Tractatus Logico-Philosophicus*, pp. 107, 108 (Propositions 6.522 and 7).

5.4.1 The Kingdom of God in Scripture and history

The idea of the Kingdom of God, the *basileia tou theou*, is foundational both for the proclamation of Jesus and his understanding of himself. The New Testament witnesses[168] of the Kingdom of God, or for Matthew, the Kingdom of Heaven, contain aspects that were taken up in the history of theology to follow, though in part they were emphasized one-sidedly. We shall mention a few of these aspects here.

First, there is the presence of a temporal aspect of the Kingdom of God. On the one hand, the Kingdom of God lies in the future, its realization has not yet come to pass and it is considered to be the ultimate destiny of the goal of the history of God with the world (Mk 10.23–25, 14.25; Lk. 13.28–30; Matt. 7.21; 1 Cor. 6.9f, 15.50; Gal. 5.21). The futurity of the Kingdom of God was emphasized particularly by Johannes Weiß[169] (d. 1914) and Albert Schweitzer (d. 1965; see section 1.1.2), though they did not evaluate the notion positively (see section 1.1). A corresponding but positive evaluation can be found in the works of Jürgen Moltmann or Wolfhart Pannenberg (see section 4.3).

On the other hand, the Kingdom of God is understood as something present, whose advent has already occurred and conditions the present (Lk. 10.9, 11.20, 16.16; 1 Thess. 2.10–12; Rom. 14.17). Views where the Kingdom of God is *purely* a present occurrence appear rather seldom in the history of Christianity, especially if one does not count interpretations that understand the Kingdom of God as an inner-personal spiritual occurrence (see below). In the twentieth century, Charles Dodd (d. 1973) said for the Bible the Kingdom of God implied a realized eschatology (see section 1.1). Fully realized conceptions of the Kingdom of God have only appeared in those times and societies that were also characterized by their religious 'enthusiasm' (*Schwärmertum*), such as the Anabaptist Kingdom of Münster during the Reformation. As in particular societal spheres that have taken effect in present times, the aspect of the presence of the Kingdom of God exercised influence on the development of the notion of the two cities

---

[168]On the New Testament background, cf. Becker, *Jesus von Nazareth*, pp. 100–398, especially pp. 176–233 and for an introduction, see also Jens Schröter, 'Kingdom of God III. New Testament', in *RPP*, vol. 7, pp. 188–95.

[169]Cf. Johannes Weiß, *Die Predigt Jesu vom Reich Gottes* (Göttingen: Vandenhoeck & Ruprecht, 1964), pp. 49–50.

(*civitates*) by Augustine (d. 430) or in the development of the doctrine of the two realms or kingdoms in the Reformation, though other elements also played a significant role at this point.

In addition to texts that describe the Kingdom of God as present or future, there are also those that attempt to override the tension by emphasizing their *unity* (Mark 4.30; Lk. 13.18–21; Mark 1.14f).

Whereas the Kingdom of God is described here with the help of temporal proximity and distance, there are other texts that attest to spatial proximity and distance.

On the one hand, there is the notion that the Kingdom of God is in a spatially remote place, namely, heaven. This notion existed prior to Jesus (Dan. 4.34; Ps. 145.10–17). In the history of theology, these notions tie into all those that depict heaven as an ideal place, as we saw in section 3.2.

On the other hand, there is the idea that the Kingdom of God is *spatially present*. This is presupposed by the notion of the temporal presence of the Kingdom of God (see above).

A combination of the notions of the spatial distance and presence of the Kingdom of God can be found where there is a combination of the notions of the heavenly and terrestrial world. A prime example of this is the notion of the descent of the heavenly Jerusalem to earth (Rev. 21.2).

Another question that one can pose with regard to conceptions of the Kingdom of God is that of personality.

On the one hand, the Kingdom of God is conceived interpersonally or socially, concerning the good order between persons (Luke 13.23–30). This aspect is emphasized wherever the Kingdom of God itself is understood primarily either in terms of its ethical significance or the influence it exercises on ethics. This distinction is important because it does not imply that it automatically concerns conceptions that understand the Kingdom of God as effected by moral action. A conception of the Kingdom of God set in the paradigm of good social order can be seen in the work of nineteenth-century German theologian Albrecht Ritschl (see section 1.1).

On the other hand, the Kingdom of God can be understood *inner-personally*, aiming at the fulfilment of particular persons and their affectivity (Luke 17.20f). This kind of spiritualization can be found in the Alexandrian theology of the early church, especially in Origen (d. 254),[170] in the mysticism of the Middle Ages, but also in modern theology, in the

[170]Cf. Robert Frick, *Die Geschichte des Reich-Gottes-Gedankens in der alten Kirche bis zu Origenes und Augustin* (Gießen: Verlag Alfred Töpelmann, 1928), pp. 100–3.

cultural Protestantism of Adolf von Harnack (d. 1930), which centres on the relationship between the individual soul and its God.[171]

Both aspects, the *social and the inner-personal, can also be combined*, as is the case when Paul describes the Kingdom of God as a unity of justice, peace and joy (Rom. 14.17). The point of this approach is nothing other than the coincidence of command and spontaneous volition, or in other words: spontaneous fulfilment of the law. This combination of inner- and interpersonal aspects of the Kingdom of God plays a significant role in the development of the Reformation doctrine of justification and in the conception of the relationship between faith and works contained within it. Luther's formulation can be used as an example of this, according to which the Holy Spirit bestows 'desire and love for all the commandments' in the hearts of believers.[172]

An additional question about the Christian understanding of the Kingdom of God consists in asking about the agents that bring about the Kingdom of God.

On the one hand, the Kingdom of God is interestingly conceived as resting on human action and can therefore be characterized as an *ethical phenomenon* (Matt. 5.17–20). The Kingdom of God is rarely understood to rest exclusively on human action in Christian thought. We did see, however, that these ideologies played a role in Enlightenment thinking, such as with Lessing (see section 4.3), as well as in subsequent ideologies that followed Enlightenment principles up to the theology of the Enlightenment.

On the other hand, the Kingdom of God, as the name implies, is understood to be the result of the reality of God's lordship to the extent that it rests exclusively on divine action and cannot therefore be judged according to human values (Luke 14.15–24). Even this idea, however, is nearly impossible to find in Christianity, because the Kingdom of God is bound constitutively to the person of Jesus Christ, which is not to be understood as being solely divine, but also as human.

Both divine and human actions are bound together in Jesus Christ as the acting subject of the Kingdom of God. On the one side, this demonstrates that the historical Jesus perceived the realization of the Kingdom of God as being present in his claims about himself to the extent that he saw the benchmark for the Kingdom of God in his action (Luke 12.8f). On the other side, this is expressed in the later confession of the first Christians in that the

---

171 Adolf von Harnack, *What is Christianity?* (trans. Thomas Bailey Saunders; New York: Harper, 1957), p. 191.

172 Cf. Luther, 'The Large Catechism', *Book of Concord*, p. 441; line 69.

Kingdom of God and the Kingdom of Christ or the Son are identified with each other (1 Cor. 15.24f; Matt. 20.21; John 18.36; Phil. 2.9–11; Col. 1.15–17). Historically, the majority of the forms of speech about the Kingdom of God could be classified within this category.

Now, we can ask *in what way* the Kingdom of God is already breaking through in Jesus' *activity*. In being mindful of this, it is not only possible to get an answer to the question of Jesus' self-understanding, but also an answer to the question of the extent of God's rule.

On the one hand, God's rule is expressed in Jesus' miracles. Among the various aspects that could be named at this point,[173] it is common to all the miracle stories that the *natural world* is included within the reach of God's lordship and that Jesus' activity discloses God's power as creator.

Likewise God's rule is something whose effects can be seen in the *personal and social world*. This comes to expression above all in Jesus' parables. The point of Jesus' telling of the parables is therefore less that his parables describe how the Kingdom of God could be, but rather that in the telling of the parable in a *perlocutionary* way, i.e. in the effect it produces among its hearers in being told,[174] the Kingdom of God itself is breaking in. To the extent, however, that the form of the appearance of the Kingdom of God is therefore to be identified as performative speech, the Kingdom of God proves itself to be an instance of communication.[175]

The third aspect in which the Kingdom of God is realized in Jesus' activity *binds the social-personal aspect with the natural aspect*. This is because the Kingdom of God is being realized in the table fellowship that Jesus maintains together with his disciples, tax collectors and sinners. The present aspect is bound up with the future at this point, because Jesus can essentially understand the eschatical reality in terms of a meal and therefore as the communal enjoyment of the gifts of creation (Mark 14.25).

> The biblical account of the Kingdom of God contains temporal aspects, in which it can be described as future, present and indeed already breaking in at present, though nonetheless also awaiting its fulfilment.

---

[173]Cf. Becker, *Jesus von Nazareth*, pp. 211–33.
[174]For a good introduction to the speech act theory of Austin and Searle as well as its theological use, cf. Vincent Brümmer, *Theology and Philosophical Inquiry* (Philadelphia: Westminster Press, 1982), pp. 9–33.
[175]Cf. Becker, *Jesus von Nazareth*, pp. 176–211.

Further, the Kingdom of God can be described spatially to the extent that it can be seen as being immanent, transcendent or as a combination of the two.

The Kingdom of God contains personal aspects, in which it can be understood as inner-personal, interpersonal or as some combination of the two.

With regard to the subject or primary agent of the Kingdom of God, it can be understood as an ethical event in such a way that it rests on human action. Conversely, it can be understood as resting on divine action. Human and divine subjectivity are bound to the person of Christ as the acting subject of the Kingdom of God.

In Jesus' activity, the Kingdom of God breaks in through his miracles, his telling of parables and his table fellowship. The miracles show that the Kingdom of God includes the natural world, the parables show that it includes the personal and social world and his table fellowship demonstrates the inclusion of combined natural and personal elements.

The circle of questions that we have addressed, by means of which we have taken in view both the biblical representation of the Kingdom of God and that of the subsequent history of theology, is certainly not the only aspects in which one can look at the notion of the Kingdom of God. Nevertheless, this makes clear that the Kingdom of God does not simply deal with the eschatical reality as a dogmatic sub-theme. On the contrary, the Kingdom of God proves to be on the one hand the origin of Christian action in the action of Jesus himself, but on the other hand as integral to the God's action collectively. To this extent, the entirety of the Christian faith could also be depicted as an explication of the Kingdom of God. Accordingly, the explicit discussion of the Kingdom of God is ultimately coextensive with that doctrine which has the unity of divine action with the world as its object: the doctrine of the economic Trinity. More precisely, we can follow Christoph Schwöbel in saying that the Kingdom of God describes 'the unity of God's work of creation, reconciliation, and consummation',[176] and indeed under the aspect that this action of God reaches its goal and implementation in creation, reconciliation and consummation.

[176]Christoph Schwöbel, 'Kingdom of God IV. Historical Theology and Dogmatics; V. Social Ethics', in *RPP*, vol. 7, pp. 191–6.

Because the Kingdom of God describes an integral part of the action of God in terms of the implementation of divine rule, reflection on Christian theology as a whole could be understood as an explication of the Kingdom of God from a *dogmatic* perspective. An *eschatological* examination of the Kingdom of God will, on the contrary, be geared towards the consummation of the Kingdom of God that has not yet been fulfilled in the here and now.

This eschatological examination would then have the task, under the title of the fulfilment of the Kingdom of God, of saying something about the eschatical reality itself that could in turn be arranged conceptually. It is to this that we shall turn next.

5.4.2 Consummation considered 'conceptually'

The fact that we will give a description of the eschatical reality in terms of the fulfilment of the Kingdom of God at this point should not be understood simply as an attempt to provide a deeper analysis of one or more the aspects of the Kingdom of God that we have just rendered above. Rather, the results of the systematic work done in the last section are not to be drawn in for usage in the conceptual language about the eschatical reality. Those who do not find themselves in agreement with the foregoing decisions, but have arrived at other ones instead, will also arrive at conclusions different from what is to follow. Since not all of the foregoing argumentation can be repeated at every step along the way, this section possesses a highly thetic character. It is nonetheless important to our account of eschatology as a whole, because this conceptual content is capable of delivering an important criteriology against which the metaphorical language used for the eschatical reality can be measured. Two skills are therefore utterly decisive for the development of theological competence in the eschatological perspective, completely independently of whether one agrees with the author on specific points in the results: the deployment of a corresponding conceptual criteriology and its application on metaphorical speech. This is because having these two skills is a necessary condition for Christian proclamation, be it in the forms of preaching, pastoral care or in Christian education.

It is nearly irrelevant whether one chooses to employ the terminology of the fulfilment of the Kingdom of God, eternal life or the consummation of the world, because all these expressions are already highly metaphorical. Nevertheless, the attempt to speak conceptually about the eschatical reality is not to be doomed to failure if conceptual language differs from metaphorical or pictorial language qualitatively or categorically, but quantitatively, and indeed precisely on account of the fact that it is a particularly generalized and controlled form of speech.[177] It is precisely at this point that 'conceptual' language is thoroughly in a position to perform its particular service by functioning as a conceptual criteriology for other forms of speech about the eschatical reality that are less conceptually controlled and appeal more strongly to visual and imaginative modes of expression.

> If the eschatical reality is described 'conceptually' in an eschatological reflexion, then this presupposes that there is no sharp distinction between literal speech and metaphorical speech. 'Conceptual' language is only a unique form of metaphorical language, which stands under a particular methodological control.
>
> This kind of 'conceptual' speaking about the eschatical reality bears the combined outcomes of every section of this book together. As a result, this section is marked by its thetic and illustrative character.

According to what was said in section 3.1, the eschatical reality can neither be timeless, nor consist of the simultaneity of all temporal events, nor simply be a time after the end of the world. Instead, the eschatical reality will be like an irreversible ordered relation, as it is itself an aspect of the Trinitarian being of God. This includes the fact that the eschatical reality itself has an event-like character.

In the same manner, the eschatical reality cannot be understood as being either without space, nor spatial. Rather, it shares with space, like God's own being, the structure of a reversible ordered relation. As a result, the eschatical reality includes the possibility of personal transcendence and alterity.

There will no longer be any falsehood in the eschatical reality, but only truth. Since the eschatical reality has to be understood as the fulfilment of creation in such a way that the ambiguities and incomplete aspects of

---

[177]Cf. Mühling, *Gott ist Liebe*, pp. 24–43.

how creatures attempt to implement sets of rules based on the twofold love command will be abolished and the world will be fulfilled through the transferal of creatures by grace from their worldly, penultimate frameworks of individuation to the Trinitarian relational framework, then there will be perfect consonance of creaturely knowledge and symbolic action with divine action. In section 3.3, we saw that truth, in the sense of an ethical theory of truth, consists in the resonance of discerning creaturely action with divine action and its results. We can now finally understand this theory of truth to be an eschatical one, because such entire compatibility is only realized in the eschatical situation.

However, it is not only the case that truth is completely actualized in the eschatical reality, but also goodness. If the event-like character and the personal transcendence are abolished in the eschatical character as little as the possibility of symbolic creaturely action, then constitutive action will also not be abolished. But, since the concept of action also includes intentionality and therefore freedom of choice, then this also cannot be minimized in the eschatical reality. If on the other hand the eschatical reality is to be good and only good, then this is only conceivable if there is complete consonance between the will of creation with the twofold law of love as the divine will. It is at this point that the ethical understanding of the Kingdom of God, such as that formulated by Albrecht Ritschl, has its relative justification. Complete consonance between the creaturely will and the twofold love command can only be conceived in such a way that that one of the two relata merges into the other: creatures simply do the will of God, the existence of pure facticity. Hubertus Hubbeling (d. 1986) proposed that it would be possible to define the Kingdom of God as a whole by means of formal logic, namely, as perfect consonance between modal and deontic logic.[178]

Modal logic[179] deals with the formalization of modal concepts such as 'possible', 'impossible', 'necessary', 'accidental' and 'contingent'. These concepts are expressed by means of modal operators (P for 'it is possible that…', I for 'it is impossible that…', L for 'it is (logically) necessary that…' and C for 'it is contingent that…') that precede given statements (abbreviated

---

[178]Cf. Hubertus Gezinus Hubbeling and H.C.M. De Swart, *Inleiding tot de symbolica logica* (Assen: Van Gorcum, 1976), p. 114.

[179]A short introduction to modal logic can be found in Albert Menne, *Einführung in die formale Logik* (Darmstadt: Wissenschaftliche Buchgesellschaft, 1985), pp. 55–64. A detailed presentation of the various modalities and their meaning for theology can be seen in Dirk Evers, *Gott und mögliche Welten: Studien zur Logik theologischer Aussagen über das Mögliche* (Tübingen: Mohr Siebeck, 2006).

by the letter p). A sentence such as 'It is possible that Narnia exists' can be rendered formally as follows: Pp, if p = 'Narnia exists'. In this kind of modal logic, the particular content of any statement p is therefore irrelevant to the formal semantics of the proposition. Similar to our clarification of concepts used to express our understanding of the future in everyday language (see section 1.3), these propositions can be formalized without any regard to their particular content, only by the use of the operation of negation (¬).

$\neg Pp = Ip = L\neg p$	'it is not possible that…' = 'it is impossible that…' = 'it is necessary that…is not…'
$\neg P\neg p = I\neg p = Lp$	'it is not possible that…is not…' = 'it is impossible that…is not…' = 'it is necessary that…'
$\neg Lp = P\neg p$	'it is not necessary that…' = 'it is possible that…is not…'
$\neg L\neg p = Pp$	'it is not necessary that…is not…' = 'it is possible that…'
$Pp \,\&\neg\, P\neg p = Cp$	'it is possible that…and it is possible that…is not…' = 'it is contingent that…'

Facticity does not have its own modal operator. This is because if someone says that it is a fact that there are houses made of bricks, what is essentially being said is that: 'There are brick houses.' Facticity is therefore expressed simply by means of the corresponding expression p, without a modal operator.

Further, next to these formal expressions there are still a few other important laws of modal logic:

$p \rightarrow Ip$	'if…, then it is also possible that…' E.g., if it is factually correct that there are houses made of bricks, then it also has to be possible for there to be houses made of bricks.
$Lp \rightarrow p$	'if it is necessary that…, then…' E.g., if it is necessary that the sum of the angles in a triangle in Euclidean space is 180°, then the sum of the angles is factually also 180°.

The last law above obviously applies to necessity, but not to possibility. As a result, we can say that the following is not a law of modal logic:

false: $Pp \rightarrow p$	'if it is possible that…, then…' E.g., if it is possible that Snow White exists, then Snow White also exists. This conclusion is false.

Deontic logic, on the other hand, deals with concepts such as 'obligatory', 'permitted' and 'forbidden'. Similar to modal logic, deontic concepts can also be formalized by means of modal operators placed before a given statement. O_d now stands for 'it is obligatory' (= 'it is compulsory' = 'one must ...'), P_d for 'it is permitted', F_d for 'it is forbidden' and C_d for 'it is ethically indifferent'. The subscript $_d$ following the modal operator simply indicates that we are now working within the framework of deontic logic.

$\neg P_d p = F_d p = O_d \neg p$	'it is not permitted that ...' = 'it is forbidden that ...' = 'it is obligatory that ... is not ...'
$\neg P_d \neg p = F_d \neg p = O_d p$	'it is not permitted that ... is not ...' = 'it is forbidden that ... is not ...' = 'it is obligatory that ...'
$\neg O_d p = P_d \neg p$	'it is not obligatory that ...' = 'it is permitted that ... is not ...'
$\neg O_d \neg p = P_d p$	'it is not obligatory that ... is not ...' = 'it is permitted that ...'
$P_d p$ & $P_d \neg p = C_d p$	'it is permitted that ... and it is permitted that ... is not ...' = 'it is ethically indifferent that ...'

The falsity of the conclusion about the possibility of facticity that arose in modal logic also appears similarly in deontic logic, because it is obvious that the facticity of something cannot be inferred from its permissibility

invalid: $P_d p \rightarrow p$	'if it is permitted that ..., then ...' E.g., if it is permissible for trucks to become obsolete, then trucks will always become obsolete. This conclusion is false.

The formalization of modal concepts also corresponds precisely to the formation of deontic concepts, as well as to the one corresponding declaration of the falsity named above. The consonance of deontic and modal logic is, however, not complete in our world. This can be seen when we focus on the laws named above. This is because the fact that an event is permitted does not follow necessarily on from that fact that it is factual, just as little as the actuality of an event follows on from that fact that it is obligatory:

false: $p \rightarrow P_d p$	'if ..., then it is also allowable that ...' E.g., if it is factually correct that motorcycles are stolen, then it is also allowable for motorcycles to be stolen. This conclusion is false.
false: $O_d p \rightarrow p$	'if it is obligatory that ..., then ...' E.g., if it is obligatory that no one drive faster than 65 mph, then everyone will always drive 65 mph. This conclusion is false.

In the eschatical reality, there must nevertheless be complete consonance and correspondence between modal logic and deontic logic, i.e. the final two propositions above would be true, and indeed, this would be the case without also denying the ability of any agents to act freely. This is what Hubbeling means in his discussion of a purely formal description of the Kingdom of God. This purely formal description is undoubtedly still highly abstract, because content p of the proposition is altogether arbitrary. From a Christian perspective, this formal definition does not sufficiently describe the Kingdom of God, since the concrete content still has yet to be added: p cannot consist in just any arbitrarily defined content, but only in the rule of love for God and neighbour.

It is not only possible to describe the eschatical reality in purely formal terms, but deontic logic also allows possibility for ethically indifferent actions and events, that is, those events that are permissible, and whose opposites are also permissible. As we saw in section 3.3, this would be the same sphere in which existing differences are only aesthetic, but never ethical. This sphere is also not precluded by the eschatical reality, but the ethical differences are to be thought of as concerning eschatic events that would be just as good as their opposites. This allows for the possibility that our here and now can contribute something to the eschatical reality, because there can be multiple conceivable but equally good eschatical realities, which nonetheless will not all be realized. As such, it is conceivable that in the eschatical reality, which is constituted by Godself, divine and created persons can continue to act together in cooperation. What is excluded, however, is the notion that there is only one conceivable best possible world, along with the notion that the eschatical reality is full because there is no longer any difference between possibility and actuality. On the contrary, the eschatical reality ought to be understood in such a way that it forms an infinitely open connection of events in which God brings about an infinite number of possibilities that are infinitely realized, without realization and possibility ever coinciding. This does not present any difficulties for the logic of infinity.

According to the results developed from section 4.1, it is also well possible that not only persons participate in the eschatical reality, but non-personal creatures will also be deified through divine grace. This includes the notion that God can allow for eschatic contingency, if indeed only in the sense of what is equally good, so that even this contingency only affects the aesthetic sphere and therefore all that is ethically indifferent. This is also necessary from the perspective of the relational anthropology that we have developed here, because if no persons are to be eschatically annihilated, and persons are constituted by the entirety of the relational structures in which they are involved, including their relationships to the non-personal environment, then it is imperative for non-personal creatures to be deified through divine grace. The question of whether one sees this then as a renewal of the world or as an annihilation of the world ultimately depends on the concept of the world in question. If space-time is held to be constitutive for the world, then one will not only be able to speak of an *annihilatio*, but also of a *renovatio*. With respect to the questions about which non-personal entities will be attributed eschatical relevance by God and how the non-personal realm of the eschatical world will look, there is only one possible answer: we do not know.

We have already presupposed that created persons will be able to participate in the eschatical reality through divine grace, interact with one another and communicate. This includes the living body, presupposing the living body is defined in the right way. However, what is definitely excluded is the notion of a purely individual soul that either lives with God devoid of every relation to others or is fused into an undifferentiated identity. If one sees the body as determined by physical materiality (= mass-energy equivalences), then we can only say that we do not yet know whether this is of eschatical relevance. However, if bodiliness or embodiment has its character as the medium of personal being-and-becoming-in-relation, then it will be necessary to speak of an embodied eschatical reality. The form of the living body as the medium of personhood will nevertheless no longer be arbitrarily determined by whatever relationships in which it currently stands, but exclusively by the action of the Holy Spirit so that it will be necessary to speak of a spiritual bodiliness. It is precisely through this action that the living body will receive its graceful integrity, because it is now to be understood as inviolable, since violability as a characteristic of corporeality (instead of embodiment) is defined through others as identity constituting relations.

Since it is not only necessary for personal identity to stand not only in relation to one's self, to non-personal entities and to God, but also in relation to other created persons, the eschatical reality *per se* is to be understood as having a social form. In this social form, there is no longer any difference between those forms of communication that are ordained by the Spirit of God and those that are not. This means that, eschatically (and only eschatically) speaking, the difference between the church and the world disappears, God's regiment to the right and God's regiment to the left. It is also possible to say that in the Kingdom of God there will no longer be any church in so far as it is characterized by a difference in significance to the 'world'. However, in understanding the church solely as the communion of the saints, then it can be thought of as being ever present.

Nearly all characterizations of the eschatical reality to this point have been formal, and have not pertained to its actual content. There is, however, such a characterization of its content, and indeed, altogether concretely: the eschatical reality consists for us in the fact that we will be immediately together with the Lord Jesus Christ in eternity. Since by this we mean the second person of the Trinity, who lives and reigns in an unmediated relationship with the Father and the Spirit in eternity, the concept of the Parousia as being together with Christ in eternity is coextensive with *theosis* in the sense of being incorporated into the relational structure of the Trinity, in other words, we will 'see' God immediately, 'face to face'. Or, one could say that we will interact directly with the Trinitarian persons. From this comes what already happens in Christ in the here and now – the realization of true love – which will also be the defining characteristic of the eschatical reality: faith in the sense of not-knowing can cease, though certainly not in the sense of trust, since trust is an essential and constitutive component of love. Likewise, hope, in the sense of experiencing a difference between an unfulfilled present and a perfected future, will no longer be meaningful in the eschatical reality.

In order for us to be able to conceive of this eschatical life, it is factually necessary for persons to be able to be justified, i.e. to be able to participate in the eschatical reality through grace alone without contribution of their own merit and worthiness. This means, however, that not only death as the end of this life in the here and now is indispensable in so far as it serves as a confirmation of justification, but the resurrection of the person by God is also indispensable because it provides the necessary element of continuity by which God's fidelity to creation is preserved.

Next to the resurrection, however, the judgement is also of continued significance, because only it affords the necessary transformations. If the judgement is understood as the transformation of evil into evil that has been overcome yet also remembered, then evil can also make a contribution to the eschatical reality, though only aesthetically. It is as *remembered evil* no longer *evil*. This means that evil is neither dualistically eternalized as in the classic notion of the twofold outcome in terms of eternal life on the one hand and eternal pain as punished evil on the other, nor declared to be nothing as in the case of annihilation: if evil were not present in the eschaton in the aesthetic form to which it has been transformed, then it will not be remembered in eternity. But, what will not be remembered in eternity does not have any relevance for our life in the here and now. Jesus Christ is the paradigm for evil that has been suffered: even the resurrected Christ bears his scars. They are signs of his identity, but, as signs of his having overcome suffering, they are now also signs of his beauty. We can also think about the evil that has been the source of suffering in the here and now in the same way, as 'scarred'. This possibility can be conceived, but how are we actually to depict it? We do not know. If the judgement is not only the process of the transformation of the person, but the actual process of the constitution of the person, then all the difficulties of conceiving continuity and discontinuity together fall away. At the same time, however, this means that our eschatic life will be and is already our real life. Everything that persons experience at present, what befalls them and what they themselves actually do, is just as little inconsequential as the world is in its temporal reality as a whole for the eschatical reality. However, compared with what happens in the eschatical reality, everything that happens in the here and now is still in a metaphorical sense 'quantitatively' more minor. Nonetheless, at this point, our conceptual speech fails, because the penultimate and the ultimate cannot be measured. All our knowledge at present, including theology in the eschatological perspective, remains *theologia viatorum* and, compared with the eschatical knowledge, knowledge only in the same sense that the knowledge of an unborn baby could be called scientific in comparison to all of the scientific knowledge of intellectual history.

The eschatical reality is event-like and process-like in that it shares in common with time and space the characteristics of what is in one perspective a reversible (like space), but in another perspective irreversible (like time) order of events, which is asymmetric, irreflexive and transitive, but without comprising time and space. It includes personal transcendence, alterity (otherness) and novelty (newness), yet excludes falsehood and ambiguity. Truth now becomes an eschatical concept. The eschatical reality includes creaturely and divine interaction and cooperation. Now persons spontaneously fulfil God's rules, so that what we want and what we ought to want always coincide without ever dissolving into each other. The eschatical reality includes not only personal, but also non-personal creatures, even if we do not yet know to what extent. If the living body is taken to be the medium of personal being-as-becoming-in-relation, then bodiliness or embodiment is also determined by the Holy Spirit as a whole, including unscathed embodiment. The eschatical reality further includes sociality. Concretely, this means being together personally with Jesus Christ in an unmediated way, and therefore also together with Father, Son and Holy Spirit simultaneously. From this, the substance of divine rule giving emerges as the realization of true love. For human persons, the eschatical reality is only reached through death as the confirmation of their justification and resurrection by God. The eschatical reality is attained through the judgement as a process of transformation, which guarantees that the world's evil is included in so far as it is remembered, but also overcome. To the extent that the judgement is also the process which actually brings created personhood about, the eschatical life of created persons is what constitutes their life at present and is in fact the very condition of its possibility. All these statements remain, as *theologia viatorum* itself, pre-eschatical statements and therefore also require the transformative process of judgement themselves.

5.4.3 Images of consummation

At the beginning of this chapter, we mentioned a series of biblical images that could make our talk about the eschatical reality somewhat more plastic and conceivable. We will now discuss these biblical images along with two further ones that do not come directly out of Scripture and then compare them with our prior conceptual analysis of the eschatical reality. This procedure should in no way replace an exegetical analysis of the respective images in their context but rather can only supplement it. Both would be necessary for the concrete reckoning with them in preaching and teaching. Similarly to how it did not come down to a direct agreement with the content, it is also the case here that it is left to the concrete decisions of the critical judgement of the readers. Nevertheless, the practice of correlating the 'conceptual' criteriology and the images is important, because it demonstrates empirically how the work put into making decisions in systematic theology not only grows out of questions about Christian practice (see section 1.1.1), but which steps and competencies are necessary in order to lead into this practice. In the background of the following criteriological procedure is the search for the implementation of positive, negative and *neutral* analogies, originating with the scientific theory developed by Mary Hesse.[180] The neutral analogies are important at this point. This is because if we were to only pursue positive or negative analogies, the 'conceptual' criteriology would then be the only standard by which the eschatic imagery of the proclamation could be measured. Were this actually the case, then it would be possible to say: 'Speaking of Paradise is meaningful in this regard, but not in that one.' This procedure would ultimately mean that the imagery is nothing more than a series of illustrations that are ultimately unnecessary had one been able to understand the 'conceptual' version. This would further presuppose a strict distinction between literal and metaphorical speech. However, we have already seen that speech does not function quite so simply and that our language itself participates in the ambiguities of the here and now and is therefore not infallible. Neutral analogies are those that we are unsure whether they apply or not. It is possible within the frame of our discursive work that one or the other neutral analogies could be converted into positive or negative analogies, although under pre-eschatical conditions neutral analogies will as a rule always remain. The existence of neutral analogies is therefore an essential expression of the 'soft' distinction that is being presented here between conceptual and metaphorical speech. Further, these analogies also make it possible for the relationship between our 'conceptual' criteriology and the eschatic imagery to be more than a one-way street. In this discourse, it is altogether possible that the relationship between 'conceptual' criteriology and the imagery of eschatic hope can completely or partially reverse, with the images directing the criteriology, since the distinction between 'conceptual' criteriology and 'imagery of eschatic hope' is ultimately only a pragmatic one. The corresponding images are not being newly introduced here but have been consistently drawn in throughout the entire book. In order to avoid an overly detailed analysis, the focal point in what follows has been placed on the diagnosis of positive analogies.

The results of the 'conceptual' analysis of the eschatical reality can be used as a criteriology in order to analyse critically various biblical and non-biblical images used for the eschatical reality. Since 'conceptual'

[180]Cf. Mary B. Hesse, *Models and Analogies in Science* (London: Sheed and Ward, 1963), pp. 9–10.

speech is only a particular form of metaphorical speech, there are not only positive and negative analogies between the 'conceptual' analysis of the eschatical reality and eschatical imagery, but also neutral analogies. Of these neutral analogies, we do not yet know whether they apply or not in the here and now. In this regard, the relationship between the 'conceptual' criteriology and the eschatical reality can also reverse, so that eschatic imagery not only possesses illustrative, but also cognitive character.

5.4.3.1 The new or heavenly Jerusalem (Rev. 21.10–27)

The notion of the new or heavenly Jerusalem expresses among other things that the eschatical reality has a social content and therefore affords cooperation and culture. This necessarily excludes the possibility that Christianity could teach a simple and romanticized doctrine of 'back to nature'. Also to note is that within the biblical description of the new Jerusalem, there is no church and the temple is explicitly rejected because the distinction between church and world, or the realms to the right and to the left, is to be abolished in the eschatical reality. Negative analogies can be seen in the fact that the church is not to be abolished in the sense that it is understood to be the communion of saints. Another negative analogy consists in the fact that those things that are of importance for a modern large city – size of over 100,000 residents, an independent city government, etc. – are surely not of eschatical relevance. It also appears questionable whether one is to speak of walls and towers or of precious stones. Here, it seems that we are dealing with negative analogies, though it is impossible to be certain at this point. In fact, cut gemstones and walls could stand for the products of human culture themselves. Have we therefore already advanced into the realm of neutral analogies?

What we can say is that the image of the heavenly Jerusalem elucidates the eschatical reality to the extent that it consists in a perfected social form, including products of human culture.

5.4.3.2 The peace of the animals (Is. 11.6–9)

The image of the universal peace of the animals on the contrary expresses that the eschatical reality is not simply a cultural affair, but rather that it must also be understood as the fulfilment of the natural world. If the notion of 'eat or be eaten' in the natural world at present rests on the fact that nature is unfulfilled and open to partial arbitrariness, then the fact that nature is now fulfilled and that arbitrariness and chaotic suffering have been excluded is expressed by means of this image. However, this can under no circumstances be a product of human cultural achievement or a product of the course of the world at present. Negative analogies arise when this image is concretely depicted: it does not appear meaningful to speak of babies playing with poisonous snakes in the eschatical reality or of lions eating hay. However, it is clear that one ought not to be all too certain about the apportionment of positive and negative analogies at this point, and therefore also allow space for neutral analogies.

> The image of the peace of the animals stands for, among other things, the eschatical fulfilment of the natural, non-personal world.

5.4.3.3 Paradise (Lk. 23.43; Rev. 2.7)

Paradise is only mentioned occasionally in the New Testament. Descriptions of its material qualities are found in Old Testament imagery, extra-canonical literature and the literature of the peoples and cultures neighbouring ancient Israel. The notion of paradise is interesting because it consists in the combination of social and cultural aspects native to the idea of the eschatical city with the image of the fulfilment of nature, resulting in the image of paradise as a garden. The account of the protological paradise (Gen. 2f.) reflects the dreams of the ancient near easterner living under difficult climatic conditions and no longer having to be a bedouin or having to cultivate large areas for little return but instead being a gardener.

> The image of paradise as a garden exemplifies the notion that the eschatical reality constitutes both the fulfilment of the natural and the cultural world, and there is no separation of nature and nurture.

5.4.3.4 A new heaven and a new earth (Rev. 21.1)

The imagery mentioned up to this point describes the eschatical reality as the fulfilment of the world, not as its end. This comes summarily to expression in the image of a new heavens and earth, even if in this description there is not only an element of continuity between the eschatical and the present reality, but also discontinuity.

> What can be positively maintained regarding this image is that the created non-personal world will be relevant to the form of the eschatical reality in its spheres that are both accessible and inaccessible to us, if the creature is not to be altogether judged meaningless. However, with respect to the question about the extent to which this will be the case, we can only remain silent at this point.

5.4.3.5 The eschatical vineyard (Mic. 4.4; Zech. 3.10)

The description of the eschatical reality as a vineyard is one that is undoubtedly frequently present throughout the Old Testament, though it seemingly appears less often in the general consciousness, making it worthwhile to deal with this image in a bit more detail at this point:

> In days to come the mountain of the LORD's house shall be established as the highest of the mountains, and shall be raised up above the hills. Peoples shall stream to it, and many nations shall come and say: 'Come, let us go up to the mountain of the LORD, to the house of the God of Jacob; that he may teach us his ways and that we may walk in his paths.' For out of Zion shall go forth instruction, and the word of the LORD from Jerusalem. He shall judge between many peoples, and shall arbitrate between strong nations far away; they shall beat their swords into plowshares, and their spears into pruning hooks; nation shall not lift up sword against nation, neither shall they learn war any more; but they shall all sit under their own vines and under their own fig trees, and no one shall make them afraid; for the mouth of the LORD of hosts has spoken. (Micah 4.1–4)

This pericope was actually transmitted twice, as the same material also appears in Is. 2.2–5. It deals with the well-known idea of the pilgrimage of the nations of the earth to Zion. The vineyard actually only appears in Micah and we will accordingly direct our concentration to this image. Wine itself has eschatical significance representing salvation. What is clear is that the image is not concerned with a kind of salvation within history. If Mount Zion is to be higher, then this will be a matter of a comprehensive future reformation or fulfilment, also of nature. The social form in this comprehensive depiction of salvation will also be changed: justice will reign and every war will come to an end and the opposite of war is peace. Whereas war can be described as the conflict between competing ends fought by means of force, a positive description of peace is more difficult. This is where wine is significant in Micah: 'They shall all sit under their own vines.' Does this mean a life of idleness where we all become drunkards? The grapevine, at least in hot lands such as Palestine, does have another meaning: when it is growing on an arbour or bower above the ground, it can also provide protection from the sun and heat. This accordingly brings in the social function of the image for the eschatical reality that is being described here, one that comes even more clearly into expression in Zech 3.10: The vineyard is not only the location of the fulfilment of nature, but also of the fulfilment of sociality and communication: one invites the other to meet under the vines for conversation. This also reflects the ancient near eastern dream of having one's own vineyard, not only with respect to the heat, but also as a sign of abundance and wealth.

If we look at the wine motif in the New Testament that sees Jesus as the paradigmatic glutton and drunkard (Luke 7.34), we then see that Jesus' proclamation of the Kingdom of God possesses similarities to that of the Old Testament imagery: the Kingdom of God is breaking in where Jesus celebrates table fellowship with sinners, where he, as in the vineyard, enjoys the gifts of creation with them and communicates with them. Even if this were to have begun during Christ's earthly life, a reconciliation and fulfilment of the world would still have been necessary. This is expressed in John 15.1–11, where Christ himself is the vine bower, so that the image of the eschatical vineyard can also be understood with the Parousia as the being in the unmediated presence of Christ. The image of the enjoyment of the goods of creation and sociality under the wine bower is only eschatically possible because Christ has transformed the world. The world was changed by Christ's surrender to humanity on the cross and in the resurrection, and this change is attained through the wine and blood of the vine that is Christ. Since we have nothing to hope for beyond Christ, this means that our eschatic hope no longer simply consists in enjoying the pacification of nature and conversation with the rest of humanity as friends under the wine bower, but it also means, even if the wine and bower is a person, being together with Christ and enjoying conversation with him. The enjoyment of creation and of unmediated communion with Christ is anticipated in the mediated presence of Christ in the Eucharist.

> In summary, we can say that the eschatical, ultimate reality will be one in which not only humanity, but also nature, embodied in the vineyard, has a meaning and this reality will be one of communal interaction and communication among neighbours through shared enjoyment of the gifts of creation. Beyond this, it will entail unmediated communication with Christ through our being gathered together with him.

5.4.3.6 Assembly with the Lord (1 Thes. 4.17)

In our examination of the last image, we already drew in the Parousia in terms of being directly in Christ's presence, though it now appears here as its own separate image. The Parousia not only forms an image that depicts Christian hope, but it also – on the basis of its significance in the history of theology – constitutes one of the last things, or eschata, as detailed in this book (see section 4.1). To go any further at this point on the Parousia would only result in repetition.

5.4.3.7 Theosis (Rom. 8.14; Acts 17.28f.; 2 Pet. 1.4)

The aforementioned immediate communication with Christ in the idea of the Parousia and in the idea of the eschatical vineyard ultimately also means unmediated communication with the Father and the Spirit, since the Son also lives with them in his Trinitarian relatedness. In this regard, it is also appropriate to speak of the *theosis* or deification of humanity. This makes clear that the eschatical reality is not merely a hope for the world, but also for God, in so far as the eschatical world means incorporation into the inner divine relational structure. We even said a few things about this in section 5.1. In any case, one will also have to maintain negative analogies at this point. If Acts 17.28f speaks of divine 'offspring' and 2 Peter 1.4 of participation in the 'divine nature', then it is not possible to bring the term 'offspring' together with the concept of genus as found in the *arbor porphyriana* (see section 3.3) and also not understand the concept of nature from its medieval usage. On the contrary, it will be necessary to emphasize along with Rom. 8.14 that it is a relational occurrence by the action of the Holy Spirit through grace, which always means presupposing an eschatic incorporation into the inner-Trinitarian relational structure.

5.4.3.8 Seeing God 'face to face' (1 Cor. 15.28)

An immediate implication of the description of the eschatical reality as permanent, unmediated togetherness with Christ as the Son and as *theosis* in the sense of incorporation into the individuating Trinitarian framework is that it can also be described in such a way we will see God face to face. This means being together with God in a personal, loving relationship. Negative analogies will have to apply because of the use of terms such as 'face' and 'seeing' whose ultimate semantic concern is to depict the immediacy of interpersonal communication. This combines with another expression, that 'then we will know, just as we have been known', i.e. expressed as a positive analogy that our own identity claims in the eschatical reality will correspond to our true identities as they have been constituted in the judgement. If love is understood as a form of personal relationship that involves the identities of the participants themselves, 1 Cor. 13 can be drawn in precisely for this aspect. This also makes clear that the conflicts brought about by the interaction of mercantile, manipulative and loving relationships that characterize our lives at present will be abolished and only relationships based on love will be of eschatical relevance.

5.4.3.9 God is 'all in all' (1 Cor. 15.28)

The unmediated communication between God and humanity in the Parousia, *theosis* and immediate vision of God, which implies the agreement of all creaturely identity claims with the identities ascribed to them by God, also means that God will be 'all in all' in so far as there will be no more conflicts of interest and God will become the world of creation. This does not in any way indicate that there could be a reduction of alterity and therefore a dissolution of personal identities, which would have to be rejected as a negative analogy.

In summary, we can say that the image of the Parousia as immediate togetherness with Christ shows that personal, loving relationships are not of penultimate, but of eschatical and ultimate relevance.

The notion of the divinization of humanity means incorporation into the relational structure of the Trinity through grace.

The image of the vision of God from face to face refers to the immediacy of communication and interaction with God in personal, loving relationships, which in contrast to manipulative and mercantile relationships are alone of eschatical significance.

The notion that God will be all in all relates to the end of every intentional conflict and agreement with the will of God.

5.4.3.10 Eternal life (Matt. 25.46; Mk 10.30; John 3.16; Rom. 6.22)

It is possible to summarize the foregoing images in the notion of 'eternal life', which means nothing less than life in eternity. This means, according to our decisions in section 3.1, a life within the relational structure of the Trinity, since this constitutes a precise representation of eternity. It is now the meaning of the word 'life' that remains in question.

Up to the end of the nineteenth century, the concept of life did not have any central theological meaning and, despite its fundamental significance in the philosophy of life and in theology of the twentieth century among theologians such as Albert Schweitzer (d. 1965), the later Paul Tillich (d. 1965), Dietrich Bonhoeffer (d. 1945), Gerhard Ebeling (d. 2001) and Trutz Rendtorff, it has never attained the status of a fundamental theological concept. This is due to the fact that the various concepts for life (such as *zoe* in Greek for life as such and *bios* for the concrete human life, *vita* in Latin and the terminology found in various modern languages) were always positively connoted but at the same time referred to different phenomena seen by means of different philosophical perspectives. As a result, in the course of the Western intellectual tradition, the understanding of life was always dependent on various fundamental concepts that were indeed foundational for their respective intellectual traditions, meaning they did not therefore make recourse to a unified or common stock of phenomena. An analysis of the history of the concept accordingly does not deliver any satisfactory clarification. The current boom of the so-called life sciences, with biology leading the way, clearly necessitates a theological analysis and clarification of the concept. This elucidation will have to relate pragmatically to the biological observation of life, supported by a phenomenological basis in the framework of the Christian understanding of reality. In the following, we will distinguish between creaturely, divine and successful life, before we are able to explicate 'eternal' life.[181]

Creaturely life can be defined as a specific, inner-worldly, differentiated and emergent process of becoming applicable to various orders of organisms. This can be clarified in the following way:

1. Life is an event-like process, in the course of which particular possibilities are selectively actualized from a pre-existing set of possibilities.
2. The nature of the process and selection is controlled by a rule that does not emanate from the process itself and thereby defines the origin and goal of the process. As a result, creaturely life cannot select its own processuality, but this is always experienced as a given and therefore not at the disposal of creatures themselves.
3. The process of life is integrated with and determined by other processes in the world, concretely physical and chemical processes, but without being able to be reduced to these.
4. Life is distinct from these others processes by the fact that it is a process of the reciprocating production of organisms, which as an open system integrates with other systems and possesses some amount of latitude to establish its own rules on the basis of its rule-governed particularity.
5. Within the process of life there are emergent, sub-processes that build upon one another and that must be distinguished from one another: the non-personal (plant and animal) life and personal life. Non-personal life is distinct from personal life in that its capacity for self-direction rests on certain pre-existing rules, whereas personal life can itself determine its matter of choice within given limits and can increase its options within certain limits.
6. The basis of the expansive possibilities of personal life is its experience and disclosedness and not only perception of the act of choice itself (self-consciousness) in a reciprocally conditioning and constituting relational nexus of individual and species.

[181] Für das Folgende cf. Eilert Herms, 'Leben', *Marburger Jahrbuch Theologie* 14 (Marburg: Elwert, 2002), pp. 93–119; Eilert Herms (ed.), *Leben* (Gütersloh: Gütersloher Verlagshaus, 2005); P. Hadot, H. Hübner, J. Vennebusch, R. Piepmeier, U. Dierse and K. Rothe, 'Leben', *Historisches Wörterbuch der Philosophie*, vol. 5, 13 vols (eds Joachim Ritter et al.; Basel: Schwabe & Co, 1980), pp. 52–103; Jürgen Hübner, 'Leben V', in Müller, Gehard et al. (eds), *Theologische Realenzyklopädie*, vol. 20 (Berlin: De Gruyter, 1990), pp. 530–61; Wolfgang Drechsel, 'Der lange Schatten des Mythos vom gelungenen Leben', *Pastoraltheologie* 95 (2006), pp. 314–28.

7. This processual, graduated order of life is itself an emergent process, i.e. subsequent stages in the process cannot be sufficiently inferred from the earlier stages, but only constitute a necessary condition for the subsequent stages in the process.

The so-called life sciences including biology are only occupied with one segment of creaturely life, namely, only in so far as this process is observable. Those self-enclosed aspects of life, including a large part of its determination by rules, are not empirically observable and remain closed to the corresponding branches of science, so that phenomenological, anthropological and theological analyses are indispensible for a thorough grasp of life in the world. This, however, shows that a non-theoretical, world-view neutral description of life is ultimately not possible. Descriptions of interactions between various life processes that always live within the organic nexus through the exhaustibility of creaturely organisms (death) vary between the model of struggle and the model of surrender, as we have already seen in section 4.2.

Creaturely life is to be distinguished from the *divine life*, which according to God's self-disclosure takes place in eternity as Trinitarian life between the persons of the Father, Son and Holy Spirit. Divine life therefore denotes God as such and is to be defined as a process of choice led by certain rules, though with the distinction that God constitutes God's own rule so that this is not withdrawn and God has to be understood as life itself. As a result, the divine life is also to be understood as identical with other descriptions of the relational structure that is the Trinity, first and foremost that of love. Divine life is related positively to creaturely life, in that it is seen as the condition of the possibility of creaturely life, especially in terms of its regulated specificity and therefore at its origin and goal.

At present, creaturely personal life exists under the alternative of either conforming to or contradicting the regulated determinacy conditioned by the divine life. The Christian notion of original sin thereby signifies the circumstance that it is no longer possible for creaturely personal life in the here and now to undertake an act of choice corresponding to the conditions of its own constitution. Rather, the possibility for such a correspondence is first brought about by the reconciling work of the Son and the Spirit (see section 2.2.4.4). However, since the process of creaturely life nonetheless remains ambiguous, as the possibility of correspondence never transitions into the possibility of autonomous choice (*simul justus et peccator*), the term 'successful life' can never itself signify the correspondence of creaturely, personal life to the actual conditions of its own constitution but rather relates to a personal life, whose experience – in both contradiction and correspondence to the conditions of its constitution – is deduced from its need for justification and therefore its dependence on the life giving inspiration of the Holy Spirit. The disclosedness of particular creaturely life also includes a specific view of the inter-organic process of creaturely life to the extent that it is explicitly understood to be life *primarily* for and through others and remains indisposable, despite being subject to a kind of partial self-disclosure. It is therefore necessary to demarcate the concept of the truly successful life from the concept of the quality of life: successful life in the here and now is exclusively defined by the experience of the need for justification from and through the divine life, not, on the contrary, by a particular quality of experience (feelings of happiness, sadness, doubt, satisfactory or surplus possession of the necessities for life, etc.). Where this difference is not observed, the language of 'successful life' turns into a myth, the relation to the divine life is functionalized as religion and this reversal of the end-means structure reveals the idolatry of the talk of 'successful life'.[182] The reversal of the end-means structure consists in the fact that the act of choice in the personal life now is no longer orientated on the conditions of the constitution and definition of goals established by the divine life, but its act of choice is aligned towards a specific quality of experience only accessible to the individual (and generally experienced as pleasurable), and so life is once again in contradiction to its own constitution and goals.

Based on this clarification of the concept of life, we can understand *eternal life* in three ways. First, eternal life is a synonym for the divine life (see above). Second, it is a synonym for successful life (see above), especially in the Johannine writings. Third, eternal life is a designation for the eschatical incorporation of creaturely life into the inner-Trinitarian divine life by grace and therefore means unmediated vision and enjoyment of God. The concept of life does go beyond the previously mentioned imagery used to depict the eschatical reality to the extent that it includes permanency of choice, even in the eschatical reality, and therefore actually novelty (newness) for both God and creation.

> The concept of eternal life goes beyond that of the other images since, in addition to the permanent event-like nature of the eschatical reality, it also includes perpetual novelty.

[182]Cf. Wolfgang Drechsel, 'Der lange Schatten des Mythos vom gelungenen Leben', pp. 314–28.

5.4.3.11 Music

At the end of our analysis of the imagery used to depict the eschatical reality, we can further mention two suitable images that do not directly derive from the biblical material. This should help exemplify the fact that reflection about a 'conceptual' criteriology cannot only be used to explicate types of speech that are already to hand, but also in being creative with regard to the development of additional forms of speech. The first example comes from the American Lutheran Robert W. Jenson. At the end of his dogmatics, he nearly completely eschews 'conceptual' language, speaking nearly 'hymnically'. At this point, we shall forgo the attempt to render a conceptual clarification of what Jenson writes at that point. A criteriological examination of Jenson's musical imagery can be left for the reader to pursue:

> The last word to be said about God's triune being is that he "is a great fugue". Therefore the last word to be said about the redeemed is Jonathan Edwards's beautiful saying… "When I would form an idea of a society in the highest degree happy, I think of them… sweetly singing to each other."
>
> The point of identity, infinitely approachable and finitely to be approached, the enlivening *telos* of the Kingdom's own life, is perfect harmony between the conversation of the redeemed and the conversation that God is. In the conversation God is, meaning and melody are one.
>
> The end is music.[183]

> Robert Jenson describes the eschatical reality as music, in which meaning and melody are identical.

5.4.3.12 The content of a good book

Conceptually controlled but nevertheless pictorial language about the eschatical reality can not only produce new images and combine old ones, it can also appear in the various spheres of the Christian faith and its lifeworld. C.S. Lewis (d. 1963), for example, offers a number of different images for the eschatical reality in the last volume of his *Chronicles of Narnia*, a series of children's books. A few of these images will be introduced in what follows. We will also eschew a critical explication of these images at this point as

[183]Jenson, *Systematic Theology II*, p. 369.

well and leave any necessary theological judgements in the matter to the reader. As a small aid, however, we can suggest that Lewis's understanding of reality is largely indebted to either a creative Christian Platonism or a platonizing Christianity:

> 'There *was* a real railway accident,' said Aslan softly. 'Your father and mother and all of you are – as you used to call it in the Shadowlands – dead. The term is over: the holidays have begun. The dream is ended: this is the morning.'
>
> And as He spoke, He no longer looked to them like a lion; but the things that began to happen after that were so great and beautiful that I cannot write them. And for us this is the end of all the stories, and we can most truly say that they all lived happily every after. But for them it was only the beginning of the real story. All their life in this world and all their adventures in Narnia had only been the cover and the title page: now at last they were beginning Chapter One of the Great Story which no one on earth has read: which goes on for ever: in which every chapter is better than the one before.[184]

C. S. Lewis describes the relationship between our life in the here and now to our life in the eschatical reality by means of the relationship of the title page of a book to its content.

5.4.4 Back to the present

We shall now come back into the present from our attempts to describe the eschatical reality. We are not *in patria*, in the homeland, but *in via*, on the way. Still, this way is transformed through hope into the eschatical reality. It is not like with the atomist Democritus (d. 371 BCE), a way that offers an inn for recovery along the way and then ends pointlessly,[185] but a way with a destination that is also present along the way. It is certainly true that the eschatical reality can be seen in the here and now during the celebration of the worship service, as the Eastern Orthodox Churches emphasize. But, even the Sunday worship service is solidly interlocked with our service to God in everyday life. If, following Augustine, Christians are to utter

---

[184]C.S. Lewis, *The Last Battle* (London: Collins, 2001), p. 224.

[185]The saying, 'a life without a festival is like a long road without an inn', is attributed to Democritus. For his understanding of hope and death, see section 4.2.

'our heart is unquiet until it rests in you',[186] then this does not mean that Christians are to long to be out of the busyness of everyday life and in the absolute peace of God. Since we saw that both God and the eschatical reality share the same kind of event-like structure as the world, then the busyness can only relate to the ambiguity of the here and now, and peace and rest to the unambiguity of the eschatical reality. Christian hope and the occupation with eschatology can therefore be consistent with attempts to flee the world. Even the medieval mystic Richard of St. Victor (d. 1173), who longed to be completely in God, still recognized with the Paul (Rom. 9.3) that the highest form of longing was the wish to step back out from God once again for the sake of one's neighbour: 'The soul goes out from God and descends below… and is willing to be apart from Christ for the sake of the neighbour.'[187] Christian hope therefore drives us to action in everyday life in the here and now. In sections 4.1–5.3, we have attempted to identify a few of the ethical implications that stem from our occupation with eschatology. It would therefore be amiss to attempt to summarize these implications or convey them into a unified ethical principle, because this would be the subject matter of systematic theology as ethics, not, however, of eschatology. It would further be amiss because Christian ethics is more a matter of perceiving and leading life in the divine story than a matter of establishing principles for action. Finally, it would also be amiss because the unspeakable speakability of Christian hope for the eschatical reality would thereby lose in its dignity: the influences of this hope on our life and action in the here and now are just as diverse and manifold as this life is itself. It is from this standpoint that we will now have to amend Richard's statement: Does life and action in the here and now really mean being separated from Christ? If Christians also want to long for his immediate presence, they will always find him again in a mediated way (Rom. 14.7–8):

> We do not live to ourselves, and we do not die to ourselves. If we live, we live to the Lord, and if we die, we die to the Lord; so then, whether we live or whether we die, we are the Lord's.

---

[186] Augustine, *Confessions*, p. 39 (1,1).

[187] Richard von St. Victor, *De quattuor gradibus violentiae caritatis – Über die Gewalt der Liebe: Ihre vier Stufen* (Munich: Schöningh, 1969), pp. 29, 46.

Bibliography

Albertus Magnus, 'De ressurectione', in Bernhard Geyer (ed.), *Opera Omnia*, vol. 26 (Münster: Aschendorff, 1958), pp. 286–7.

Alexander of Hales, *Glossa in quattuor libros Sententiarum Petri Lombardi* (Quaracchi: Collegii S. Bonaventurae, 1960).

Althaus, Paul, *Die letzten Dinge: Entwurf einer christlichen Eschatologie* (Gütersloh: Bertelsman, 1924, 2nd edn).

———, *Die Theologie Martin Luthers* (Gütersloh: Gütersloher Verlagshaus, 1984, 7th edn).

Anastasius of Sinai, *Wegweiser* (ed. J.P. Migne; Patrologiae Graeca 89; Paris: Imprimerie Catholique, 1865).

Anselm of Canterbury, 'Proslogion' (trans. M.J. Charlesworth), in Brian Davies and G.R. Evans (eds), *Anselm of Canterbury: The Major Works* (Oxford: Oxford, 1998), pp. 87–8.

Aquinas Thomas, *Summa contra Gentiles I–IV* (trans. and ed. Anton C. Pegis et al.; 5 vols; Notre Dame: Notre Dame, 1975).

———, *Summa Theologica* (trans. Fathers of the English Dominican Province; 5 vols; Notre Dame: Ave Maria, 1981).

Ariès, Philippe, *Geschichte des Todes* (Munich: Dt. Taschenbuch-Verl., 1993, 6th edn).

Athanasius, *On the Incarnation of the Word* (trans. Archibald Robertson; London: Nutt, 1891).

Auffarth, Christoph, 'Parousia I. Classic Antiquity', in Hans Dieter Betz et al. (eds), *Religion Past and Present*, vol. 9, 14 vols (Leiden: Brill, 2006–2013), p. 555.

Augustine, 'De Trinitate I-XII', in W.J. Mountain (ed.), *Corpus Christianorum Series Latina*, vol. 50 (Turnhout: Brepols, 1968).

———, *The Trinity* (trans. Edmund Hill; ed. John E. Rotelle; New York: New City Press, 2002).

———, *The Confessions* (trans. Maria Boulding; ed. John E. Rotelle; New York: New City Press, 2012, 2nd edn).

———, *The City of God Against the Pagans* (trans. and ed. R.W. Dyson; Cambridge: Cambridge University Press, 2013, 10th edn).

Axt-Piscalar, Christine, 'Trinitarische Entzauberung des patriarchalen Vatergottes', *Zeitschrift für Theologie und Kirche* 91 (1994), pp. 476–86.

Balthasar, Hans Urs von, 'Eschatologie', in Johnannes Feiner, Josef Trütsch and Franz Böckle (eds), *Fragen der Theologie heute* (Einsiedeln: Benziger, 1957).
———, *Theo-Drama I–V* (San Francisco: Ignatius, 1988–1998).
Barrow, John D. and Tipler, Frank J., *The Anthropic Cosmological Principle* (Oxford: Oxford, 1986).
Bartelmus, Rüdiger, 'Himmel', in G.J. Botterweck, H.J. Fabry and H. Ringgren (eds) *Theologisches Wörterbuch zum Alten Testament*, 10 vols. (Stuttgart: Kohlhammer, 1995), pp. 204–39.
Barth, Karl, *The Epistle of the Romans* (trans. Edwyn C. Hoskyns; London: Oxford, 1968).
———, *Church Dogmatics II/1: The Doctrine of God, Part 1* (trans. T.H.L. Parker et al.; eds G.W. Bromiley and T.F. Torrance; London: T&T Clark, 2004a).
———, *Church Dogmatics III/2: The Doctrine of Creation* (trans. H, Knight et al.; eds G.W. Bromiley and T.F. Torrance; London: T&T Clark, 2004b).
———, *Church Dogmatics IV/3.1: The Doctrine of Reconciliation* (trans. Geoffrey Bromiley; London: T&T Clark, 2004c).
Barth, Ulrich, 'Abschied von der Kosmologie – Befreiung der Religion zu sich selbst', in Wilhelm Gräb (ed.), *Urknall oder Schöpfung? Zum Dialog von Naturwissenschaft und Theologie* (Gütersloh: Kaiser, 1995), pp. 14–42.
Baumgarten, Sigmund Jacob, *Evangelische Glaubenslehre*, vol. 3 (ed. J. S. Semler; Halle: Gebauer, 1760).
Becker, Jürgen, *Auferstehung der Toten im Urchristentum* (Stuttgart: Katholisches Bibelwerk, 1976).
———, *Das Urchristentum als gegliederte Epoche* (Stuttgart: Katholisches Bibelwerk, 1993).
———, *Jesus of Nazareth* (trans. James E. Crouch; New York: De Gruyter, 1998).
Beierwaltes, Werner, 'Einleitung' in Plotin, *Über Ewigkeit und Zeit (Enneade III, 7)* (trans. and ed. Werner Beierwaltes; Frankfurt am Main: Klostermann, 1995, 4th edn), pp. 43–9.
Beisser, Friedrich, *Hoffnung und Vollendung* (Gütersloh: Gütersloher Verlagshaus, 1993).
Bellah, Robert N., 'Civil Religion in America', *Dædalus* 96.1 (winter 1967), pp. 1–21.
Berger, Peter L., *The Heretical Imperative: Contemporary Possibilities of Religious Affirmation* (New York: Doubleday, 1979).
Beyschlag, Karlmann, *Grundriß der Dogmengeschichte I* (Darmstadt: Wissenschaftliche Buchgesellschaft, 1987).
———, *Die Erlanger Theologie* (Erlangen: Martin-Luther-Verlag, 1993).
Bloch-Smith, Elizabeth, *Judahite Burial Practices and Beliefs about the Dead* (Sheffield: JSOT Press, 1992).

Bloch, Ernst, *Das Prinzip Hoffnung* (Frankfurt am Main: Suhrkamp, 1990, 3rd edn).

Blum, G.G., 'Chiliasmus II', in Gehard Müller et al. (eds), *Theologische Realenzyklopädie*, vol. 7 (Berlin: De Gruyter, 1981), pp. 729–33.

Boethius, *The Theological Tractates and The Consolation of Philosophy* (trans. S.J. Tester et al.; Loeb Classic Library; Cambridge: Harvard, 1973).

Braaten, Carl E. and Jenson, Robert W., *Union with Christ: The New Finnish Interpretation of Luther* (Grand Rapids: Eerdmans, 1998).

Brandenburger, Egon, 'Gerichtskonzeptionen im Urchristentum und ihre Voraussetzungen', in Egon Brandenburger (ed.), *Studien zur Geschichte und Theologie des Urchristentums* (Stuttgart: Katholisches Bibelwerk, 1993), pp. 289–338.

Breidert, Wolfgang, 'Raum II', in Joachim Ritter et al. (eds), *Historisches Wörterbuch der Philosophie*, vol. 8, 13 vols (Basel: Schwabe & Co, 1992), pp. 82–8.

Brom, Luco Johan van den, *Divine Presence in the World: A Critical Analysis of the Notion of Divine Omnipresence* (Kampen: Kok, 1993).

———, 'Space I. Philosophy of Religion; Space II. Dogmatics', in Hans Dieter Betz et al. (eds), *Religion Past and Present*, vol. 12, 14 vols (Leiden: Brill, 2006–2013), pp. 179–80.

Brümmer, Vincent, *Theology and Philosophical Inquiry* (Philadelphia: Westminster Press, 1982).

———, *The Model of Love* (New York: Cambridge University Press, 1993).

———, *What are We Doing When We Pray? On Prayer and the Nature of Faith* (Burlington: Ashgate, 2008).

Brunner, Emil, *The Christian Doctrine of God: Dogmatics I* (trans. Olive Wyon; Philadelphia: Westminster Press, 1949).

Bultmann, Rudolf, *Jesus and the Word* (New York: Scribner's, 1934).

———, *Geschichten und Eschatologie* (Tübingen: Mohr Siebeck, 1958).

———, 'The Eschatology of the Gospel of John', in *Faith and Understanding I* (London: SCM, 1969), pp. 165–83.

———, 'What Does it Mean to Speak of God?', in *Faith and Understanding I* (trans. Louise Pettibone Smith; Philadelphia: Fortress, 1987), pp. 53–65.

———, 'New Testament and Mythology', in *New Testament and Mythology and Other Basic Writings* (Minneapolis: Fortress, 1990), p. 1–44.

Burkett, Delbert Royce, *The Son of Man Debate: A History and Evaluation* (Cambridge: Cambridge University Press, 1999).

Busch, Wilhelm, *Schein und Sein: Nachgelassene Gedichte* (Munich: Joachim, 1909).

Calvin, John, 'Psychopannychia; Or, Imaginary Sleep of the Soul between Death and Judgment', in *Calvin's Tracts*, vol. III (trans. Henry Beveridge; Edinburgh: Constable, 1851), pp. 413–90.

——, *Commentarius in Harmoniam Evangelicam*, in Eduard Reuss et al. (eds), *Corpus Reformatorum*, vol. 73 (Brauschweig: Appelhans und Pfenningstorff, 1890).

——, *Institutes of the Christian Religion* (trans. Ford Lewis Battles; ed. John T. McNeill; 2 vols; Louisville: Westminster, 1960).

Chisholm, Roderick M., 'Events without Times: An Essay on Ontology', *Nous* 24 (1990), pp. 413–28.

Clarke, Samuel and Leibniz, Gottfried Wilhelm, *Der Briefwechsel mit G.W. Leibniz von 1715/1716 = A collection of papers which passed between the late learned Mr. Leibniz and Dr. Clarke in the years 1715/1716 relating to the principles of natural philosophy and religion* (ed. Ed Dellian; Hamburg: Meiner, 1990).

Clayton, Philip, 'Neurowissenschaft, Mensch und Gott', in Ted Peters, Gaymon Bennett and Kang Phee Seng (eds), *Brücken bauen: Neurowissenschaft und Religion* (Göttingen: Vandenhoeck & Ruprecht, 2006), pp. 169–86.

Cone, James H., *A Black Theology of Liberation* (Philadelphia: J. P. Lippencott, 1970).

Conte, Amedeo G., 'Konstitutive Regeln und Deontik', in Edgar Morscher and Rudolf Stranzinger (eds), *Ethik: Grundlagen, Probleme, Anwendungen* (Vienna: Hölder-Pichler-Tempsky, 1981), pp. 82–6.

Cullmann, Oscar, *Christ and Time* (London: SCM, 1963a, 3rd edn).

——, *Christus und die Zeit* (Zurich: Evangelischer Verlag, 1963b, 3rd edn).

Daley, Brian, *Eschatologie in der Schrift und Patristik* (Freiburg: Herder, 1986).

Dalferth, Ingolf U., *Der auferweckte Gekreuzigte: Zur Grammatik der Christologie* (Tübingen: Mohr Siebeck, 1994).

Davidson, Donald, *Essays on Actions and Events* (Oxford: Clarendon, 2002).

Deane-Drummond, Celia, *Christ and Evolution* (Minneapolis: Fortress, 2009).

Denzinger, Heinrich, *Compendium of Creeds, Definitions and Declarations on Matters of Faith and Morals* (ed. Peter Hünermann et al.; San Francisco: Ignatius Press, 2012).

Derrida, Jacques, 'Of an Apocalyptic Tone Recently Adopted in Philosophy', *Oxford Literary Review* 6.2 (1984), pp. 3–37.

Dieckmann, Elisabeth, *Personalität Gottes – Personalität des Menschen. Ihre Deutung im theologischen Denken Wolfhart Pannenbergs* (Altenberge: Oros-Verlag, 1995).

Diels, Hermann, *Die Fragmente der Vorsokratiker.*, vol. 2 (Hamburg: Rowohlt, 1964).

Digest, Luther, *An Annual Abridgment of Luther Studies* (Shorewood: Luther Academy, 1995).

Dodd, Charles Harold, *The Parables of the Kingdom* (London: Nisbet & Co, 1948).

Dorner, Isaak August, *The Future State: The Doctrine of the Last Things* (trans. Newman Smyth; New York: Scribner's, 1883).

Drechsel, Wolfgang, 'Das Schweigen der Hirten? Altenseelsorge als (kein) Thema poimenischer Theoriebildung', in Susanne Kobler-von-Komorowski and Heinz Schmidt (eds), *Seelsorge im Alltag* (Heidelberg: Winter, 2005a), pp. 45–64.

——, 'Der bittere Geschmack des Unendlichen. Annäherungen an eine Seelsorge im Bedeutungshorizont des Themas Krebs', in *Wege zum Menschen* 57 (2005b), pp. 459–81.

——, 'Der lange Schatten des Mythos vom gelungenen Leben', *Pastoraltheologie* 95 (2006), pp. 314–28.

Ebeling, Gerhard, *Die theologische Definition des Menschen* (Tübingen: Mohr Siebeck, 1989).

Echternach, Helmut, 'Ewigkeit', in Joachim Ritter et al. (eds), *Historisches Wörterbuch der Philosophie*, vol. 2, 13 vols (Basel: Schwabe & Co, 1972), p. 842.

Elert, Werner, *Der Kampf um das Christentum: Geschichte der Beziehungen zwischen dem evangelischen Christentum in Deutschland und dem allgemeinen Denken seit Schleiermacher und Hegel* (Munich: Beck, 1921).

——, *Theodor von Pharan: Der Ausgang der altkirchlichen Christologie* (Berlin: Lutherisches Verlagshaus, 1957).

——, *Der christliche Glaube: Grundlinien der lutherischen Dogmatik* (ed. Ernst Kinder; Hamburg: Furche-Verlag, 1960, 5th edn).

Engels, Friedrich, 'Schelling und die Offenbarung', in Karl Marx and Friedrich Engels (eds), *Gesamtausgabe I/3* (Berlin: Dietz, 1985).

Epicurus of Samos, 'Epicurus to Menoeceus' (trans. C. Bailey), in Whitney J. Oates (ed.), *The Stoic and Epicurean Philosophers: The Complete Extant Writings of Epicurus, Epictetus, Lucretius, Marcus Aurelius* (New York: Random House, 1940), pp. 30–3.

Erlemann, Kurt, *Naherwartung und Parusieverzögerung im Neuen Testament: Ein Beitrag zur Frage religiöser Zeiterfahrung* (Tübingen: Francke, 1995).

Etzelmüller, Gregor, "*… zu richten die Lebendigen und die Toten*": *Zur Rede vom jüngsten Gericht im Anschluß an Karl Barth* (Neukirchen-Vluyn: Neukirchener Verlag, 2001).

Evers, Dirk, *Raum – Materie – Zeit: Schöpfungstheologie im Dialog mit naturwissenschaftlicher Kosmologie* (Tübingen: Mohr Siebeck, 2000).

——, *Gott und mögliche Welte: Studien zur Logik theologischer Aussagen über das Mögliche* (Tübingen: Mohr Siebeck, 2006).

Feuerbach, Ludwig, *The Essence of Christianity* (trans. George Eliot; Amherst: Prometheus, 1989).

Finé, Heinz, *Die Terminologie der Jenseitsvorstellungen bei Tertullian* (Bonn: Hanstein, 1957).

Flasch, Kurt, *Was ist Zeit? Augustinus von Hippo, das XI. Buch der Confessiones: Historisch-philosophische Studie: Text – Übersetzung – Kommentar* (Frankfurt am Main: Klostermann, 1993).

Fleischer, Margot, 'Friedrich Nietzsche. Dionysische Bejahung der Welt' in Margot Fleischer and Jochen Hennigfeld (eds), *Philosophen des 19. Jahrhunderts* (Darmstadt: Primus Verlag, 2004, 2nd edn), pp. 179–98.

Flew, Antony, *Body, Mind and Death* (New York: Macmillan, 1964).

———, *The Logic of Mortality* (Oxford: Blackwell, 1987).

Frankfurt, Harry G., 'The Freedom of Will and the Concept of a Person', *The Journal of Philosophy* 68.1 (1971), pp. 5–20.

Frei, Hans, *Theology and Narrative* (New York: Oxford, 1993).

Frick, Robert, *Die Geschichte des Reich-Gottes-Gedankens in der alten Kirche bis zu Origenes und Augustin* (Gießen: Verlag Alfred Töpelmann, 1928).

Fuentes, Agustín, *Biological Anthropology: Concepts and Connections* (New York: McGraw Hill, 2011).

———, 'Blurring the Biological and Social in Human Becomings', in Tim Ingold and Gisli Palsson (eds), *Biosocial Becomings: Integrating Social and Biological Anthropology* (Cambridge: Cambridge University Press, 2013a), pp. 42–58.

———, 'Evolutionary Perspectives and Transdisciplinary Intersections: A Roadmap to Generative Areas of Overlap in Discussing Human Nature', *Theology and Science* 11 (2013b), pp. 106–29.

Fukuyama, Francis, *The End of History and the Last Man* (London: Hamilton, 1992).

Geach, Peter T., *Providence and Evil* (Cambridge: Cambridge University Press, 1977).

Geertz, Jan Christian et al. (eds), *T&T Clark Handbook of the Old Testament: An Introduction to the Literature, Religion and History of the Old Testament* (London: T&T Clark, 2012).

Gerhard, Johann, *Ioannis Gerhardi Loci Theologici cum pro adstruenda veritate tum pro destruenda quarumvis contradicentium falsitate per theses nervose solide et copiose explicati* (Lipsiae: Hinrichs, 1885).

Goffman, Erving, *Stigma: Notes on the Management of Spoiled Identity* (New York: Simon and Schuster, 1963).

Grässer, Erich, *Das Problem der Parusieverzögerung in den synoptischen Evangelien und in der Apostelgeschichte* (Berlin: De Gruyter, 1977, 3rd edn).

Greshake, Gisbert, *Auferstehung der Toten* (Essen: Ludgerus, 1969).

Griffin, David Ray, *God, Power and Evil: A Process Theodicy* (Philadelphia: Westminster, 1976).

Gunton, Colin E., *The Actuality of Atonement: A Study of Metaphor, Rationality and the Christian Tradition* (Edinburgh: T&T Clark, 1988).

——, 'Relation and Relativity: The Trinity and the Doctrine of Creation', in Colin E. Gunton (ed.), *The Promise of Trinitarian Theology* (Edinburgh: T&T Clark, 1991), pp. 142–61.

Gutiérrez, Gustavo, *A Theology of Liberation: History, Politics and Salvation* (London: SCM, 2001).

Haas, Alois, 'Meister Eckharts Auffassungen von der Zeit', in *Naturphilosophische Studien* (ed. Evangelische Studiengemeinschaft; Heidelberg: Forschungsstätte d. Evang. Studiengemeinschaft, 1982), pp. 27–62.

Hadot, P., Hübner, H., Vennebusch, J., Piepmeier, R., Dierse, U. and Rothe, K., 'Leben', in Joachim Ritter et al. (eds), *Historisches Wörterbuch der Philosophie*, vol. 5, 13 vols (Basel: Schwabe & Co, 1980), pp. 52–103.

Härle, Wilfried, 'Luthers Zwei-Regimenten-Lehre als Lehre vom Handeln Gottes', in Wilfried Härle (ed.), *Marburger Jahrbuch Theologie I* (Marburg: Elwert, 1987a), pp. 37–77.

——, *Systematische Philosophie* (Munich: Kaiser, 1987b, 2nd edn).

——, 'Der Glaube als Gottes- und/oder Menschenwerk in der Theologie Martin Luthers', in Wilfried Härle (ed.), *Marburger Jahrbuch für Theologie IV* (Marburg: Elwert, 1992), pp. 37–77.

——, *Dogmatik* (Berlin: De Gruyter, 1995).

——, 'Die weltanschaulichen Voraussetzungen jeder normativen Ethik', in Wilfried Härle (ed.), *Marburger Jahrbuch Theologie XIII* (Marburg: Elwert, 2001), pp. 15–38.

Harnack, Adolf von, *Lehrbuch der Dogmengeschichte I* (Tübingen: Mohr Siebeck, 1909, 4th edn).

——, *What is Christianity?* (trans. Thomas Bailey Saunders; New York: Harper, 1957).

Hauerwas, Stanley, *A Community of Character* (Notre Dame: Notre Dame, 1981).

Heesch, Matthias, *Transzendentale Theorie und religiöse Erfahrung: Ihre Vermittlung als erkenntnistheoretische Grundintention in Richard Rothes Theologischer Ethik* (Frankfurt am Main: Lang, 1990).

Hegel, Georg Wilhelm Friedrich, Wissenschaft der Logik I/1: Die Objektive Logic: Erstes Buch: Die Lehre vom Sein (1832), in Walter Jaeschke and Friedrich Hogemann (eds), *Gesammelte Werke*, vol. 21 (Hamburg: Felix Meiner, 1984).

——, *Elements of the Philosophy of Right* (ed. Allen Wood; trans. H.B. Nisbet; Cambridge: Cambridge University Press, 2012).

Heim, Karl, *Die Wandlung im naturwissenschaftlichen Weltbild: Die modern Naturwissenschaft vor der Gottesfrage* (Hamburg: Furche, 1954).

Hempel, Carl G. and Oppenheim, Paul, 'Studies in the Logic of Explanation', *Philosophy of Science* 15.2 (April 1948), pp. 135–75.

Hermanni, Friedrich, *Das Böse und die Theodizee: Eine philosophisch-theologische Grundlegung* (Gütersloh: Gütersloher Verlagshaus, 2002).
Herms, Eilert, *Gesellschaft gestalten* (Tübingen: Mohr Siebeck, 1991).
———, *Offenbarung und Glaube* (Tübingen: Mohr Siebeck, 1992).
———, *Kirche für die Welt* (Tübingen: Mohr Siebeck, 1995a).
———, 'Offenbarung V', in Gehard Müller et al. (eds), *Theologische Realenzyklopädie*, vol. 25 (Berlin: De Gruyter, 1995b), pp. 146–210.
———, 'Leben', in Wilfried Härle (ed.), *Marburger Jahrbuch Theologie XIV* (Marburg: Elwert, 2002a), pp. 93–119.
———, 'Theologische Ethik und Rechtsbegründung', in Wilfried Härle (ed.), *Marburger Jahrbuch Theologie XIV* (Marburg: Elwert, 2002b), pp. 13–40.
Herms, Eilert (ed.), *Leben* (Gütersloh: Gütersloher Verlagshaus, 2005).
Hesse, Mary B., *Models and Analogies in Science* (London: Sheed and Ward, 1963).
Hick, John, *Death and Eternal Life* (London: Collins, 1976).
Hjelde, Sigurd, *Das Eschaton und die Eschata: Eine Studie über Sprachgebrauch und Sprachverwirrung in protestantischer Theologie von der Orthodoxie bis zur Gegenwart* (Munich: Kaiser, 1987).
———, 'Divine Judgement I. Religious Studies', in Hans Dieter Betz et al. (eds), *Religion Past and Present*, vol. 4, 14 vols (Leiden: Brill, 2006–2013), pp. 109–10.
Hörning, Martin, 'Medizinische Aspekte', in Martin Hörning and Peter Leppin (eds), *Der Tod gehört zum Leben. Sterben und Sterbebegleitung aus interdisziplinärer Sicht* (Münster: Lit, 2005), pp. 5–24.
Hubbeling, Hubertus Gezinus, *Einführung in die Religionsphilosophie* (Göttingen: Vandenhoeck & Ruprecht, 1981).
Hubbeling, Hubertus Gezinus and De Swart, H.C.M, *Inleiding tot de symbolica logica* (Assen: Van Gorcum, 1976).
Hübner, Jürgen, *Die Theologie Johannes Keplers zwischen Orthodoxie und Naturwissenschaft* (Tübingen: Mohr Siebeck, 1975).
———, 'Leben V', in Gehard Müller et al. (eds), *Theologische Realenzyklopädie*, vol. 20 (Berlin: De Gruyter, 1990), pp. 530–61.
Hucklenbroich, Peter, 'Tod und Sterben – Was ist das? Medizinische und philosophische Aspekte', in Peter Hucklenbroich and Petra Gelhaus (eds), *Tod und Sterben: Medizinische Perspektiven* (Münster: Lit, 2001), pp. 3–20.
Huntington, Samuel P., 'The Clash of Civilizations', *Foreign Affairs* 72.3 (1993), pp. 22–8.
Huxel, Kirsten, 'Untersterblichkeit der Seele versus Ganztodthese? – Ein Grundproblem christlicher Eschatologie in ökumenischer Perspektive', *Neue Zeitschrift für Systematische Theologie* 48 (2006), pp. 342–66.
Ingold, Tim, 'Becoming Persons: Consciousness and Sociality in Human Evolution', *Cultural Dynamics* 4.3 (1991), pp. 355–78.

———, 'To Human is a Verb', in Agustín Fuentes and Aku Visala (eds), *Verbs, Bones and Brains: Interdisciplinary Perspectives on Human Nature* (Notre Dame: Notre Dame, forthcoming).

Ingold, Tim and Palsson, Gisli (eds), *Biosocial Becomings: Integrating Social and Biological Anthropology* (Cambridge: Cambridge University Press, 2013).

Irenaeus, 'Against Heresies', in Alexander Roberts and James Donaldson (eds), *The Ante-Nicene Fathers, Vol. 1: The Apostolic Fathers* (New York: Scribner's, 1899), pp. 309–567.

Janowski, Bernd, 'Der barmherzige Richter', in R. Scoralick (ed.), *Das Drama der Barmherzigkeit Gottes: Studien zur biblischen Gottesrede und ihrer Wirkungsgeschichte in Judentum und Christentum* (Stuttgart: Katholisches Bibelwerk, 2000), pp. 33–91.

———, 'Divine Judgment II. Old Testament', in Hans Dieter Betz et al. (eds), *Religion Past and Present*, vol. 4, 14 vols (Leiden: Brill, 2006–2013), pp. 110–11.

Janowski, Johanna Christine, *Allerlösung: Annäherungen an eine entdualisierte Eschatologie*, vol. 2 (Neukirchen-Vluyn: Neukirchener Verlag, 2000).

Jenson, Robert W., 'The Triune God', in Robert W. Jenson and Carl E. Braaten (eds), *Christian Dogmatics I* (Philadelphia: Fortress, 1984), pp. 83–191.

———, *Systematic Theology I: The Triune God* (New York: Oxford, 1997).

———, *Systematic Theology II: The Works of God* (New York: Oxford, 1999).

Jeremias, Jörg, *Kultprophetie und Gerichtsverkündigung in der späten Königszeit Israels* (Göttingen: Neukirchener Verlag, 1970).

———, 'Der 'Tag Jahwes' in Jes 13 und Joel 2', in Reinhard Gregor Kratz, Thomas Krüger and Konrad Schmid (eds), *Festschrift für Odil Hannes Steck*, (Beihefte zur Zeitschrift für die alttestamentliche Wissenschaft 300; Berlin: De Gruyter, 2000), pp. 129–38.

Jewett, Robert and Lawrence, John Shelton, *Captain America and the Crusade against Evil* (Grand Rapids: Eerdmans, 2003).

Jinkins, Michael, *A Comparative Study in the Theology of Atonement on Jonathan Edwards and John McLeod Campbell* (San Fransisco: Mellen, 1993).

Joachim of Fiore, *Liber Concordia Novi ac Veteris Testamenti* (Venice: 1519).

Joest, Wilfried, *Ontologie der Person bei Luther* (Göttingen: Vandenhoeck & Ruprecht, 1987, 2nd edn).

Johannes Buridanus, *Kommentar zur Aristotelischen Physik* (Paris: 1509).

Johannes Scotus Eriugena, *De divisione naturae*.

John of Damascus, 'The Orthodox Faith', in *Writings: The Fount of Knowledge: The Philosophical Chapters, On Heresies and On the Orthodox Faith* (trans. Frederic H. Chase; The Fathers of the Church, vol. 37; Washington D.C.: Catholic University, 1958), pp. 165–406.

Jonas, Hans, 'The Concept of God after Auschwitz: A Jewish Voice', *The Journal of Religion* 67.1 (Jan. 1987), pp. 1–13.
Jooss, Elisabeth, *Raum: Eine theologische Interpretation* (Gütersloh: Gütersloher Verlagshaus, 2005).
Jüngel, Eberhard, 'Death: History of Dogma and Dogmatics', in Hans Dieter Betz et al. (eds), *Religion Past and Present*, vol. 3, 14 vols (Leiden: Brill, 2006–2013), pp. 697–9.
———, *Death: The Riddle and The Mystery* (trans. Iain and Ute Nichol; Edinburgh: Saint Andrew, 1975).
———, 'The Relationship between "Economic" and "Immanent" Trinity', *Theology Digest* 24 (1976), pp. 179–84.
———, *God as the Mystery of the World: On the Foundation of the Theology of the Crucified One in the Dispute between Theism and Atheism* (trans. Darrell Guder; Grand Rapids: Eerdmans, 1983).
———, 'Gottes ursprüngliches Anfangen als schöpferische Selbstbegrenzung', in, *Wertlose Wahrheit: Zur Identität und Relevanz des christlichen Glaubens* (Munich: Kaiser, 1990), pp. 151–62.
Jüngel, Eberhard and Ricoeur, Paul, 'Thesen zur theologischen Metaphorologie', in Jean-Pierre von Noppen (ed.), *Erinnern um Neues zu sagen* (Frankfurt am Main: Athenaeum, 1988).
Kähler, Martin, *Dogmatische Zeitfragen* (Leipzig: Deichert, 1908).
———, *Die Wissenschaft der christlichen Lehre von dem evangelischen Grundartikel aus im Abrisse dargestellt* (Waltrop: Spenner, 1994, 3rd edn).
———, *Zur Lehre von der Versöhnung* (Gütersloh: Bertelsmann, 1998, 2nd.n).
Kant, Immanuel, *Critique of Practical Reason*, in *Practical Philosophy* (trans. and ed. Mary J. Gregor; Cambridge: Cambridge University Press, 2005), pp. 133–271.
———, *The End of all Things*, in *Religion and Rational Theology* (trans. and ed. Allen W. Wood and George di Giovanni; Cambridge: Cambridge University Press, 1996a), pp. 221–31.
———, *Groundwork of the Metaphysics of Moral*, in *Practical Philosophy* (trans. and ed. Mary J. Gregor; Cambridge: Cambridge University Press, 1996b), pp. 37–108.
———, *Critique of Pure Reason* (trans. and ed. Paul Guyer and Allen W. Wood; Cambridge: Cambridge University Press, 1998).
Karl, Rahner, *The Trinity* (trans. Joseph Donceel; ed. Catherine Mowry LaCugna; New York: Crossroad, 2010).
Kenny, Anthony, *Action, Emotion and Will* (London: Routledge, 1963).
Kepler, Johannes, *Mysterium Cosmographicum* (Munich: Beck, 1938).
Koch, Klaus, 'Gibt es ein Vergeltungsdogma im AT?', *Zeitschrift für Theologie und Kirche* 52 (1955), pp. 1–42.

Kolb, Robert and Timothy J. Wengert (eds), *The Book of Concord: The Confessions of the Evangelical Lutheran Church* (trans. Charles Arand et al.; Minneapolis: Fortress, 2000).

Körtner, Ulrich H.J., *Weltangst und Weltende: Eine theologische Interpretation der Apokalyptik* (Göttingen: Vandenhoeck & Ruprecht, 1988).

Kreck, Walter, *Die Zukunft des Gekommenen: Grundprobleme der Eschatologie* (Munich: Kaiser, 1961).

Kunz, Erhard, *Protestantische Eschatologie von der Reformation bis zur Aufklärung* (Freiburg: Herder, 1980).

Lammer, Kerstin, *Den Tod begreifen: Neue Wege in der Trauerbegleitung* (Neukirchen-Vluyn: Neukirchener Verlag, 2006, 4th edn).

Lampe, Peter, 'Paul's Concept of a Spiritual Body', in Ted Peters, Robert John Russell and Michael Welker (eds), *Resurrection: Theological and Scientific Assessments* (Cambridge: Cambridge University Press, 2002), pp. 102–14.

Lang, Bernhard and McDannell, Colleen, *Der Himmel: Eine Kulturgeschichte des ewigen Lebens* (Frankfurt am Main: Suhrkamp, 1990).

Lea, Thomas D., 'A Survey of the Doctrine of the Return of Christ in the Ante-Nicene Fathers', *Journal of the Evangelical Theological Society* 29.2 (1986), pp. 163–77.

Leibniz, Gottfried Wilhelm, *Theodicy: Essays on the Goodness of God, the Freedom of Man, and the Origin of Evil* (trans. E.M. Huggard; La Salle: Open Court, 1985).

Lem, Stanislaw, *Die phantastischen Erzählungen* (Frankfurt am Main: Insel, 1980).

———, *The Star Diaries* (trans. Michael Kandel; New York: Harcourt, 1985).

Leppin, Volker, 'Millenarianism/Chiliasm: III. Church History, 3. Reformation and Modern Times', in Hans Dieter Betz et al. (eds), *Religion Past and Present*, vol. 8, 14 vols (Leiden: Brill, 2006–2013), p. 360.

Lessing, Gotthold Ephraim, 'On the Proof of the Spirit and of the Power', in Henry Chadwick (ed.), *Lessing's Theological Writings* (Stanford: Stanford, 1956), pp. 51–6.

———, *The Education of the Human Race* (trans. John Dearling Haney; New York: Columbia, 1908).

Lewis, C.S., *The Great Divorce* (London: Collins, 1946).

———, *The Last Battle* (London: Collins, 2001).

Lindbeck, George A., *The Nature of Doctrine* (Philadelphia: Westminster, 1984).

Löhe, Wilhelm, 'Das Entgegenkommen zur Auferstehung der Toten. Predigt über Phil 3, 7–11. 1857', in Klaus Ganzert (ed.), *Gesammelte Werke*, vol. 6.1 (Neuendettelsau: Freimund-Verlag, 1957), pp. 695–706.

Lohse, Bernhard, *Martin Luther's Theology: Its Historical and Systematic Development* (trans. and ed. Roy A. Harrisville; Minneapolis: Fortress, 1999).

Lovejoy, Arthur Oncken, *The Great Chain of Being* (Cambridge: Harvard, 1961).

Luther, Martin, *D. Martin Luthers Werke: kritische Gesamtausgabe* (WA) (120 vols, Böhlau: Weimar, 1883–2009).

——, *Sermons on the Gospel of St. John Chapters 14–16, in Luther's Works*, vol. 24 (eds Jaroslav Pelikan, and Daniel E. Poellot; St. Louis: Concordia, 1961a).

——, *Word and Sacrament III*, in *Luther's Works*, vol. 37: (trans. and ed. Fischer, Robert; Philadelphia: Fortress, 1961b).

——, *Lectures on Genesis: Chapters 26–30*, in *Luther's Works*, vol. 5 (eds Jaroslav Pelikan and Walter A. Hansen; St Louis: Concordia, 1968).

——, *On the Bondage of the Will, in Luther and Erasmus: Free Will and Salvation* (eds and trans. E. Gordon Rupp et al.; Philadelphia: Westminster, 1969).

MacCormac, Earl R., *Metaphor and Myth in Science and Religion* (Durham, NC: Duke, 1976).

Mannermaa, Tuomo, *Der im Glauben gegenwärtige Christus: Rechtfertigung und Vergottung; zum ökumenischen Dialog* (Hannover: Lutherisches Verlagshaus, 1989).

Marquard, Odo, 'Rechtfertigung: Bemerkungen zum Interesse der Philosophie an der Theologie', *Gießener Universitätsblätter* 13.1 (1980), pp. 78–87.

Marquardt, Friedrich-Wilhelm, *Was dürfen wir hoffen, wenn wir hoffen dürfen? Eine Eschatologie*, vol. 1 (Gütersloh: Kaiser Gütersloher Verlagshaus, 1993).

Mathys, Hans-Peter (ed.), *Ebenbild Gottes – Herrscher über die Welt* (Neukirchen-Vluyn: Neukirchener Verlag, 1998).

McDougall, Duncan, 'Hypothesis Concerning Soul Substance together with Experimental Evidence of the Existence of Such Substance', *Journal of the American Society for Psychical Research* 1.5 (1907), pp. 237–64.

McTaggart, John M.E., 'The Unreality of Time', *Mind* 17 (1908), pp. 457–74.

——, *The Nature of Existence*, vol. 2 (Cambridge: Cambridge University Press, 1927).

Mead, George Herbert, *Mind, Self and Society* (Chicago: University of Chicago, 1934).

Melanchthon, Philipp and Stupperich, Robert, *Loci praecipui theologici von 1559 (2. Teil) und Definitiones* (Gütersloh: Gütersloher Verlagshaus, 1980, 2nd edn).

Menne, Albert, *Einführung in die formale Logik* (Darmstadt: Wissenschaftliche Buchgesellschaft, 1985).

Minkowski, Hermann, 'Raum und Zeit', in Hendrik A. Lorentz, Albert Einstein and Hermann Minkowski (eds), *Das Relativitätsprinzip: Eine Sammlung von Abhandlungen* (Darmstadt: Wissenschaftliche Buchgesellschaft, 1958, 6th edn), pp. 54–66.

Moltmann, Jürgen, *Theology of Hope* (trans. James W. Leitch; London: SCM, 1967).

——, 'Christian Hope: Messianic Or Transcendent? A Theological Discussion With Joachim of Fiore And Thomas Aquinas', *Horizons* 12.2 (1985), pp. 328–48.

——, *The Trinity and the Kingdom* (trans. Margaret Kohl; Minneapolis: Fortress, 1993a).

——, *The Way of Jesus Christ: Christology in Messianic Dimensions* (trans. Margaret Kohl; Minneapolis: Fortress, 1993b).

Moody, Raymond A., *Life after Life: The Investigation of a Phenomenon – Survival of Bodily Death* (New York: Mockingbird, 1975).

Moskopp, Dag, 'Zum Hirntod aus der Sicht eines Neurochirurgen', in Peter Hucklenbroich and Petra Gelhaus (eds), *Tod und Sterben: Medizinische Perspektiven* (Münster: Lit, 2001), pp. 21–43.

Mühling, Markus, 'Ascension of Christ IV: History of Dogma and Dogmatics: Protestantism,' in Hans Dieter Betz et al. (eds), *Religion Past and Present*, vol. 1, 14 vols (Leiden: Brill, 2006–2013).

——, *Gott ist Liebe: Studien zum Verständnis der Liebe als Modell des trinitarischen Redens von Gott* (Marburg: Elwert, 2005a, 2nd edn).

——, *Versöhnendes Handeln – Handeln in Versöhnung: Gottes Opfer an die Menschen* (Göttingen: Vandenhoeck & Ruprecht, 2005b).

——, *A Theological Journey into Narnia: An analysis of the message beneath the text of the 'Lion, the Witch and the Wardrobe' by C. S. Lewis* (trans. Sarah Draper; Göttingen: Vandenhoeck & Ruprecht, 2006).

——, *Liebesgeschichte Gott* (Göttingen: Vandenhoeck & Ruprecht, 2013).

——, 'Logic', in Hans Dieter Betz et al. (eds), *Religion Past and Present*, vol. 7, 14 vols (Leiden: Brill, 2006–2013), pp. 583–6.

——, *Resonances: Evolution, Neurobiology and Theology: Evolutionary Niche Construction, the Ecological Brain and Relational-Narrative Theology* (Göttingen: Vandenhoeck & Ruprecht, 2014).

——, '"Voller Gnade und Wahrheit". Eine theologische Resonanztheorie der Wahrheit', in Ulrich Beuttler and Martin Rothgangel (eds), *Glaube und Denken, Jahrbuch der Karl Heim Gesellschaft* 27 (2014), pp. 81–102.

Müller, Thomas, 'Arthur Priors Zeitlogik' (Unpublished doctoral dissertation, Freiburg, 2001).

Müller, Ulrich B., 'Parusie und Menschensohn', *Zeitschrift für die Neutestamentliche Wissenschaft* 92 (2001), pp. 1–19.

Nesse, Randolph M., Williams, George C. and Kuhlmann-Krieg, Susanne, *Warum wir krank werden: Die Antworten der Evolutionsmedizin* (Munich: Beck, 1998, 2nd edn).
Newton, Isaak, 'Optics', in *Opera quae exstant omnia*, vol. 4 (London: 1782), pp. 1–264.
Normore, Calvin, Kretzmann, Norman, Kenny, Anthony and Pinborg, Jan (eds), *The Cambridge History of Later Medieval Philosophy* (Cambridge: Cambridge University Press, 1982).
Oberdorfer, Bernd, *Filioque: Geschichte und Theologie eines ökumenischen Problems* (Göttingen: Vandenhoeck & Ruprecht, 2001).
Oort, Johannes van, 'Manichaeism', in Hans Dieter Betz et al. (eds), *Religion Past and Present*, vol. 8, 14 vols (Leiden: Brill, 2006–2013), pp. 25–30.
Origen, *On First Principles* (trans. G. W. Butterworth; ed. Tania M. Geist; Notre Dame: Ave Maria Press, 2013).
Ott, Ludwig, *Eschatologie in der Scholastik* (ed. Erich Naab; Freiburg: Herder, 1990).
Owen, G.E.L., 'Plato and Parmenides on the Timeless Present', *The Monist* 50 (1966), pp. 317–40.
Pannenberg, Wolfhart, 'Dogmatische Thesen zur Lehre von der Offenbarung', in *Offenbarung als Geschichte* (Göttingen: Vandenhoeck & Ruprecht, 1961), pp. 91–114.
———, *Was ist der Mensch? Die Anthropologie der Gegenwart im Lichte der Theologie* (Göttingen: Vandenhoeck & Ruprecht, 1962).
———, *Wissenschaftstheorie und Theologie* (Frankfurt am Main: Suhrkamp, 1973).
———, *Grundfragen systematischer Theologie II* (Göttingen: Vandenhoeck & Ruprecht, 1980).
———, *Anthropologie in theologischer Perspektive* (Göttingen: Vandenhoeck & Ruprecht, 1983).
———, *Systematic Theology I–III* (trans. Geoffrey W. Bromiley; 3 vols; Grand Rapids: Eerdmans, 1991–1998).
———, 'Unendlichkeit', in Joachim Ritter et al. (eds), *Historisches Wörterbuch der Philosophie*, vol. 11, 13 vols (Basel: Schwabe & Co, 2001), pp. 140–5.
Parrot, Andre, *Le 'Refrigerium' dans l'au-dela* (Paris: Librairie Leroux, 1937).
Peirce, Charles Sanders, *Collected Papers*, vol. 5 (Cambridge, MA: Harvard, 1960).
Peters, Albrecht, *Glaube und Werk: Luthers Rechtfertigungslehre im Lichte der Heiligen Schrift* (Berlin: Lutherisches Verlagshaus, 1967, 2nd edn).
Peura, Simon and Raunio, Antti, *Luther und Theosis: Vergöttlichung als Thema der abendländischen Theologie* (Erlangen: Luther-Agricola-Gesellschaft, 1990).

Pike, Nelson, *God and Timelessness* (London: Routledge, 1970).
Plato, *Complete Works* (ed. John M. Cooper; Indianapolis: Hackett, 1997).
Plotinus, *The Enneads* (trans. Stephen MacKenna; London: Penguin, 1991).
Porphyry, 'The Introduction', in, *The Organon, or Logical Treatises of Aristotle* (trans. and ed. Octavius Freire Owen; London: Bell, 1902), pp. 609–33.
Poulet, Georges, 'Timelessness and Romanticism', *Journal of the History of Ideas* 15.1 (1954), pp. 3–22.
Preul, Reiner, 'Problemskizze zur Rede vom Handeln Gottes', in Wilfried Härle and Reiner Preul (eds), *Marburger Jahrbuch Theologie I: Handeln Gottes* (Marburg: Elwert, 1987).
Puntel, Lorenz Bruno, *Wahrheitstheorien in der neueren Philosophie: Eine kritisch-systematische Darstellung* (Darmstadt: Wissenschaftliche Buchgesellschaft, 1993, 3rd edn).
Quine, Willard Van Orman, *Word and Object* (Cambridge: MIT, 2013).
Ratzinger, Joseph, *Eschatology: Death and Eternal Life* (trans. Michael Waldstein; Washington, D.C.: Catholic University of America Press, 2006, 2nd edn).
Reinhard, Volkmar, *Vorlesungen über die Dogmatik* (ed. J. G. I. Berger; Amberg: Seidl, 1801).
Reinhuber, Thomas, *Kämpfender Glaube: Studien zu Luthers Bekenntnis am Ende von de servo arbitrio* (Berlin: De Gruyter, 2000).
Reuter, Michael, *Abschied von Sterben und Tod? Ansprüche und Grenzen der Hirntodtheorie* (Stuttgart: Kohlhammer, 2001).
Richard of St Victor, *De quattuor gradibus violentiae caritatis – Über die Gewalt der Liebe. Ihre vier Stufen* (Munich: Schöningh, 1969).
——, *On the Trinity* (trans. and ed. Ruben Angelici; Eugene: Cascade, 2011).
Riemann, Bernhard, 'Über die Hypothesen, welche der Geometrie zugrunde liegen', in Richard Dedekind and Heinrich Weber (eds.), *Gesammelte mathematische Werke, wissenschaftlicher Nachlass und Nachträge* (Berlin: Springer, 1990).
Rietdijk, Cornelius W., 'A Rigorous Proof of Determinism derived from the Special Theory of Relativity', *Philosophy of Science* 33 (1966), pp. 341–4.
——, 'Special Relativity and Determinism', *Philosophy of Science* 43 (1976), pp. 598–609.
Ritschl, Albrecht, *The Christian Doctrine of Justification and Reconciliation: The Positive Development of the Doctrine* (trans. and ed. H. R. Mackintosh and A.B. Macaulay; Edinburgh: T&T Clark, 1902, 2nd edn).
——, 'Die christliche Vollkommenheit', in, *Kleine Schriften* (Waltrop: Spenner, 1999), pp. 41–65.
——, 'Instruction in the Christian Religion', in *Three Essays* (trans. Philip Hefner; Eugene: Wipf and Stock, 2005), pp. 219–91.

Robinson, John A.T., *In the End God … A Study of the Christian Doctrine of the Last Things* (London: T&T Clarke, 1958).
Rohls, Jan, 'Person und Selbstbewußtsein', *Neue Zeitschrift für Systematische Theologie und Religionsphilosophie* 21 (1979), pp. 54–70.
Rosenau, Hartmut, *Allversöhnung: Ein transzendentaltheologischer Grundlegungsversuch* (Berlin: De Gruyter, 1993).
Rössler, Reimara, Kloeden, Peter E. and Rössler, Otto E., *Das Thanatosprinzip: Biologische Grundlagen des Alterns* (Munich: Beck, 1997).
Rothe, Richard, *Theologische Ethik II* (Wittenberg: Zimmerman, 1869, 2nd edn).
Runggaldier, Edmund, *Was sind Handlungen? Eine philosophische Auseinandersetzung mit dem Naturalismus* (Stuttgart: Kohlhammer, 1996).
Sagan, Carl, *Cosmos* (New York: Ballantine, 1985).
——, *Contact* (New York: Pocket Books, 1997a).
——, *Pale Blue Dot: A Vision of the Human Future in Space* (New York: Ballantine, 1997b).
Sartorius, Ernst Wilhelm, *Die Lehre von der Heiligen Liebe oder Grundzüge der evangelisch-kirchlichen Moraltheologie* (Stuttgart: Liesching, 1861, 2nd edn).
Schleiermacher, Friedrich, *Der christliche Glaube (1821–1822)* (ed. Hermann Peiter; 2 vols; Berlin: De Gruyter, 1984).
——, *The Christian Faith* (trans. H. R. Mackintosh and J. S. Stewart; Berkeley: Apocryphile, 2001, 2nd edn).
Schmidt-Japing, Johannes Wilhelm, *Lotzes Religionsphilosophie in ihrer Entwicklung* (Göttingen: Vandenhoeck & Ruprecht, 1925).
Schnelle, Udo, *Neutestamentliche Anthropologie: Jesus, Paulus, Johannes* (Neukirchen-Vluyn: Neukirchener Verlag, 1991).
Scholtz, Gunter, 'Historismus' in Joachim Ritter et al. (eds), *Historisches Wörterbuch der Philosophie*, vol. 3, 13 vols (Basel: Schwabe & Co, 1974), pp. 1141–7.
Schröter, Jens, 'Kingdom of God III. New Testament', in Hans Dieter Betz et al. (eds), *Religion Past and Present*, vol. 7, 14 vols (Leiden: Brill, 2006–2013), pp. 188–95.
Schwarz, Hans, 'Eschatology', in Robert W. Jenson and Carl E. Braaten (eds), *Christian Dogmatics II* (Philadelphia: Fortress, 1984), pp. 529–37.
——, *Jenseits von Utopie und Resignation* (Wuppertal: Brockhaus, 1990).
——, *Die christliche Hoffnung: Grundkurs Eschatologie* (Göttingen: Vandenhoeck & Ruprecht, 2002).
Schwarz, Reinhard, *Die apokalyptische Theologie Thomas Müntzers und der Taboriten* (Tübingen: Mohr Siebeck, 1977).

Schwöbel, Christoph, 'Wahrheit', in E. Fahlbusch (ed.), *Taschenlexikon Religion und Theologie*, vol. 5 (Göttingen: Vandenhoeck & Ruprecht, 1983, 4th edn), pp. 283–9.

———, 'Die Rede vom Handeln Gottes im christlichen Glauben', in Wilfried Härle and Reiner Preul (eds), *Marburger Jahrbuch Theologie I: Handeln Gottes* (Marburg: Elwert, 1987).

———, *God: Action and Revelation* (Kampen: Kok, 1992).

———, 'Christology and Trinitarian Thought', in Christoph Schwöbel (ed.), *Trinitarian Theology Today* (Edinburgh: T&T Clark, 1995), pp. 113–46.

———, 'Verdrängte Geschöpflichkeit: Die Flucht vom Tod', *Pharmazeutische Zeitung* 44 (1997), pp. 11–17.

———, 'Trinitätslehre als Rahmentheorie des christlichen Glaubens', *Marburger Jahrbuch Theologie* 10 (Marburg: Elwert, 1998), pp. 129–54.

———, *Gott in Beziehung: Studien zur Dogmatik* (Tübingen: Mohr Siebeck, 2002).

———, *Gott im Gespräch* (Tübingen: Mohr Siebeck 2011).

———, 'Kingdom of God IV. Historical Theology and Dogmatics; V. Social Ethics', in Hans Dieter Betz et al. (eds), *Religion Past and Present*, vol. 7,14 vols (Leiden: Brill, 2006–2013), pp. 191–6.

Sellin, Gerhard, *Der Streit um die Auferstehung der Toten: Eine religionsgeschichtliche und exegetische Untersuchung von 1. Korinther 15* (Göttingen: Vandenhoeck & Ruprecht, 1986).

Seuse, Heinrich, *Das Buch der Wahrheit: mittelhochdt.-dt.= Daz buechli der warheit* (eds Loris Sturlese and Rüdiger Blumrich; Hamburg: Meiner, 1993).

Sextus Empiricus, *Adversus Mathematicos – Gegen die Wissenschaftler* (Würzburg: Königshausen & Neumann, 2001).

Shibutani, Tamotsu, 'Human Agency from the Standpoint of Pragmatism', in Horst Jürgen Helle (ed.), *Verstehen and Pragmatism: Essays in interpretive Sociology* (Frankfurt am Main: Lang, 1991), pp. 183–94.

———, 'Reference Groups as Perspectives', *American Journal of Sociology* 60.6 (May, 1955), pp. 562–9.

Singer, Peter, *Practical Ethics* (Cambridge: Cambridge University Press, 2006).

Sölle, Dorothee, 'Gott und das Leiden', in Michael Welker (ed.), *Diskussion über Jürgen Moltmanns Buch 'Der gekreuzigte Gott'* (Munich: Kaiser, 1979).

Spengler, Oswald, *Pessimismus?* (Schriftenreihe der Preußischen Jahrbücher 4; Berlin: Stilke, 1921).

———, *The Decline of the West I: Form and Actuality* (New York: Knopf, 1928).

Spinoza, Baruch de, *Ethics*, in Micheal L. Morgan (ed.), *The Essential Spinoza: Ethics and Related Writings* (trans. Samuel Shirley; Indianapolis: Hackett, 2006).

Staats, Reinhard, 'Auferstehung I/4', in Gehard Müller et al. (eds), *Theologische Realenzyklopädie*, vol. 4 (Berlin: De Gruyter, 1979), pp. 467–77.

Stange, Carl, *Das Ende aller Dinge* (Gütersloh: Bertelsmann, 1930).

Stausberg, Michael, *Zarathustra und seine Religion* (Munich: C. H. Beck, 2005).

Steck, Odil Hannes, *Der Schöpfungsbericht der Priesterschrift* (Göttingen: Vandenhoeck & Ruprecht, 1981, 2nd edn).

Stegmüller, Wolfgang, *Das Universalienproblem einst und jetzt* (Darmstadt: Wissenschaftliche Buchgesellschaft, 1974, 3rd edn).

Stock, Konrad, *Annihilatio Mundi: Johann Gerhards Eschatologie der Welt* (Munich: Kaiser, 1971).

——, 'Gott der Richter. Der Gerichtsgedanke als Horizont der Rechtfertigungslehre', *Evangelische Theologie* 40 (1980), pp. 240–56.

Strawson, Peter, *Individuals: An Essay in Descriptive Metaphysics* (London: Routledge, 1971).

Stuiber, Alfred, *Refrigerium interim: Die Vorstellungen vom Zwischenzustand und die frühchristliche Grabeskunst* (Bonn: Hanstein, 1957).

Swinburne, Richard, *The Christian God* (Oxford: Oxford, 1994).

Teilhard de Chardin, Pierre, *The Divine Milieu* (New York: Harper & Row, 1965).

Thomasius, Gottfried, *Christi Person und Werk: Darstellung der evangelisch-lutherischen Dogmatik vom Mittelpunkt der Christologie aus*, vol. 1 (Erlangen: Bläsing, 1856, 2nd edn).

Theißen, Henning, *Die evangelische Eschatologie und das Judentum: Strukturprobleme der Konzeption seit Schleiermacher* (Göttingen: Vandenhoeck & Ruprecht, 2004).

Tillich, Paul, 'Eschatologie und Geschichte', in *Religiöse Verwirklichung* (Berlin: Furche-Verlag, 1930), pp. 128–41.

——, 'Eschatology and History', in *The Interpretation of History* (trans. N.A. Rasetzki and Elsa L. Talmey; New York: Scribner's, 1936), pp. 266–84.

——, *Symbol und Wirklichkeit* (Göttingen: Vandenhoeck & Ruprecht, 1962).

——, *Systematic Theology*, 1 vol. (Chicago: University of Chicago, 1967).

——, *Main Works/Hauptwerke*, vol. 6: *Theologische Schriften/Theological Writings* (ed. Carl Heinz Ratschow; Berlin: De Gruyter, 1992).

Tipler, Frank J., *The Physics of Immortality: Modern Cosmology, God and the Resurrection of the Dead* (New York: Doubleday, 1994).

Troeltsch, Ernst, Troeltsch, Marta and Le Fort, Gertrud von, *Glaubenslehre: Nach Heidelberger Vorlesungen aus den Jahren 1911 und 1912* (Munich: Duncker und Humblot, 1925).

Tuveson, Ernest Lee, *Redeemer Nation* (Chicago: University of Chicago, 1968).

Vate, Dwight Van de, Jr., *Romantic Love: A Philosophical Inquiry* (University Park: Pennsylvania State, 1981).

Verweyen, Hansjürgen, *Osterglaube ohne Auferstehung* (Freiburg: Herder, 1995).

Volkmann, Stefan, *Der Zorn Gottes: Studien zur Rede vom Zorn Gottes in der evangelischen Theologie* (Marburg: Elwert 2004).

Vorgrimler, Herbert, 'Das Fegefeuer', in Franz Böckle et al. (eds), *Zwischenzeit und Vollendung der Heilsgeschichte Mysterium Salutis*, vol. 5 (Zurich: Benzinger, 1976), pp. 453–7.

——, *Geschichte der Hölle* (Munich: Fink, 1993).

Weber, Otto 'Die Lehre von der Erwählung und die Verkündigung', in Otto Weber, Walter Kreck and Ernst Wolf (eds), *Die Predigt von der Gnadenwahl* (Munich: Kaiser-Verlag, 1951), pp. 9–36.

Weidemann, Volker, 'Cosmology – Science or Speculation?', in A. V. Diemer (ed.), *World Congress of Philosophy* vol. 16 (1978) (Frankfurt am Main: Lang, 1983).

——, 'Das inflationäre Universum', in Helmut A. Müller (ed.), *Naturwissenschaft und Glaube* (Bern: Scherz, 1988), pp. 346–65.

Weir, David Alexander, *Foedus natural: The Origin of Federal Theology in 16th Century Reformation Thought* (Unpublished doctoral dissertation, St. Andrew's University, 1984).

Weiß, Johannes, *Die Predigt Jesu vom Reich Gottes* (Göttingen: Vandenhoeck & Ruprecht, 1964).

Welker, Michael, *Universalität Gottes und Relativität der Welt* (Neukirchen-Vluyn: Neukirchener Verlag, 1988, 2nd edn).

——, 'Konzepte von "Leben" in Nietzsches Werk', in Wilfried Härle (ed.), *Marburger Jahrbuch Theologie IX* (Marburg: Elwert, 1997), pp. 41–52.

Weyl, Hermann, *Was ist Materie?* (Berlin: Julius Springer, 1924).

Whitehead, Alfred North, *Process and Reality: An Essay in Cosmology* (eds David Ray Griffin and Donald W. Sherburne; New York: Macmillan, 1978).

Wilkens, Ulrich, *Der Brief an die Römer* (Zürich: Brenzinger, 1980).

Wittgenstein, Ludwig, *Tractatus Logico-Philosophicus* (trans. C. K. Ogden; New York: Cosimo, 2007).

Wölfel, Eberhard, 'Endet die Zeit? Bemerkungen zum Zeitproblem im Aspekt naturwissenschaftlicher Erschließung', in Konrad Stock (ed.), *Zeit und Schöpfung* (Gütersloh: Gütersloher Verlagshaus, 1997), pp. 11–40.

Wolf, Ernst (ed.), *Die Bekenntnisschriften der evangelisch-lutherischen Kirchen* (Göttingen: Vandenhoek & Ruprecht, 1967).

Wolff, Hans Walter, *Anthropology of the Old Testament* (Norwich: SCM, 2011).

Wright, Georg Henrik von, *Erklären und Verstehen* (Frankfurt am Main: Athäneum Fischer, 1974).

Zahrnt, Heinz, *Die Sache mit Gott* (Munich: Piper, 1966).
Zizioulas, John, 'Human Capacity and Human Incapacity', *Scottish Journal of Theology* 28 (1975), pp. 401–48.
——, *Being as Communion* (Crestwood: St Vladimir's Seminary Press, 1985).
——, 'On Being a Person: Towards an Ontology of Personhood', in Christoph Schwöbel and Colin E. Gunton (eds), *Persons, Divine and Human* (Edinburgh: T&T Clark, 1991), pp. 33–46.
——, 'The Doctrine of the Holy Trinity: The Significance of the Cappadocian Contribution', in Christoph Schwöbel (ed.), *Trinitarian Theology Today* (Edinburgh: T&T Clark, 1995), pp. 44–60.
Zwingli, Huldrych, 'An Account of the Faith (*Fidei Ratio*, 1530)', in *The Latin Works and Correspondence of Huldreich Zwingli*, vol. 2 (trans. S. M. Macauley; Philadelphia: Heidelberg Press, 1922), pp. 33–61.
——, 'Action or Use of the Lord's Supper, Easter 1525', in Bard Thompson (ed.), *Liturgies of the Western Church* (Philadelphia: Fortress, 1980), pp. 149–56.

Scripture Index

Old Testament

Gen. 1.1 81, 87
Gen. 1.6 113
Gen. 1.26f 184, 204
Gen. 2.4–3, 24 211
Gen. 2.7 183, 186
Gen. 2.17 186
Gen. 2f 357
Gen. 3.5 211
Gen. 3.15 166
Gen. 25.8 185
Gen. 26.3 48

Exod. 3.12 48
Exod. 3.14 53

Lev. 11.24f 185
Lev. 19.31, 28 185

Deut. 18.10f 185

Judg. 2.10 184

2 Sam. 12.23 185

1 Kgs 2.9 184
2 Kgs 21.6 185

Job 3.19 185
Job 7.9f 185
Job 10.21 185
Job 42.17 185

Ps. 8 139
Ps. 23 139
Ps. 28.1 184
Ps. 31.16 184
Ps. 49.15 185
Ps. 84 139
Ps. 88.4, 6 184
Ps. 88.13 185
Ps. 90.4 225
Ps. 90.5 184
Ps. 94.17 185
Ps. 102.25f 152
Ps. 104 139
Ps. 115.17 185
Ps. 139.16 184
Ps. 143.7 184
Ps. 145.10–17 341

Prov. 1.12 184

Isa. 2.2–5 358
Isa. 2.12–17 256
Isa. 10.18 183
Isa. 11.6–9 338, 357
Isa. 13.9 256
Isa. 24.21 304
Isa. 24–27 55
Isa. 25.8 185
Isa. 33 55
Isa. 38.18f 185
Isa. 43.2 48
Isa. 51.6 152
Isa. 65.17 152
Isa. 66.15–24 304

Ezek. 37 185
Ezek. 37–48 225

Dan. 4.34 341
Dan. 7.9, 26f 304

Dan. 7.13f 256
Dan. 12.2 185, 278

Joel 2.1–12 256
Joel 4.14 304
Joel 4.14–15 256
Joel 4.16–17 256

Amos 5.18–20 255

Mic. 4.1ff 55
Mic. 4.1–4 358
Mic. 4.4 338

Zeph. 1.7, 14–18 256

Zech. 3.10 358

Apocrypha or Deutero-Canonical Books

Sir. 7.36 3

2 Macc. 7.14–28 61
2 Macc. 7.14 185, 308
2 Macc. 7.14, 23 278
2 Macc. 12.42–45 294

1 Enoch 33.6 93
1 Enoch 91.12–17 225
1 Enoch 37–71 256
1 Enoch 84.2-4 55
1 Enoch 91.5 304

2 Enoch 25.16 256
2 Enoch 32.1–33 225

2 Baruch 24–32 225

4 Esdras 7.26–30 225
4 Esdras 7.28–33 225
4 Esdras 13.3 256

As. Mos. 10 55

New Testament

Matt. 3.1par 304
Matt. 3.7par 304
Matt. 3.9par 304
Matt. 5.17–20 342
Matt. 5.20 338
Matt. 5.45 62
Matt. 6.4–18 330
Matt. 7.21 338, 340
Matt. 7.22f 330
Matt. 8.11 55, 338
Matt. 10.23 257
Matt. 10.28par 330
Matt. 13.11 338
Matt. 13.36–43 330
Matt. 18.1.4 338
Matt. 19.28 330
Matt. 20.21 343
Matt. 23.35 152
Matt. 24.23 258
Matt. 24.27 258
Matt. 24.29 154
Matt. 24.30 248
Matt. 24.42–44 256
Matt. 24–25 248, 257, 326
Matt. 25.31–46 305, 330
Matt. 25.46 338, 362
Matt. 28.20b 254

Mk 1.14 15
Mk 1.14f 341
Mk 1.14, 62 257
Mk 1.9–11parr 122, 124
Mk 4.30 341
Mk 9.43–48 304
Mk 9.48 304
Mk 10.15 15
Mk 10.23 340
Mk 10.23–25 340
Mk 10.30 338, 362
Mk 12.18–27par 291
Mk 13 248

Mk 13.21, 32	248
Mk 13.24–27	258
Mk 13.31	152
Mk 13.31parr	159
Mk 13.32–37	258
Mk 14.25	55, 340, 343
Mk 14.25par	55
Lk. 3.8par	304
Lk. 7.34	359
Lk. 10.9	340
Lk. 11.20	340
Lk. 12.8f	342
Lk. 12.8f par	55
Lk. 12.16–20	304
Lk. 13.1–5	304
Lk. 13.18–21	341
Lk. 13.23–30	341
Lk. 13.25–27	330
Lk. 13.28–30	340
Lk. 14.15–24	342
Lk. 16.1–7	304
Lk. 16.16	340
Lk. 17.20f	341
Lk. 17.34f	304
Lk. 21	248, 257
Lk. 21.33	152
Lk. 23.43	281, 282, 288, 338, 357
Jn 3.5	282
Jn 3.16	313, 338, 362
Jn 3.16f	151
Jn 3.17f	254, 282
Jn 3.18–20	305
Jn 3.36	305
Jn 5.18	56
Jn 5.24	186, 305
Jn 5.24f	254
Jn 5.24ff	282
Jn 9.39	305
Jn 12.46	305
Jn 14.2	45
Jn 15.1–11	359
Jn 18.36	343
Acts 17.28f	338, 360
Acts 17.28	110
Rom. 1.3b–4	60
Rom. 1.4	61
Rom. 1.18	305
Rom. 1.18f	326
Rom. 2.1–3.20	305
Rom. 2.3	330
Rom. 3.6	330
Rom. 3.9	305
Rom. 3.20	305
Rom. 3.24f	305
Rom. 4.17	61
Rom. 4.24b	60
Rom. 4.25	60
Rom. 5.14, 17	186
Rom. 6	280
Rom. 6.3	186
Rom. 6.3f, 8f	60
Rom. 6.8	223
Rom. 6.22	338, 362
Rom. 6.23	186, 196
Rom. 7.19	212
Rom. 8.11	60
Rom. 8.14	360
Rom. 8.18–25	166, 167
Rom. 8.19–22	159
Rom. 8.19–23	152
Rom. 8.38	112
Rom. 8.38	275
Rom. 9.3	368
Rom. 10.9	60
Rom. 14.7f	368
Rom. 14.10	330
Rom. 14.17	340, 342
Rom. 14.9	186
1 Cor. 1.7	257
1 Cor. 3.5	280

1 Cor. 3.11–15 305, 306, 308
1 Cor. 4.4f 330
1 Cor. 5.13 330
1 Cor. 6.2f 330
1 Cor. 6.9f 340
1 Cor. 7.31 152
1 Cor. 8.4–6 60
1 Cor. 10.4 253
1 Cor. 11.32 330
1 Cor. 13 361
1 Cor. 13.3 60
1 Cor. 13.12 159, 338
1 Cor. 13.13 32
1 Cor. 15 44, 152, 189, 258, 280, 282, 288
1 Cor. 15.3b–4 60
1 Cor. 15.12 279
1 Cor. 15.14, 19 56
1 Cor. 15.14–19 280
1 Cor. 15.23–28 257
1 Cor. 15.24f 343
1 Cor. 15.26 186
1 Cor. 15.28 338, 361
1 Cor. 15.29 253
1 Cor. 15.40f 281
1 Cor. 15.44 45, 281
1 Cor. 15.50 281
1 Cor. 15.51 281
1 Cor. 16.22 60, 257

2 Cor. 4.14 60
2 Cor. 5.7 299
2 Cor. 5.10 330
2 Cor. 5.17 152

Gal. 1.1 60
Gal. 3.22 305
Gal. 5.21 340
Gal. 6.15 152

Eph. 2.4ff 253–254

Phil. 1.20f 186
Phil. 1.23 281, 282, 288
Phil. 2.6–11 60
Phil. 2.9–11 343

Col. 1.15–17 343
Col. 1.16 112
Col. 1.20 305, 306
Col. 3.1–4 253

1.Thess. 1.9f 60
1.Thess. 2.10–12 340
1.Thess. 4.6 330
1.Thess. 4.13 288
1.Thess. 4.13–18 248, 257, 258, 278, 280, 282
1.Thess. 4.14a 60
1.Thess. 4.15–17 279
1.Thess. 4.17 279, 338
1.Thess. 5.1–11 248, 257, 258
1.Thess. 5.2 248
1.Thess. 5.8 256
1.Thess. 5.9f 278, 305
1.Thess. 5.11 256
1.Thess. 5.23 257

2.Thess 1.5 330
2.Thess 2.2–8 257

1.Tim 3.16 60

Heb. 1.10f 152

Jas 5.7 257

1 Pet. 1.3–12 253
1 Pet. 1.7 257
1 Pet. 3.13 152
1 Pet. 4.7 253

2 Pet. 1.4 338, 360
2 Pet. 1.16 257
2 Pet. 3.10 256

1 Jn 2.28 257
1 Jn 4.17f 338

Rev. 1.3	253
Rev. 1.7	257
Rev. 2.7	338, 357
Rev. 3.3	256
Rev. 3.11	253
Rev. 6	257
Rev. 8f	257
Rev. 16	257
Rev. 16.15	256
Rev. 16.16	248
Rev. 19.11–16	257
Rev. 20.1–7	225, 244
Rev. 20.6, 14	186
Rev. 20.11	152
Rev. 20.14	304
Rev. 21.8	304
Rev. 21.1	338, 358
Rev. 21.2	341
Rev. 21.1, 5	152
Rev. 21.10–27	338, 356
Rev. 22.20	60, 257

Author Index

Albertus Magnus 127
Alexander of Hales 205
Althaus, P. 16–17, 138–9, 154, 163, 190, 262–3, 267, 273
Anastasius Sinaiticus 299
Angelus Silesius 268
Anselm of Canterbury 51, 75
Aquinas, Th. 91, 112–13, 127, 153, 163, 195, 227, 244, 248, 289, 299, 310, 312
Ariès, Ph. 179
Aristotle 81–3, 112, 122, 182
Athanasius 298
Auffarth, Chr. 257
Augustine 81–9, 116, 134, 172, 187–8, 226, 243–4, 288–90, 299, 310–11, 313–14, 318, 341, 367, 368
Axt-Piscalar, Chr. 65

Balthasar, H.U.v. 14, 68
Barrow, J.D. 156
Bartelmus, R. 113
Barth, K. 13–15, 17, 87, 128, 190, 198, 263–4, 266, 268, 287, 321
Barth, U. 110, 115, 160
Basil of Caesarea 243
Basilides 57
Battles, F.L. 117
Becker, J. 55–6, 60–1, 254, 257, 271, 278–9, 281–2, 304–5, 340, 343
Beierwaltes, W. 84, 88
Beisser, F. 189–92, 201, 292
Bellah, R.N. 236
Bengel, J.A. 233
Bennett, G. 171
Berger, P.L. 25, 154
Betz, H.D. 128, 132, 193, 227
Beuttler, U. 148
Beveridge, H. 188
Beyschlag, K. 6, 57, 170
Black, M. 19, 21
Bloch, E. 19, 232
Block-Smith, E. 184
Blum, G.G. 85, 226
Böckle, F. 295
Boethius, A.M.S. 8, 88–101, 142, 204–5, 262–3
Bonaventure 205, 330, 332
Bonhoeffer, D. 362
Botterweck, G.J. 113
Boulding, M. 81
Braaten, C.E. 50, 169, 299
Brandenburg, E. 304
Breidert, W. 113
Brenz, J. 128
Bretschneider, K.G. 4
Brom, L.J.v.d. 131, 132
Bromiley, G.W. 18, 87, 168, 190, 199, 266
Brümmer, V. 90, 94, 95, 203, 343
Brunner, E. 322
Bultmann, R. 15, 16, 18, 52, 62, 128, 263, 287
Buridanus, J. 122
Burkett, D.R. 257
Busch, W. 203

Calvin, J. 95, 116, 117, 118, 125, 127, 128, 154, 160, 188, 189, 221, 240, 295, 314
Cameron, J. 241
Cartwright, N. 241
Charlesworth, M.J. 51

Chisholm, R. 27
Clarke, S. 13, 110, 122
Clemens Alexandrinus 285, 318
Cocceius, J. 241
Coleridge, S. 85
Cone, J.H. 19
Conte, A.G. 143, 164, 207
Crancach, L. 142
Crouch, J.E. 304

Daley, B. 282, 288–9, 312
Dalferth, I.U. 59
Darby, J.N. 241
Davidson, D. 26
Davies, B. 51
Deane-Drummond, C. 68
Democritus 108, 367
Denzinger, H. 118–19
Derrida, J. 239
Descartes, R. 183
Dieckmann, E. 209
Diels, H. 108, 112
Dierse, U. 363
Dodd, Ch.H. 15–16, 43, 340
Dorner, I.A. 11–12, 43, 242–3, 264–6, 271, 273
Drechsel, W. 219, 363, 365
Duns Scotus, J. 95
Dyson, R.W. 244

Ebeling, G. 189, 362
Echternach, H. 91
Edwards, J. 235, 241, 366
Einstein, A. 92, 123
Elert, W. 135, 187, 190, 237–8, 249
Engels, F. 232
Epictetus 172
Epicurus of Samos 172, 181
Erasmus 137
Eriugena, J. 284, 290
Erlemann, K. 253
Erskine of Linlathen, Th. 62, 295, 320, 332

Erving, E. 209
Etzelmüller, G. 321, 324
Euclid 109
Eusebius 243
Eutyches 204
Evans, G.R. 51
Evers, D. 109, 112–13, 115, 120, 122–3, 131–2, 155–6, 169, 347

Fabry, H.J. 113
Feiner, J. 14
Feuerbach, L. 197
Finé, H. 318
Flasch, K. 83
Fleischer, M. 23
Flew, A. 202, 291–2
Francke, A.H. 233, 253
Frank, F.R.H.v. 6, 20, 102, 155–6, 161, 197, 291
Frei H. 68
Frick, R. 341
Fuentes, A. 209, 323
Fukuyama, F. 24, 232

Gauß, C.F. 123
Geach, P.T. 95, 142
Gelhaus, P. 173, 175
Gerhard, J. 3, 4, 46, 158–62, 168, 171, 189, 226, 280, 285, 327, 362–3
Gertz, J.Ch. 211
Geyer, B. 127
Goffman, E. 209
Gräb, W. 110
Grässer, E. 253
Greshake, G. 273
Griffin, D.R. 97, 135
Grube, D.-M. 181
Gunton, C.E. 148, 165, 210
Gutiérrez, G. 19

Haas, A. 85
Hadot, P. 363

Härle, W. 38, 48, 65, 111, 146, 166, 192–3, 195, 205, 247, 253, 292
Harnack, A.v. 187, 342
Hartshorne, Ch. 135
Hauerwas, S. 68
Heesch, M. 233
Hegel G.W.F. 11, 23, 66, 124, 130, 224, 232, 238, 246
Heidegger, M. 15, 199
Heim, K. 124, 148
Hempel, C.G. 27
Henningfeld, J. 23
Hermanni, F. 134
Herms, E. 46, 66, 224, 236, 247, 363
Hesse, M.B. 355
Hick, J. 202
Hill, E. 82, 209
Hippolytus 226
Hjelde, S. 3–6, 8, 12, 17, 304
Hörning, M. 174–6, 178
Hoskyns, E.C. 15
Hubbeling, H.G. 347, 350
Hübner, J. 114–15, 363
Hucklenbroich, P. 173–5, 179–80
Hünermann, P. 118
Huntington, S.P. 238, 239
Huxel, K. 192

Iñárritu, A.G. 192
Ingold, T. 209, 323
Irenaeus of Lyon 153, 162, 226
Irving, E. 240
Issac Luria 120, 269

Janowski, J.Chr. & B. 200, 303, 308–9, 324
Jenson, R.W. 50, 52, 68, 169, 251, 299, 366
Jeremias, J. 256, 303
Jewett, R. 235–6, 240–1
Jinkins, M. 241
Joachim of Fioe 226–7
Joest, W. 189
Johannes Buridanus 114
John of Damascus 119
Jonas, H. 135–6
Jooss, E. 109
Jüngel, E. 62, 66, 71, 121, 148, 175, 182, 184, 187–8, 190–3, 198–200
Justin Martyr 226, 264

Kähler, M. 12–13, 43–5, 61–2, 154, 332
Kant, I. 9, 23, 71–2, 85–6, 109, 114–15, 183, 205
Kenny, A. 27, 95
Kepler, J. 114–15
Kinder, E. 190
Kloeden, P.E. 179
Knight, H. 190
Koch, K. 303
Kolb, R. 6
Körtner, U. 237, 239
Kreck, W. 13, 321
Kretzman, N. 95
Krüger, Th. 256
Kübler-Ross, E. 178
Kuhlmann-Krieg, S. 180
Kunz, E. 154, 233

Labriolle, P. 318
LaCugna, C.M. 66
Lammer, K. 221
Lampe, P. 281
Lang, B. 156, 209, 233, 339
Lawrence, J.S. 235–6, 240–1
Lea, Th.D. 264
Leibniz, G.W. 110, 122–3, 133–4
Lem, S. 202, 212–13, 291–2
Leppin, V. 174, 227
Lessing, G.E. 12, 229–32, 342
Leucippus 108
Lewis, C.S. 62, 313, 318, 366–7
Lindbeck, G. 68
Locke, J. 204
Löhe, W. 6, 242
Lohse, B. 138

Lorentz, H. 92
Lotze, H. 9, 23, 91
Lovejoy, A.O. 284
Lucretius 172–3
Lüdemann, G. 57
Luther, M. 48, 50–1, 53, 62, 105, 107, 124–30, 135, 137–40, 153–4, 160, 165–6, 188–9, 194–5, 208, 211, 246–7, 273, 292, 295, 298–9, 310, 334–5, 337, 342

MacCormac, E.A. 27
Mach, E. 123
Mahlmann, Th. 128
Mannermaa, T. 299
Marius Victorinus 82
Marquard, O. 136
Marquardt, F.W. 21
Marx, K. 232
Mathys, H.P. 184
McDannell, C. 339
McDonald, G. 313
McDougall, D. 192
McLeod Campbell, J. 241
McTaggart, J.M.E. 92–3, 95, 99, 103–4
Mead, G.H. 209
Melanchthon, Ph. 6, 240, 244, 300, 311
Menne, A. 347
Migne, J.P. 299
Minkowski, H. 92, 123
Moltmann, J. 18–19, 21, 32, 66, 120, 136, 226–7, 233–5, 254, 268–70, 340
Moody, R.A. 178
Morscher, E. 143
Moskopp, D. 175, 177
Mountain, W.J. 82
Mühling, M. 62, 68–9, 71, 128, 148, 164, 193, 209, 295, 314, 346
Müntzer, Th. 227

Nesse, R.M. 180
Nestorius 204
Newton, I. 86, 109–10, 122–3
Nietzsche, F. 23, 166
Noppen, J.P. 148
Normore, C. 95

Oberdorfer, B. 70
Olevianus, K. 240
Oort, J.v. 135
Oppenheim, P. 27
Origen of Alexandria 282, 288–9, 295, 315–18, 322, 341
Ott, L. 4, 153, 248, 259, 284, 289–90, 294, 327, 330–2, 334

Palsson, G. 209, 323
Pannenberg, W. 10, 17–18, 20–1, 32, 52, 57–9, 62, 66, 69, 130, 166, 168–9, 190, 199–200, 209, 225, 246, 267, 272–3, 277, 322, 340
Papias of Hierapolis 226
Parker, T.H.L. 87
Parmenides 53, 85, 112
Parrot, A. 318
Peirce, Ch.S. 23
Peiter, H. 319
Pelikan, J. 105, 107
Peters, T. 171, 281, 334
Petrus Lombardus 158, 205, 226, 290
Peura, S. 298
Philo of Alexandria 280
Piepmeyer, R. 363
Pike, N. 102
Planck, M. 104
Plato 85, 88–9, 181–2, 201–3, 260, 294
Plotinus 84, 88
Porphyry 82, 145
Poulet, G. 85
Preul, R. 111
Puntel, L.B. 147, 148

Quine, W.V.O. 26

Rahner, K. 66, 69, 199
Ratschow, C.H. 10

Ratzinger, J. 183, 195, 282, 289
Raunio, A. 298
Reimarus, H.S. 57
Reinhuber, T. 139
Rendtorff, T. 362
Reuter, M. 175
Richard of St. Victor 70–1, 206, 330, 332, 334, 368
Ricoeur, P. 148
Riemann, B. 108, 114, 123
Rietdijk, C.W. 92
Ringgren, H. 113
Ritschl, A. 9–10, 91, 94, 160–1, 199–200, 341, 347
Ritter, J. 23, 91, 113, 130, 363
Robinson, J.A.T. 13, 43
Rohls, J. 209
Rollock, R. 241
Rosenau, H. 305, 312, 316–22
Rotelle, J.E. 81–2
Rothe, R. 233, 363
Rothgangel, M. 148
Runggaldier, E. 26

Sagan, C. 170
Sartorius, E.W.Chr. 76
Sartre, J.P. 199
Schelling, F.W.J. 224, 232
Schleiermacher, F.D.E. 7–9, 11, 21, 32, 44–5, 85–6, 110, 128, 160–1, 166, 199–200, 238, 252, 318–20, 332
Schmid, K. 256
Schmidt-Japing, J.W. 23
Schnelle, U. 186
Scholtz, G. 23
Schröter, J. 340
Schumacher, J. 178
Schwarz, H. 23, 169, 228–9, 241–2
Schwarz, R. 227
Schweitzer, A. 8–9, 12, 15–16, 43, 340
Schwöbel, Chr. 16, 30, 46, 65, 70, 76, 105, 111, 139, 147, 169, 171, 210, 219, 344
Searle, J. 343
Sellin, G. 280
Semler, J.S. 154
Seng, K.P. 171
Seuse, H. 85, 203, 298
Sextus Empiricus 53
Shibutani, T. 209
Singer, P. 204
Socrates 181
Sölle D. 136
Spener, Ph.J. 233
Spengler, O. 24, 237
Spinoza, B. 110
Staats, R. 285, 288, 295
Stange, C. 190, 308
Stausberg, M. 135
Steck, O.H. 113, 256
Stegmüller, W. 146
Stock, K. 10, 86, 158–61, 327–9
Stranzinger, R. 143
Strauß, D.F. 57
Strawson, P.F. 49, 296, 297
Stuiber, A. 318
Stupperich, R. 300
Sturlese, L. 85
Swart, H.C.M.de 347
Swinburne, R. 8, 94, 97–101

Talmey, M. 10
Tarski, A. 147
Teilhard de Chardin, P. 18, 20–1, 156, 273
Tertullian 226, 312, 318
Tester, S.J. 88
Theißen, H. 21
Thomasius, G. 74
Tillich, P. 10, 12, 15–16, 50–1, 53, 95, 97, 128, 259–63, 265, 267–8, 287, 322, 362
Tipler, F.J. 20, 102, 155–7, 163, 170, 197, 291–3
Torrance, J.B. 241
Torrance, T.F. 87, 190

Troeltsch, E. 14
Tuveson, E.L. 229, 235

Vate, D.v.d.jr. 209
Vennebusch, J. 363
Verweyen, H. 57
Visala, A. 209
Volkmann, S. 135, 209
Vorgrimler, H. 295, 306, 311

Weber, O. 108, 321
Weidemann, V. 104, 156
Weiss, J. 8–9, 12, 15, 340
Weizel, K.L. 8
Welker, M. 95, 129, 135–6, 166, 281
Wengert, T.J. 6
Weyl, H. 92
Whitehead, A.N. 18, 97, 135, 286
Wilkens, U. 166
William of Auxerre 289
Williams, G.C. 180
Wittgenstein, L. 34, 95, 339
Wolf, E. 312, 321
Wölfel, E. 86, 103
Wolff, H.W. 184
Wright, G.H.v. 27
Wycliffe 125–6
Wyon, O. 322

Zahrnt, H. 322
Zizioulas, J. 70, 210
Zwingli, H. 116–17

Subject Index

abba 64
Abraham 241, 304, 318
accidents 68, 82–5, 110, 119, 347, 367
act/action/agency 1, 8, 11, 16, 19, 25–32, 37–41, 46–55, 59–74, 87, 93–6, 98, 100, 102, 106, 111, 116, 133, 137–50, 158–9, 163–5, 168–72, 177, 185, 193, 199, 202, 205, 207–10, 214–17, 220–2, 230–1, 245–8, 252, 254, 263, 267, 274–5, 281, 293, 299, 302–5, 313, 315, 317, 319, 323–30, 332, 337–44, 347, 350–1, 360, 363–5, 368
activity 9, 51, 58, 61–2, 81, 93, 131–2, 138–41, 144, 149, 175–6, 188, 214–16, 234, 246–7, 252, 337, 343
actuality 7–8, 11, 19, 27, 46, 51, 57, 72, 88, 104, 135, 139, 142–8, 159, 161, 167, 172, 176, 192, 195, 200, 202, 208, 211, 232–3, 237, 251, 267, 316, 321–2, 327, 330, 349–53, 364
actualization 9, 138, 161, 339, 347, 363
adoption 24, 28, 121, 282, 320
advent 257, 265, 340
Adventists 240
adventure 27, 69, 367
aeon 269
aesthetics 141, 149, 167, 326, 330, 350, 352–3
affectivity 143, 207–8, 341
agent 25, 27, 29, 30, 39, 98, 139, 141, 314, 330, 331, 332, 342, 350
aims 6, 49, 137, 161, 200, 207–8, 232, 237, 327
alienation 191, 260, 261
all-encompasing/all-embracing activity of God 76, 138–9, 141, 144, 149, 270
alterity/otherness 67, 71, 87, 104–6, 111, 165, 299, 300, 346, 361
amillennialism 239, 243–4, 246, 299
Anabaptists 227, 340
angels 158–9, 204, 206, 258, 269, 275, 316, 330
annihilation 136, 144, 151–63, 168–71, 184, 193–4, 200, 234, 244, 256, 304, 306–12, 317, 319–30, 351, 353
anthropic principle 156
anthropology 30, 172, 183–9, 192–5, 198, 204, 209, 215, 217, 220–3, 253, 268, 277, 283, 290, 296–7, 323, 334, 350, 364
Anti-Christ 242, 248–9
anticipation 20–1, 57–8, 159, 216, 251, 329, 360
antinomy 127
anxiety 6, 213, 298
apocalypticism 58, 93, 185, 223–7, 236–9, 243, 245–8, 256, 278, 304
arbor porphyriana 145, 146, 360
Armageddon 248
Arminians 314
ascension 124, 127–30, 146, 160, 254
asceticism 170, 301
atomism 104, 108–9, 112, 195, 323, 326, 367
atonement 62, 148, 241, 265, 374, 377
autonomy 267, 290
axiology 16, 17, 21

babies 353, 357
baptism 122, 124, 186, 222–3, 304, 331
Baptists 54–5, 248, 278, 304–6
basileia tou theou 340
beauty 7, 133–4, 138, 141, 145–50, 154, 167, 291, 325, 353, 366–7
being as becoming in relation 206, 298, 300, 351
big bang 110, 160
blessing 138, 181, 266, 295, 319, 334
blood 20, 116, 118–19, 125, 281, 288, 359
body/bodiliness/embodiment 57, 83, 112, 117–19, 123–8, 146, 153, 161, 170, 174–8, 180–8, 190–2, 195, 197, 202, 222–3, 247–8, 252, 267, 271, 276–94, 296–302, 334, 351
brain 69, 99, 175–7, 192, 209, 377
burial 179, 184, 221–2

calamity 189, 213, 249
cancer 219
cannibals 289
Cappadocians 70
catastrophes 227, 249
causality 27, 85, 98–100, 111, 135, 303
cells 173–6, 179
certainty 18, 28, 30, 44, 178–9, 220, 262, 265
chaos 113, 214–17, 357
chiliasm 225–7, 235, 371
choice 25, 81, 101, 125, 140, 144, 196, 201–2, 309, 315, 347, 363–5
Christ 6–8, 11–21, 39, 42–7, 56–64, 68, 72, 75–7, 102, 112, 116–20, 124–31, 136, 138, 160–1, 171, 173, 186–91, 198–200, 203–4, 216–17, 223–30, 235, 241, 243–4, 248–78, 280, 282, 284, 286, 288, 293, 295, 298–301, 305–17, 321–2, 328–37, 342–3, 352–3, 359, 360–1, 368
christocentrism 12, 13, 45, 62
christogenesis 20, 273
christology 59–60, 65, 74–6, 96, 117, 126–8, 187, 253–4, 260, 268, 270–1, 280
chromosomes 179
church 61, 64–5, 69–70, 75, 87, 116, 119, 127–8, 132, 135, 153, 158, 187–90, 192, 198, 210, 221–2, 226–7, 233, 236, 240, 242, 244, 249, 252–3, 259–60, 264, 266–7, 276, 278, 282, 284, 287–8, 294, 298, 303, 308, 312, 314–16, 319, 321, 336, 339, 341, 351–2, 356, 367
coherence 18, 52, 97, 111, 135, 137, 147, 163, 193, 200, 225, 284, 287
collectivism 206
coma 175, 218
commandments 143, 208, 238, 342
communication 46–7, 54, 65, 96, 102, 105, 107, 125, 129, 132, 149, 160, 172, 195, 206, 222, 224, 246, 260, 266, 297–301, 338, 343, 351, 359–61
communion 46, 55, 116–31, 210, 265–6, 343, 352, 356, 360
community 44, 46, 61, 65–71, 132, 171, 185, 198, 230, 233, 257, 260, 267, 278–9, 314
compassion 87, 312, 319
condemnation 311–12, 314
confession 42, 60, 125, 139, 152, 242, 311–12, 315, 342
confidence 234
confirmation 62, 214, 217, 219, 265, 308, 352
conflict 55–6, 76, 100, 110, 128, 236, 328, 359
conscience 311
consciousness 20, 27, 86, 99, 101, 104, 110, 156–7, 175–7, 194, 209, 239, 241, 246, 249, 296, 319, 329, 358

consolation 88–90, 97, 204, 337
consummation 88, 133, 137, 144, 157–8, 163, 168, 221, 252–3, 262–5, 307, 311, 338, 344–6, 354
contingency 24, 29, 68, 96, 99, 106, 142–4, 147, 165–8, 213, 215, 245, 347–50
cooperation 139, 141–3, 147–8, 309, 317, 350, 356
corporeality 83, 107, 160, 182, 231, 267, 280–1, 287, 295, 297, 351. *See also* body
corruption 117, 152, 249, 282
cosmology 20, 97, 109–10, 114, 154–6, 160, 162
cosmos 20, 153–6, 170
cosmosphere 20
covenant 240–1, 387
creatio ex nihilo 61, 81, 87, 89, 163–4, 167, 292
creation 18, 36, 46–7, 54–5, 59, 61, 64, 71, 74, 76, 81, 83, 86–7, 89, 91, 106, 110, 113, 116, 120, 127, 129, 133, 136–7, 141–4, 149, 152, 157, 160, 163–71, 184, 190, 192–4, 198, 200, 206–8, 215–17, 222, 267, 269–75, 277, 282, 284, 292, 299, 300–7, 309, 313, 315–16, 328–33, 343–7, 352, 359–61, 363–5
creator 55, 153, 167, 185, 196, 207, 221, 278–9, 292, 299, 343
creature 101, 105–6, 111, 128, 138–9, 143–7, 149–50, 158–9, 164–9, 194, 196, 201, 207, 209, 224, 272–4, 284, 299, 309–10, 315–17, 327, 347, 350–1, 363
creatureliness 98, 195–9, 219
creed 42, 70, 118–19, 282
cremation 222–3
cross 19, 26, 56–9, 61–4, 71, 106, 116, 136–8, 145, 161, 173, 189, 191, 199–200, 216, 223, 246, 248, 251, 267, 275, 293, 295, 305, 311, 327–9, 335, 337, 359
damnation 306, 309, 312, 316, 318, 322, 331, 334, 337
Darwinism 23
death 2, 4, 13, 20, 41, 44, 55–63, 72, 116, 135–6, 143, 155, 162, 166–7, 172–204, 211–13, 215–23, 235, 237, 243–4, 248, 252, 254, 258, 262, 264, 267, 273, 275–84, 287–8, 290–8, 300, 302–4, 308–9, 311–14, 320, 329, 332, 334, 352, 364, 367
death, brain-death 175, 177
dehistoricization 259, 264
deification 298–300, 338, 350–1, 360
democracy 24, 237
deontic rules 143, 164, 207–8, 213–15, 347, 349–50
deprivation 178, 316
determinism 24, 92–3, 96, 215
devil 166, 189, 244, 311–12, 334
devotion 62, 165, 216, 217, 328
dignity 205, 368
dilemma 23, 127, 321, 332
disclosedness 46, 48, 65–6, 73, 103, 138, 245, 314, 343, 363, 365
disembodiment 296
dispensationalism 240–1
dissolution 233, 235, 237, 249, 270, 272, 306, 361
distentio animi 83–4, 92, 123
divinity 75–6, 127, 161, 204
doxa 281, 289
drama 68, 189, 227, 303, 377
dream 32, 181, 219, 233, 357, 359, 367
dualism 26, 135, 183–4, 187, 192, 195, 283, 290, 296–7, 314, 318, 324, 334, 352
duration 28, 155, 333
dying 172–5, 177, 179–80, 376, 381, 383

elimination 83, 124, 218, 245, 261, 326
emergence 14, 65, 75, 153, 156, 248–9
emotions 27, 35–6, 176, 182, 337, 378
enjoyment 55, 343, 359, 365

enlightenment 4, 22, 57, 128, 154, 163, 228–33, 239, 245, 308, 310, 342
eritis sicus deus 211
eschata 3–8, 10, 12, 17, 38–9, 133, 151, 194, 200, 218, 242, 251–5, 257, 259, 261, 263, 265, 267, 269, 271, 273, 275–7, 279–367
eschatoi 7–8, 39, 41, 43–77, 121, 133, 162, 164, 332
eschaton 3–18, 39, 81–101, 103, 105, 107, 109, 111, 113, 115, 117, 119, 121, 123, 125, 127, 129, 131, 133, 135, 137, 139, 141, 143, 145, 147, 149–50, 164, 172, 283, 309, 353
eschatos 7–8, 11–13, 39, 43, 75
essence 18, 49–50, 67, 70–1, 74, 76, 81–2, 98, 104–6, 110, 117, 119, 122–4, 127, 129, 134, 146, 160–1, 166, 189, 196–7, 201, 215, 260, 299–300
eternalization 94, 97, 107, 352
eternity 14–17, 21, 39, 72, 81, 84–91, 93–108, 129, 133, 141–2, 161, 168, 194, 213, 241, 254, 258–9, 262–3, 268–9, 283, 285–7, 304, 313, 328, 333, 335–6, 352–3, 362, 364
eternity as atemporality 84, 259, 268–9, 284
eternity as simultaneity 88–100, 103, 122–3, 262, 283, 286, 333, 346
ethics 14, 19, 21, 30, 37, 110, 133, 140–5, 148–50, 164, 169–73, 176, 204–5, 207, 215, 218, 222, 232–4, 236, 243, 245, 247, 249, 253, 258, 273–5, 277, 300–2, 304–5, 326, 329, 336, 341–2, 344, 347, 349–50
ethos 170, 215, 236
etsi mundus non daretur 74, 216–17
eucharist 20, 117–18, 125–6, 160, 266, 276, 336, 360
event 16–17, 23, 25–9, 33–6, 39, 41, 44–5, 47, 50–9, 61–3, 66, 71, 87–90, 92–3, 95–6, 98–104, 106–8, 118, 132, 135–6, 138–9, 141–5, 147–8, 150, 154, 168, 186, 191, 193, 204, 208, 216, 223, 225, 248, 251, 255, 262–3, 266–7, 269, 272–3, 279, 286–7, 308, 314, 323, 325, 327–9, 331–2, 335, 337, 346–7, 349–50, 363
evidence 58, 87, 151–2, 185, 192, 203, 294
evil 91, 94–5, 133–6, 138, 140–2, 144–5, 150, 153, 162, 166, 197, 200–1, 211–12, 221, 230–2, 235, 242, 247–8, 264, 282, 304, 309, 314–17, 322, 326, 329, 352–3
evolution 18, 20–1, 23, 68–9, 166, 179–80, 197, 209
exhortation 249, 256, 258
existence 20, 25, 30, 46–8, 50–1, 53–4, 70–1, 81, 83, 93, 98–9, 108–9, 133–4, 136, 141, 146, 149, 155, 159–60, 163, 165, 169, 184, 189, 192, 200, 203, 206–7, 214–15, 249, 260–1, 288, 296, 301, 322, 347, 355
expectations 19, 29–42, 51, 55, 57, 59, 62–4, 67, 75–6, 79, 83, 109, 162–4, 170, 172, 178, 180, 197, 204, 214, 224–9, 234–5, 242, 245–6, 251, 254–5, 256–7, 260, 262, 268, 275, 277–8, 288, 337
experience 17, 19, 21, 24–5, 32, 34–5, 39, 42–9, 53, 56, 59–60, 64–5, 72, 85–6, 91–2, 99, 102–4, 107, 109, 139, 144–5, 177–8, 198–202, 208, 213, 215, 220, 222, 234, 237, 246, 253, 260–3, 271, 277, 280–1, 286, 294, 296, 300, 309, 312, 315, 320, 327–8, 334, 337–8, 353, 363, 365
extrapolation 75, 155, 162, 178, 337

faith 15, 17–19, 23, 25–33, 28, 32, 34–5, 42–56, 59–67, 73, 76, 86, 90, 103–4, 110–11, 117–19, 121, 125, 128, 137, 139, 148, 161, 166,

172, 179, 189–90, 199, 217, 222, 225, 241, 245–6, 249, 251–3, 265, 275, 299, 305–6, 310, 313–14, 319–20, 327, 331, 334–8, 342, 344, 352, 366
faithfulness 62, 64, 66, 71, 74, 77, 153, 159, 162, 164, 193, 201, 266, 276, 301, 309, 314
fall 42, 52, 85–6, 138, 149, 154, 160, 165, 197, 205, 210, 223, 233, 235, 241, 249, 252, 258, 284, 305, 308, 314, 316, 333, 353
falsification 56, 188, 202
fear 35–6, 181, 189, 213, 257, 334, 336–7
fellowship 55, 343, 359
filioque 70, 382
finitude 110, 114–18, 122, 131, 195–200, 219
finitum capax/non capax infiniti 130
formation 46–7, 64, 215, 224, 234, 349
fragment 99, 108, 112, 199, 215, 219, 372
freedom 28, 37, 63, 68, 74, 88–90, 93, 106, 133, 143–4, 159, 165, 167, 188, 190, 208, 232, 295, 315–16, 318, 332–3, 347, 374, 379
functionalization 212, 219, 220, 253, 263, 291, 365

gift 34, 48, 55, 60, 117, 146, 187, 241, 265, 282, 313, 314, 343, 359
glory 159, 235, 256, 258–9, 261, 266–7, 269–70, 281, 289
Gnosticism 57, 153, 158, 162, 170, 282, 288
God-consciousness 7–8, 86
God the Father 8, 45, 54, 62, 65, 68–72, 76, 91, 105–6, 114, 118–19, 127–8, 149, 153, 188, 217, 226, 241, 254, 262, 264, 271–3, 315, 352, 360, 364
God the Holy Spirit 3, 12, 45, 60–72, 76, 88, 105–6, 115, 117–18, 131–2, 149, 166, 188, 216–17, 226–7, 234, 254, 263, 265–7, 271–6, 281–2, 299, 305, 309, 313, 327–8, 342, 351–2, 360, 364, 365
God the Son 68–72, 76–7, 105–6, 114, 116, 121, 126, 149, 152, 188, 216–17, 226, 241, 248, 254, 256–8, 271–3, 305–6, 327, 343, 360–1, 364
goodness 115, 134, 140–1, 150, 167, 196, 315, 317, 325–6, 347
gospel 44, 46, 47–8, 51, 54, 65, 105, 107, 149, 187, 232, 236, 246, 256, 272, 275, 282, 336, 339
grace 106–7, 116, 137, 145, 148, 163, 168, 171, 191, 194, 199, 226, 241, 265, 271–2, 284, 287, 295–6, 299, 304–5, 313–15, 317, 321, 332–3, 337, 347, 350–2, 360, 365
guilt 210, 213, 275, 332

harmony 122, 306, 330, 366
heaven 76, 81, 83, 93, 112–13, 116–18, 122, 124, 127–8, 130, 132, 152–4, 158, 160, 168, 235, 248, 256, 258, 265, 269–70, 318, 338–41, 356, 358
hell 81, 154, 306, 311–12, 318, 337
hellenism 181–3, 185, 187, 222, 224, 255, 280, 288
hope 7, 18–21, 23–4, 29, 32, 35–9, 46, 48–51, 54, 56, 59, 62–7, 72–3, 84, 86–7, 97, 102, 105–7, 132–3, 138, 144, 160, 162, 169–71, 179, 181, 183–6, 189–92, 201–2, 211, 222, 227, 232, 234–5, 241–2, 245, 249–51, 254, 256–7, 265, 267, 272–3, 275–7, 279, 284, 287, 292, 298, 301, 305, 336–9, 352, 355, 359, 360, 367–8
horizon 29–30, 41, 51, 57, 59, 62–7, 75–7, 109, 163, 172, 178, 180, 197, 204, 219, 227, 229, 234–5, 245–6, 251, 255, 277, 327, 337
human, becomings 9, 171, 189, 209, 219, 277

identification 49–50, 54, 64, 66, 104, 109, 110–11, 114–15, 140, 198, 249, 254
identity 24, 49–50, 56, 62–7, 77, 106, 121, 150, 162–3, 176, 182–3, 193–5, 199–200, 202, 209–12, 219, 221, 224, 238, 271–2, 274, 288–93, 298, 323, 325–6, 330, 337, 351, 353, 361, 366
ideology 184, 232, 234, 238, 342
imagination 176, 306, 310, 346
imago dei 10, 86, 88–90, 94–6, 108, 132, 138, 142–3, 170, 172, 184–5, 188, 204–6, 213, 217, 225, 256, 307, 322, 327, 357–60
imminentism 253, 373
immortality 20, 23, 102, 157, 182–3, 187, 194–5, 197, 200, 288, 300
immortalization 194, 197, 313, 323, 326
incarnation 12, 76–7, 96, 106, 129, 202, 216, 261, 265, 267, 270–2, 298, 332
incommunicable-from-another-and-to-another-becoming 206
individualism 206, 296, 323–4, 326
individuation 104–5, 182, 205, 271–2, 298, 335–6, 347, 361
infinity 88, 98, 100–2, 107–11, 114–16, 118–21, 123–5, 127, 130–3, 157, 168, 196–7, 201, 219, 254, 283–4, 287, 290, 295, 318, 333, 350
inspiration 234–5, 274, 365
interaction 24, 29, 42, 62, 68, 71, 74, 179, 202, 207, 209, 224, 238, 327, 361, 364
intercession 221, 295
intermediate state 295, 318

judgement 4, 6, 13, 15, 21, 29, 33, 36, 47, 54–5, 62, 64, 94, 97, 107, 117, 136, 144–5, 150, 186, 188–9, 193, 198–200, 218, 240, 244, 248, 252–3, 255–6, 258–9, 262–3, 265–6, 269–75, 277–8, 288–9, 294, 300–37, 342, 352–4, 358, 361, 367
justice 158, 203, 303, 309–10, 312, 315, 342, 359
justification 9, 42–5, 48, 51, 61, 136, 145, 148, 161, 185, 189, 203, 214, 217, 219, 221, 243, 269, 274–5, 290, 293, 299, 309, 313, 325, 327, 334, 347, 352, 365

kairos 15, 333
karma 202–3
kenosis 76
kingdom 3, 6, 8–10, 12, 15–16, 19, 21, 24, 54–5, 64, 66, 91, 120, 144, 161, 200, 224–7, 232–5, 241, 244, 251–2, 261, 263–5, 267, 270, 276–7, 281, 301–2, 304–7, 319, 322, 338–47, 350, 352, 359, 366

liberation 19, 21, 86, 158, 182, 282
libertinism 170, 301
liberty 226
lifeforms 234
lifeworld 55, 218–19, 366
limbus 277, 311, 318
localization 49–50, 127, 333
love 9, 27, 62–3, 65, 69, 71–4, 76, 105, 143–4, 152, 164–7, 193, 195, 199, 201, 203, 207–15, 222, 231, 242, 268, 272–5, 293, 309–10, 312, 327–8, 342, 346–7, 350, 352, 361, 364, 368
love, co-loved/-lover 71
love-story 68–9
Lutheranism 5, 136

manducatio indignorum 337
Manichaeism 135
manipulation 178, 246, 274, 361
marana-tha 60, 65, 257, 268
Mass-energy equivalence 351
medicine 174–8, 191–2, 218
mercy 303, 377
merit 26, 221, 241, 295, 352

messiah 227, 235, 254, 256–7
metabolism 173–4, 178, 180
metaphor 27, 59, 113, 131, 148–9, 273, 300, 307, 329, 331, 339, 345–6, 353, 355
metaphysics 49, 72, 111, 145–6, 205
Middle-Platonism 285, 316
millennialism 224–8, 232–5, 242–6
millennium 225–6, 228–9, 235, 241–2, 252, 262
mind 26, 82, 88, 93, 117, 127, 202, 209, 262, 315, 329, 336
miracle 55, 343
misplacedness 10, 211
mistrust 211
model 70, 85–6, 87, 91–6, 100, 102, 108, 110–15, 117, 120–4, 127, 129–32, 142, 151, 154–6, 158, 163, 211, 237, 262–3, 285, 287, 289–90, 308–9, 311–12, 318, 322–4, 331–3, 335, 339, 364
modernity 22, 85, 136, 165, 224–5, 227–8, 239, 252, 310
monism 26, 85, 134, 190, 283, 285, 292
morality 23, 183, 230
mortality 186, 196, 198, 202, 320
mystery 71, 115, 175, 295
mysticism 85–6, 203, 224, 268, 284, 298–9, 339, 341
myth 27, 128, 136, 203, 220, 363, 365

Narnia 62, 348, 366–7
narrative 47, 50, 60, 63, 68–9, 104, 136, 206, 327
naturalism 26, 197, 384
nature 20–1, 28, 30, 35, 46, 52, 66, 68, 75–6, 81, 89–90, 97–101, 110, 117–18, 120–1, 125–8, 130, 135, 154, 158–9, 161, 163, 165–6, 169, 196–7, 201, 203–4, 209, 215–16, 231, 234, 246, 254, 256, 269, 271, 281, 284, 286, 299, 312, 330, 356–7, 359–60, 363
near-death experiences 178
nefesh 183, 184
neo-Platonism 84, 88, 100, 134, 145–6, 188, 203, 284, 298, 316
neurobiology 46, 69, 171, 175
nirvana 203
nominalism 146
noosphere 20
novelty 101–2, 365

Omega point 156–7
omnipotence 52, 74, 76–8, 133–9, 141, 261, 269, 295, 309, 318
omnipresence 74–8, 117, 128, 131, 260, 270
omniscience 74, 76, 134
ontology 26–7, 69, 148, 182, 189, 191, 202, 210
organism 173–4, 179–80, 206, 213–15, 233, 237, 363–4
organs 99, 176
orphic tradition 57, 181–3, 187, 195, 222, 280

panentheism 121, 197
pantheism 110, 115, 121, 140, 157, 194, 197
parable 55, 343, 372
paradise 338, 355, 357
Parousia 3, 8–9, 11–12, 161, 228, 235, 251–82, 284, 287, 297, 300–1, 334, 352, 359, 360, 361
participation 47, 84, 128, 154, 168, 227, 246–7, 260–1, 295, 299, 317, 336, 360
passion 215, 231, 291
passivity 27, 50–1, 135, 189, 193, 194, 208, 217, 260, 292, 298, 318, 327
perception 85–6, 89–90, 99, 101, 104, 109–10, 114, 178, 181, 202, 219, 296, 363
perfectibility 22, 24, 163, 231

perfection 22, 137, 157, 163, 189–92, 201, 231, 252, 292, 295
perichoresis 266
perseverance 314
person 4–5, 7–8, 11–13, 20, 26–8, 37, 39, 42–5, 47, 59, 62–3, 69–70, 72, 74–6, 89, 92, 105–7, 117, 122, 125–6, 128–33, 140, 144, 151, 160, 162–5, 172, 178, 189, 191–4, 199, 202, 204–13, 216–17, 219–23, 226, 246, 248, 251–3, 263, 266, 271–8, 281, 283, 288–308, 320–1, 323–4, 326–37, 341–2, 350–3, 359, 364
personality 72, 128–9, 132, 135–6, 161, 170–2, 183, 200, 203–6, 209–10, 213–14, 217, 260, 291, 297–8, 324, 326–35, 341, 351
person as particuar whence-and-whither becoming 206–7
persons as becomings 209–10, 213, 268, 323–4, 327
pessimism 24, 26, 29, 229, 237–8, 240, 242, 245
phenomena 15, 34, 86, 110, 166, 196, 210, 334–5, 362
phenomenology 25, 362, 364
physics 20, 81, 83, 102, 114, 122, 155, 157, 197, 291–2, 377, 386
piety 112, 233, 266
pirates 182
Platonism 182, 284, 288, 367
pluralism 24, 236, 247
poimenics 174, 219
Post-liberalism 68
postmillennialism 10, 228–9, 233, 235–6, 239–40, 245, 246
postmodernity 13, 24, 239
potentiality 43, 138, 159, 200, 292, 332
practice 30–2, 36, 42–3, 45–6, 52–3, 59, 75, 87, 174, 185, 220–3, 234, 304, 354
pragmatism 209
prayer 3, 60, 81, 87, 90, 102, 221, 257, 295, 311
predestination 139, 295, 309, 313–14, 318
predetermination 37, 143
predictability 26, 248–9, 265
pre-eschata 39, 151, 153, 155, 157, 159, 161, 163, 165, 167, 169, 171, 173, 175, 177–9, 181, 183, 185, 187, 189, 191, 193, 195, 197, 199, 201, 203, 205, 207, 209, 211, 213, 215, 217–19, 221, 223–5, 227, 229, 231, 233, 235, 237, 239, 241, 243, 245, 247, 249, 251, 259, 270, 275, 279, 283, 294–5, 320, 332, 355
premillennialism 228–9, 236–40, 242, 245
presence 20, 88, 117, 120, 126–9, 160, 249, 252–5, 258, 260, 263–7, 270–6, 282, 284, 287, 300–1, 337, 340–1, 359–60, 368
privatio boni 134
process 18, 20, 23, 30, 42, 47, 54, 57, 69, 70, 73, 83, 95, 97, 109, 122, 129, 135–6, 142, 149, 153, 155, 174–6, 178–80, 191–2, 194, 199, 202, 220, 233, 234, 269, 286, 289, 295, 299, 303, 307, 317, 323–5, 327–8, 330–3, 335–6, 353, 363–5
processions 70, 73
progress 24, 175, 233, 237, 263, 324
prolepsis 18, 20, 58, 335
promise 48, 51, 63, 71, 115, 137, 163, 165, 173, 211, 217, 232, 234, 241, 254, 265, 272, 328–9, 335
prophecy 54, 161, 224, 245, 248, 252, 255, 303, 304
protology 61, 94, 313, 314, 357
providence 88–90, 95, 142
pseudo-personalization 213
punishment 188–9, 199–201, 230, 303, 307, 309–13, 326, 332, 334
purgatory 277, 294–6, 322
purification 84, 97, 153, 157, 171, 256, 288, 295, 322

rationality 90, 93, 117, 148, 204–5, 230
realism 134, 145–6
reality, eschatic 55, 72, 110, 133, 144–5, 149–50, 152, 162, 167, 251, 270, 274, 308
recapitulation 107
reconciliation 17, 19–20, 44, 52, 61–2, 75, 96, 145, 149, 161, 163, 173, 199, 217, 221, 261, 264, 266, 282, 295, 298, 305, 315, 328, 344, 359, 364
redemption 19, 61, 85–6, 91, 116, 133, 137–8, 152–3, 159, 161, 198, 229, 235–6, 245, 251, 305, 309, 316–17, 319, 327, 366
reductionism 26, 62, 102, 170, 285, 291, 293
re-embodiment 202
refrigerium 317–18, 382, 386
reincarnation 201–3
relata 11, 16, 26, 30, 33, 38, 39, 50, 52, 71, 89, 103, 121, 129, 147, 148, 193, 207, 208, 213, 214, 215, 229, 230, 244, 254, 288, 323, 324, 330, 331, 336, 339, 347, 362, 368
relatedness 104, 189, 265, 292, 300, 360
relation 10, 13–14, 16, 27, 29–30, 48–9, 51, 53, 58, 63, 67, 69–76, 87, 94, 100, 103–8, 122–4, 127, 129–33, 141–2, 145, 147–8, 164–9, 171–2, 184, 188–91, 193–5, 198–9, 204, 206–17, 219–23, 227, 233, 238, 254, 259, 262–3, 265–6, 268–9, 272, 274, 277, 280–5, 289, 291–3, 297–300, 306, 323–4, 327–30, 336–7, 346–7, 350–2, 360–5
relationality 67, 124, 165, 192–5, 206–7, 210, 221, 269, 273, 285, 291–2, 297, 301, 323–4, 329
relational-narrative 323
relationlessness 186, 190–3, 196, 216–17, 223, 298
relations, asymmetric 72–3, 104, 106, 123, 165, 168, 184, 207, 272
relationship 9, 11, 15–16, 31, 49, 66–8, 87–90, 103–8, 115, 121–2, 124, 129, 131, 133, 142, 147, 163, 165, 172, 176, 188, 190–1, 194–6, 198, 206–7, 210, 212, 219, 221, 262, 266, 272–4, 292, 296, 298, 300, 318–19, 323, 325, 327–9, 335, 342, 351–2, 355, 361
relationships, filial 207, 274
relations, irreflexive 73, 104, 106, 123, 168
relations, irreversible 174–5
relations, transitive 123
relocation 106, 181
remembrance 99, 104, 116, 118
renaissance 142
renewal/*renovatio* 24, 152–3, 157–60, 162–3, 168–71, 351
repentance 241, 304
repetition 269, 360
resonances 69, 148–9
responsibility 7, 136–7, 139, 141, 170–1, 176, 204, 210, 220, 234, 236, 279, 299, 309, 331
restoration 185, 216, 223
resurrection 3–4, 9, 13, 17–18, 20, 44, 56–64, 72, 75, 127, 137–8, 155, 185, 189, 191–2, 200, 204, 218, 220, 225, 235, 242–4, 246, 248, 251–2, 264–7, 271–3, 275–304, 308–9, 327–9, 332, 335, 337, 352, 359
revelation 17, 19, 21, 42, 45–6, 48, 56, 58, 66–7, 72, 103, 128, 132, 135, 139–40, 223–5, 230, 232, 234, 238–9, 243, 245, 248, 262–3, 267, 335
revivification 329
romanticism 85, 145, 356
rules, thetic 164, 207, 214–16, 345

sabbath 225, 318
sacrament 108, 116, 118, 125–6, 128, 223, 253, 273, 276, 282, 335

sacrifice 116, 381
Sadducees 291
salvation 5, 12, 16, 19, 48–50, 55, 61–2, 116, 137, 141, 152–3, 159–60, 163, 170, 185, 194, 222–3, 225, 228, 234–5, 240–1, 247, 249, 253, 257, 265–6, 272–3, 275, 278, 280, 282, 295, 305–7, 309, 315–22, 324, 326, 330, 334, 358–9
sanctification 203, 330
satan 225, 236, 242, 249
scholasticism 53, 74, 114, 126, 153, 158, 226, 248, 259, 284, 289–90, 294, 327, 330–2, 334
science 19–20, 27, 59, 92, 104, 111, 128, 149, 156, 170, 177, 195, 197, 209, 224, 355, 362, 364
scripture 6, 42, 44–5, 47, 54, 56–7, 61, 65, 87, 152, 159, 201, 226, 340, 354
secularization 227
self-annihilation 309
self-awareness 100
self-consciousness 74, 86, 199, 202, 232, 319, 363
self-constitution 275, 315
self-disclosure 46, 48, 103, 105, 137, 162, 251, 263, 310, 337, 364–5
self-identification 50, 54, 63, 66, 75–6, 104, 121, 132, 139, 238, 257
self-judgement 313, 332
self-limitation 120–1, 269, 270
self-relation 184
self-revelation 66, 159, 225
self-sacrifice 216–17
semi-pelagianism 309, 313–14, 318, 323, 333
sexuality 291, 302
sheol 184–6
simul iustus et peccator 210, 261, 263, 334, 364
sin 7, 15, 22, 62–3, 67, 86, 133, 139, 145, 153, 163, 165–7, 172, 178, 186, 188–90, 194–6, 198–201, 203, 210–17, 230, 241, 246, 260–1, 264, 294, 305, 312–16, 327–9, 337, 364
sleep 59, 181, 188–9, 281
sociality 209–10, 213–14, 224, 247, 295, 300, 359
society 19, 21–3, 148, 151, 192, 209, 212, 218–19, 224, 232, 235–6, 247, 249, 264, 340, 366
Socinians 200, 308
sociology 46, 179–80, 209, 219
soma pneumatikon 281, 292, 299
son of man 257, 381
soteriology 44, 145, 150, 209, 253, 265, 313–15, 319, 323, 332
soterology 12, 44, 61
soul 23, 83–8, 118, 181–3, 187–8, 190–2, 195–7, 200–3, 217, 222, 280, 282–90, 292–7, 300, 302, 315, 334, 342, 351
space 28, 49, 63–4, 68, 85–6, 92, 104, 107–15, 118, 120–4, 126–33, 153, 155–6, 159–60, 168–70, 184, 220, 254, 270, 272, 275, 284, 286, 294, 336, 346, 348, 351
spatiotemporality 49–50, 64, 76, 129, 142, 162, 216, 224, 271–3, 287, 298, 335
speculation 156, 248, 282, 295, 300, 311
speech-acts 137, 148–9
spheres 113, 153
spirituality 286
Stoics 172, 183
story 68, 90, 184, 202, 211, 367–8
sublimation/elevation (*Aufhebung*) 15, 27, 159–60, 262, 299
substance 37, 82–3, 98, 100, 110, 118–19, 125–6, 136, 153, 155, 188, 191, 195, 202, 204, 209, 283, 289, 317, 327
suffering 2, 87, 102, 133–4, 136–8, 143–4, 166–7, 186, 188, 192, 194, 200, 214–17, 257, 275, 294, 312, 328–9, 353, 357

sun 83, 89, 114, 166, 304, 359
superstition 53, 211
supra-historicity 44, 259, 263, 268, 272
supra-temporality 262
surprise 32–6, 39, 41–2, 56–7, 59, 101, 109, 173, 184, 256, 258, 273, 284
surrender 61, 71–2, 359, 364

teleology 16–17, 21, 23
telomere 179
telos 145, 251, 366
temporality 38, 52, 67, 86, 92, 96–7, 106, 129, 131, 262, 268, 285
temptation 211–12, 215, 334
theism 71, 135, 378
theodicy 133–8
Theo-drama 68
theosis 272, 298–9, 336, 352, 360, 361
thermodynamics 104, 155
time 3–8, 10–12, 14–17, 20–4, 28, 49–50, 52–3, 61, 63–5, 70, 72, 81–109, 112, 114, 122–3, 126, 128–30, 132–3, 135, 139, 141–2, 153, 155, 157, 159, 168, 174, 178, 183, 185, 189–94, 199–202, 205, 212–13, 216, 220, 225–7, 230–5, 237, 240, 244, 249, 252–4, 257, 259, 262–4, 266, 268–70, 272–5, 278–80, 286, 291, 293, 295, 299, 304–5, 309, 313, 315–16, 320, 333, 335–7, 340, 346, 353, 362
time, A-series 92–3, 95, 99
time, B-series 92, 95, 99, 103–4
time, cyclical 237, 268–9, 318
timelessness 8, 85, 87, 93, 100, 102, 142, 272, 283–5, 346
time, metric 98, 100–1, 109
time, topology 98, 100
tomb 58, 184
total-death theory 190–2, 194
totalitarianism 170, 245
transcendence 23, 34, 39, 129, 227, 235, 260, 272, 284, 346–7
transcendentals 82, 149, 235, 239
transformation 9, 20, 119, 151–6, 158, 171, 234, 253, 280–1, 284, 293, 299, 307, 325–8, 330–2, 335–6, 352–3
transition 112, 168, 173, 188, 201, 243, 270
Trinity 41, 43, 45, 47, 49–51, 53, 55, 57, 59, 61, 63, 65–7, 69–77, 82–3, 87, 104–7, 113–14, 120, 127, 129, 131, 133, 138, 162, 164–5, 189, 195, 204, 206, 209, 216–17, 226–7, 235, 245, 251, 266, 271–2, 298–300, 310, 314, 327, 332, 335–7, 344, 346–7, 352, 360–2, 364–6
trust 51–2, 59, 71, 74, 207, 211, 217, 275, 337, 352
truth 7, 11–12, 18, 21, 23, 47–8, 85, 121, 147–50, 158, 178, 192, 203, 239, 246, 253, 267, 298, 329, 346–7
truthfulness 66, 74
two regiments 247

ubiquity 128
universal redemption 194, 200, 305–6, 308–9, 312, 315–22, 324
universals 134, 145–7
universe 20, 50, 98, 100, 102, 155–7
unsurpassability 65, 67

values 16, 20, 28, 106, 116, 141, 149, 155, 163, 168, 171, 179, 238, 246, 248, 342
veracity 71, 165, 309
vine 358–9
visio beatifica 299–300
void 120–1, 184
volitions 37, 342
voluntarism 74, 293

whence-and-whither becoming 206
witness 59, 116, 198, 238, 242, 306, 308, 335, 339
world 1–2, 4, 8, 13, 15, 19–21, 26–9, 34, 39, 42, 48–9, 51, 55, 61, 63,

66, 67–71, 74–8, 84, 86–8, 90, 92–4, 96, 99, 101–8, 110–15, 122–4, 126–9, 131–6, 138–9, 141–5, 147–72, 184, 188–9, 194, 197, 200–1, 206, 210, 215–16, 223–6, 232, 234–8, 240–3, 246–9, 254–5, 260, 262–5, 268–70, 272, 275, 277, 281, 286, 294–6, 298, 300, 311, 314, 319, 323, 325–8, 333, 335, 340–1, 343–4, 346–7, 349–53, 356–61, 363–4, 366–8
worldview 16, 28, 30, 39, 47, 58–9, 96, 128, 154, 177, 180, 197, 229, 236, 237, 364
wrath 189, 326–8, 337

Yahweh 64, 136, 185–6, 255–6, 303

zim-zum 269